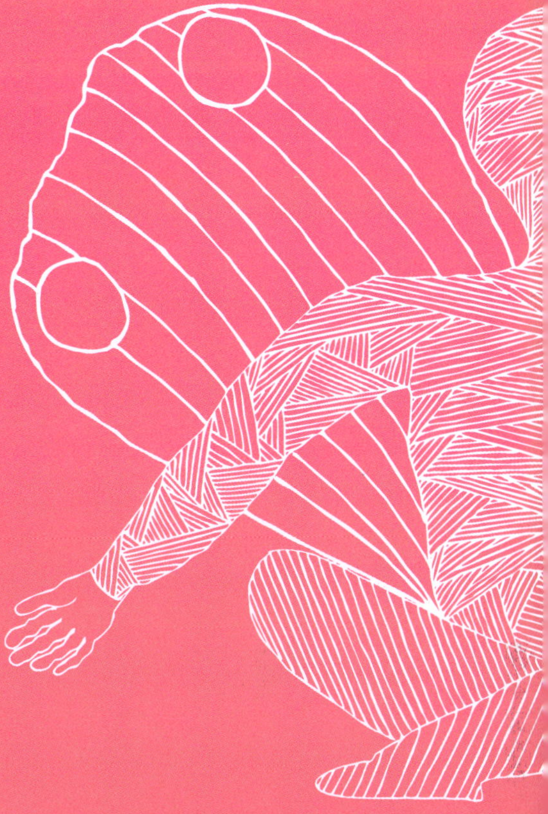

BILLY CONNOLLY

Original art, hand-signed limited edition prints and sculptures.

As the UK's leading art retailer, Castle Fine Art has been at the heart of the contemporary art movement for thirty years. We unite collectors with artworks from some of the most renowned figures in the art world. From iconic brands and major artist estates, to the new generation of artistic talent, we offer an exceptional collection of art for all.

We've had the pleasure of sharing Billy's art with the world for over a decade. His highly-collectible *Born On A Rainy Day* series of limited edition prints and sculptures is as humorous as his own comedy, with elements of his own life unexpectedly appearing throughout. Featured by *The Times* and documentaries including *Billy Connolly: It's Been a Pleasure*, his minimalist drawings have been described as 'poignant', 'funny' and 'enigmatic' by critics. According to Billy, 'They're funny in a different way from how I'm normally funny. They're odd. Some of them will make you think, and others will stop you thinking. Enjoy.'

Discover Billy's hand-signed works in our network of Castle Fine Art galleries across the UK or on our website.

The Accidental Artist

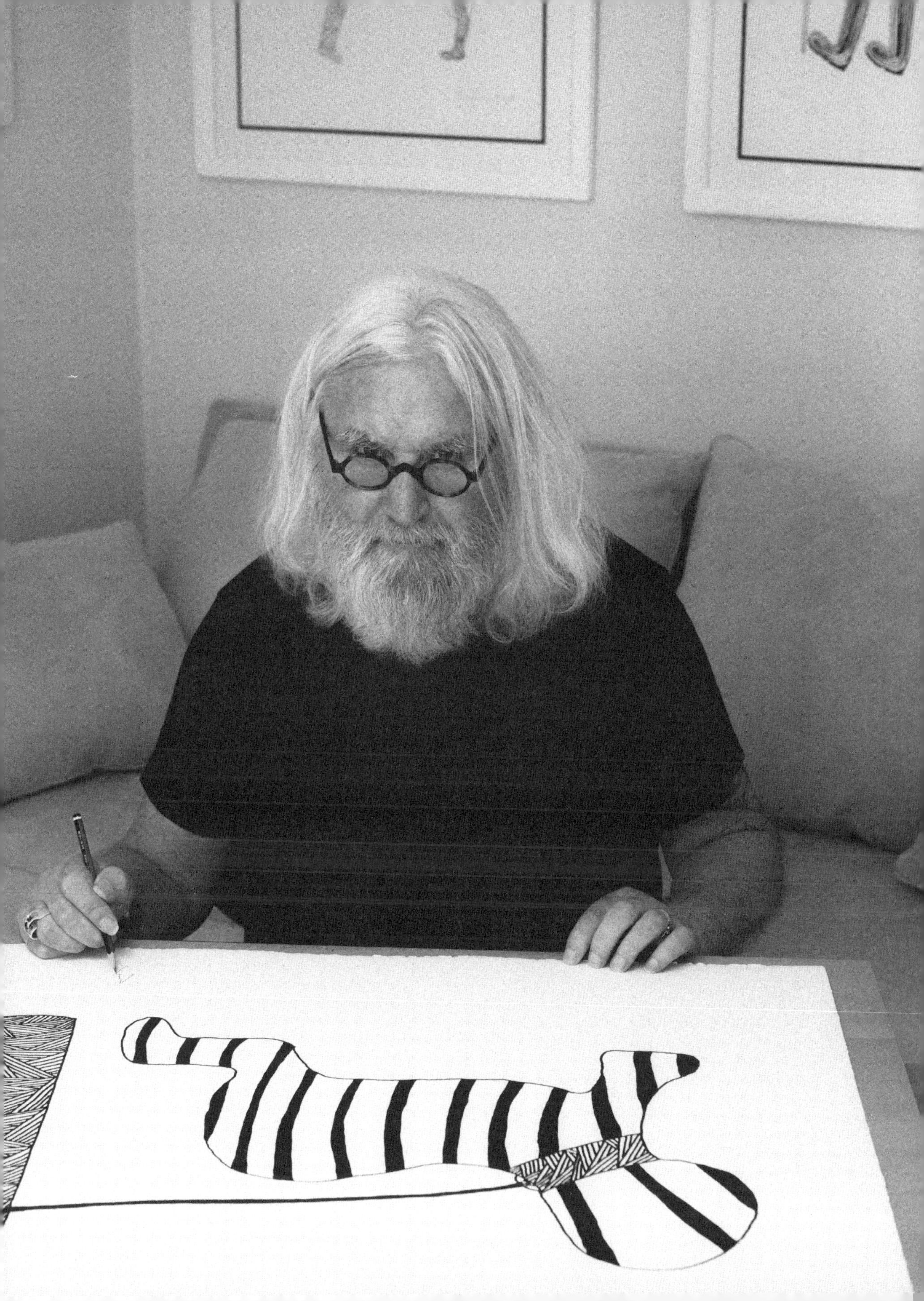

BILLY BOY CONNOLLY

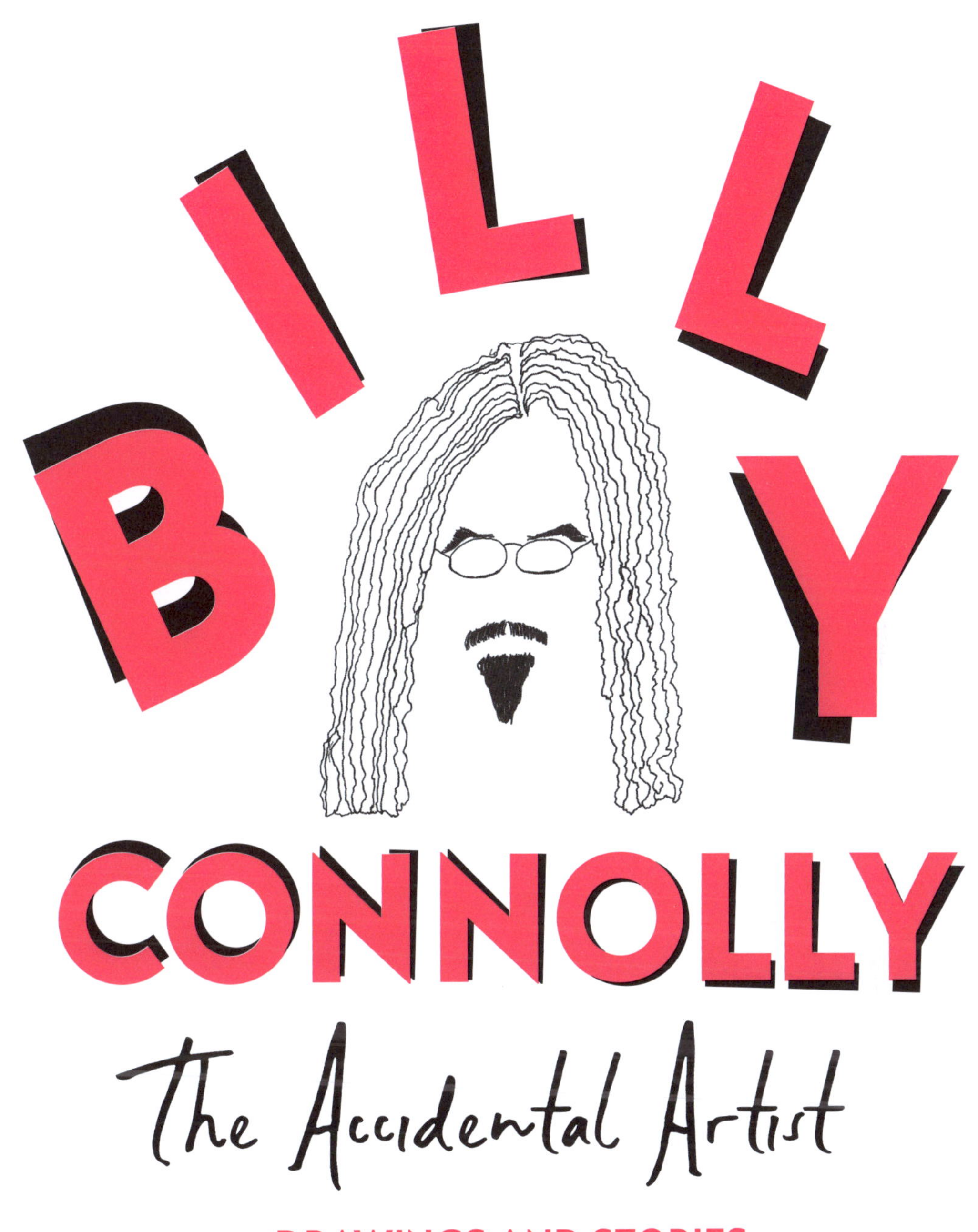

The Accidental Artist

DRAWINGS AND STORIES

JOHN MURRAY

For my wife and my family.

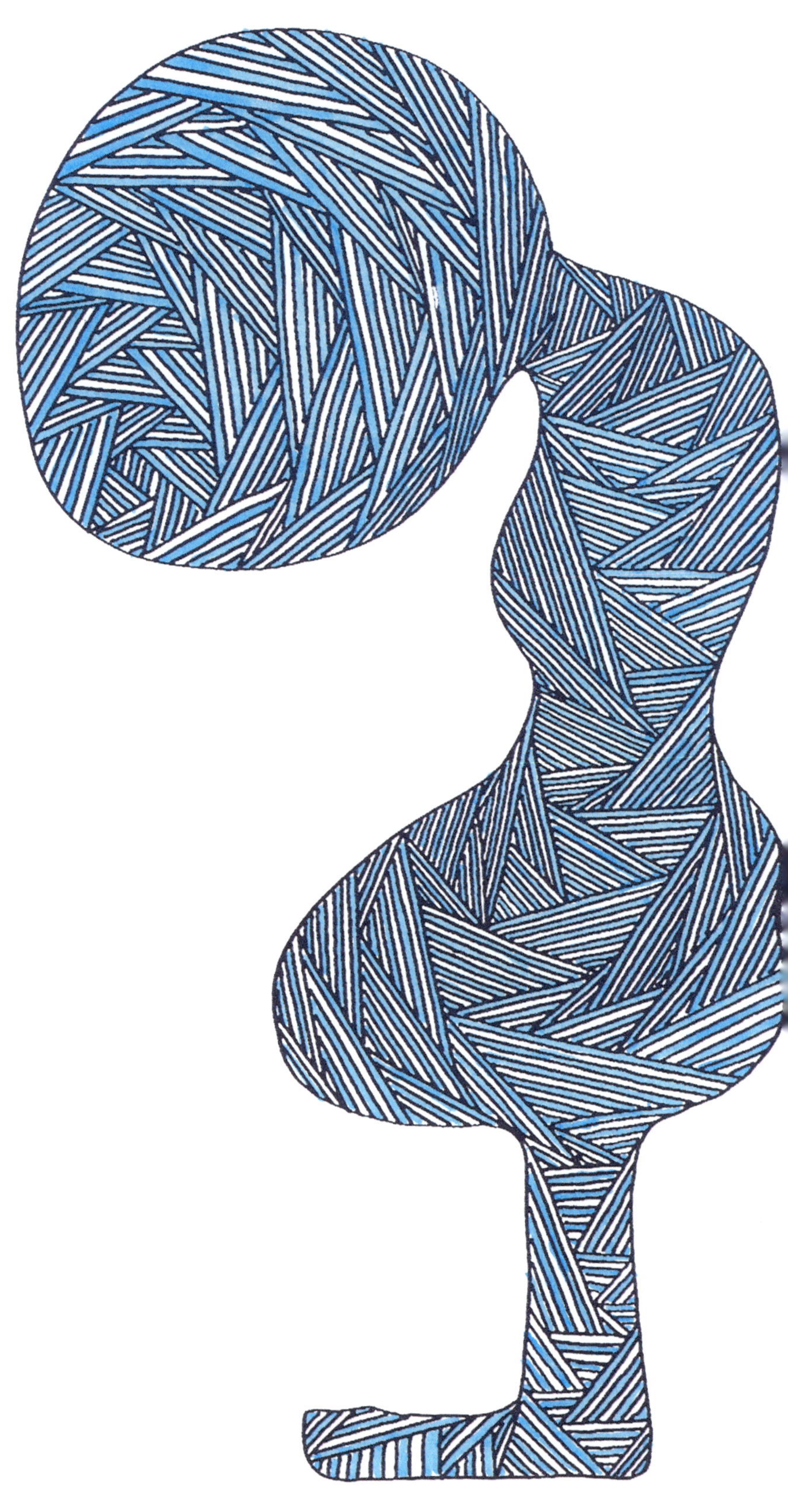

Direction, 2021

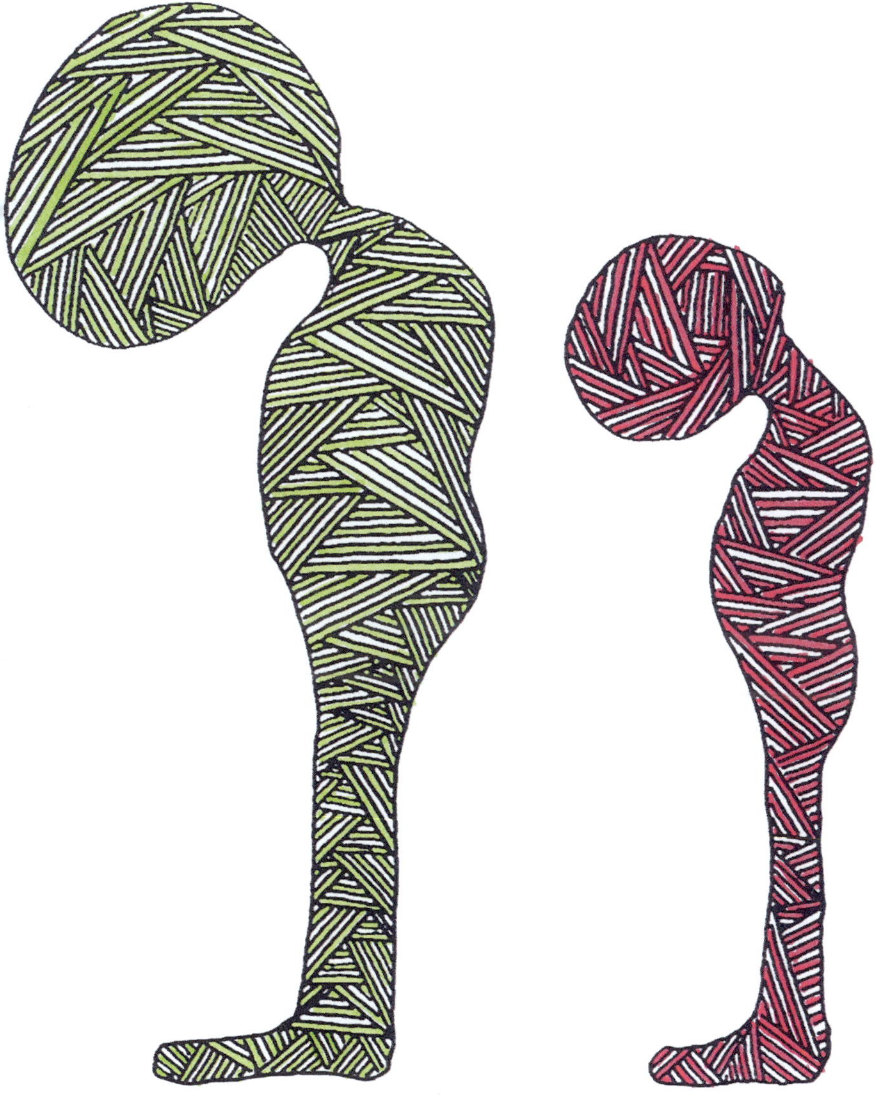

xi

Prologue

PAMELA STEPHENSON CONNOLLY

It's no secret that Billy Connolly is a complex man. On the one hand, he is a jolly, affable giggler, while on the other he revels in upsetting the established order of things. The latter has been obvious in his comedy for at least fifty years; his rebellious stand-up famously comprises fury at the status quo, razor-sharp topical commentary, irreverence for religion and sacred cows, annihilation of politicians, ample supplies of projectile swearing, and a strong dose of 'fuck you' for anyone he considers a blight on his preferred, lawless world.

When it comes to Billy's relatively new foray into the visual arts, nothing has changed. In his intriguing drawings, he again releases his oppositional self, sometimes blithely depicting a scene of pure comedic fantasy such as *The Sausage Tree* (Freud might have read far more into this drawing, but I say: 'Sometimes a sausage is just a sausage') or images of blissful daring, as in *Free Flight* where a man hovers precariously above the earth held aloft by two bunches of balloons. Sometimes Billy smacks us in the eyes with bizarre images like *It's Raining On The Moon* or the darkly satirical *Disabled American II* . . . or whisks us to the superficially fun but deeply unsettling environment of *The Wreck Room*. Many of the images have become iconic; fans used to come up to Billy in the street and ask: 'How do you remember your lines?' but nowadays they are just as likely to ask: 'Why aren't you wearing your *Pink Tie & Hanky*?'

Billy frequently dares to play God. Take his tendency to redesign the animal kingdom, creating anomalies that defy linkage to any known phylum, such as the *GoZunder Fish* that sports a rhinoceros horn, the *Gironkey* where a giraffe and donkey coexist within the same beast, or the *Purple People Eater* that (as far as we know) never ever had a spot on Noah's Ark. He even messes with human anatomy, as in *First Position* and the two-headed, unibodied creature called *Sandy & Andy McKay*. These works of human and animal fantasy are whimsical and fun, but other visual mutations such as *Steal Your Face* seem more sinister, even harking to subversive aspects of Billy's complicated unconscious mind, or at least to his psychological insightfulness. 'Are you commenting on the human tendency to don and remove our public "masks" whenever society dictates?' I asked him. 'No, fuck off,' he hinted. Of course, I deserved that, since an artist can rarely understand the fruit of his own limbic system, and it must be really trying when a person is expected to make clear sense of any kind of art.

As with Billy's comedy, it is not just the superficial elements — words spoken into a microphone or lines drawn on a page — that speak to us; we connect with his creations on a far deeper level. Just as audiences laughed despite their horror at Billy's hilarious descriptions of beatings by his father, so the viewer connects fundamentally with the longing, humiliation and despair embedded in many of Billy's best drawings.

In fact, despair seems to be a particularly common theme, an often-depicted emotion in Billy's work and — I have to say, as his partner of more than forty years — it's the one that scares me the most. I know that, as with a Rorschach inkblot test, meaning lies within the eye of the beholder, but for me the bowed heads of *Direction* for example — even *Blue Angel* — are deep and silent human cris de coeur that draw the viewer into a world of unwilling, hopeless submission. I believe such works allow a glimpse into the dark side of Billy's mythopoetic function; for example, his truly brilliant drawing *Purgatory* seems to depict two human figures, each with a different approach to an impossible challenge – one staunchly facing it with no hope of survival, the other passively accepting his fate. For me, the inherent hopelessness within that drawing was horrifying to see; it made me cry.

Fortunately, there is plenty of optimism, wonder and amusement in Billy's art. He reimagines favourite images from his childhood, such as the Teddy Boys he saw posing and strutting through Glasgow's Kelvingrove Art Gallery and Museum during Sunday afternoon visits with his sister. *The Three Teds* and *Windswept & Interesting* are recent examples of the first, red-clad Teddy Boy he drew when I asked him to create a family Christmas card a dozen years ago. And literally drawn from his favourite years in the Glasgow shipyards is the spectacular piece *And On Monday, God Made The World* in which a kneeling, helmeted, winged welder puts the finishing touches to an earthly globe. Then there are the drawings that were inspired by Billy's musical life such as *Two For The Road* in which a handless banjoist and meek little accordionist stand impotently side by side. Reminds me of one of Billy's favourite banjo jokes: 'What's the definition of perfect pitch? – When you chuck an old banjo into a skip and it collides with an accordion.'

Billy's long affair with rock 'n' roll comes to life with *Saturday Night* in which a gleeful performer plays the piano with his feet; Billy always loved Jerry Lee Lewis and the outlandish capers of the rock star glitterati. And Billy's many years on the road with a crew of pranksters, who misbehaved as much as he did, inspired *Malkie's Day Off* ('Malkie' was a small-minded, 'more than my job's worth' type of character who was invented during one of those long boozy comedy tours to keep the troupe's spirits up).

One of those endless comedy tours was titled 'Rebel Without a Clue' and in his drawing *Rebel Without A Sword*, Billy again pokes fun at the inability to sustain a rebellious stance; a sad little round samurai stands with head bowed, holding only a shield, while his sword hand hangs limply by his side. Yet another expression of frustration lies in *Count Me In* — but here, more hopefully, the blindfolded band musician marches boldly forward, confidently assuming that help will be forthcoming.

Billy is first and foremost a storyteller, including in his visual art. He has drawn some fascinating scenarios, the complexities and endings of which I, for one, am dying to know.

The Angler And The Angel seems like an illustration for a moral tale that is almost biblical in nature, while *Fly Away Peter* evokes a contemporary embodiment of St Francis of Assisi. Oh yes, Billy's early life in a Catholic primary school well and truly ingrained in him the whole candy store of parables and their protagonists.

When Billy first started drawing (inspired by a rainy, winter's day in Canada when he ducked into an art supply shop for warmth) he was naturally tentative and lacking in confidence. Now, after quite a few years of developing his art, with the support of Washington Green and Castle Fine Art and with many success-ful exhibitions behind him, he has metamorphosed into a recog-nised artist who is still tentative and lacking in confidence! Billy always second-guesses himself — but it was ever that way with his comedy. 'Will I be funny tonight?' and 'Will people laugh?' Nowadays the question is so often: 'Is this drawing any good?' 'Do people really like my drawings?' I wish Billy could see them as others see them — truly exciting representations of mysterious worlds that may be whimsical, bizarre or even grotesque, and that frequently embody extraordinary polarities of tenderness and terror, submission and savagery, frustration and 'fuck-you-ness'.

Billy's endearing sensitivity is just the outer layer. As an artist, he doesn't just please our eye, make us laugh and tinker with our emotions. What makes him able to produce drawings that drag us by our own strands of rawness to meet his is the combination of his rageful humour and his brilliant, original aesthetic sensibility; it's a marriage made somewhere between heaven and the streets of Glasgow.

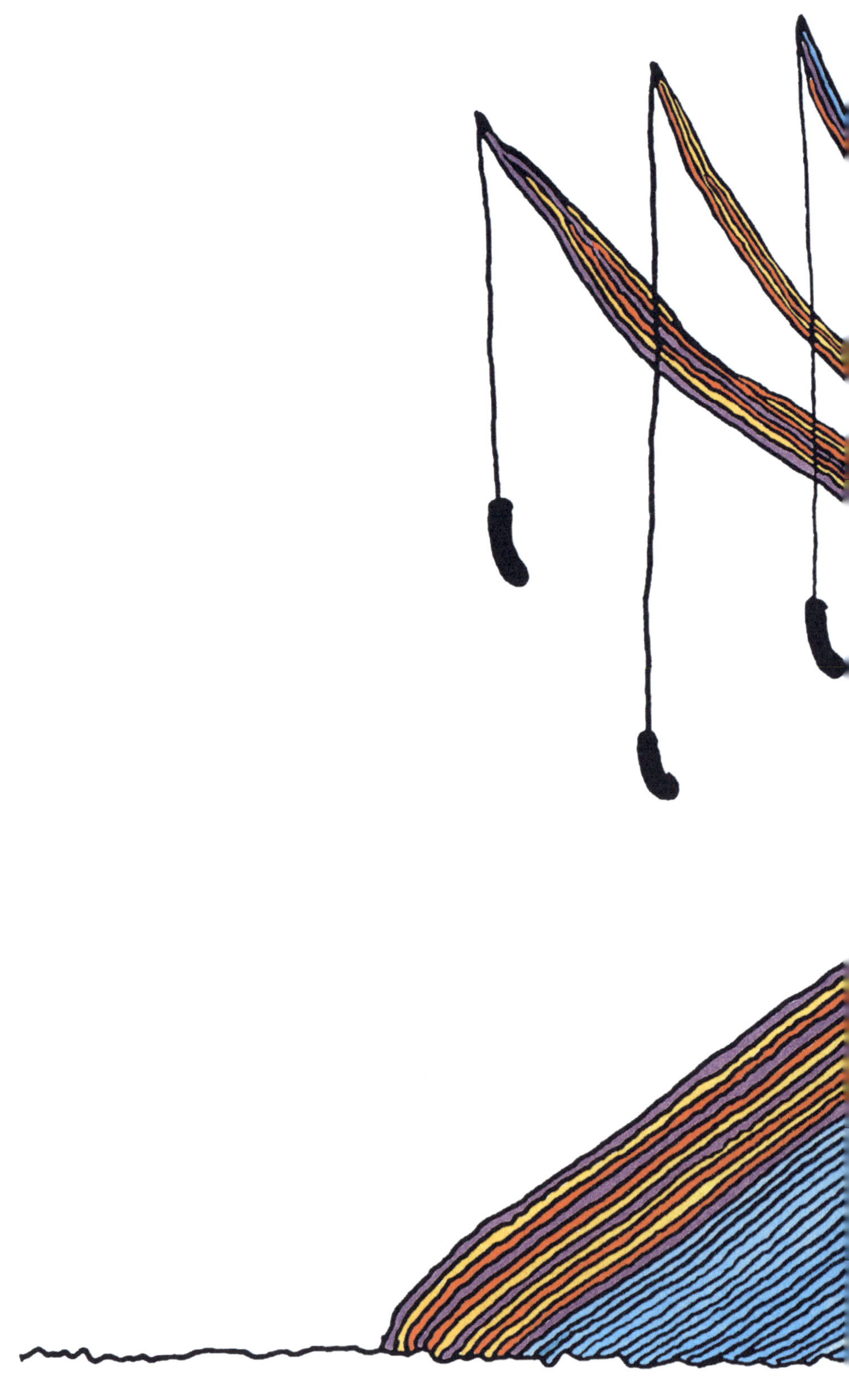

Sausage Tree, 2024

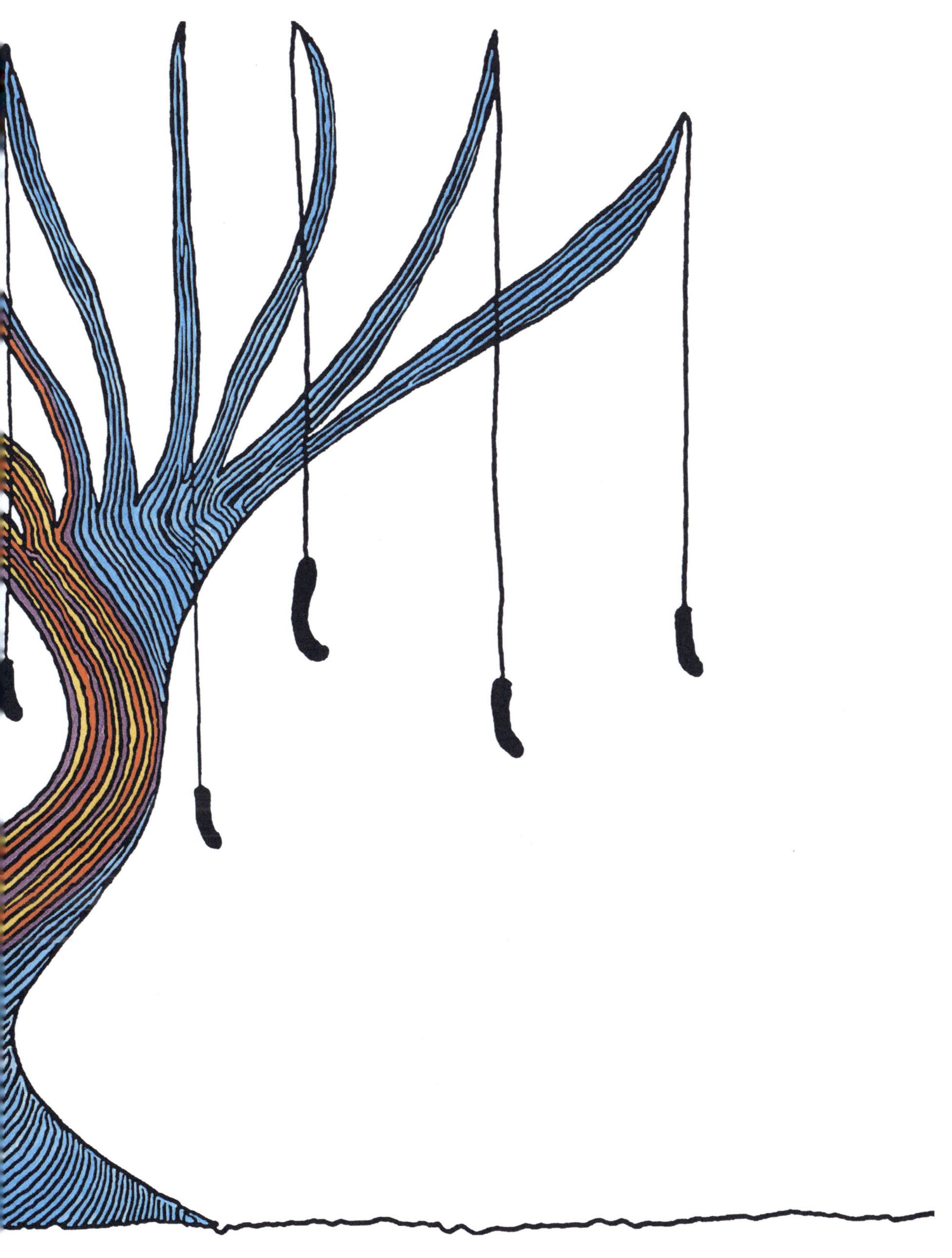

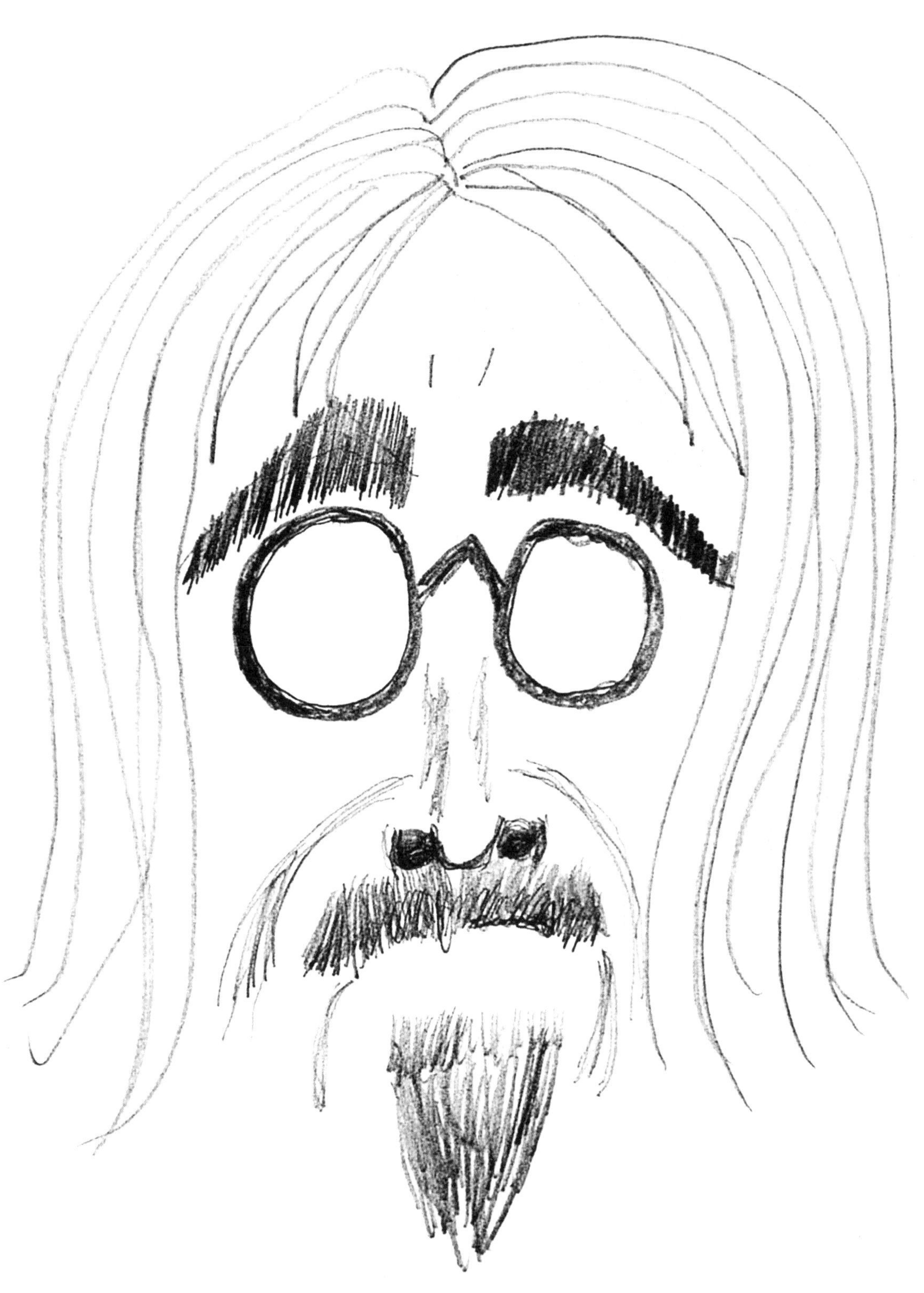

Self Portrait With Self Doubt, 2019

SIR WILLIAM CONNOLLY CBE

Rain has done me a huge favour. Changed my life. I was in Montreal on tour a few years ago, and during the day I was bored watching the telly. I went out for a walk, but it was freezing. It was pishing down that frozen rain they get in Canada that really hurts your face. After a while it got even worse. I was being bombed by blocks of ice and I couldn't even see properly, so I started walking back to my hotel. There was a pet shop opposite, so I nipped in to warm up. I watched the tortoises and puppies until the owner started looking at me like I was a kitty-rustler. Next door was an art store. I went in for a look and – for some unknown reason – bought myself some felt-tip pens and a sketchbook, then went straight back to my room and started to draw.

In the past I had never been able to draw, but I started drawing blobby-type things I called 'islands'. I divided them up into different backgrounds and colours and became utterly engrossed in that. I stuck to that style, drawing different kinds of islands for about a week. When the tour was over and I arrived home, which was in New York at the time, I said to Pamela: 'I've been drawing these things … they're pretty crap but do you think they're getting better?'

She said, 'They're definitely getting better.' So, I carried on. Then I started to develop my drawings. I started drawing people who looked as though they lived in sleeping bags, doing various things like standing in a circle, kneeling, and standing up. I liked them. I stumbled on a way of drawing the background with random lines, and eventually I changed the lines from being the background to being across the people like bandages. 'Why are they wearing bandages?' people asked. I couldn't explain. And I couldn't draw eyes, so I drew the people with blindfolds … and it went from strength to strength.

When I was a boy, my sister Florence used to take me to the Kelvingrove Art Gallery and Museum on Sundays. We would spend hours there. It had a great painting by Salvador Dalí — *Christ of St John of the Cross* — that was way superior to any of the crude religious pictures I'd been exposed to at school. It was there I was also introduced to geniuses like Vincent van Gogh, Paul Gauguin and Rembrandt, who inspire my own art today.

Over the years, I've become very friendly with a few artists including Brett Whiteley. Brett died at fifty-three of a heart attack, which was a terrible loss. Apart from being a stunning painter, Brett was one of the wildest wee men I've ever met. He came to my show at the Sydney Opera House, then arrived backstage afterwards and asked a terrible question that lots of other people have asked: 'How do you remember all that stuff?'

I patiently explained there was no 'remembering' involved, that I pretty much made it up night after night.

He said, 'Fuck off. I don't believe you.' I said, 'It's true! Everyone knows that.'

Then Brett says, 'OK. I'm coming back tomorrow night to check it out.'

He did. The following night I did a completely different show, not even bringing up one subject I'd mentioned in the previous concert … which wasn't that easy at that late point in the tour.

Brett came back after that second concert and said, 'OK, Billy. I guess you're right. That was incredible … I've never seen anything like it. But just to be sure, I'm coming back for the third time tomorrow night …'

'Fuck off,' I said.

Ken Done is another remarkable Australian painter. I just love his work. Many years ago, he taught me something important about painting and drawing. I was staying at Pearl Beach in New South Wales. He said, 'What catches your eye outside there?' I said, 'Well, I get up in the morning and eat breakfast outside on the verandah.' He said, 'What's that like?' I said, 'Well, it's really peaceful, then all these really brightly coloured galahs swoop down and try to eat my toast …' Ken said, 'So, you could use the colour of the galahs, but it's more important to try to get onto the paper the *feeling* of them swooping down.'

On a good day now, I can get a feeling onto the paper. Andrew White, the director of publishing at Washington Green/Castle Fine Art, showed interest in my drawings, which was an extraordinary thing. He's promoted my artworks and mounted exhibitions for me. I took it as a great compliment. I'm not a very confident artist, though. I keep waiting for someone to say that it's rubbish. I don't do 'art speak', so I don't know how to describe them. They're just … thoughts. I sometimes drift off what I've been doing, and the thing ends up cartoonish, which I don't like – so I toss it.

I'm immensely proud of some of my best drawings, though. I did one that is a dachshund with wheels supporting its middle body … I had to sign some prints of that one and the more I did, the more I loved it. I'm really proud of the one called *Purgatory* – it's a man standing in the bow of a boat with a box on his head. He looks like he's a prisoner of the man at the tiller steering the boat who's wearing a black cowl.

I can't quite handle it when I go to one of my exhibitions, though. I've met people who collect my stuff, which is a serious compliment, but I still can't get my head round it. Maybe you shouldn't dwell on that kind of thing. I find it extraordinarily wonderful that people want to buy my drawings. Biggest surprise of my life.

I've collected together my favourite drawings for this book and selected some of my favourite stories to sit alongside them. One doesn't illustrate the other. They are different things, but they're from the same world — my world. I hope you enjoy them as much as I have enjoyed creating them.

Love, Billy.

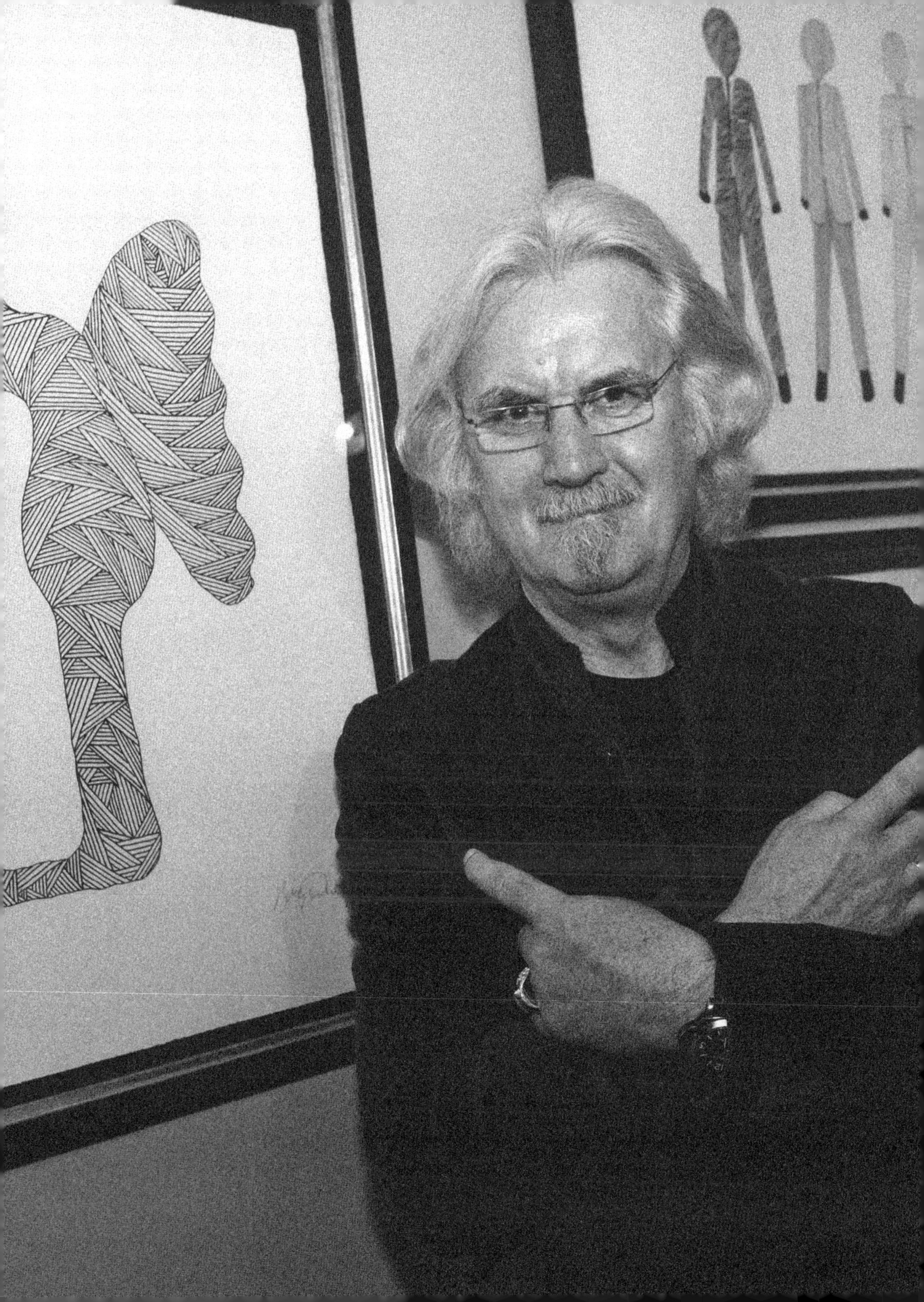

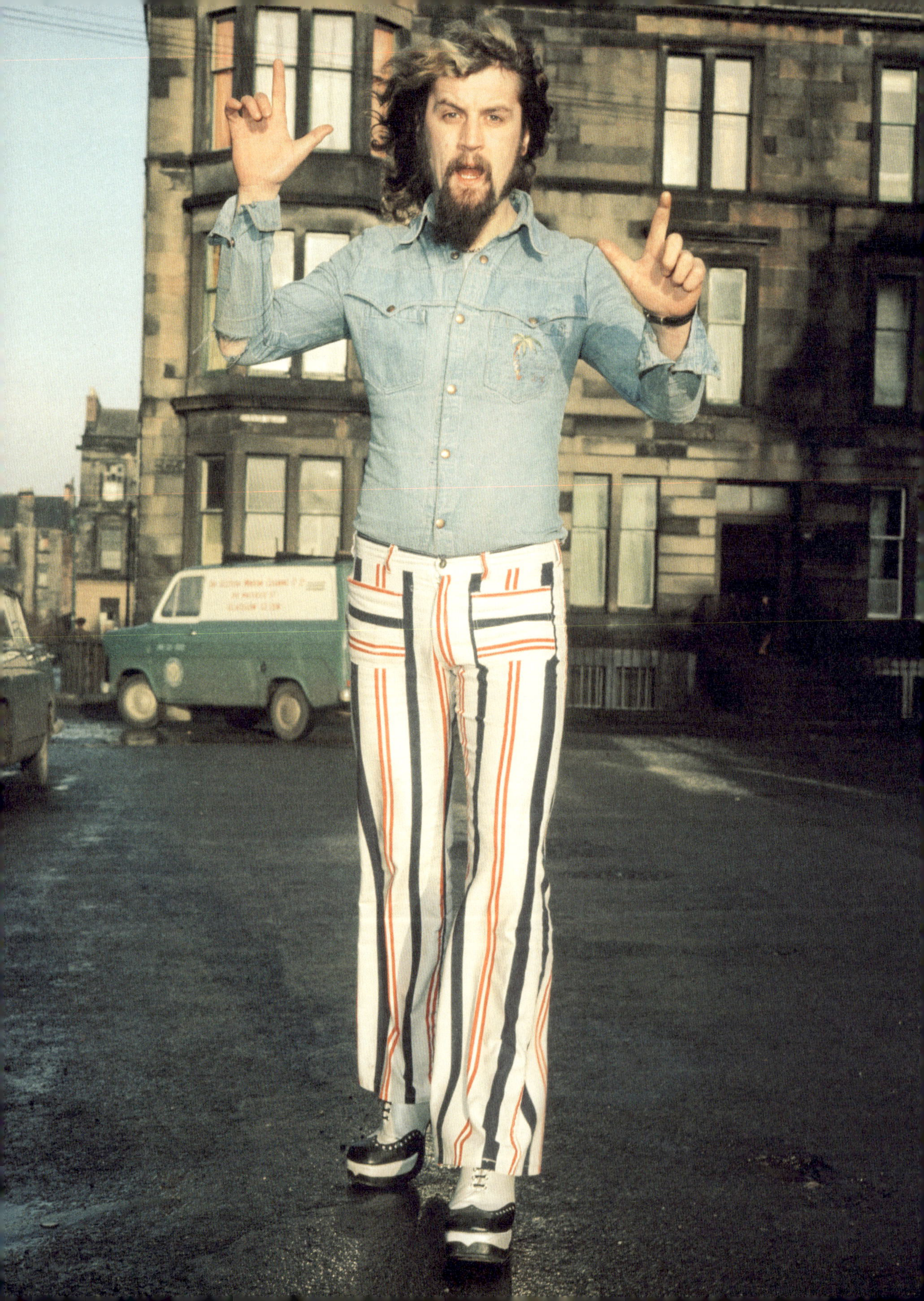

Fashion

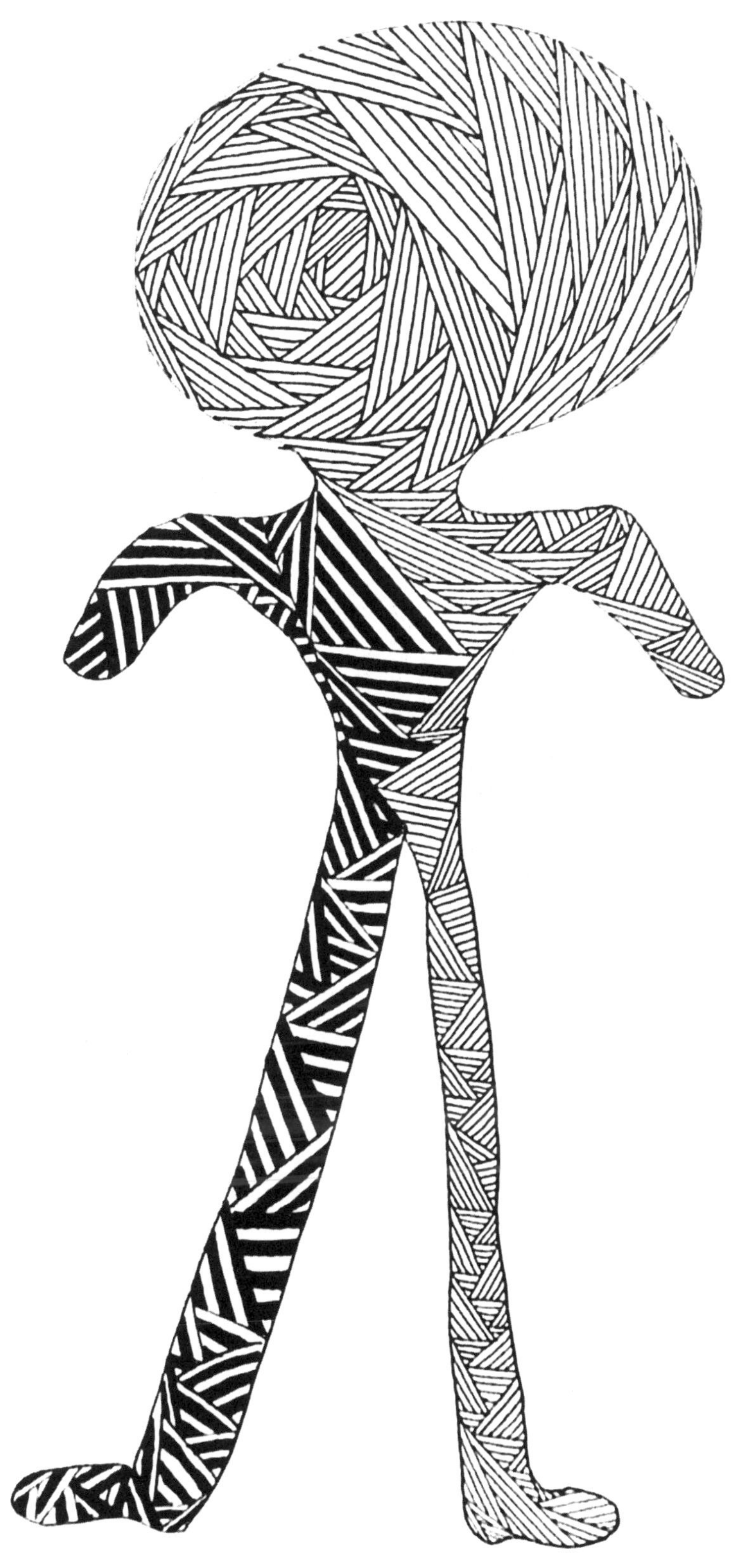

Design Boy, 2012

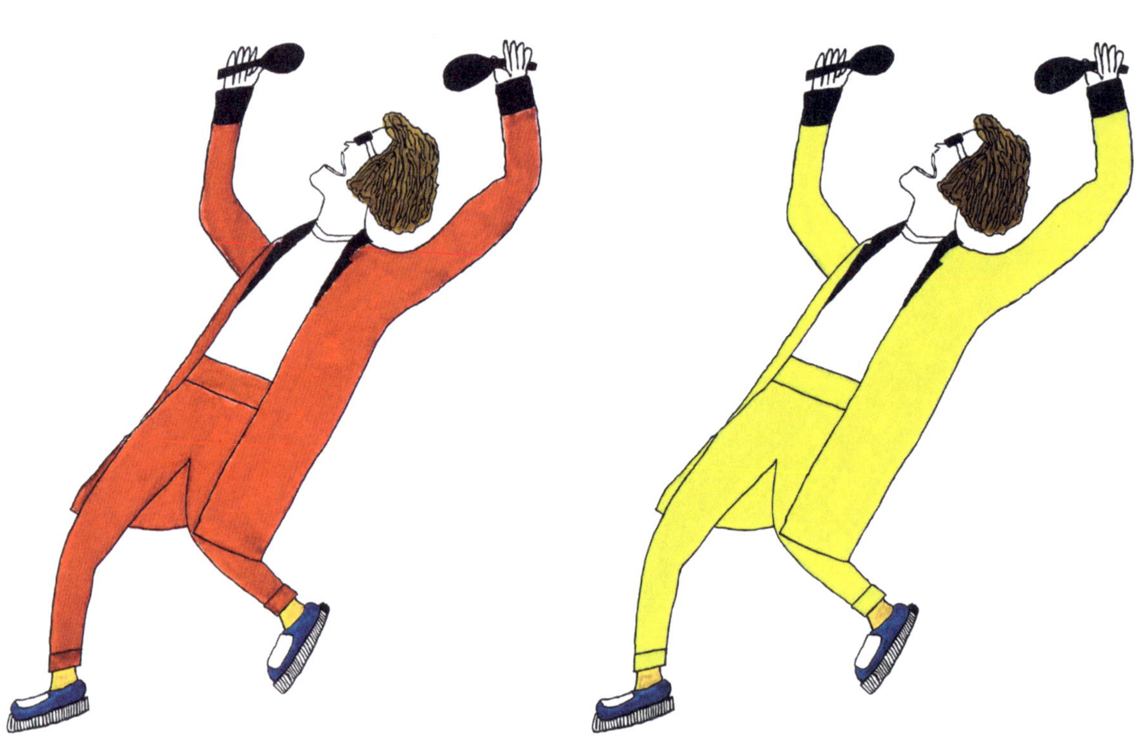

Windswept & Interesting — Red, 2020 / Windswept & Interesting — Yellow, 2020

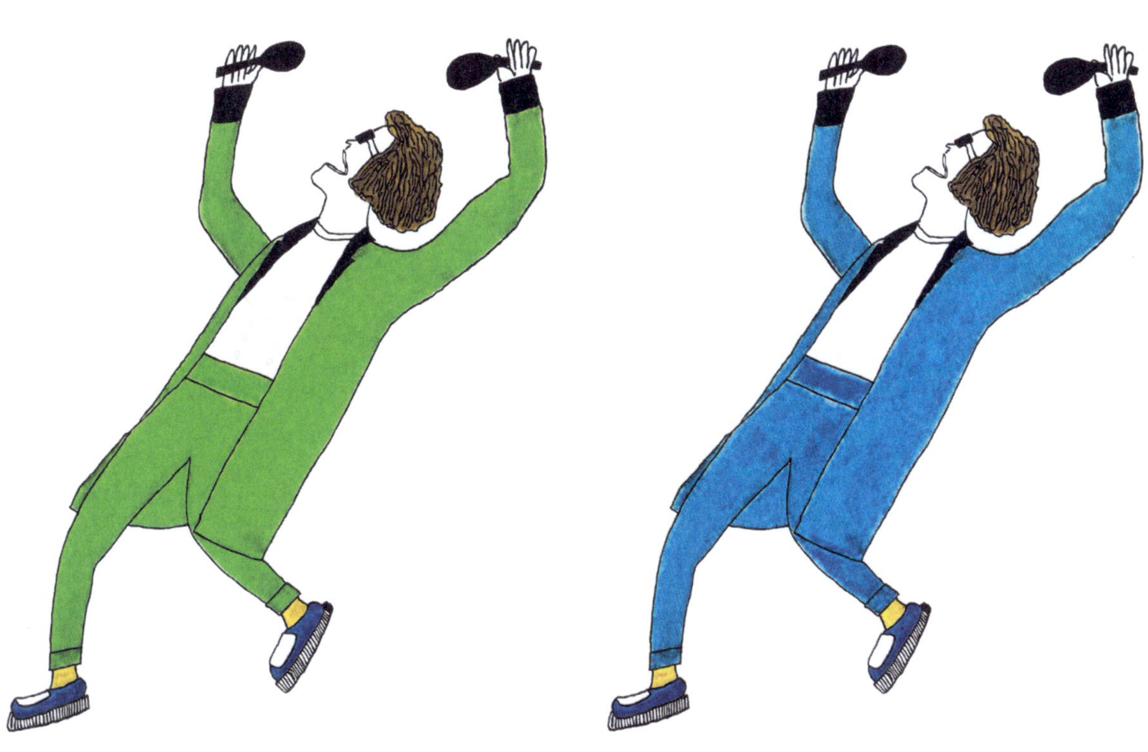

Growing up, you had to look good at the dances. 'Going on your own can' meant that you gave your father your rent money and kept the rest for clothes and other necessities. I had a suit made for me at Jackson the Tailor that I paid off every week, after my father signed a guarantee. We wore Italian-style Perry Como suits, usually in narrow blue stripes. The boxy jacket had three buttons at the front and folded-back cuffs with an inch vent and a button on each side. Some people had custom features — six buttons, or three buttons. I used to get a link button on my jacket. I was quite the fashion maven.

At one point we wore collarless shirts with separate paper collars. Some guys would draw on the points of the paper collars to make them look round — or squiggly, just to be different. I wore tight trousers that had one-inch side vents with a white button at the top. My feet had an 'Aladdin' look about them: I wore 'winkle-pickers' — narrow shoes with pointed, turned-up toes. At one point I had basket-weave winkle-pickers. They were brilliant. I was wearing them on the bus and the woman beside me said, 'You're very neat about the feet!'

My ties were one colour and dead skinny, with a tiepin. The final touch was a pair of huge, gaudy cufflinks — an eagle standing on a ruby. Thirty bob a pair, and I looked as if I owned South Africa. I got a brutal Perry Como haircut, and shaved round the acne — no mean task. I looked like a butcher's window. My father would think I'd been slashed: 'What happened to you, son??'

When we were old enough to enjoy going to pubs, we'd start the night in Gallowgate at the Sarry Heid — otherwise known as the Saracen Head pub. Angus the barman would pass pints over the heads of everybody who was standing at the bar, thus spilling beer and cider all over his patrons. Most people tolerated this, but we were all dressed up for the dancing and preferred not to arrive with a soggy arse. My pal Hughie Gilchrist came up with a novel solution: he started coming in with a pac-a-mac, a plastic raincoat that folded up into an envelope. He'd put it on and button it right up to his neck, so that he could stand at the bar and drink away without spoiling his clothes. We regarded Hughie as a natural leader.

What always staggers me is that when people blow their noses, they always look into their hankies to see what came out. What do they expect to find?

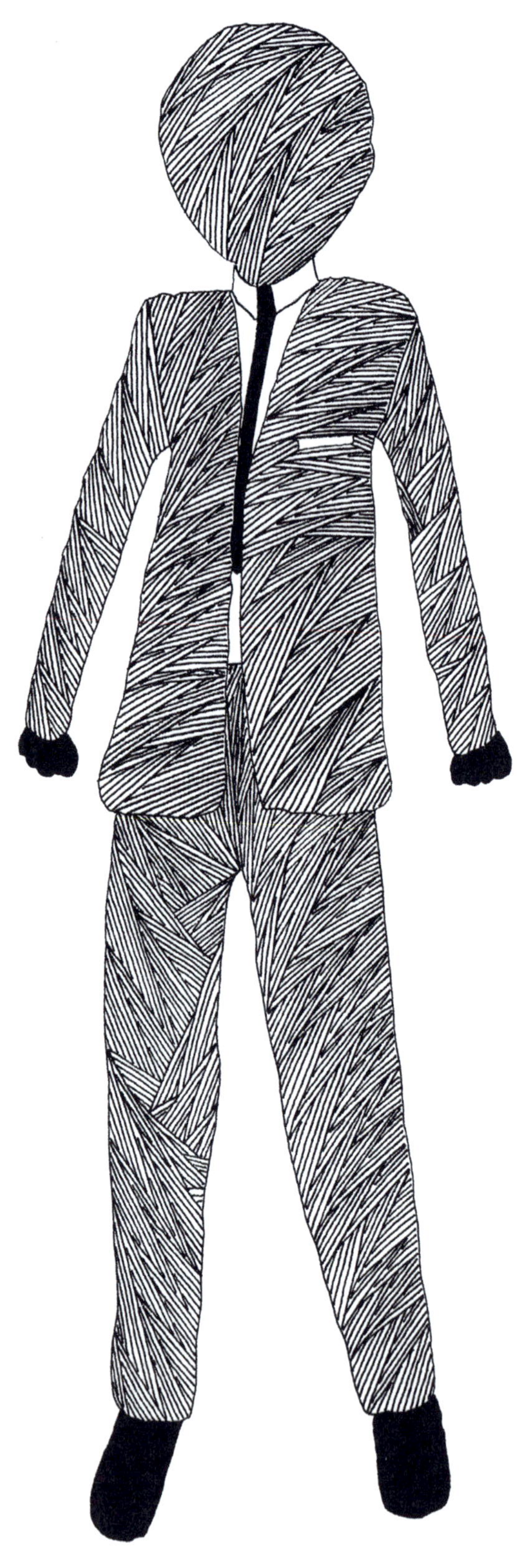

Pink Tie & Hanky, 2011

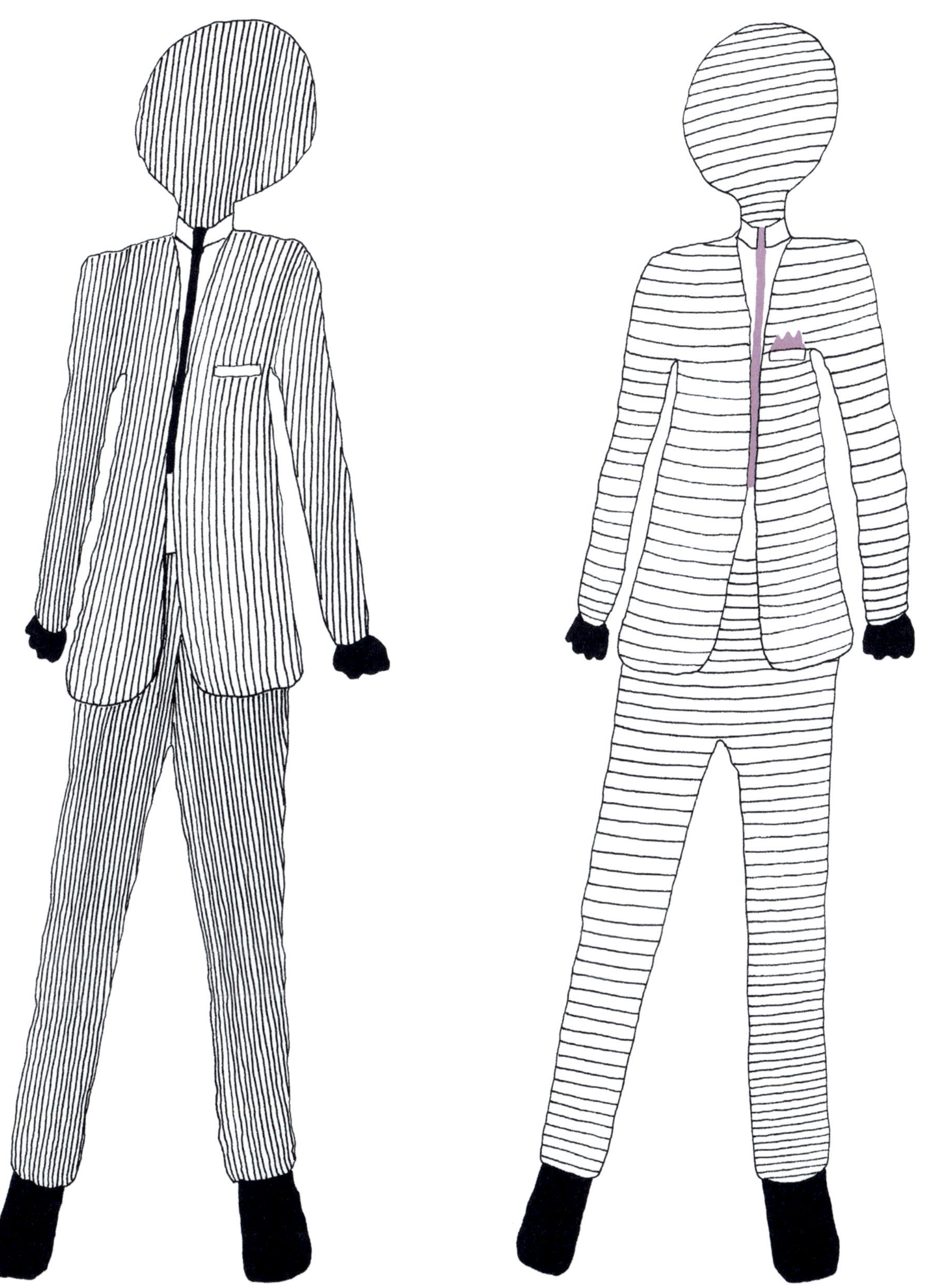

I started to become adventurous in the wardrobe department when I was a novice folkie. I decided this was necessary because when I arrived at gigs wearing jeans and a denim jacket, nobody would know who I was. I'd say, 'Where's the folk club?'

'Upstairs.'

'OK, thanks – I'm Billy Connolly.'

'Oh yeah? Didn't know what you looked like.'

I was fed up with this, so I started to dress in a way that would grab people's attention. Once I started showing up in, say, a pair of wild striped trousers with stars on my T-shirt, right away they'd say, 'Oh, you must be the guest!'

'Yes!'

From that point on I adopted an extroverted style of dress, and it never let me down. I've really had fun with it over the years. I was always on the lookout for sensational outfits. I was once walking home at night over a bridge in Amsterdam. A man came towards me, wearing fabulous suede flared trousers.

I said, 'I love your trousers.' He said, 'I love yours!'

I said, 'I'll swap you.' 'Right,' he said.

We did it. Took off our trousers in the middle of the bridge and swapped them then and there. People walking by … Perfectly normal.

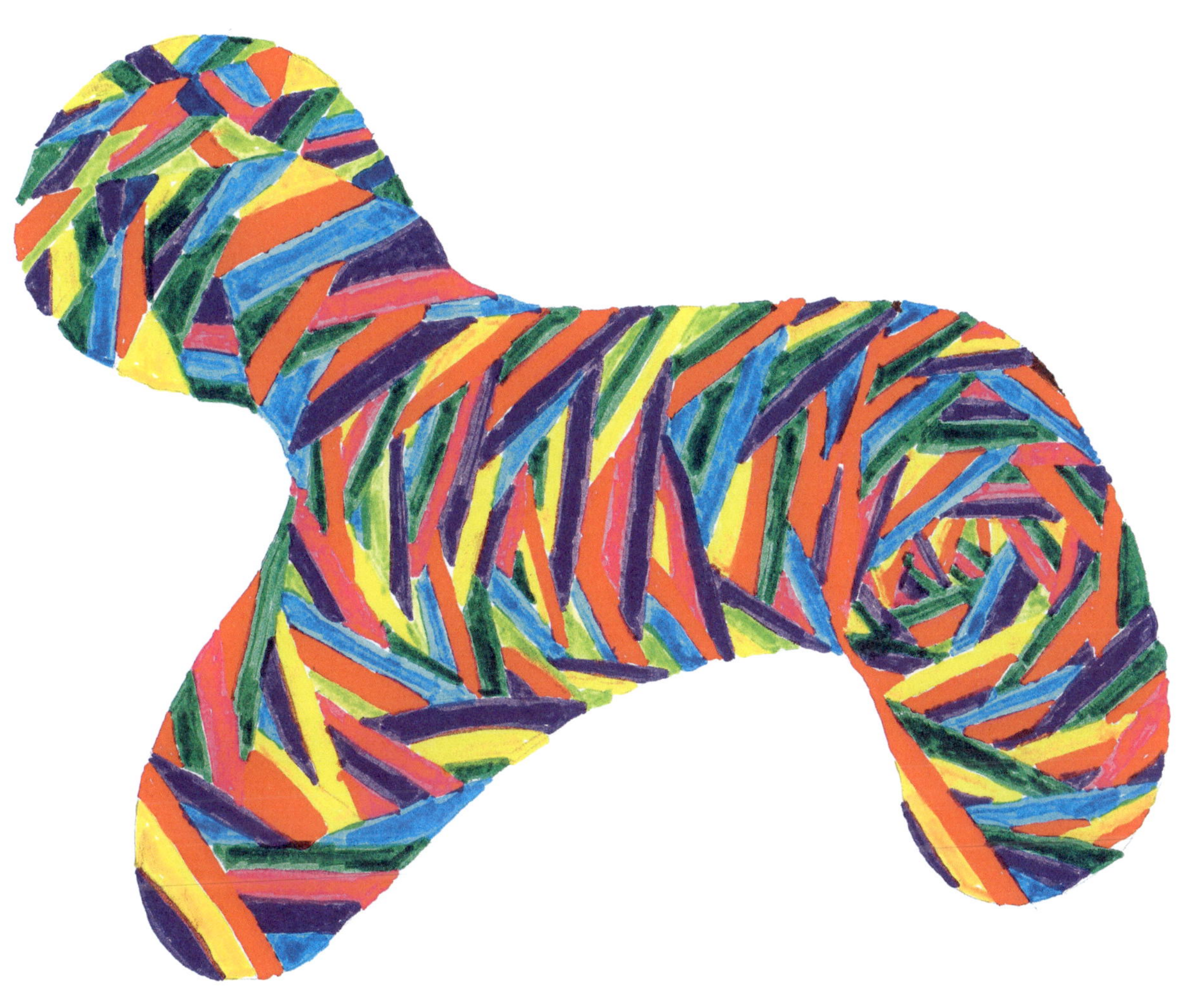

Burning Bright, 2021

My former manager, Frank Lynch, helped me develop my stage appearance; he knew people who made things. He found craftspeople to make my welly boots, my tights and leotard, and my giant boots like half-peeled bananas — they were all great ideas, but if it had been left up to me, they would have remained ideas. Frank made them happen, and those costumes became really popular. People went crazy for my 'banana boots'. They were designed by John Byrne, and Frank commissioned Edmond Smith from a design group called Artifactory to make them. My tights were designed by a London designer, Alan Jeffries, who stuck a picture of my face on the bum. Alan also made the 'scissors suit' I dreamed up, with big red handles and silver blades down my legs. I also had beautiful velvet suits with the hoods of the jackets going right down to my knees at the back, and a target on my knee. I had wanted to be in the glam rock business — and, overwhelmingly, it worked. I was being noticed by people in other fields. I was invited to do great, starry gigs like hosting the *Melody Maker* annual awards. I was giving prizes to Led Zeppelin. People were saying I was hot as a pistol.

Offstage, too, looking good was important. Wearing the right jeans was important — like Levi's 501s. In the early days, I might have been a bit too fashion-forward for my own good; when I first wore flares, people called me Popeye. I wore desert boots, cowboy boots, denim and cheesecloth shirts. My outerwear was donkey jackets, motorcycle leathers, corduroy jackets, and I flung on scarves and beads. I used to dab sandalwood oil on myself, and I wore patchouli oil for a while until I got flung out of a pub in Quebec for wearing it: 'You smell like dogs' piss.'

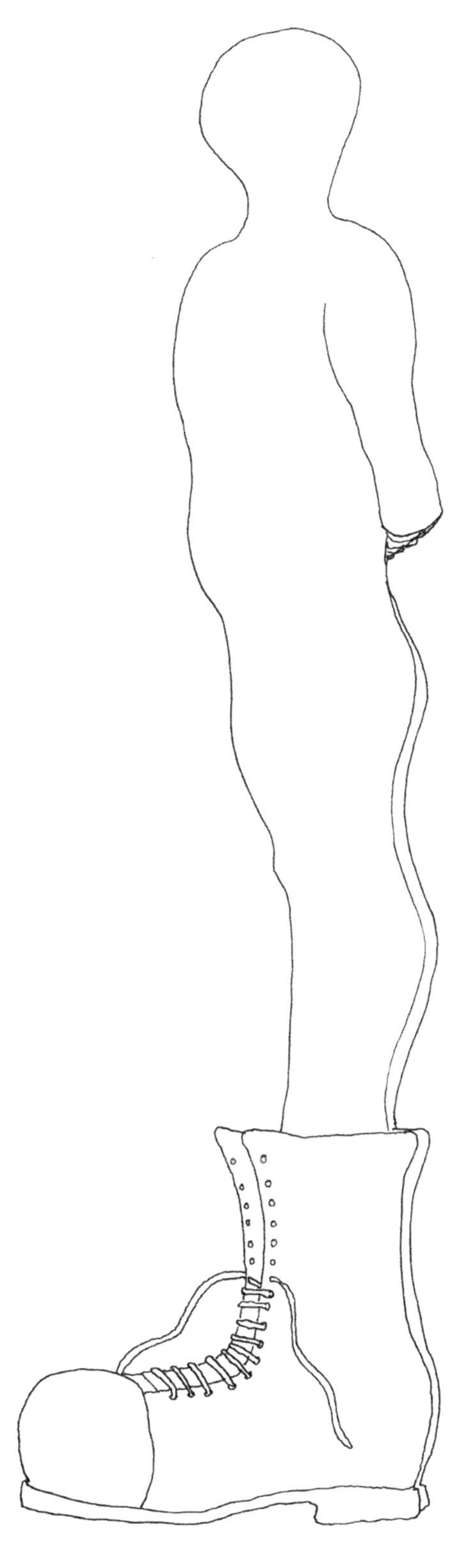

The Sentinel, 2018

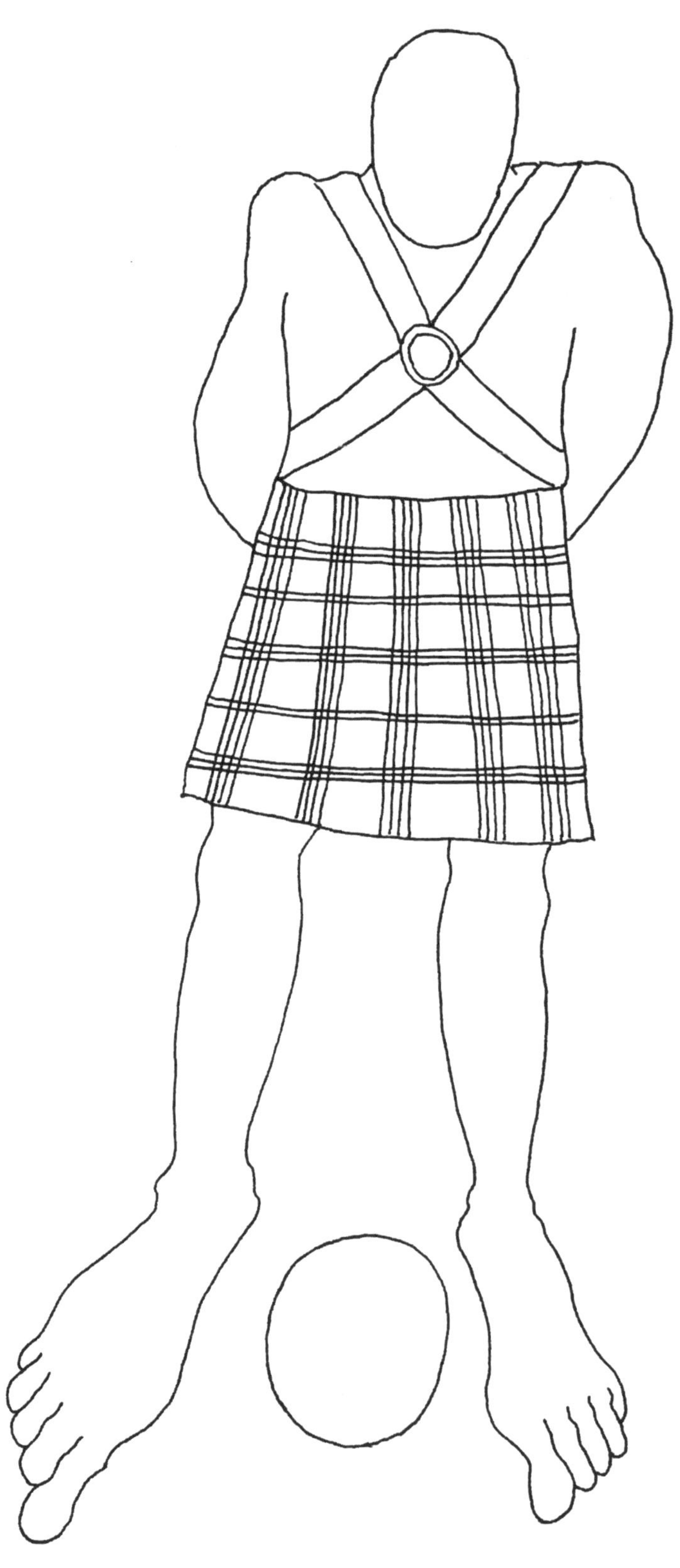

Heid The Ba', 2017

It's lovely, the way people think you do it. People think I paint or draw things on purpose. I don't, I just draw. And then as it goes on, it becomes obvious what it's going to be (to me). And then I can think about it along those lines: a horse, a man or a balloon. That's when I name it – at the end.

Sometimes I think it's a bad thing to give it a title because you force the person looking at it to think along those lines – whereas if you didn't give it a name, they would come to a different conclusion, a conclusion of their own and get a relationship with the drawing. I think that would be better, but people seem to want the titles, and they find them funny sometimes. So do I.

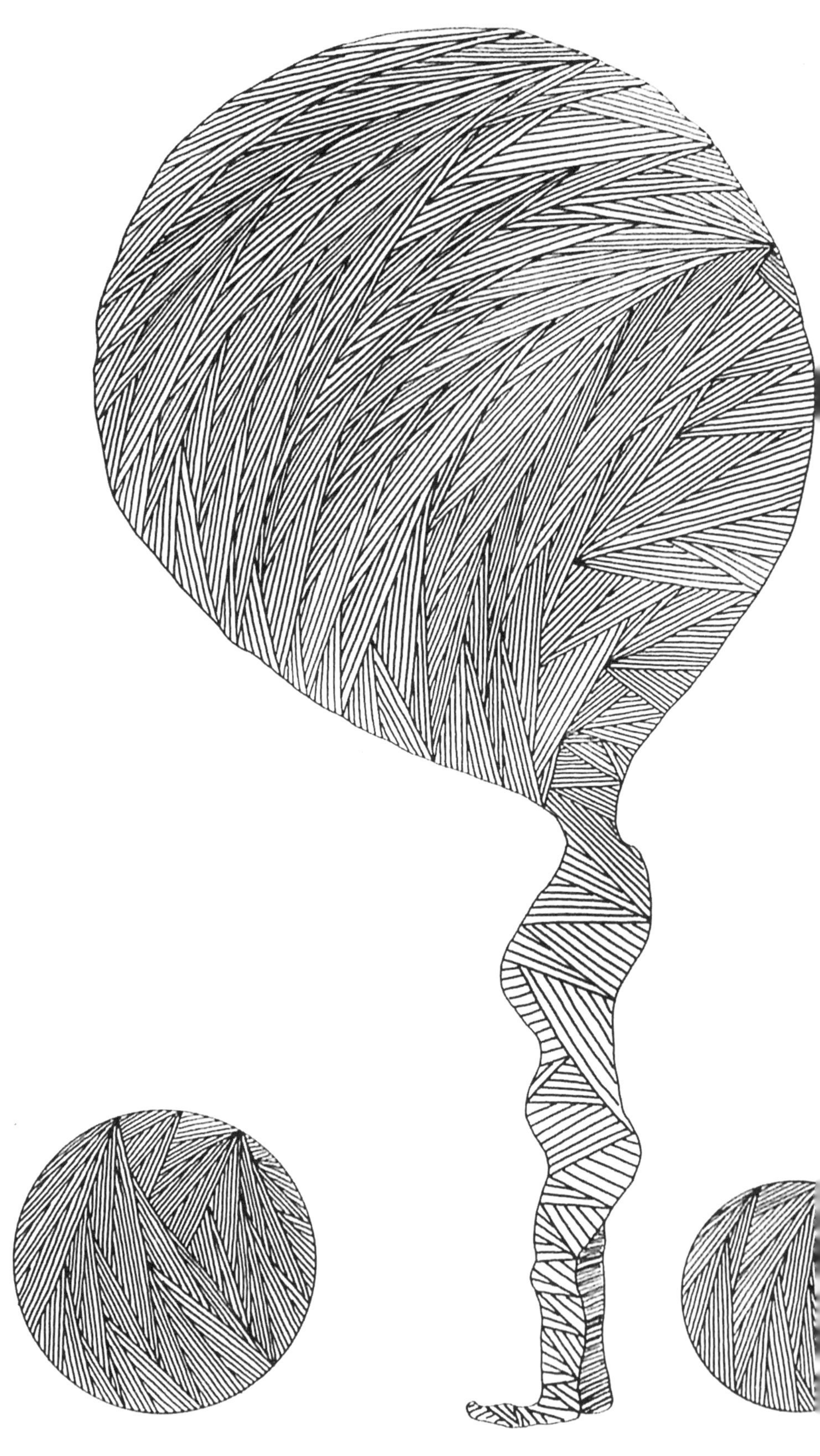

Serious Combover, 2012

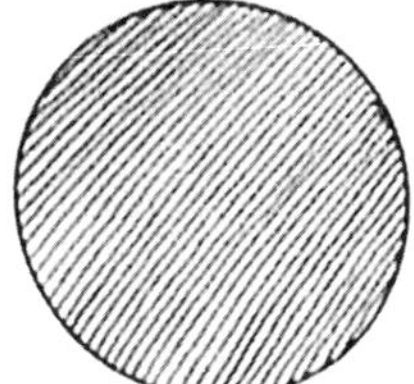

Never trust a man
who, when left alone
in a room with a tea
cosy, doesn't try it on.

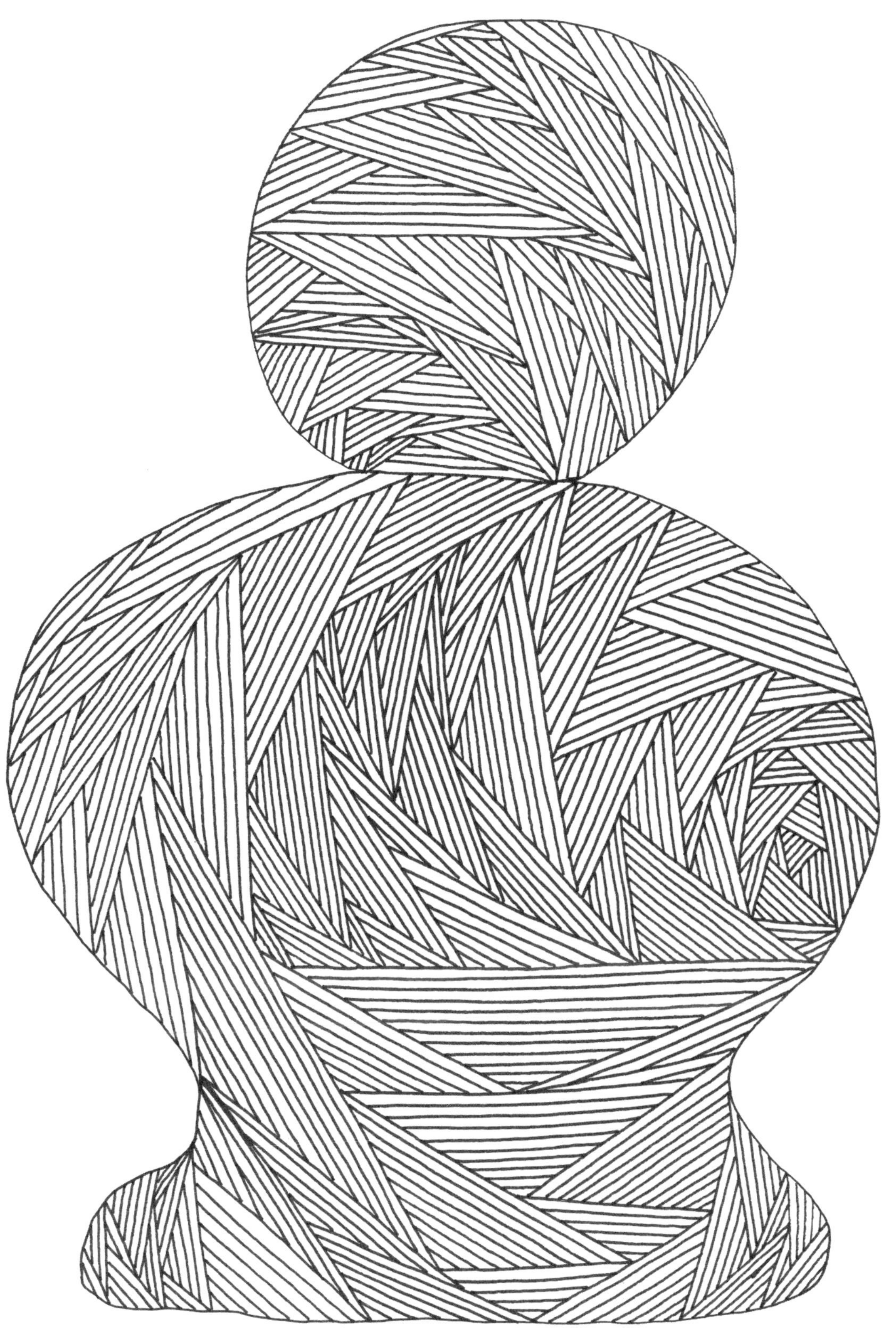

Antique Tea Caddy, 2012

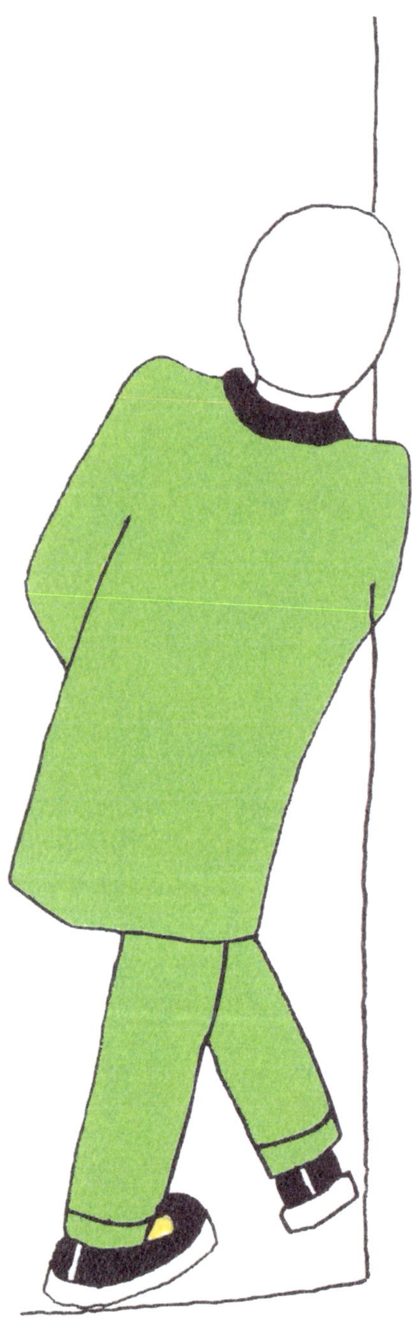 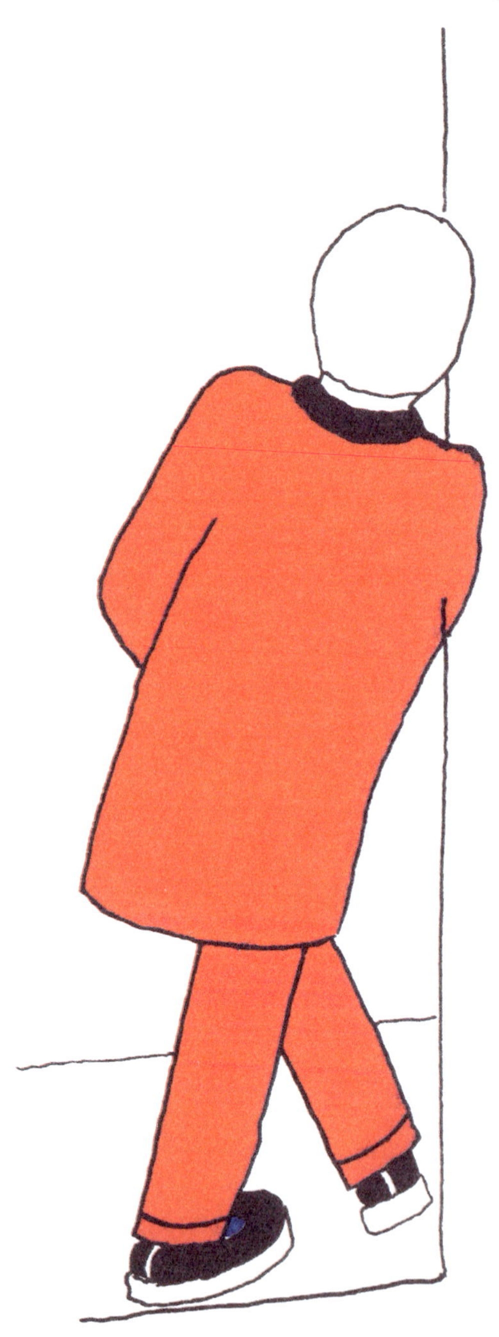

The Three Teds, 2019

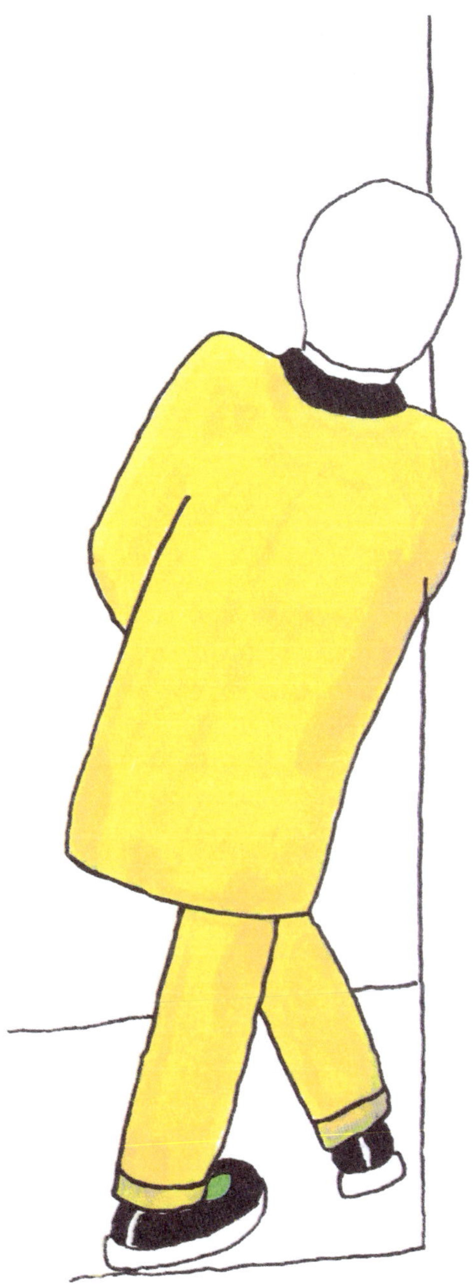

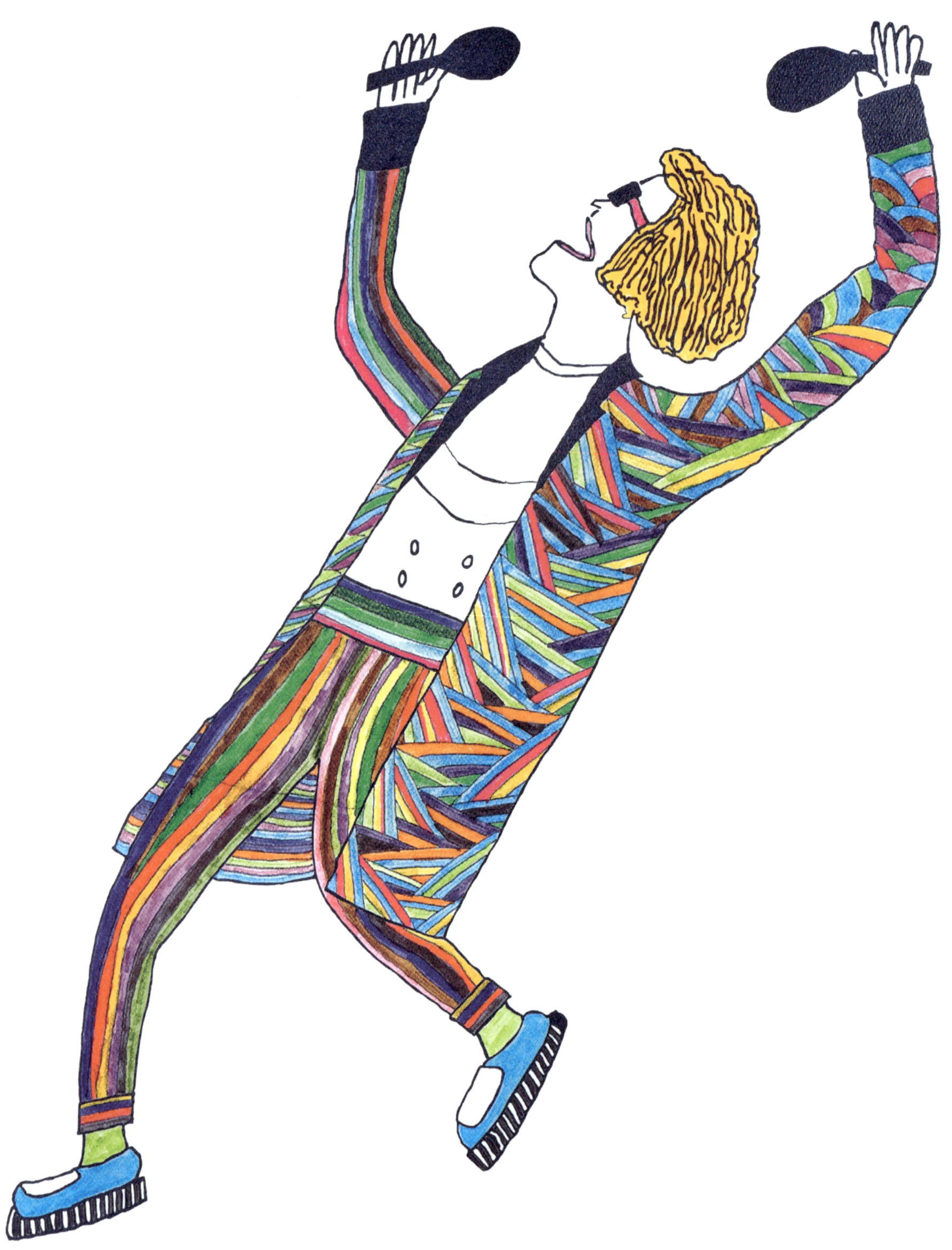

Windswept & Interesting — Multicoloured Coat, 2021

'Windswept and interesting' was a title Archie Fisher the folk singer gave me many years ago at Methil Steelworks Club in Fife. I'd been playing and I was all hairy. He saw me with all my hippy gear on, all velvet and long hair and curls and a beard. He said, 'You look windswept and interesting', and I said 'Of course I do!' and I made it my aim to be windswept and interesting from then on in.

When I was a schoolboy, about thirteen or fourteen, I saw a great Teddy Boy on one of my Sunday trips with my sister to Kelvingrove Art Gallery and Museum in Glasgow. I'd seen many Teddy Boys on the street, but this guy was amazing! He just was a Teddy Boy from his head to his toes, and his suede shoes and his soles, his beetle crushers, the drainpipe trousers and drape jacket, velvet collar and cuffs — and an earring. I'd never seen a man with an earring before — and he was with his girlfriend, and she looked great as well. They were in an art gallery, they looked like an exhibit. I thought they were brilliant, and I'd like to be one of them, but by the time I got old enough, it was gone.

Teddy Boys were windswept and interesting. They chose their clothes to differ from everyone else in society. And that was the hippie thing as well, just choosing your clothes, wearing policemen's capes and big hats with snakeskin bands. It was a good time.

I've always tried to wear windswept and interesting clothing on chat shows. And shoes — your shoes are always visible. If you look startling, the host will always have something to comment on. They like that. Once, when I went on *The Jay Leno Show* in Los Angeles, I wore a black wobbly Japanese suit and black open-toed shoes with silver buckles. Jay took in the whole thing, including my black toenail polish, and said, 'What are you — some kind of punk pilgrim?' For another appearance I wore my 'Irish Tiger' suit — a furry, green animal-print number. That earned me the title 'Tommy the Tiger's gay uncle'.

One time I went on a talk show in Canada with a famous host called Peter Gzowski. People there called him 'Captain Canada', but I called him 'Knife and Forksky'. On that occasion I wore my tights with a portrait of my face on my bum, with hair hanging down, so I could wave my hair by shaking my backside. That's where I met Robin Williams, who became my dear pal. Robin had his own views about my outfits: 'He does wear a lot of unusual clothes for a heterosexual, and I'm using the word "heterosexual" very loosely. The voice, the look, and clothes that even a drag queen would go "Oh, puhhlease…!"'

On one of my *Parkinson* appearances, I wore a jacket decorated by John Byrne. I'd run into John one day in Glasgow, when — for some reason — I was wearing a white suit. I'd had a ballpoint pen in the breast pocket, but it leaked, and ink had seeped through the cloth. I said to John, 'Look at this fucking mess.' And he said, 'Give it to me.' When he returned the jacket, the ink stain had been turned into a swallow's tail, and it was entirely covered in fabulous images — a rabbit, a dog, roses, hearts and a big baby in Victorian dress with a banjo. Brilliant.

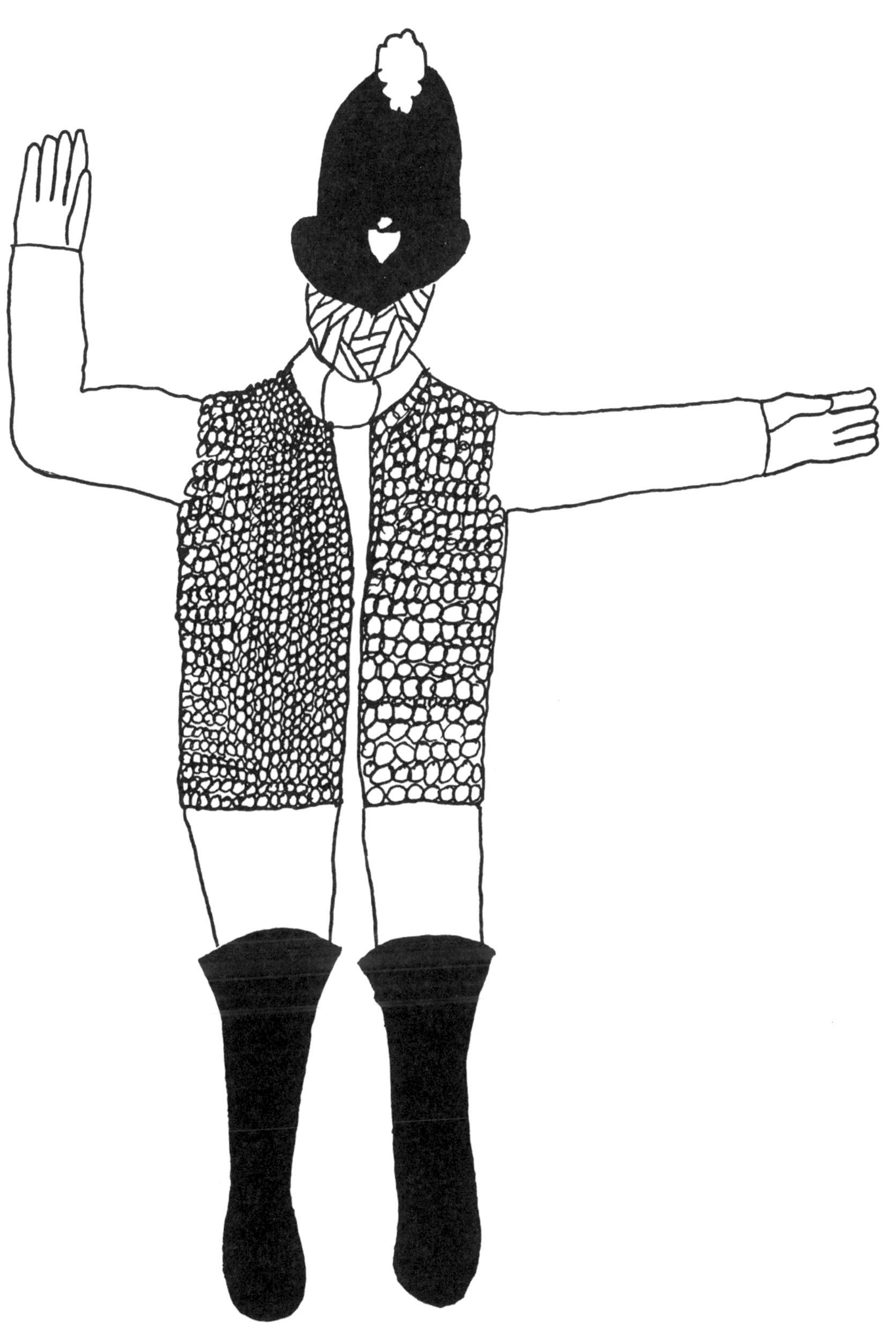

London, 2019

41

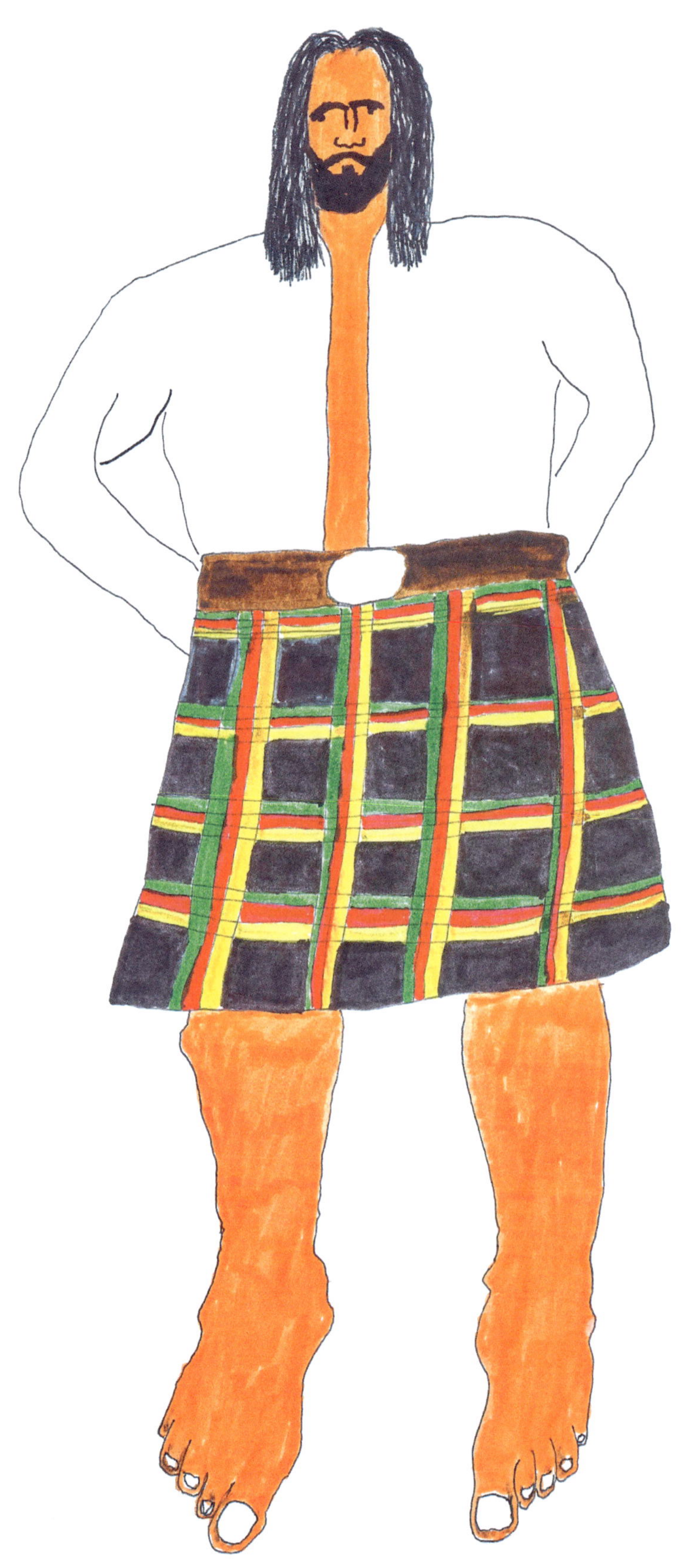

In A Casual Pose, 2021

Scottish-Americans tell you
that if you want to identify
tartans, it's easy – you simply
look under the kilt, and if it's
a quarter pounder, you know
it's a McDonald's.

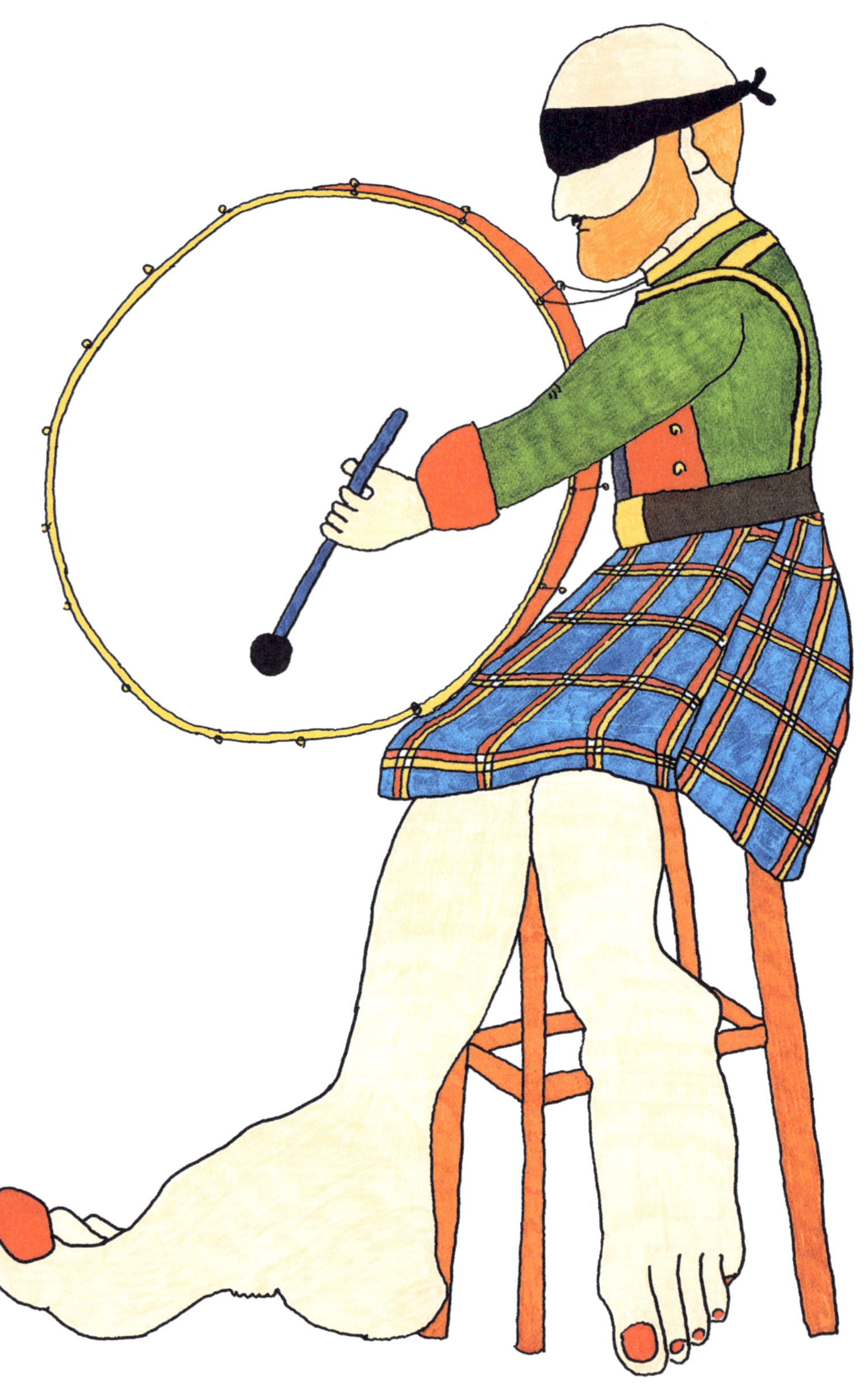

Count Me In, 2023

Magnus Barelegs apparently wore a Scottish kilt. He became the king of Norway in 1093 and was an illustrious Viking warrior who carried out many successful invasions of places like Orkney, the Hebrides and the Isle of Man. I can imagine he was dead proud of his legs. In that respect, I feel Magnus and I have something in common. In Tasmania, I won the 'Sexiest Legs in Launceston' competition. It was organised by a crowd of nutters. Launceston had just won the national basketball championships and they were doing all kinds of crazy things, including that 'sexiest legs' contest, and, in a rash moment of bravado, I had signed up. I wore pink socks with pictures of Elvis on them – I think that's what swung it for me. I wore them without shoes, and just wore my underpants.

When I was a boy, we didn't see kilts much, except on people in pipe bands and the army. Apart from them there was a definite type of person who wore a kilt – a stuffy type of person. We used to shout at them in the street: 'Kilty kilty cold bum!' Many people wear them now for weddings, but it wasn't like that when I was a boy. Well, certainly not in Glasgow.

The Highland dress keeps being reinvented. It didn't take long for the Scottish boys to fall for the jabot instead of the bow tie. You can cut a fine dash in that. Sean Connery wore it, and you can't go wrong if big Sean wore it. I think a huge change for the better has come over tartan. There was a stuffiness to it that I'm glad is disappearing. The people who are designing the new stuff don't pay any attention to the pseudo-heritage stuff. It's given rise to great new designs and a more casual attitude, with some guys even wearing leather and tweed kilts now. Beforehand, people would say, 'You're not allowed to wear such and such a tartan.' Load of crap. They seemed to make up those rules as they went along.

Sitting down in a kilt is a bit uncomfortable. I'm sensitive to wool, and it's rough on my bum. It can chafe. It's OK having the sporran banging into your willy, though. If you get a good rhythm going, your kilt swings at the right pace. It just gives your willy a wee dunt. Reminds you it's there. No bad thing. I know this because I was invited to lead the Tartan Parade along Sixth Avenue in New York City a couple of years ago, with thousands of Scottish people and Scotophiles lining the route. I was nervous that I wouldn't be up to it, but I managed to stride out the whole way, keeping ahead of all the great pipe bands and other groups. A Scottish kilt-maker called Howie Nicholsby had made me a fantastic kilt for the occasion. He's at the head of the movement to make the kilt a windswept and interesting alternative to trousers all over the world; I love that.

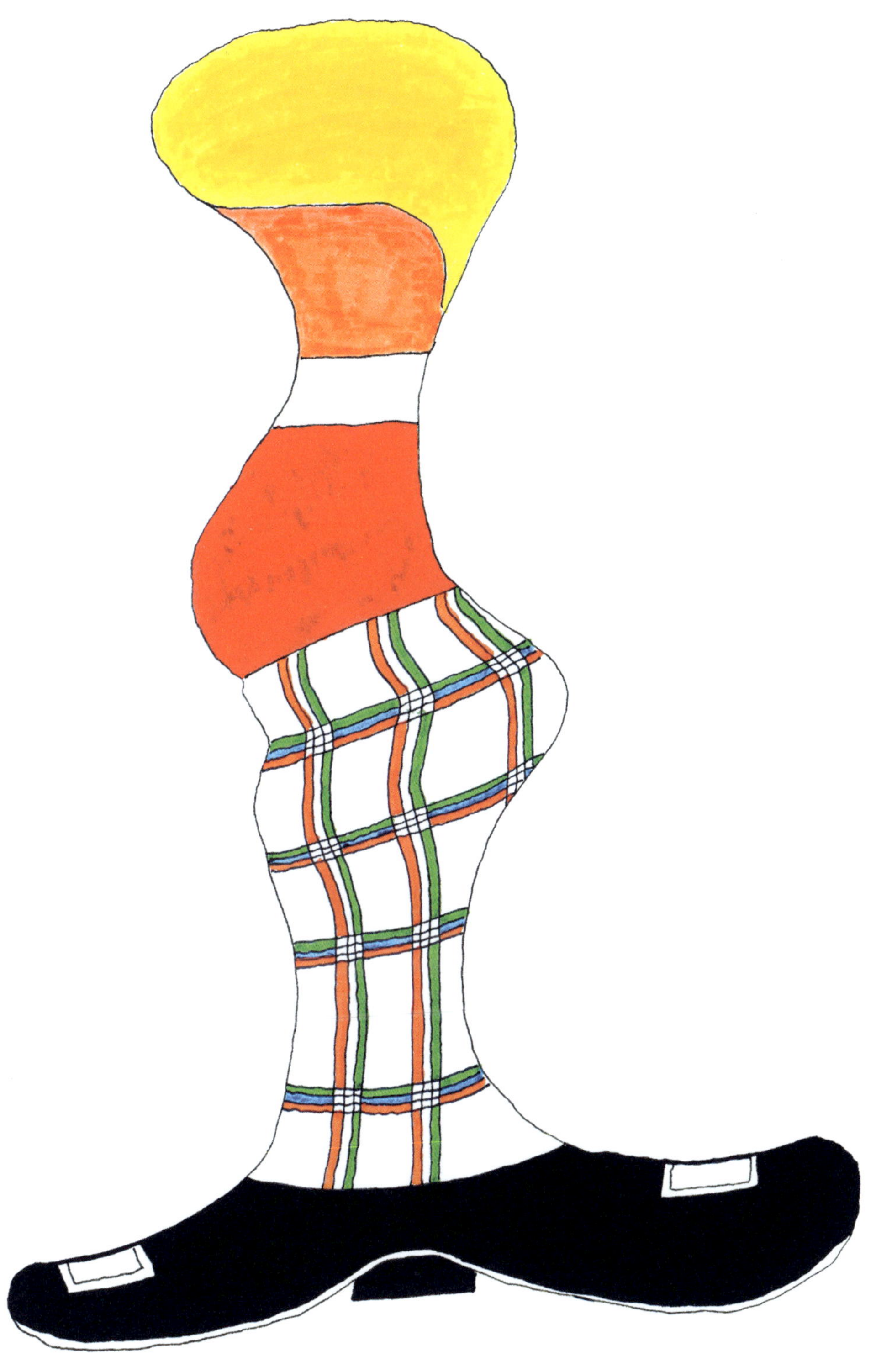

First Position, 2019

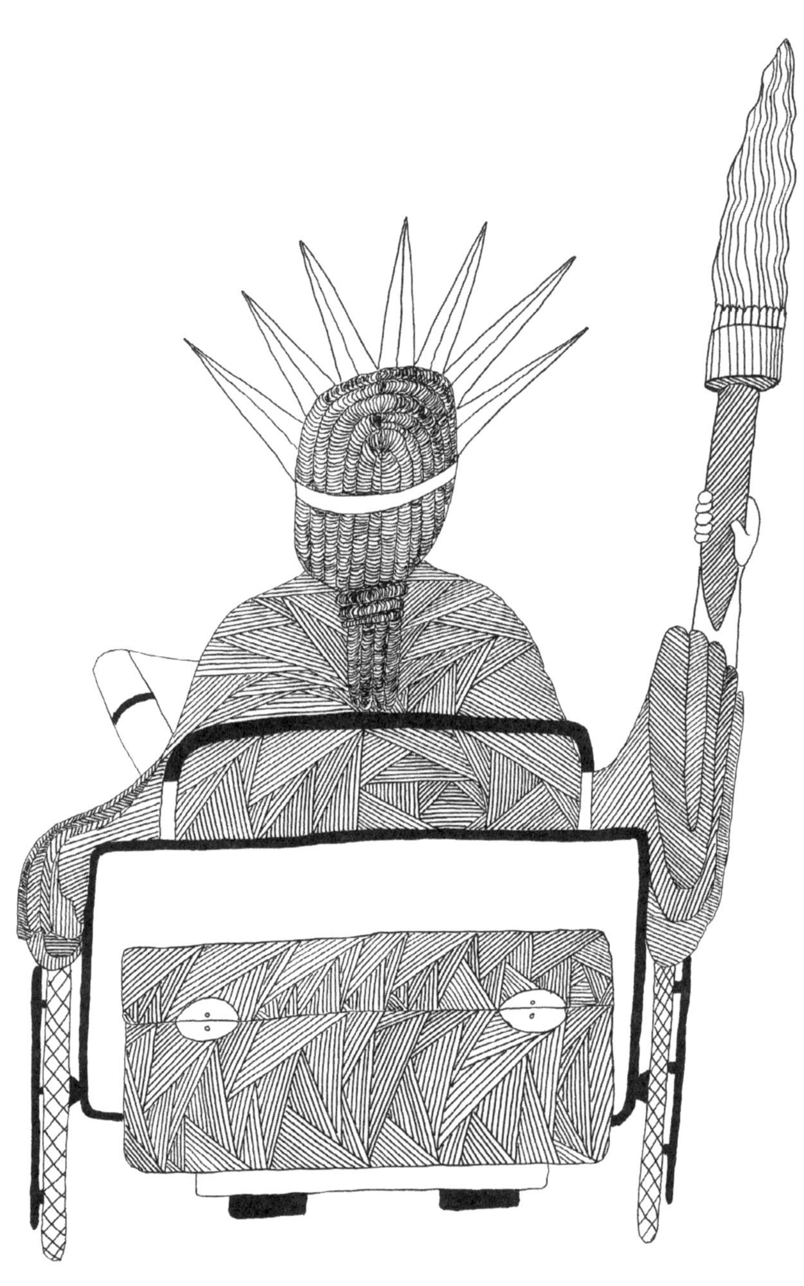

Disabled American II, 2015

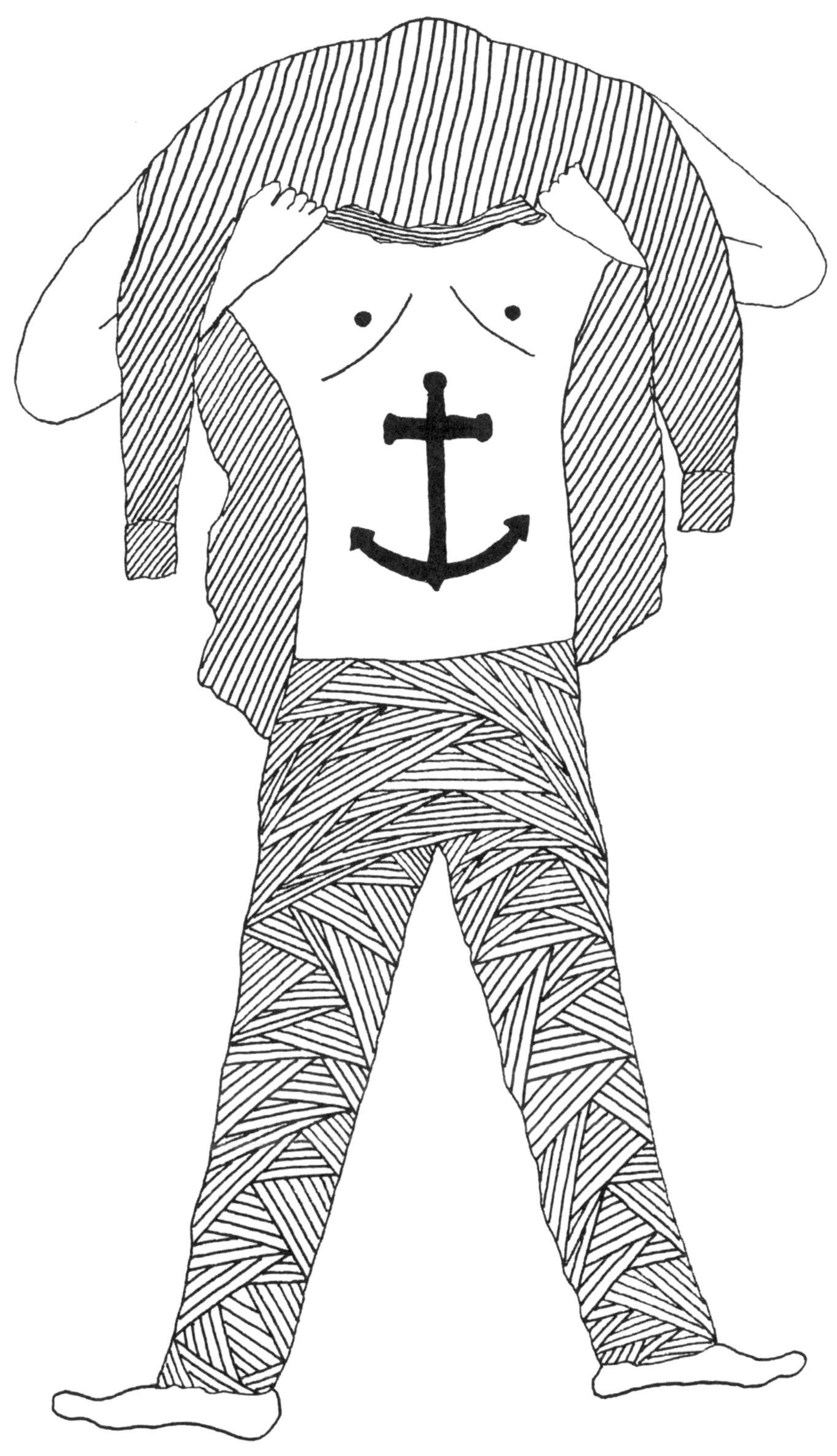

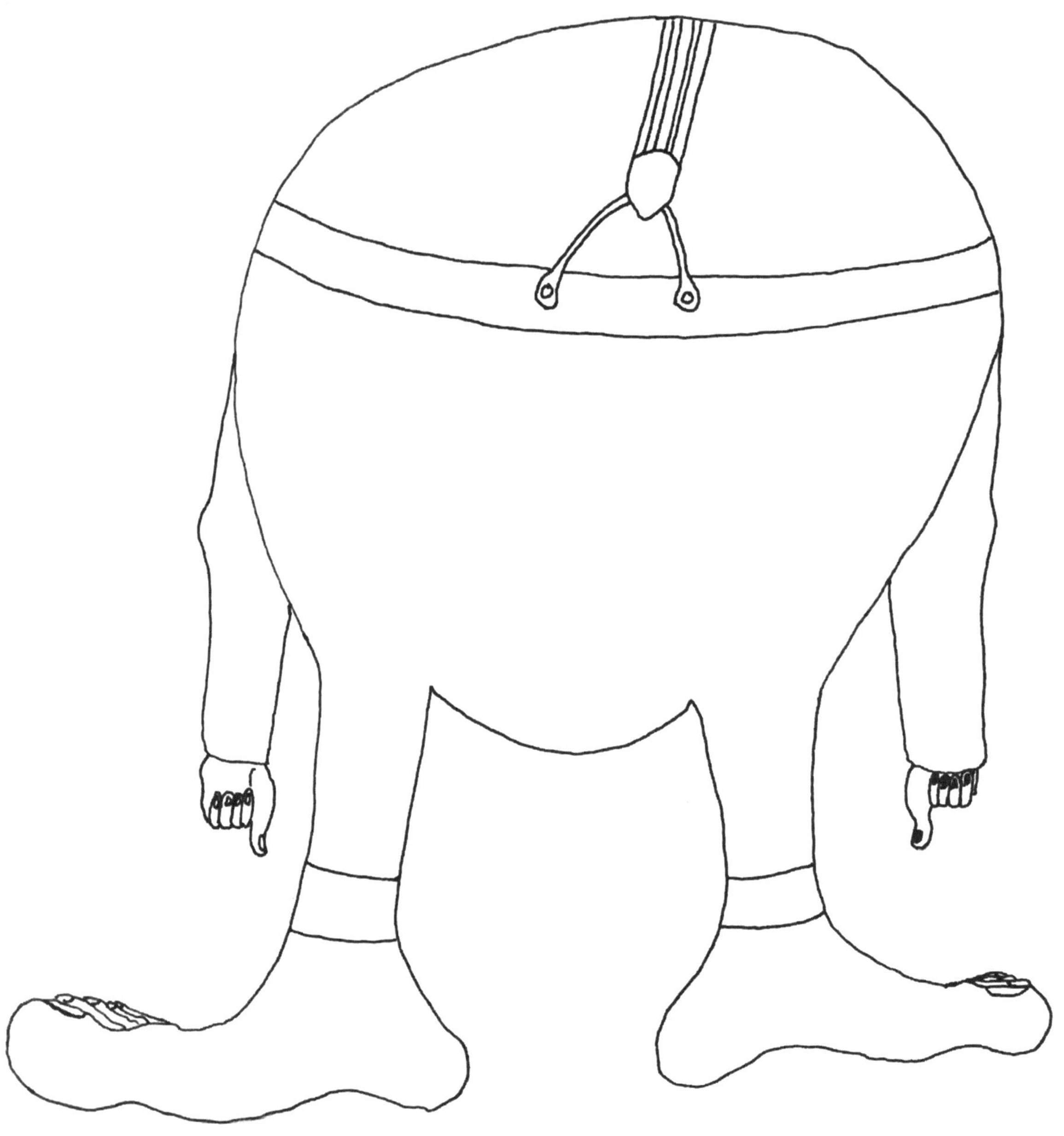

Yoga Day One, 2016

The Florida Keys, where I live now, is full of tropical clothing. It isn't a kick in the arse off what I've always been wearing — loud, gaudy colours. Mixing colours and patterns most tasteful people think should not sit side by side — I've always had a penchant for that kind of thing. I still want to look windswept and interesting, but I can't be arsed to put too much thought into it. I always wanted to dress like Mark Twain — to buy six identical suits and look the same every day and not have to make decisions. I've almost achieved it — I wear similar stuff most days. My footwear now is bare feet or sandals that show off the fabulous flowery tattoos on my feet. I miss wearing cowboy boots, though. You can't find good jeans or get your shoes repaired here, but you can buy all the T-shirts you need — with terrible jokes on them.

Tropical clothing can be a bit on the awful side. I was in Sydney, Australia, and I saw a man in a pale-blue crimplene safari suit. Now, that's enough to get you put in jail, as far as I'm concerned. Because I am into animal rights, and killing baby crimples is just a fucking disgrace. Have you any idea how many crimples it takes to make a safari suit? They hit them with big sticks! Every time a crimple dies, part of me dies too. The worst thing about that pale-blue crimplene suit was — the jacket had short sleeves. He was in long trousers, but the jacket had short sleeves. And he was wearing a long-sleeved shirt! I followed him everywhere, just to marvel. It was the best thing I've seen since I saw a guy with platform shoes and a kilt! Oh God, it was brillo! Hot weather is a great excuse to swish around in a panama hat. I put artificial flowers on mine, and I think it's a great look. I'm pretty much a floral boy. But the flowery stuff — feet tattoos, shirt and hat — is offset by my skull bracelet. I like Keith Richards's reason for wearing skulls — it's proof that human beings are the same under the skin.

There are a lot of tourists in the Florida Keys. People coming from colder places like Colorado and Minnesota to flop into pools with giant pink inflatable flamingos. I see them wandering around the touristy streets in their shorts and T-shirts, drinking margaritas out of pineapples. Some of those poor wee souls suffer from a terrible affliction — the Hungry Bum Syndrome. That's where your arse eats everything in its way: Chomp-Chomp-Chomp! You see this when they walk up the street with their Bermuda shorts way up their arse. That's Hungry Bum. Chomp-Chomp-Chomp! You take your clothes off and there's no fucking underwear there — your arse has eaten it. You have to retrieve it with a crochet needle.

Some ladies in a knitting circle kindly knitted me and Pamela matching woolly bathing suits, a kind of homage to my 'Pale Blue Scottish Person' routine. The suits are in frames on our wall. When I venture in the sea these days — in water that's a good eighty degrees warmer than what I endured when I was a boy swimming in Aberdeen — I don my favourite boxer-style cotton swim shorts. They're pink, with flamingos and palm trees dotted all over them. I could wear them to a restaurant here if I wished, with flip-flops and a cowboy hat. 'No shirt, no shoes, no problem'. But I wouldn't dream of it. I'm a Windswept and Interesting Showbiz Personality. Times may change, but standards must remain.

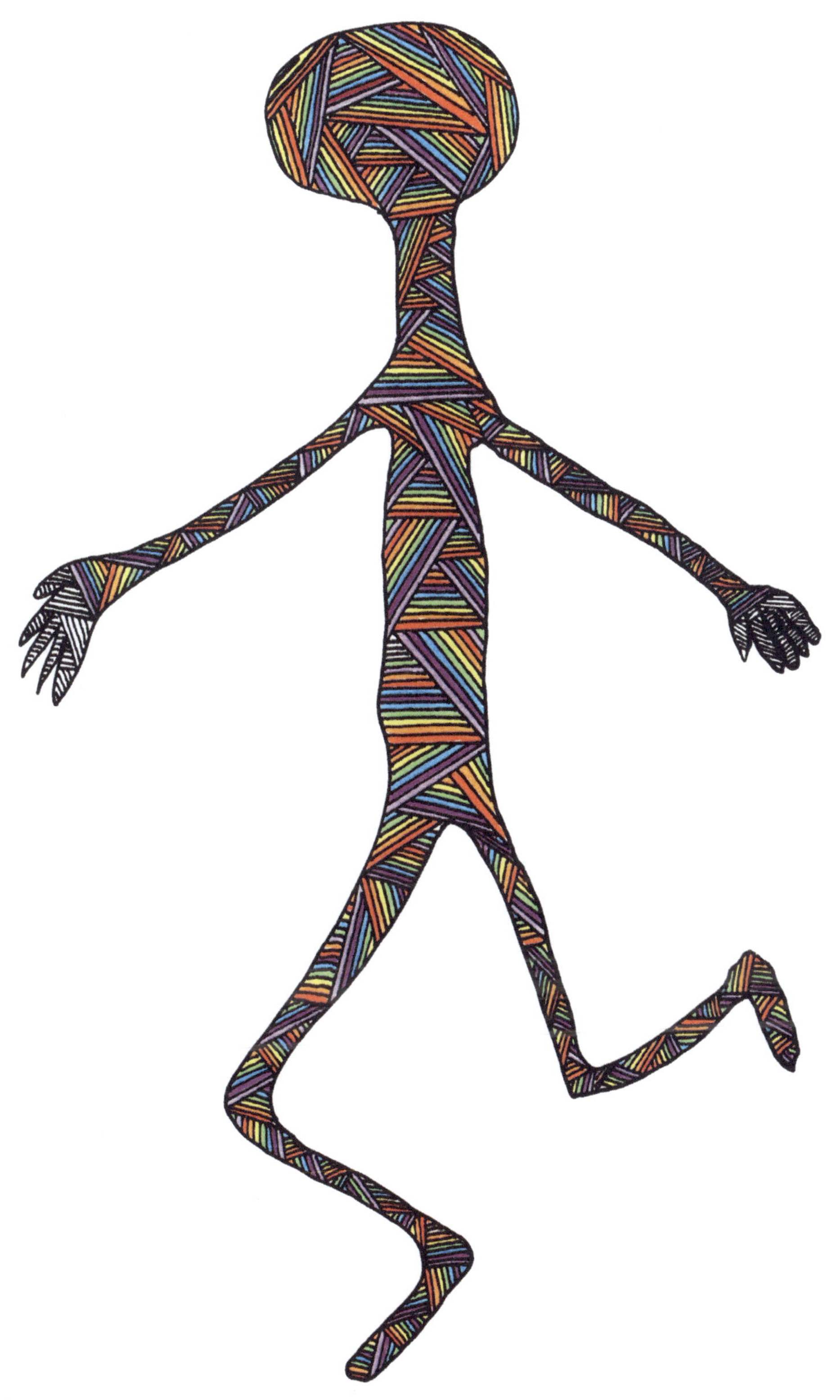

Step We Gaily, On We Go, 2023

Whenever I wear
something expensive
it looks stolen …
When I buy a *Big
Issue*, people take it
out of my hand and
give me a pound.

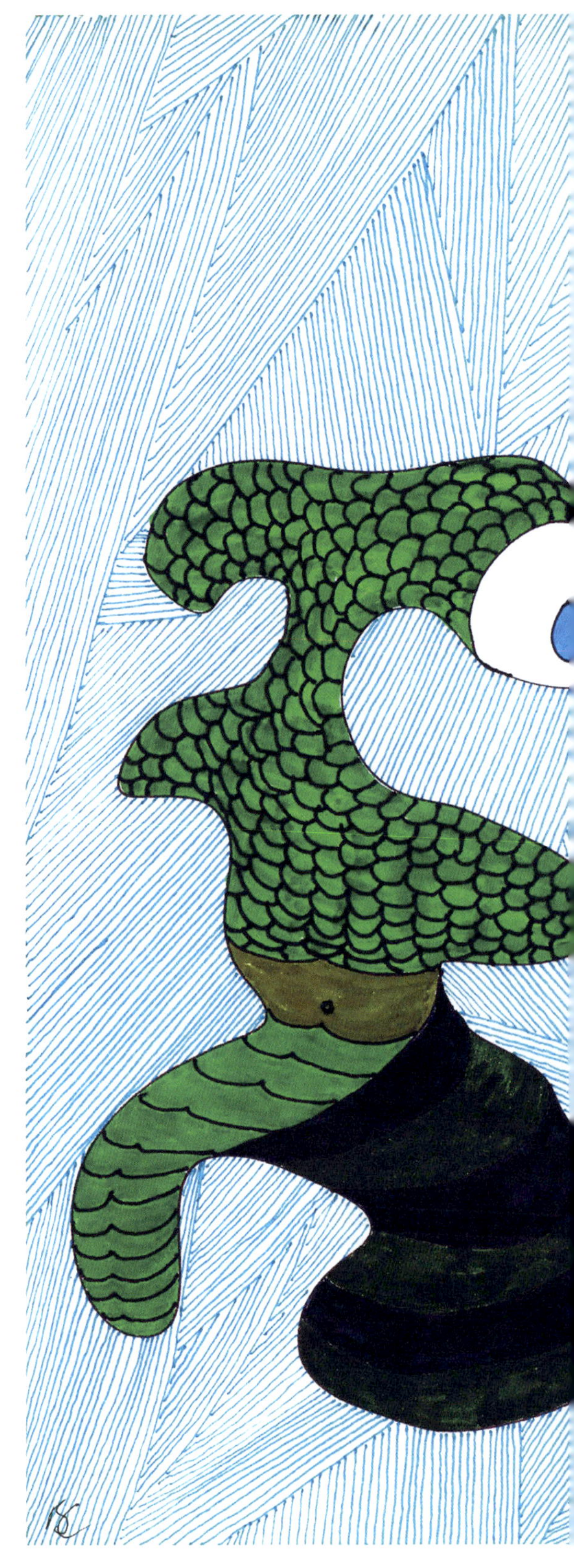

Last Night But The Night Before, 2010

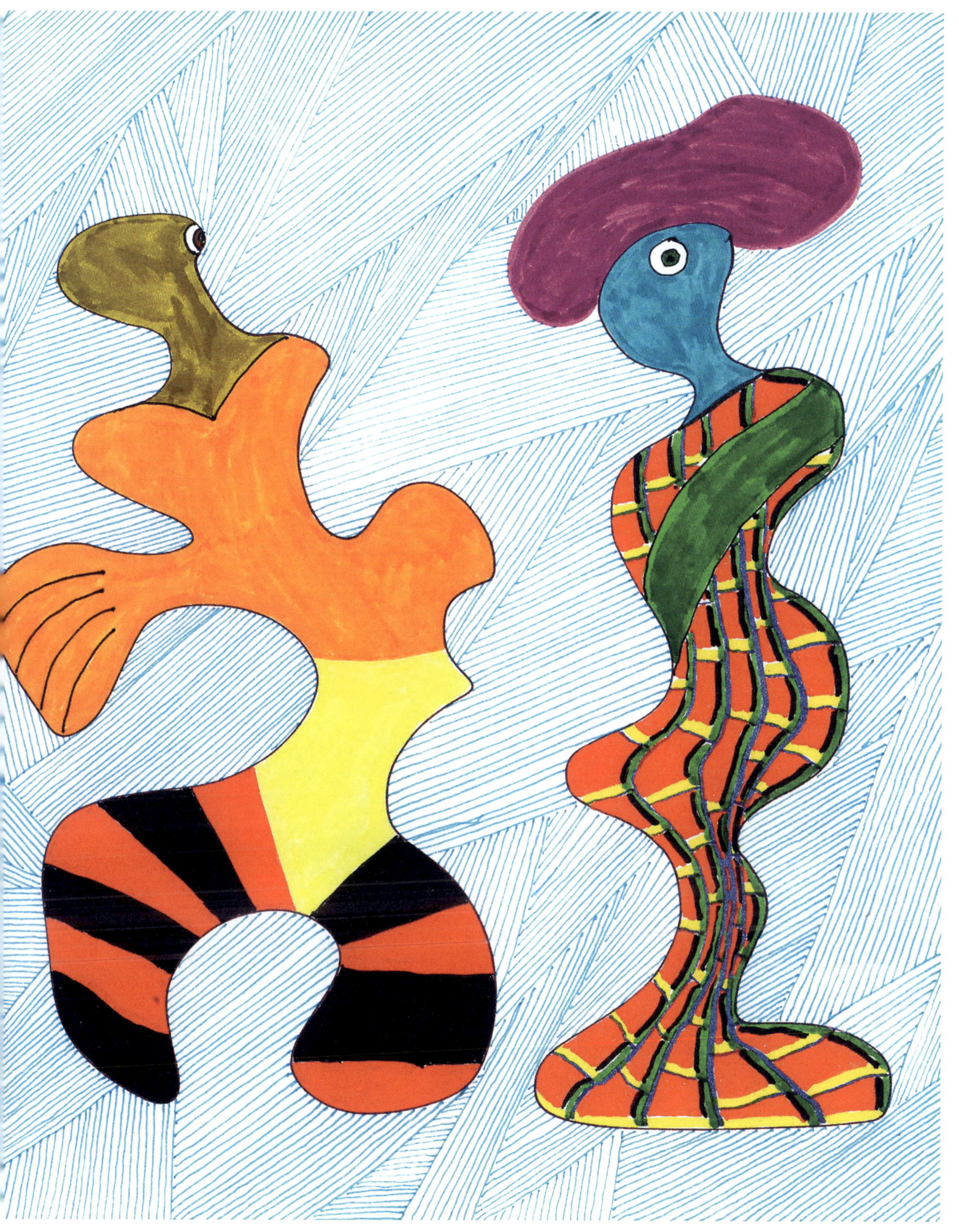

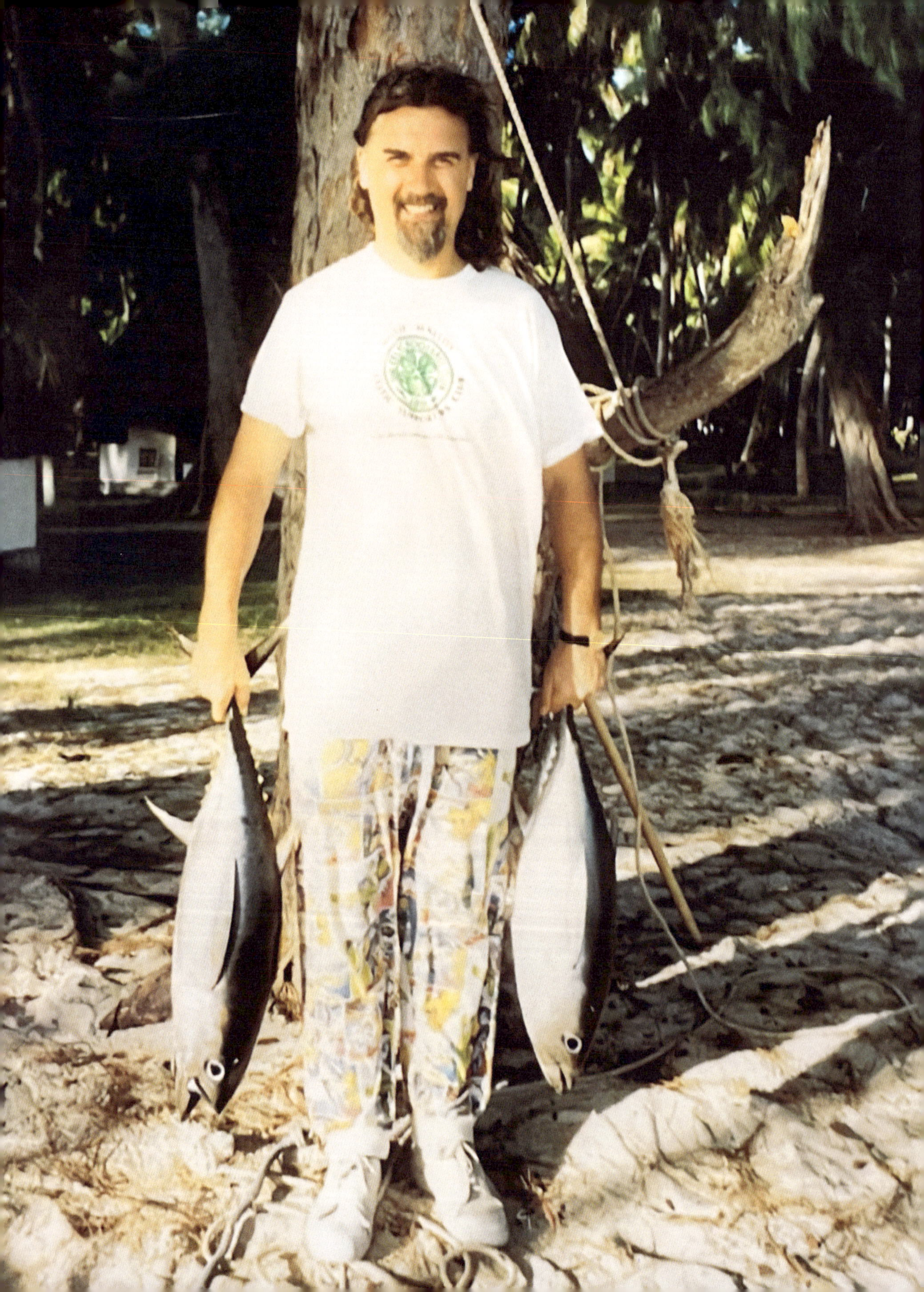

Leisure

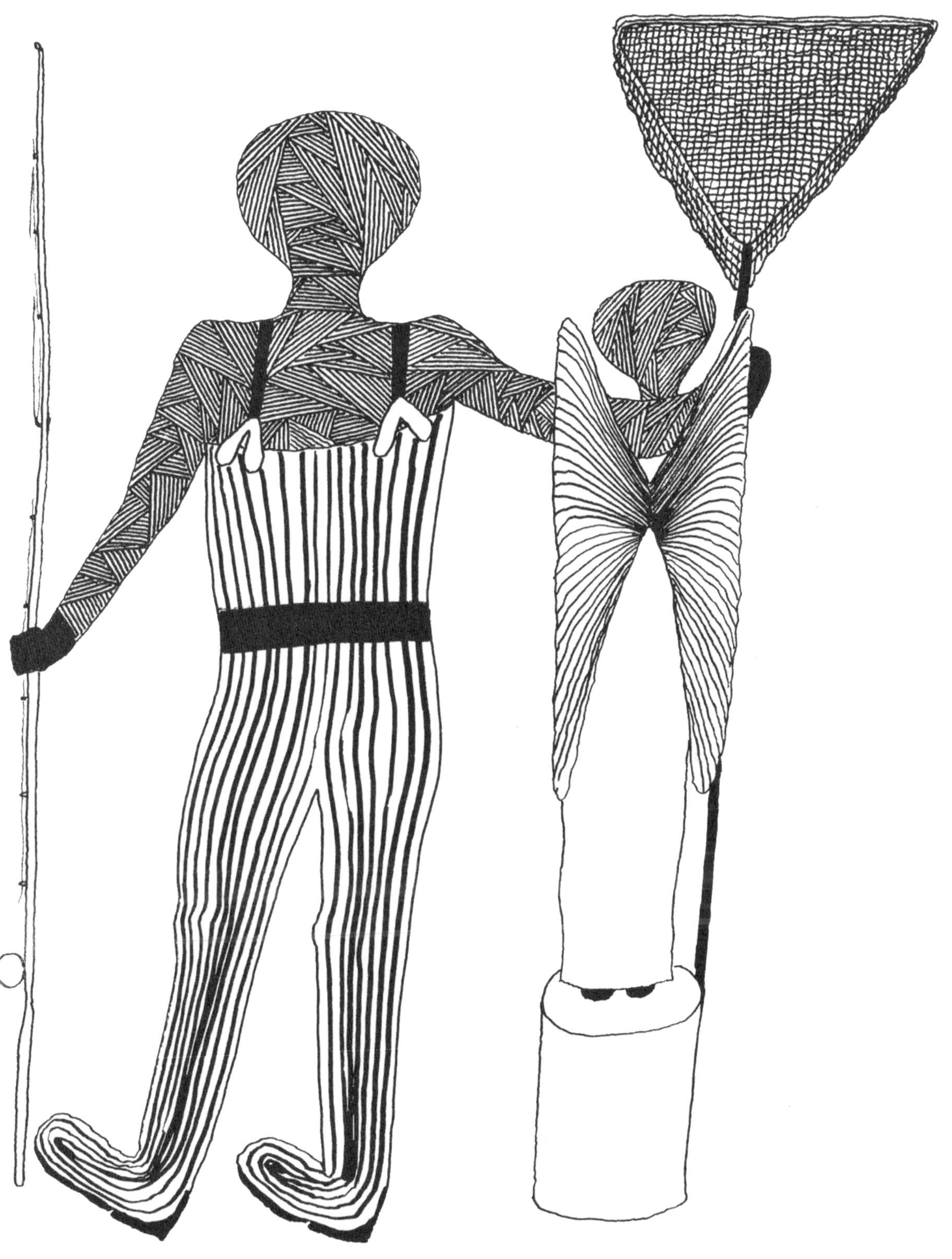

The Angler And The Angel, 2018

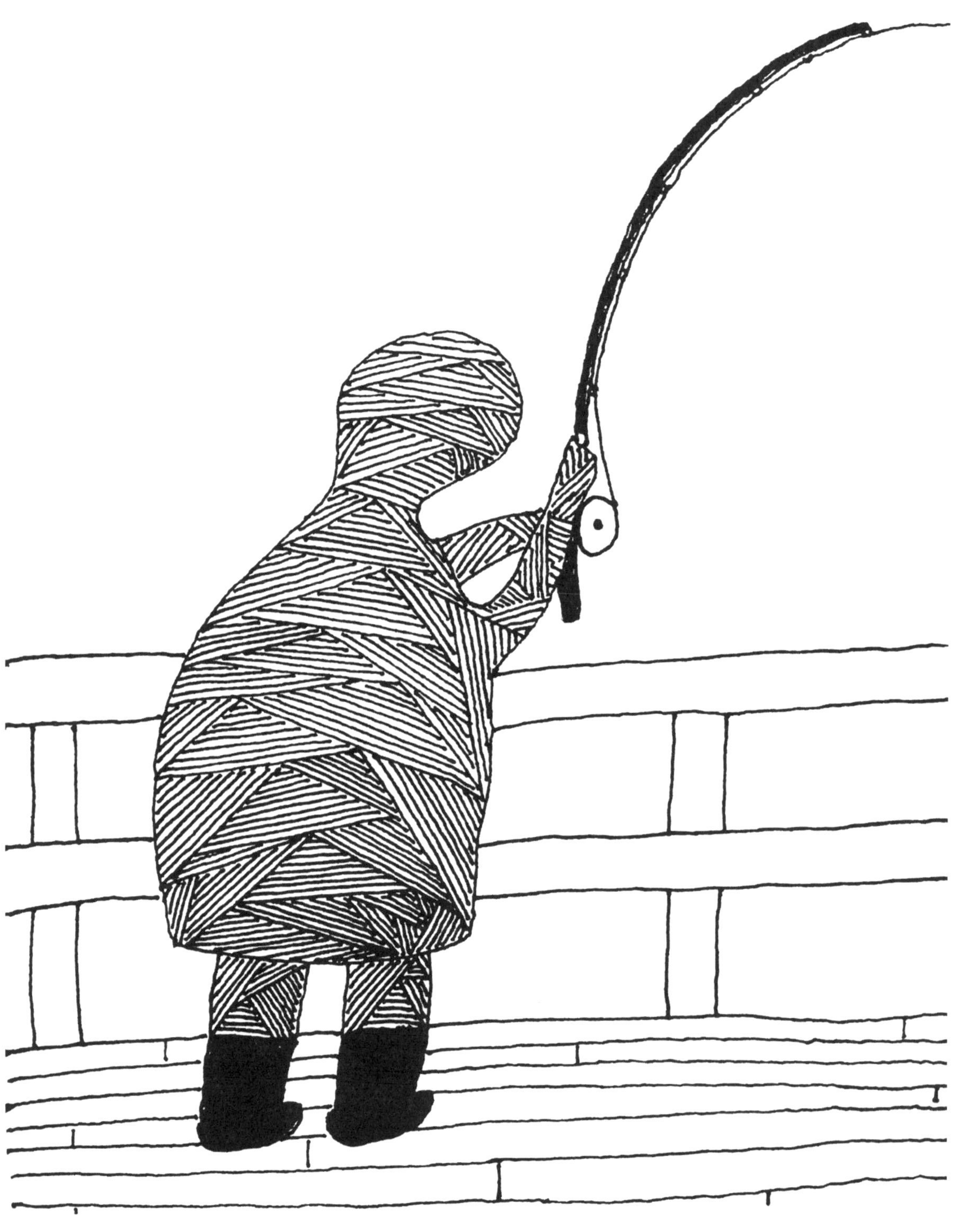

The Cast, 2018

I love fishing. I'll fish anywhere … Years before I moved to the Florida Keys, I used to nip there to catch tarpon. I love fishing in the back country off Key West and Sugarloaf Key. Some people there catch fish while standing up on their paddleboard. Not this soldier. And there's a fishing lodge in Tulum, Mexico that I loved. It's a simple wooden structure on the beach that has about six lodges and they serve great Mexican food. I went there with my son Jamie. We'd get up in the morning and go out on the boat with a guide, then come back at night for dinner. There was room on the boat to stand up and fly-fish in the shallows of the sea at about six feet deep — the bonefish, tarpon and permit like to swim there. I usually release fish after catching them, but one of my fellow guests in Mexico took umbrage at that. He said, 'I've never understood the idea of catching fish with all that special equipment and the clothing and the special flies — then letting it go.' The guy who owned the fishing lodge intervened. He asked the guest: 'Do you take part in any sport yourself?' 'Yeah,' he said, 'tennis.' 'When the game's finished,' asked the owner, 'do you eat the ball?'

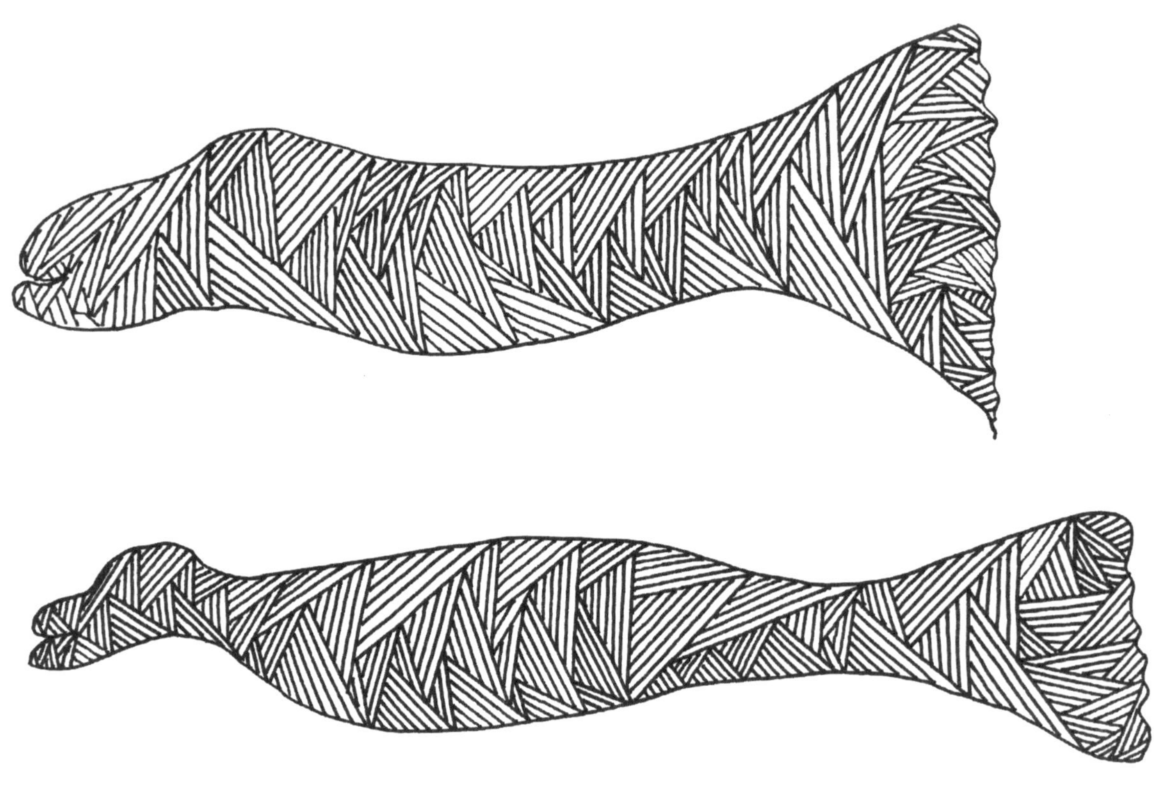

Queer Fish, 2012

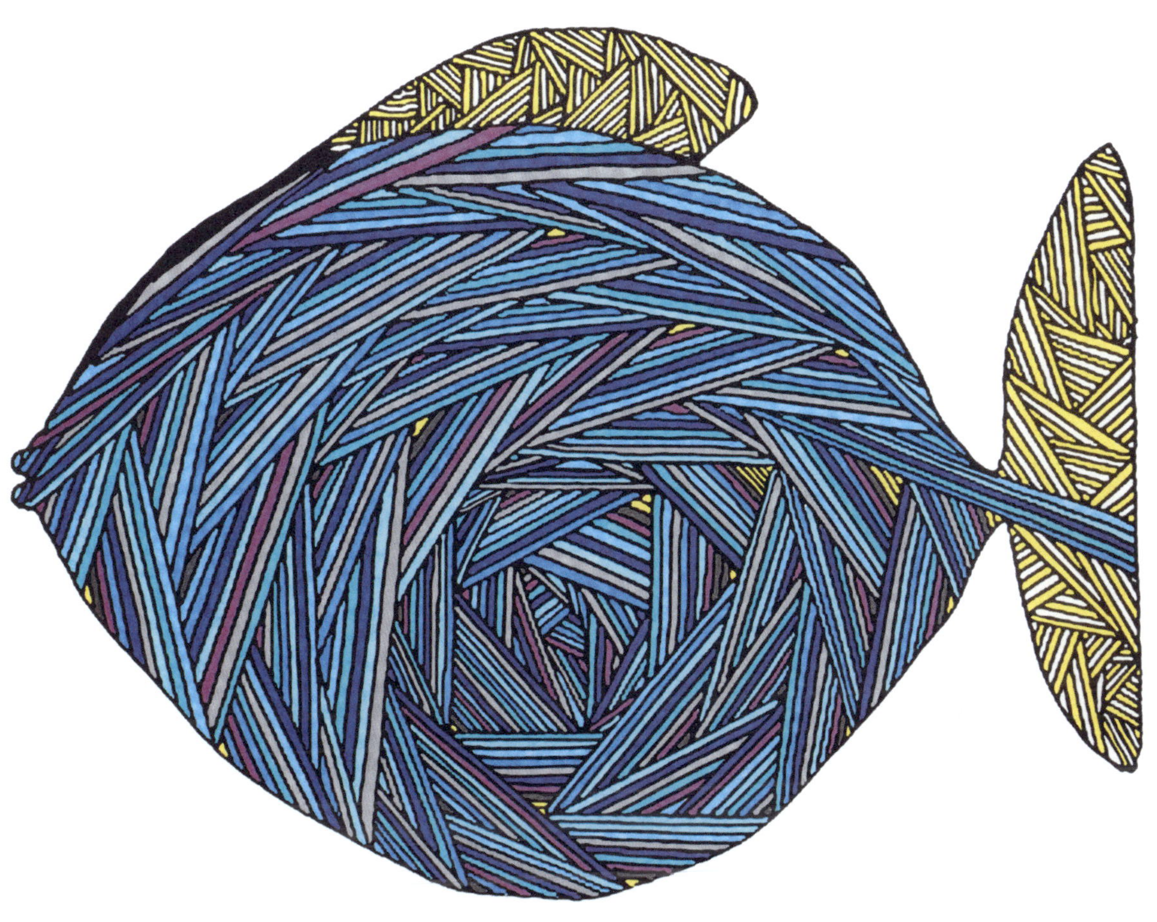

Permit From Memory, 2023

When you set out to catch a salmon in Scotland, the weather conditions will always be perfect: howling gale, blazing sunshine, snow, occasional rain, soggy underfoot or very dry — it's going to be a wonderful day! You've got to be dressed for any weather. I was once fishing in a Scottish stream and came out of the water freezing. As I was bagging my gear, I spotted a wee Glasgow man walking past. I was wearing a Highland bonnet called a Glengarry — just to be windswept and interesting — and he was wearing brand-new plus fours that were a weird blue that doesn't exist in nature, with socks to match. He was a mess, but he had the gall to say to me: 'If I had a hat like that, I wouldn't fucking wear it.'

I made it on to the front cover of the fishing magazine in Tasmania because I caught the same fish twice on two consecutive days. I almost landed it and it got away, but then I caught it the following day — it still had the fly in its mouth from the day before. So, it made me quite famous among Tasmanian anglers. It's a relief to fish in the warmer seas and rivers of Australia, New Zealand, Mexico and Florida. There's only so much freezing water my bollocks can take.

I wanted to catch fish when I visited the Arctic but there's bugger all available there. There is a most unfortunately named creature there though — it's called an 'ugly fish'. Aptly named. It's huge with a wee tail and a big fucking ugly head like a giant wart. The only edible bit is just before the tail … which is its arse. Imagine going through life being called 'ugly' and your best feature's your arse!

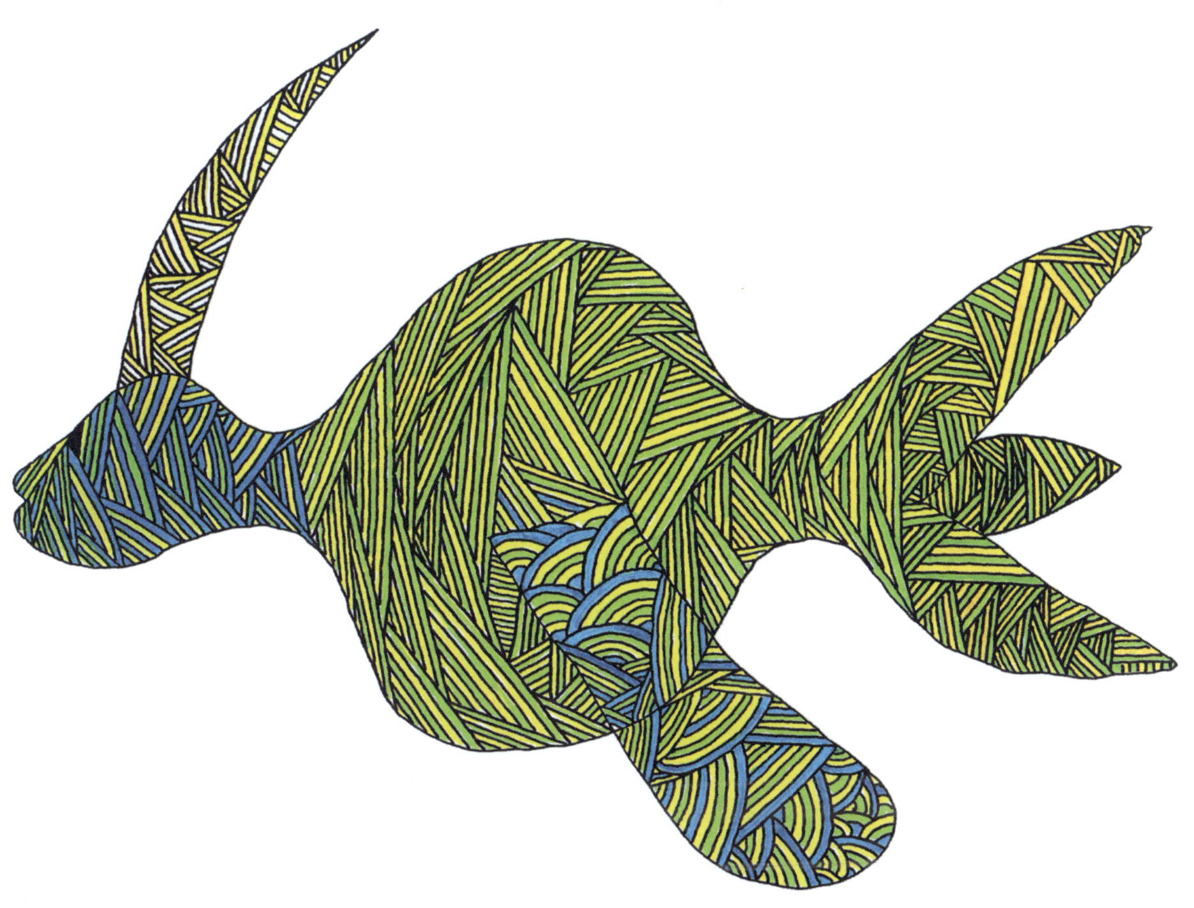

GoZunder Fish, 2021

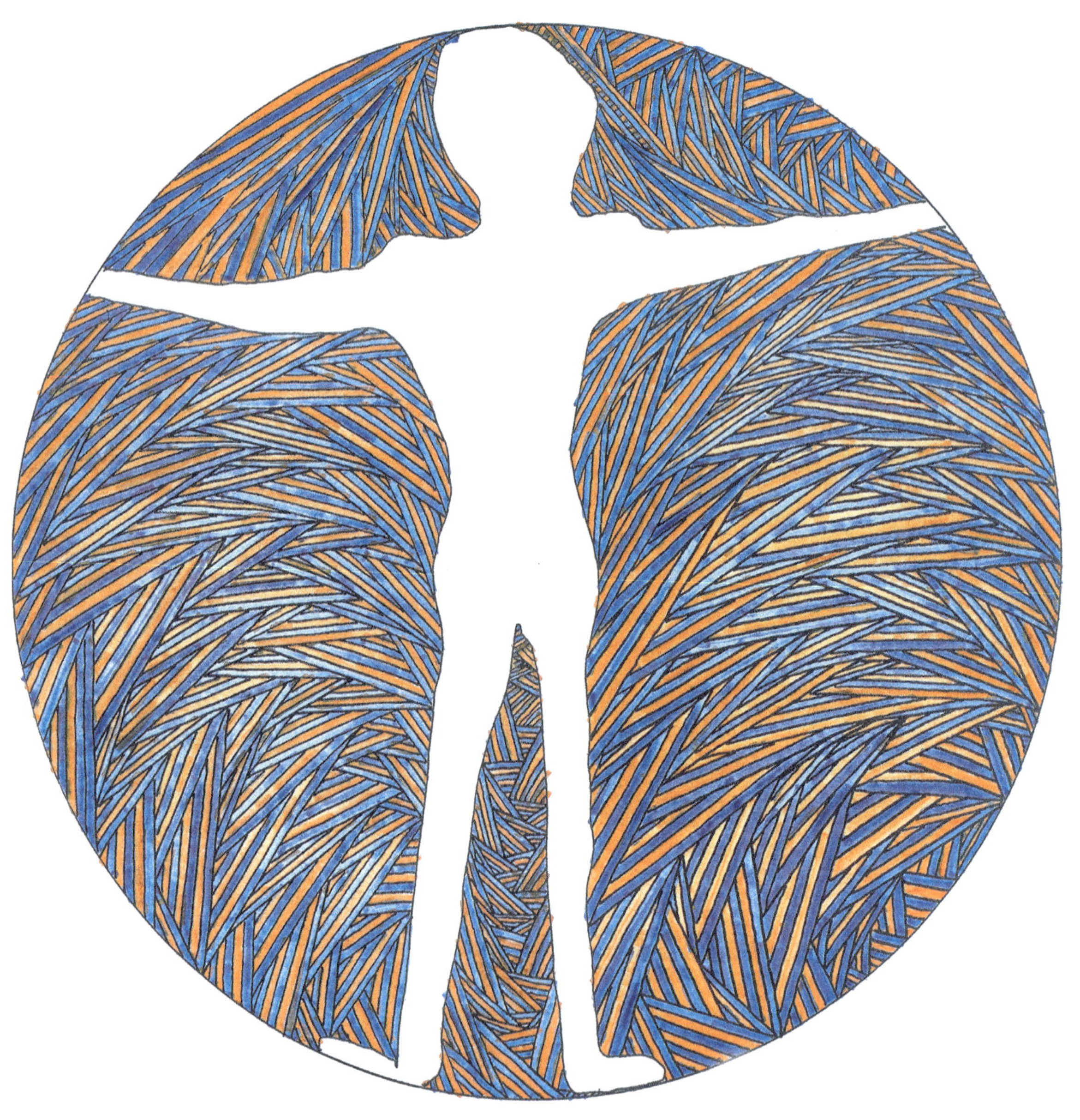

Angler's Tale, 2021

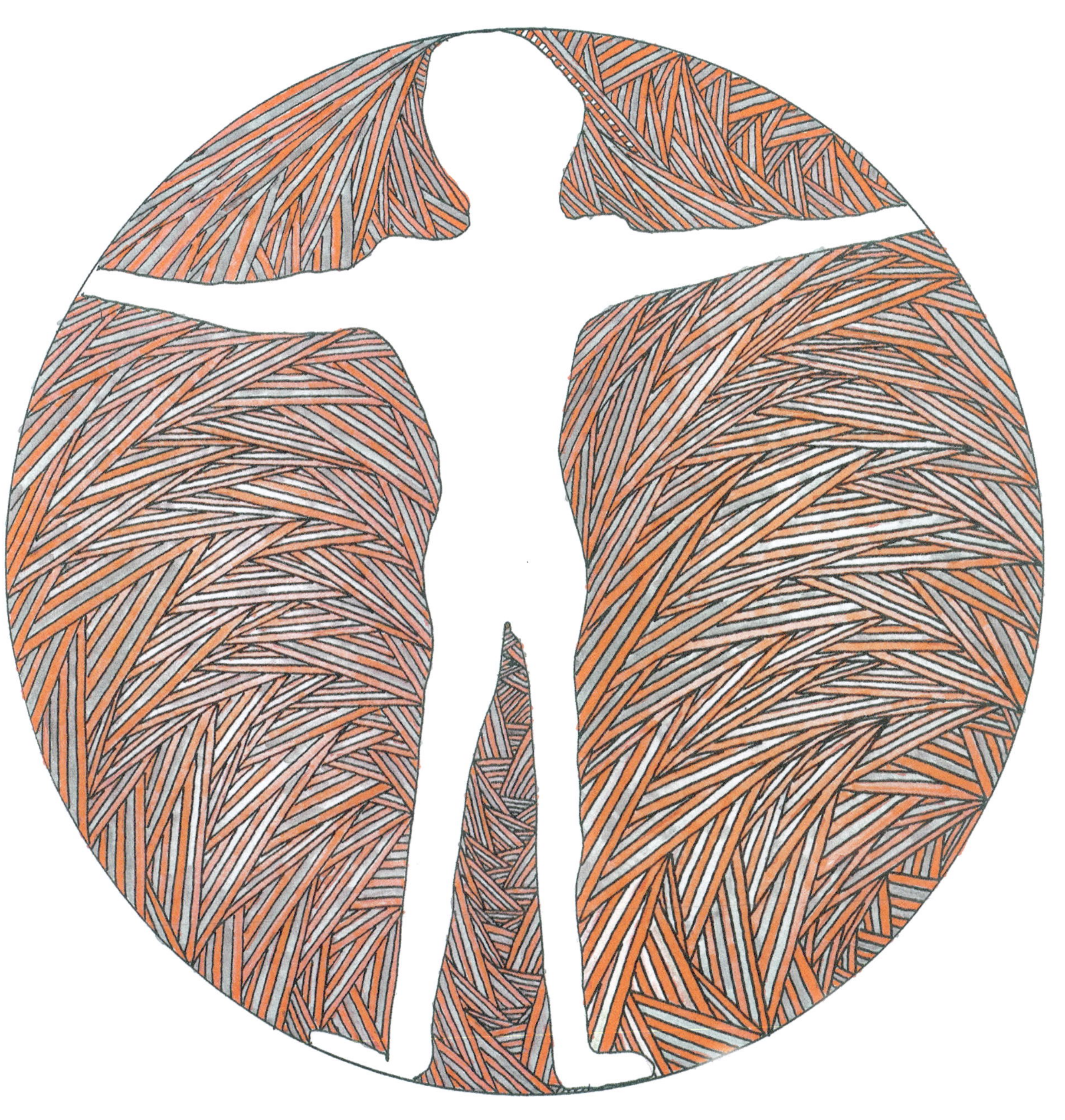

Angler's Tale, 2021

I earned money as a busker from time to time when I was hitch-hiking around France, before I could get proper gigs as a folk singer, so I know it takes extraordinary courage to be a street performer. Your audience will always be terrifyingly unpredictable. Since then, I've always loved coming across great street musicians, especially if they are doing something I've never seen before. I found some excellent buskers in Australia, like India Bhauti, the one-man band I came across in Sydney. It was a joy to see him playing weird electronic drum music with a solar panel on his head that powered his handmade instruments. And Johannes O'rinda, who performs extraordinary feats of full-body coordination by whistling classical music while conducting with his arms at the same time. Then there was the sensational Kokatahi Band, playing 'bush music' with a line-up of accordion, fiddle, banjo, drums, spoons and more. There was a lovely moment in an Inuit town when I drove up on my skidoo and witnessed something extraordinary. There was a girl singing in a very unusual way. She was facing another girl who had her mouth half-open and was making shapes with it, so the first girl could project her voice into the other girl's mouth and the echo created different noises. I learned this was throat singing, and it was the most unusual sound. I came up on my bike and I said, 'How are you doing that? It's amazing!' Then a head came round from the first girl's head and I realised she had a baby in the back of her anorak. I said, 'I know! He's doing it!' I was blown away by that style of music-making, and it's still a mystery to me. It was a rare and beautiful sound they made.

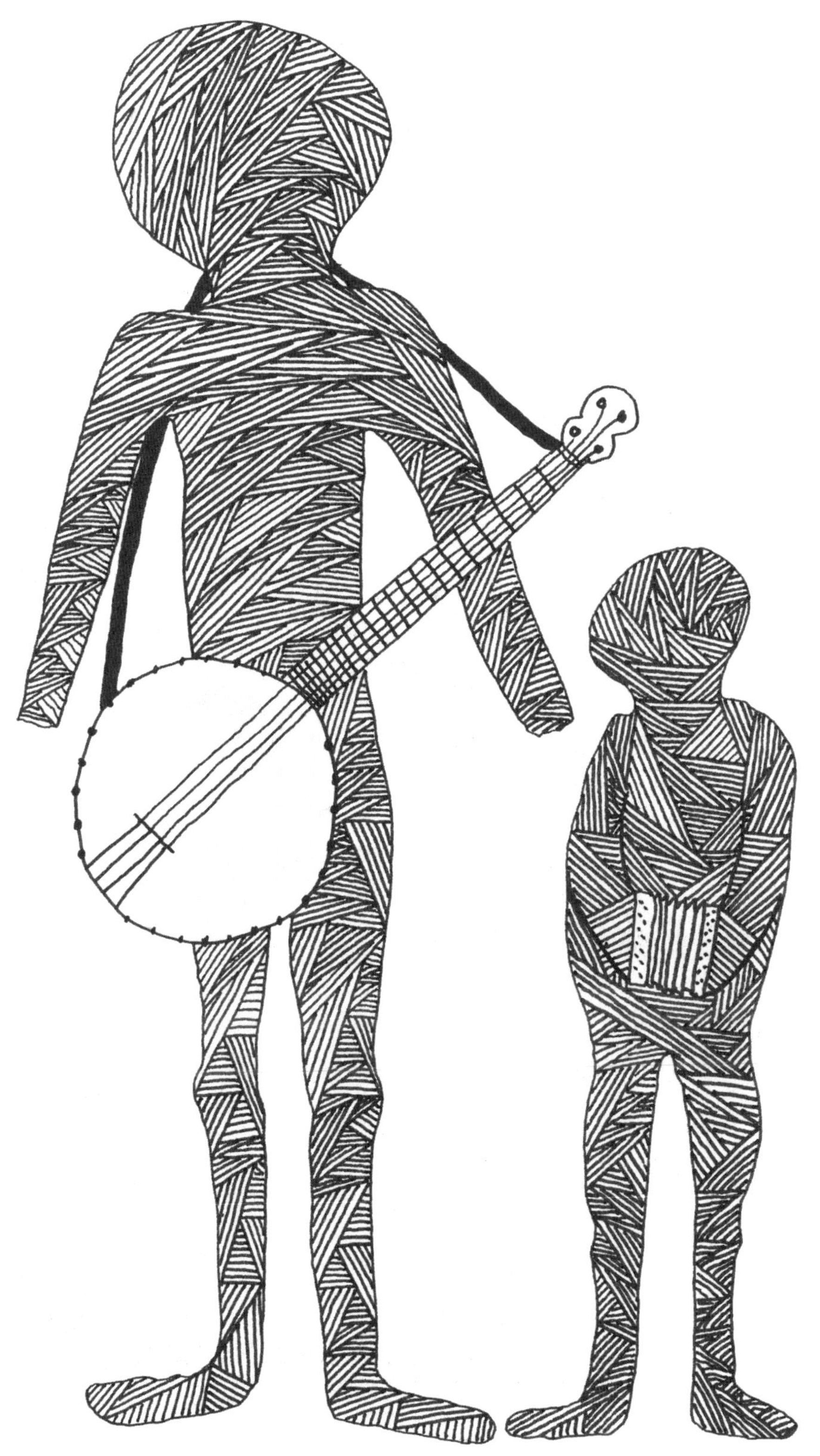

Two For The Road, 2012

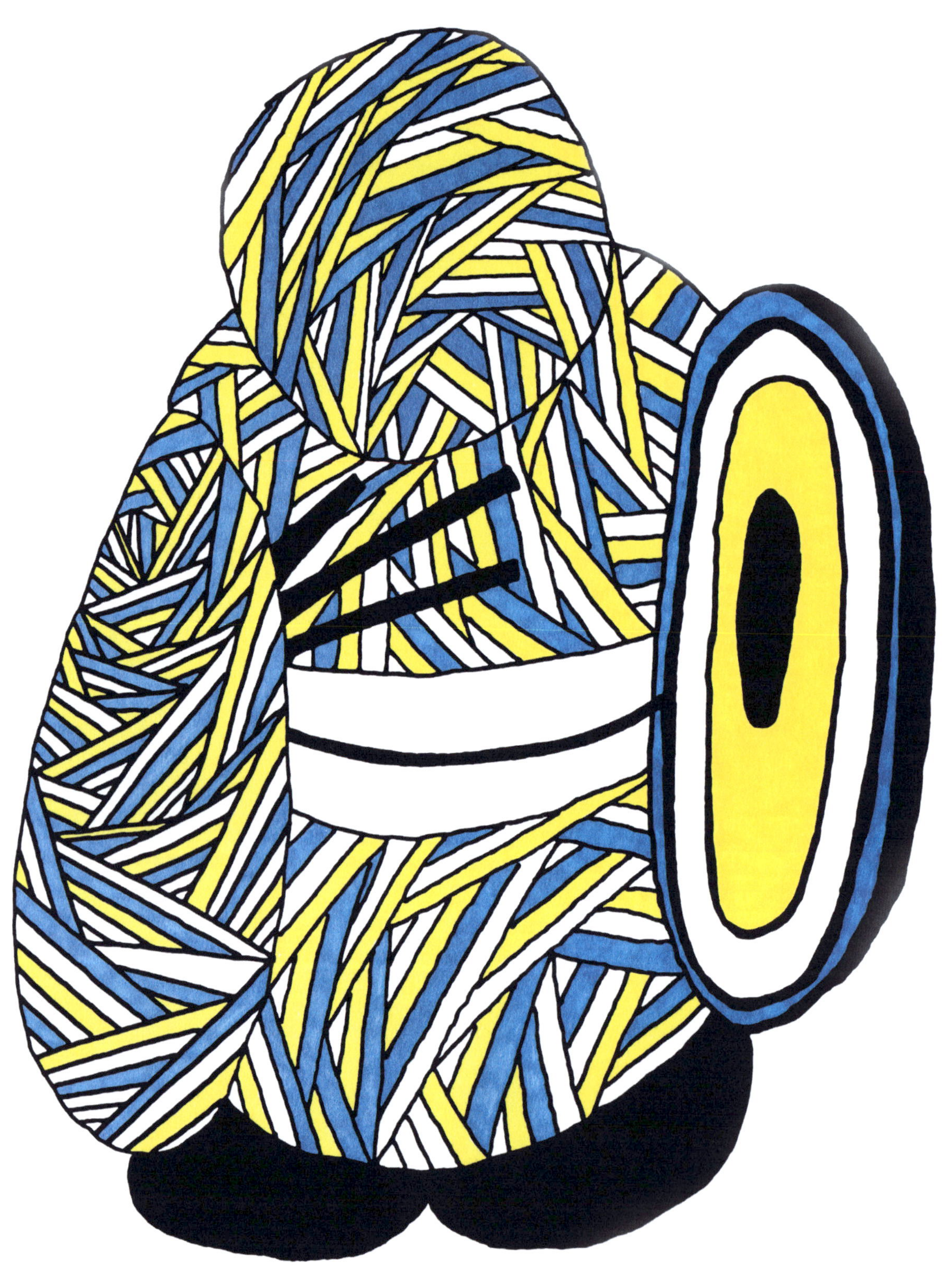

Rebel Without A Sword, 2023

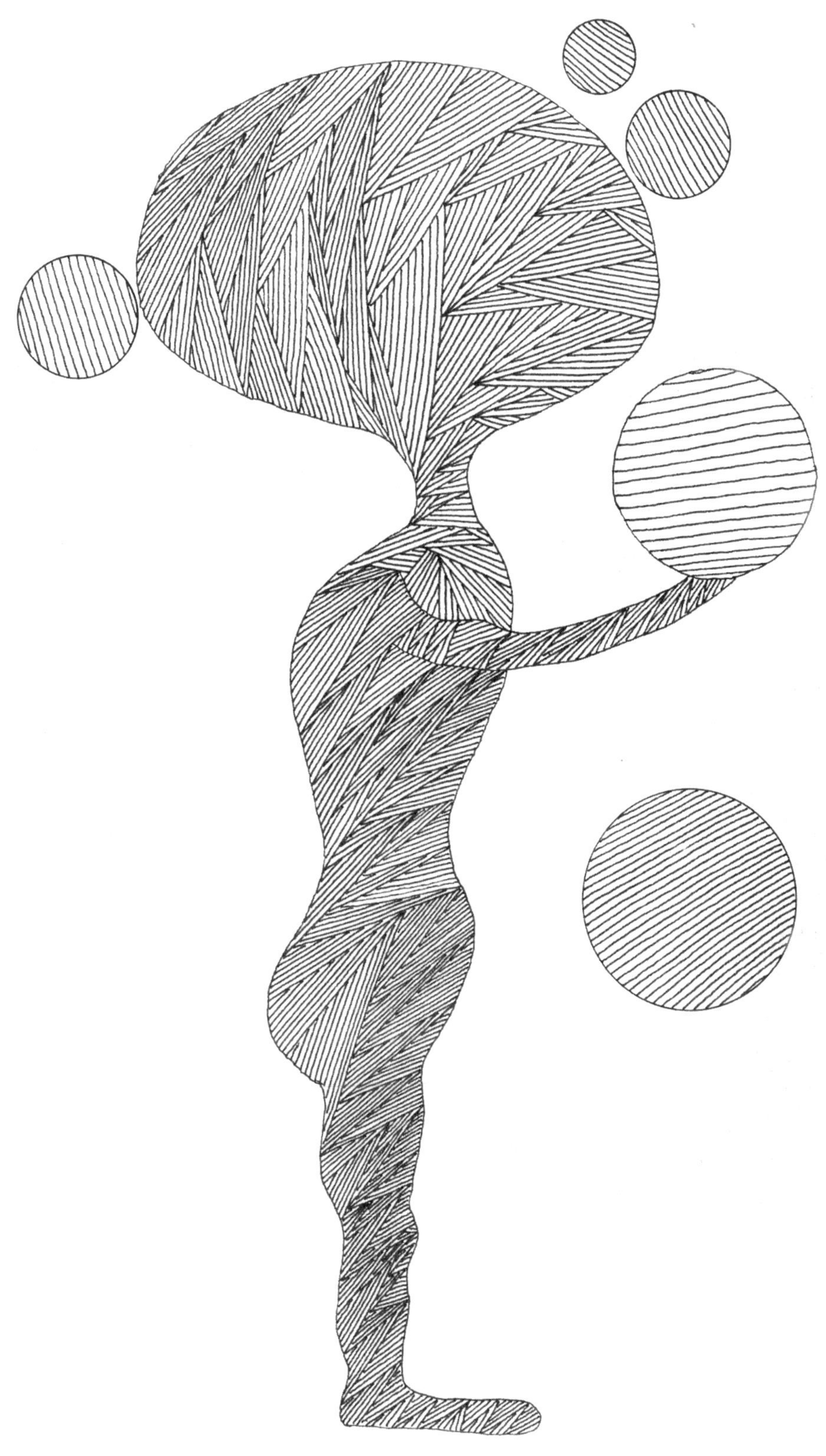

One Armed Juggler, 2012

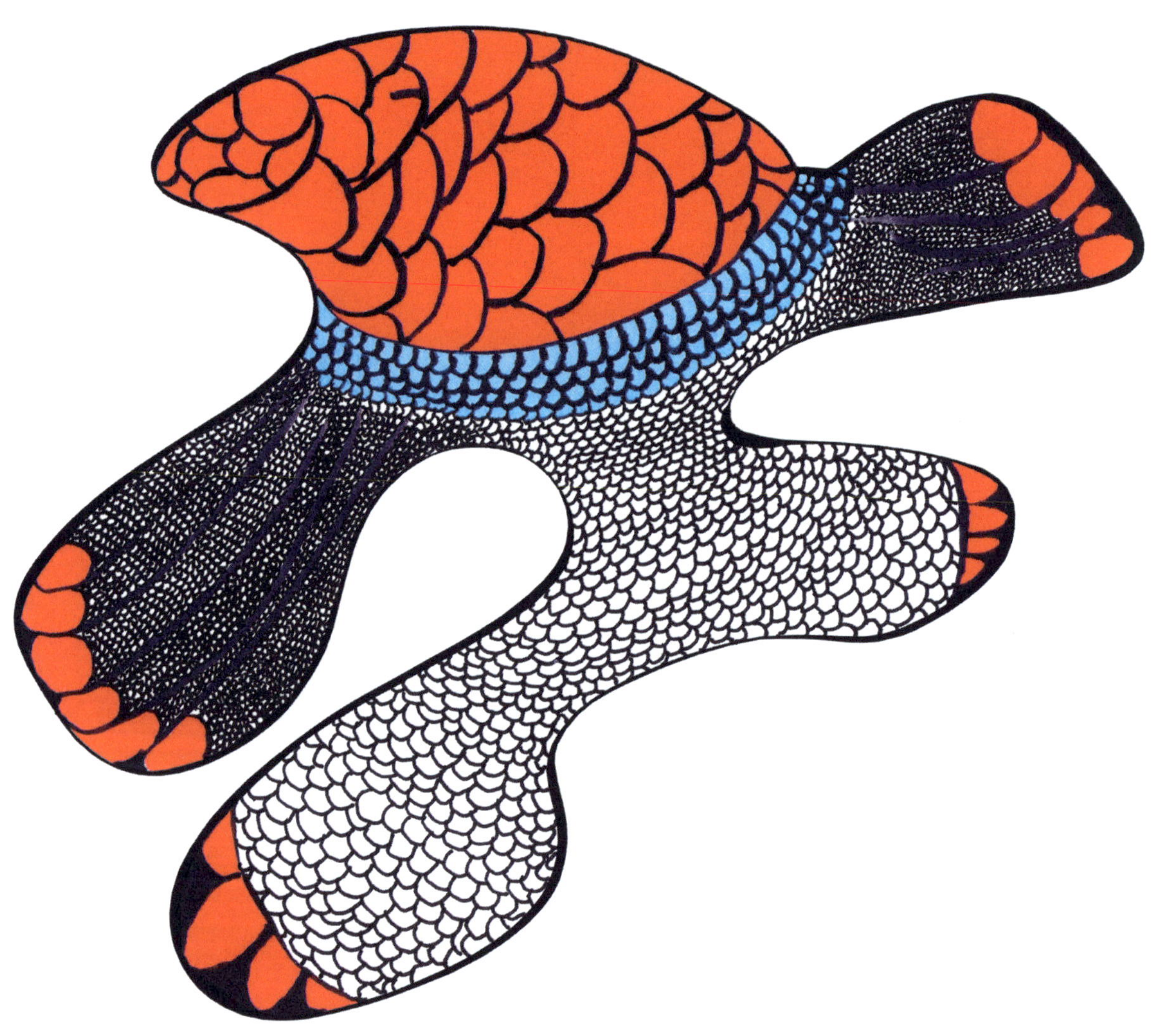

1–2–3, 1–2–3, 2010

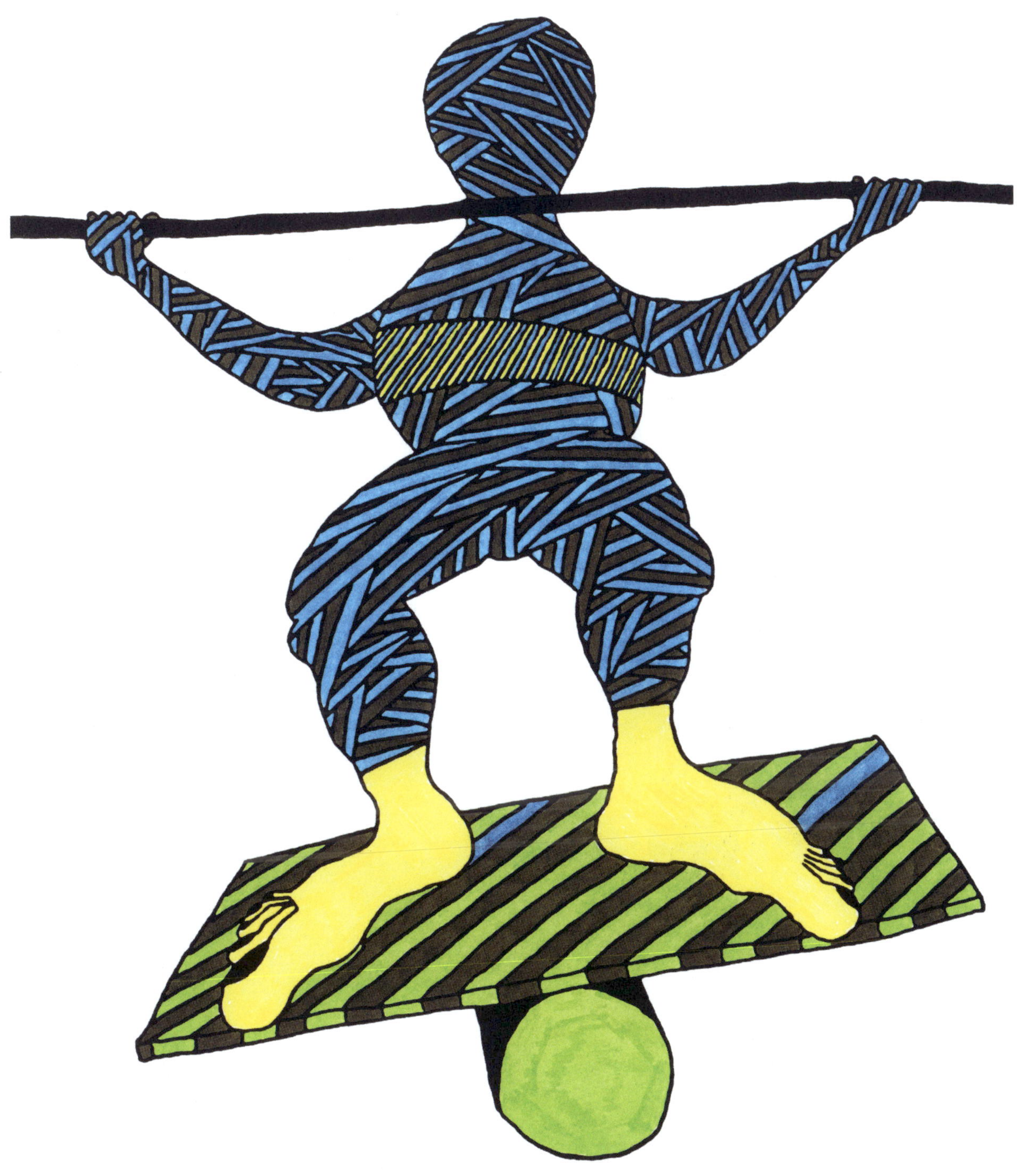

Marshall Art, 2023

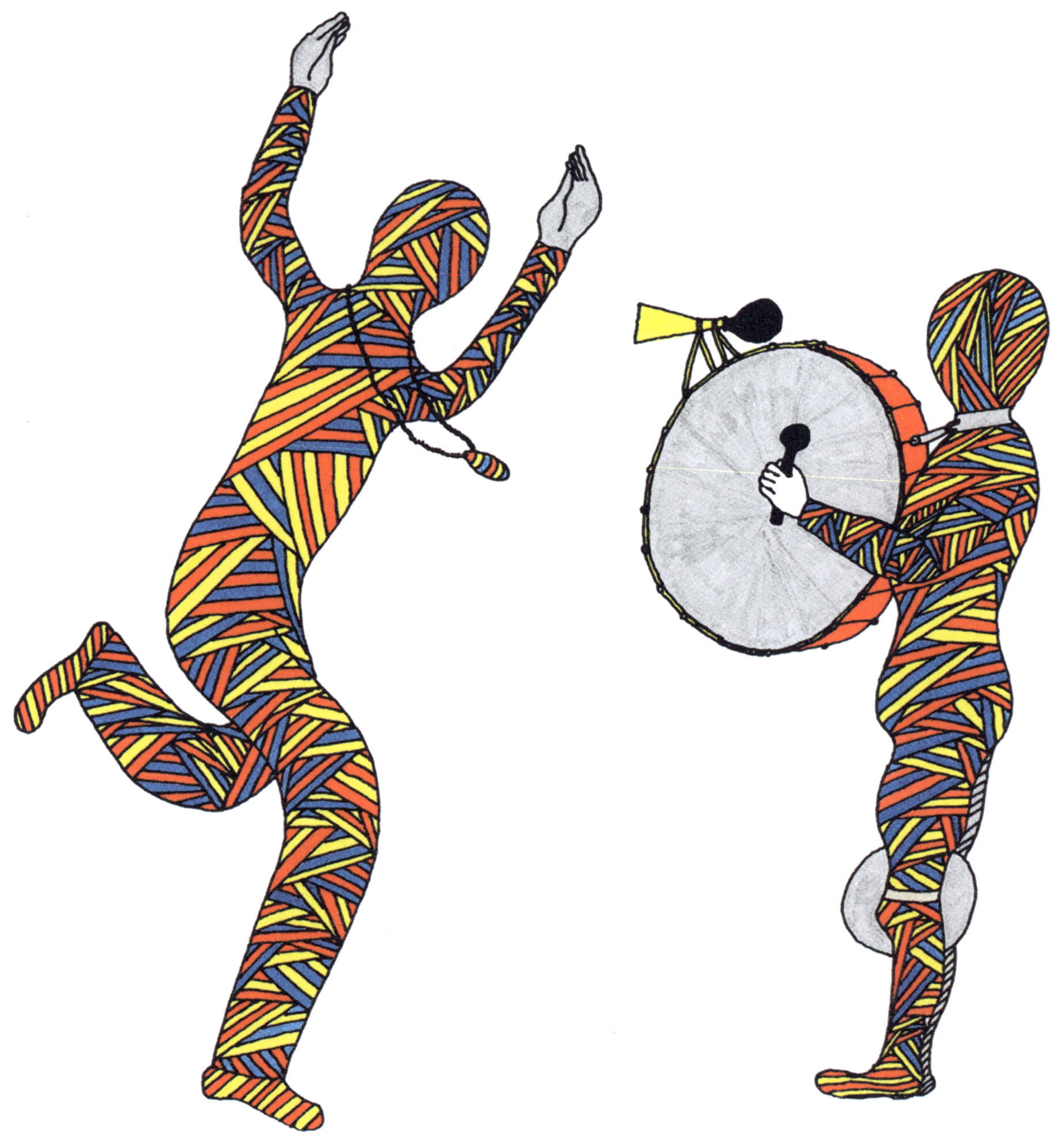

One Man's Band, 2023

The best loony I ever saw was in George Square in Glasgow. When I was a kid, I lived way out in this housing estate called Drumchapel. The one with the vans, y'know? There were no pubs out there. There are now. But, when I lived there, there were no pubs or discos or entertainment or anything like that. As a matter of fact, there were no discos anywhere — they hadn't been fucking invented yet.

There were dance halls, where you went dancin' with people. You got to touch them and everythin', it was fab. You'd been broke all week but on Fridays we'd get paid, and we'd put the Old Spice on and come into town. It was like *Seven Brides for Seven Brothers*.

You couldn't take women home, because they lived the other way — fuckin' miles that way to go home — but there were special buses at midnight or one o'clock in the morning, and we'd all gather there.

There were an awful lot of drunk guys, and waifs and strays and scoundrels, footpads and vagabonds. You'd be sitting on the bus and they'd come on, with their drunken attempts at singing: 'Oh-ohh-yehh-ehhhh …' Four coats on. All with only the top button done up. The helmet all buckled up. Four pairs of troosers, all with the fly open. A big dark cave. You could see somethin' jiggling around in there. You didnae know where to look. Once you've seen it, you can't …

It's like seeing a woman's knickers — like when you're in an airport and those seats that go back and the knees come up. Airport seats are designed to embarrass you. They're that Kentucky Fried Furniture stuff. They've got farting chairs. That vinyl — pffftttt! But you feel, as soon as you make the noise, you want to say, 'Excuse me,' but if you say that you're admitting you did something, so you're better off to go and move your arse around – pfffttt-pfffttttttt!

Sometimes women sit down and their knees come up. Zhooom! You're on it like a flash. Now, I'm not … Well, I am a dirty person, but there's just something that makes you go: Zhooom! And have a look.

You know when you see a deer running away from you and its white tail goes fiz-fiz-fiz? Or a rabbit's tail comes up: flash! Well, that wee white diamond of knicker … It has that same animal attraction. 'Oh God, it's a woman's knickers, I'd better look away!' But something drags your head to it. Your eye's coming out your ear trying to get a fuckin' look at it!

Oh, I was talking about these loonies on the bus.

These guys come on, and there's one seat beside you: Oh, fuck, no!

'D'ya wanna sweetie?' 'No, thank you, no!' 'Take a fuckin' sweetie!!'

'Ah. I'll, er, have it after.'

'You'll have it now! Eat it! Fuckin' now!'

'OK, OK, take it easy!'

Gulp.

'That's been up ma bum! Ha-ha-ha-ha!'

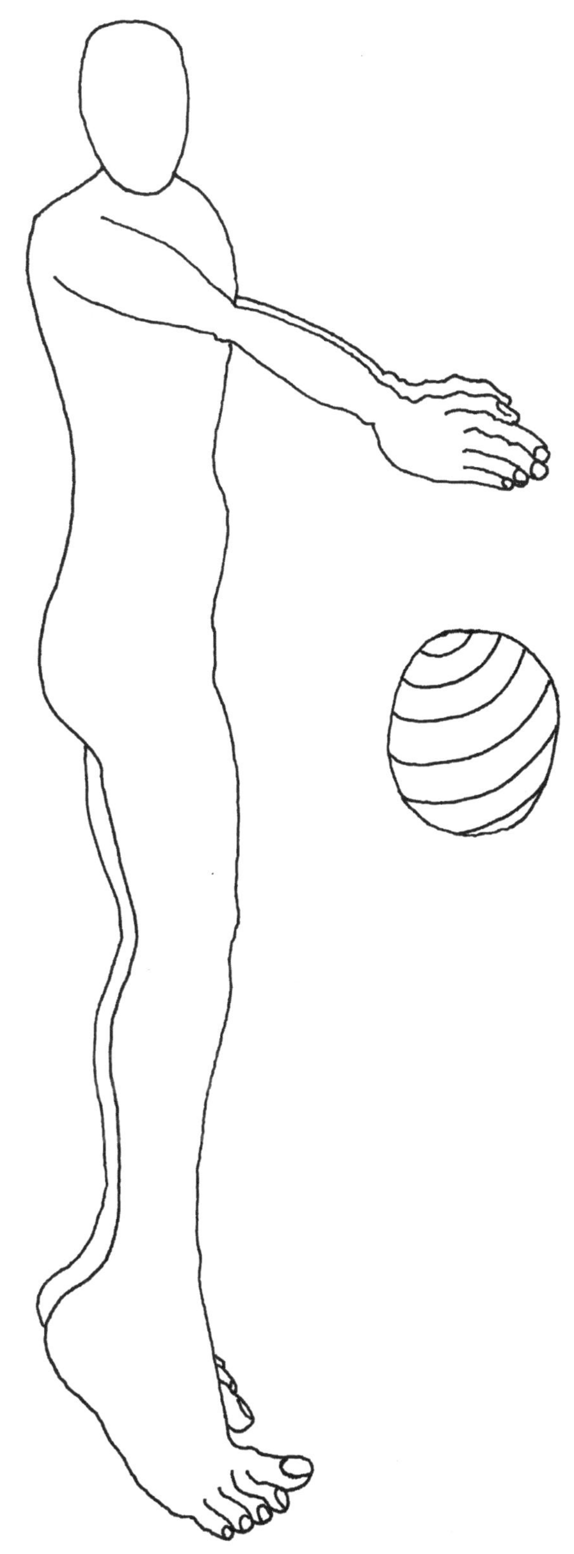

The Hoopist, 2017

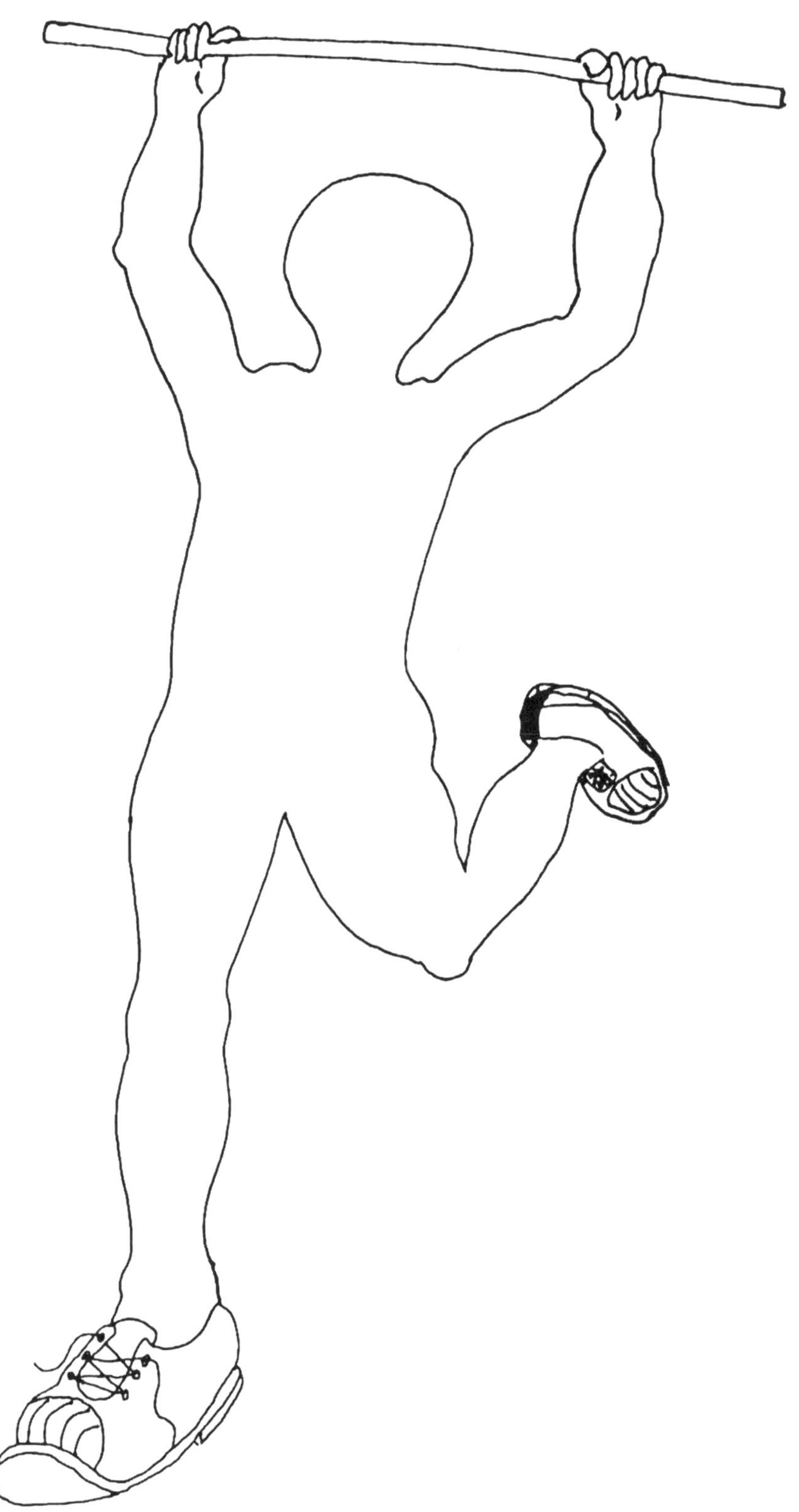

Le Joggist, 2015

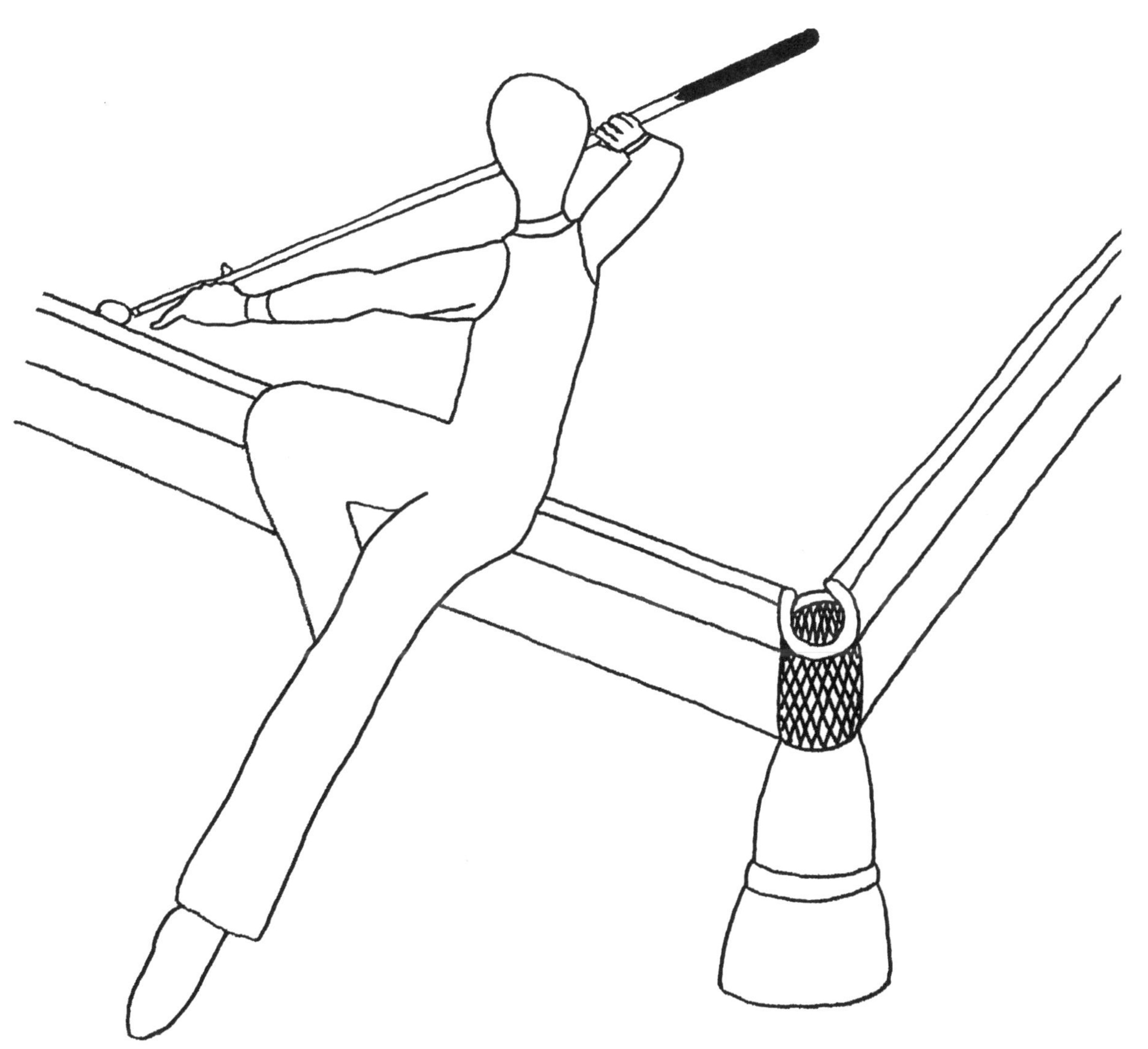

Plenty Of Side, 2018

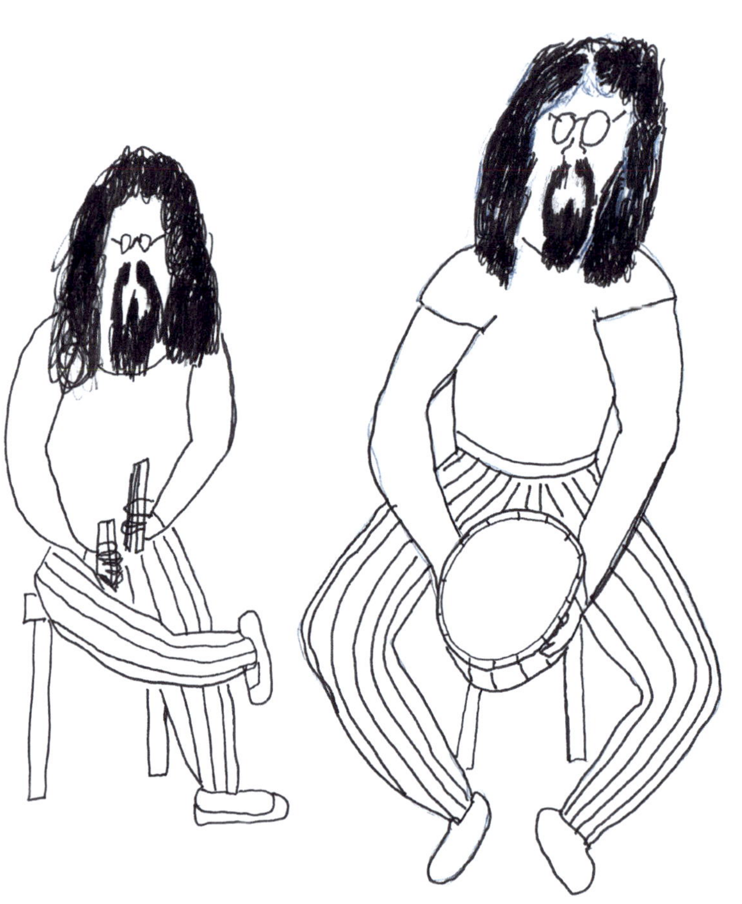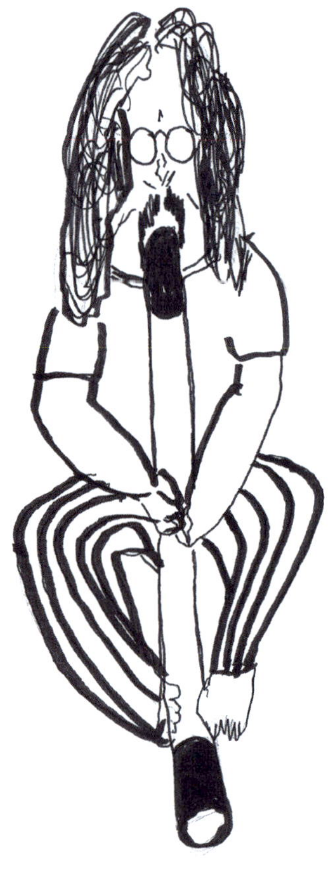

Did You Read Do?, 2022

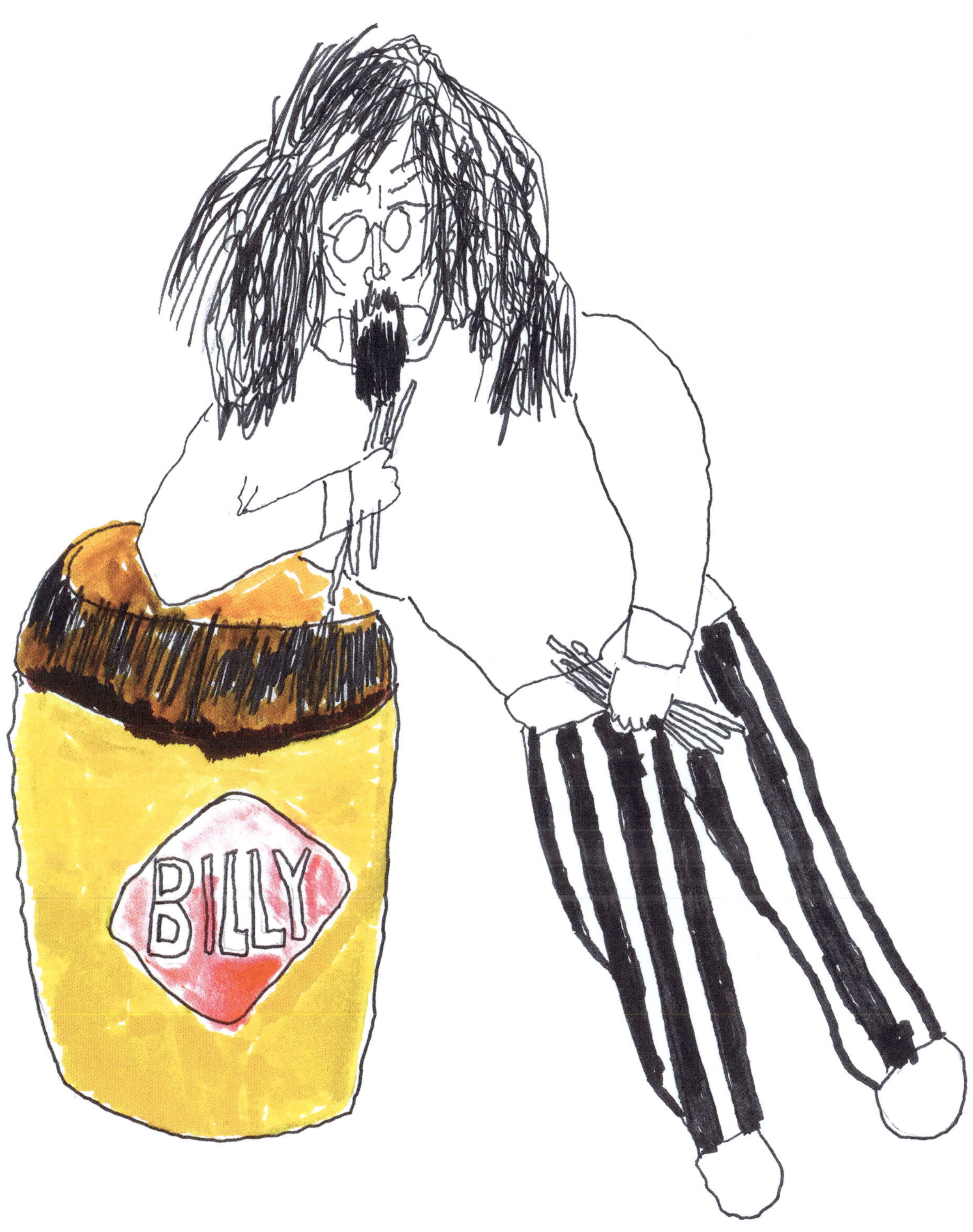
BILLY

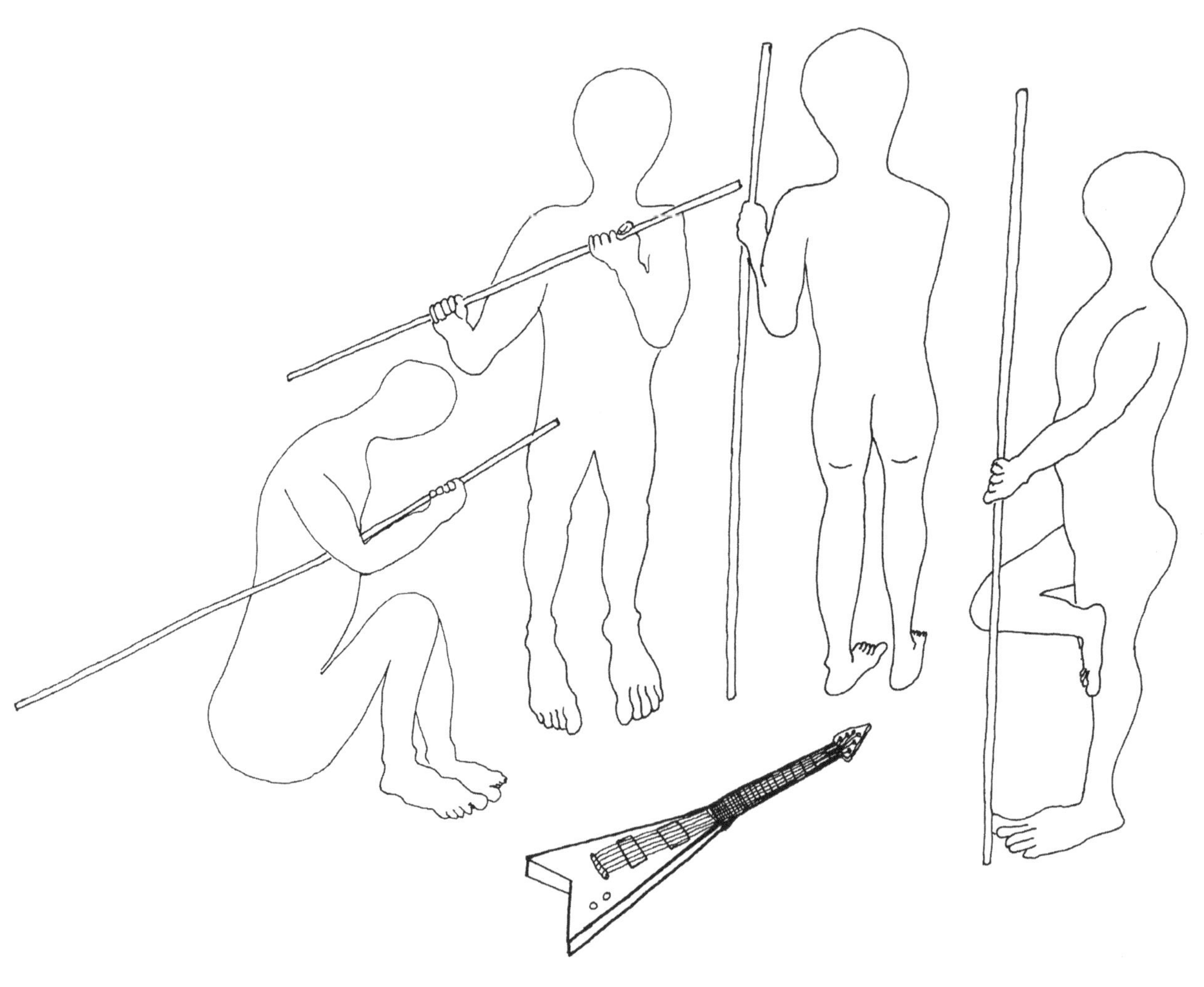

We Thought It Headed South, 2016

The most incredible impromptu musical performance I ever witnessed was a private one – only I and one other person saw it – and it remains a highlight of my life. It happened on a totally unplanned trip to Malta. My manager at the time was going there for a couple of days to do some business. He had clients filming on location for the movie *Popeye* starring Robin Williams. 'You wanna come along for the ride?' he asked. 'We'll have a laugh.' 'Sure.'

That first night I was there, we all met up – me, Robin, Ray Cooper the percussionist, a genius banjo player called Doug Dillard, and Harry Nilsson, the brilliant composer and singer.

I'd loved his music for years. He was doing the music for the movie.

The plan for that night was for us all to get shit-faced. We started drinking and it was all very jolly, and then Harry said to me, 'Before you can become one of the gang – a Member of the Knights of the Maltese Cross – you have to write your name on that castle where everybody can see it!' He pointed to a huge, towering, limestone fort sticking out of the landscape up a steep hill. Everybody looked at me as though they were thinking, 'Surely he's not going to fall for that?' But, undaunted, I climbed the hill and scaled the tower and wrote BILLY on it in large white letters with chalky white stones I found lying around.

Primary mission accomplished (getting shit-faced), we ended up in a nightclub. That's where we got into a fight. The legendary roadie Booby Daniels had showed up, and – true to form – he was chatting a woman up next to me. On her other side there was a Maltese guy and, after a while, he mumbled something to Booby, and Booby mumbled something back, and then the Maltese guy hit him in the head with an ashtray. It was a real cowboy fight — people walking backwards, kicking. We all exited the club at high speed. Outside, after taking another one on the chin, Booby stumbled and knocked down the marquee. After that, everybody dispersed for the night. We dropped Booby off to attend to his injuries and likely concussion, and then it was only me and Harry left. Harry said: 'There's a guy here who plays great guitar. He works in a garage.' Well, we found this guitarist on the way back to our hotel, but he hadn't brought his guitar. There was a piano sitting there — a terrible mess of a piano. It was painted green. So, Harry sat on a bar stool above the keys, fiddled around with the instrument for a bit, and then he turned to me and said: 'What do you want to hear?' I said, '"Remember Christmas."' I love that song of his. Harry played it, just for me and the guy in the garage, and it was one of the best moments of my life. Not many of them in a pound.

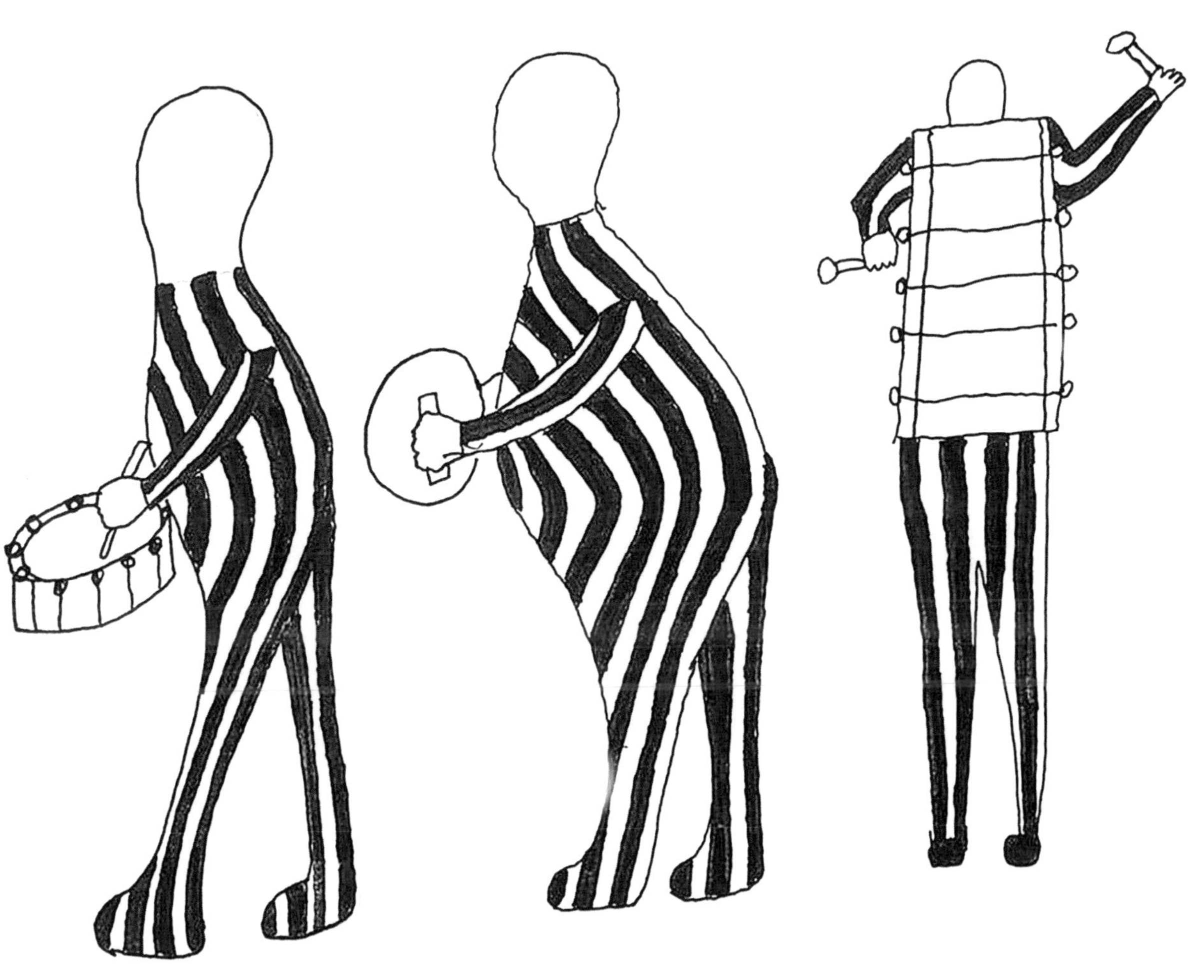

Rhythm Section, 2020

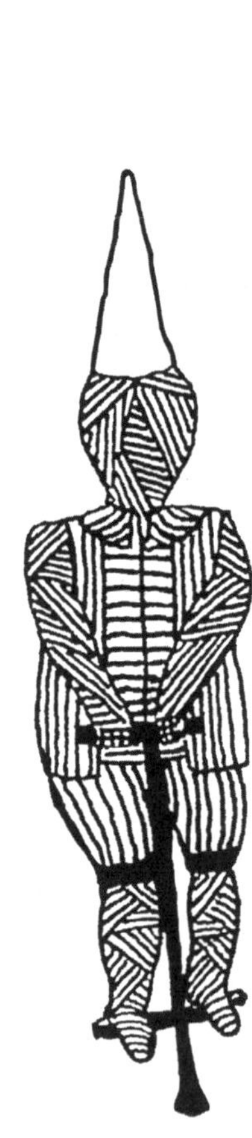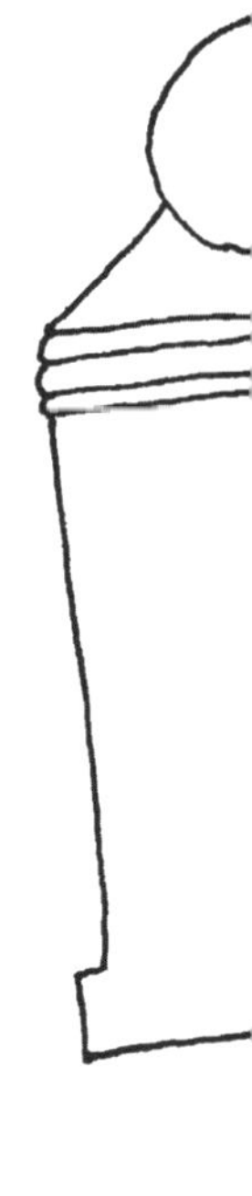

The Wreck Room, 2018

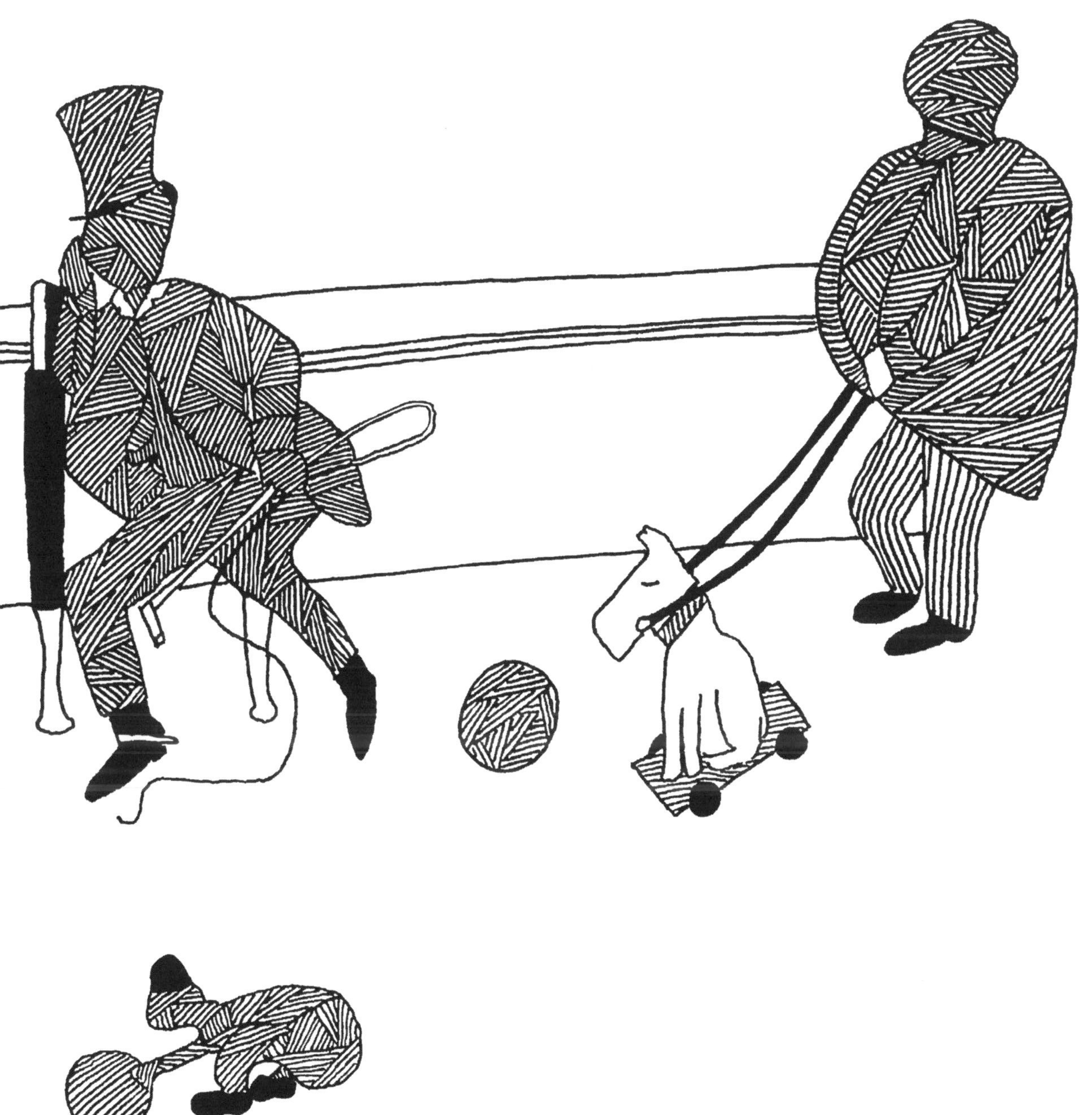

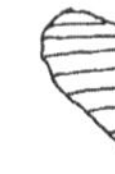
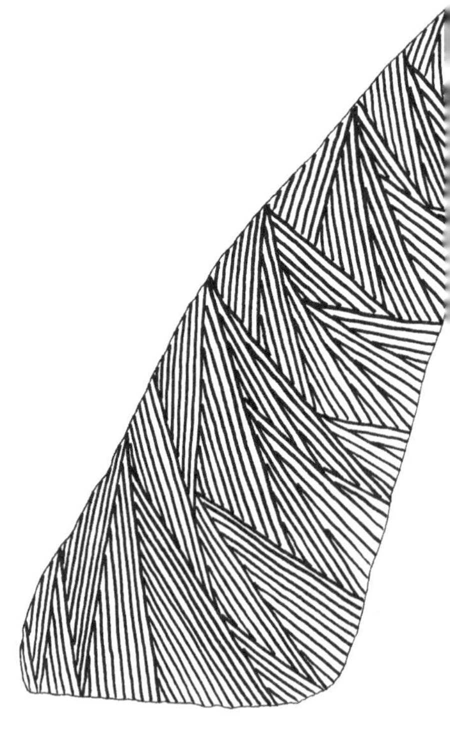

Ball Roller, 2012

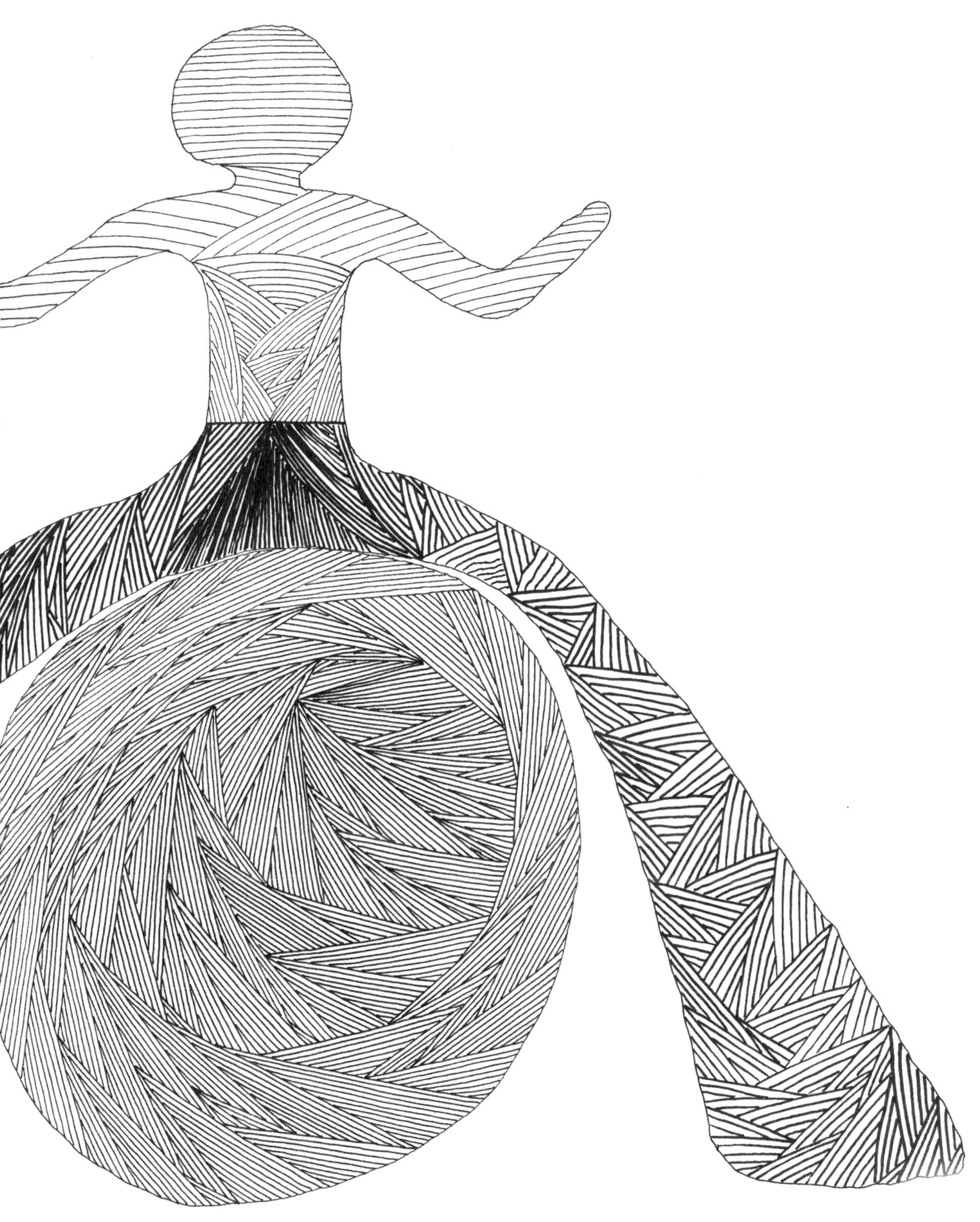

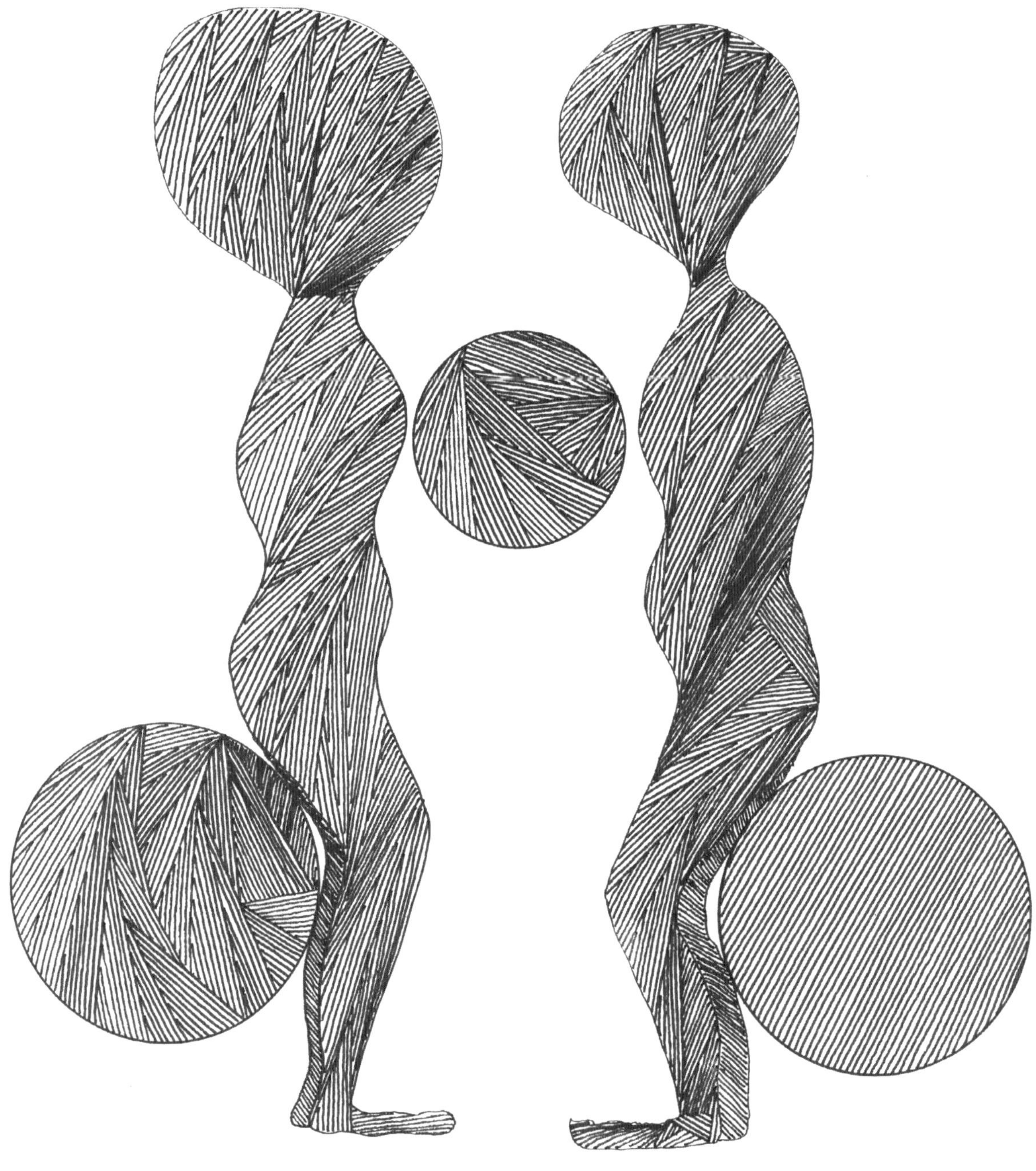

A Chat At The Gym, 2012

I made a TV show once called *Tracks Across America*, where I travelled through Minnesota, North Dakota and Montana by train. It was a brilliant journey. My favourite state along the train route was Montana. The people there were cowboys … and Native Americans. And the occasional yodeller. I met a true yodeller in a town called Shelby. He stood playing his guitar for me next to the railroad tracks, and when he started singing I could barely believe my ears — it was amazing, a real joy to listen to. He called it 'fancy cowboy yodelling', something he learned from his father when he was a boy. He told me his father would yodel old cowboy songs whenever he was happy. As he started to play another tune, I heard a 'whooo hooo' in the distance, and a train flew past us as we sang together:

All around the water tanks, waiting for a train
A thousand miles away from home, sleeping in the rain
I walked up to a brakeman, to give him a line of talk
He says 'If you've got money, I'll see that you don't walk.'

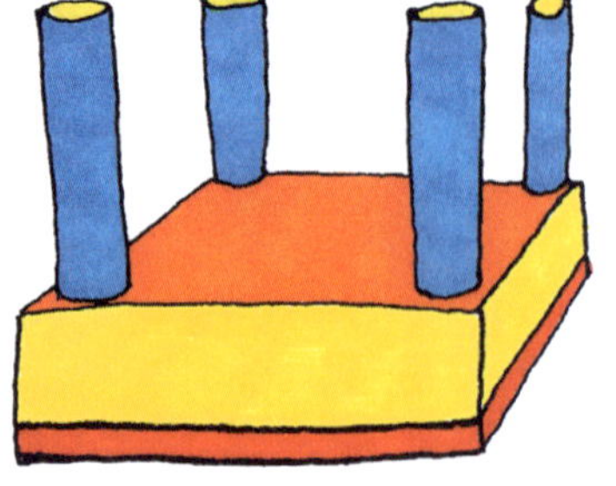

Saturday Night, 2023

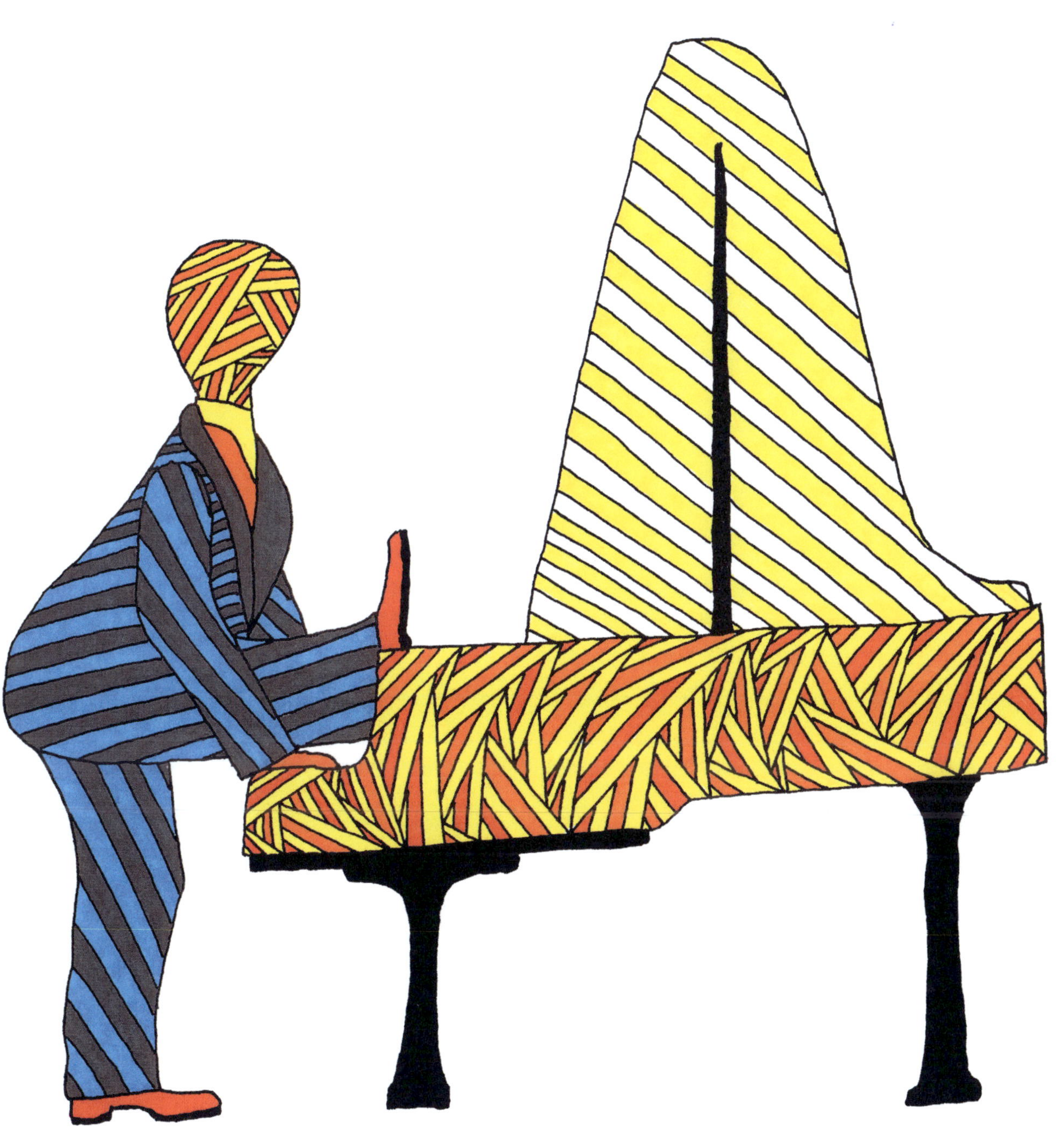

first met Elton John's guitarist, Davey Johnstone, when he was fifteen. He was a talented schoolboy with long blond hair, playing fantastic banjo in the folk clubs. Always laughing. Davey's still the same — finds everything funny. At the beginning of his career, he did a session playing the mandolin for one of Elton's albums, and afterwards Elton said, 'That was great — do you play guitar?' Davey said 'Yes' and ran out and bought one. Soon after, Davey joined Elton's band as his guitarist. One night I went to see Elton at the Apollo in Glasgow. We had a great laugh afterwards with Elton and his crew — and his manager John Reid. That night, someone — maybe it was Davey — said, 'Why not get Billy for the American tour?' John said, 'Good idea.'

John Reid drove a Rolls-Royce. I had met him years before in Paisley when he worked in a fashion shop called Stylecraft. Then he disappeared to London and became massively successful, managing Elton John. His mother had lived on a housing estate in Paisley, and John used to drive up to see her in his Rolls-Royce. I knew a folk singer called Helen Gilderson who lived with her granny in the same estate. She told me her granny said: 'That John Reid . . . I think he's a motor mechanic. They let him bring cars home.'

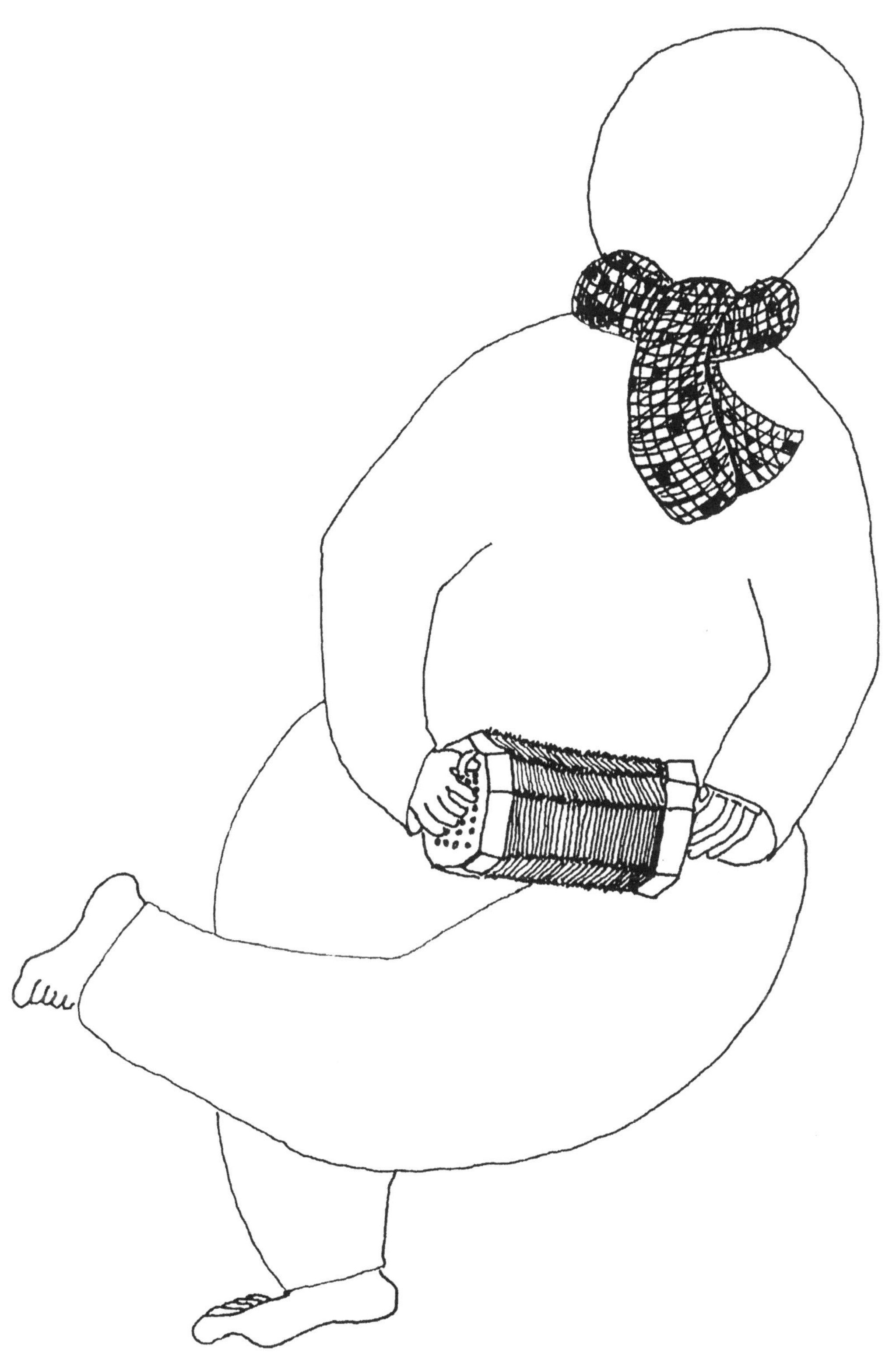

Squeezebox, 2017

At first, I thought opening for Elton was a great idea — but then I got nervous, because I'd never played such huge arenas or opened for anybody before. I was right to be concerned. Opening for rock 'n' roll stars is a mistake, because their audiences are not interested in anybody else. The roadies just stick you on with a microphone — no lights. 'That'll do you.' Then they use you to fiddle with the lights and sound. People are wandering into the auditorium as you're doing your thing. I wasn't on the marquee or the ticket or the T-shirt, so the first thing they knew of me was: 'Ladies and gentlemen, please welcome Elton — (Hrrrraaaaaayyyyy!!!) — John's friend — (Oooooooohhhhh!!) BILLY CONNOLLY!!! …' I'd be booed ON.

Elton's 1976 Bicentennial Tour was ten weeks long. I had some good nights, like Madison Square Garden — but they were very few. There'd usually be a pocket of about twenty people at the front going, 'Fuck off! Fuck off!' In Washington DC someone threw a brass smoking pipe and it hit me between the eyes. I fell to the ground and had to come offstage.

Elton is loved by other stars. Some great people came to see Elton. Elvis turned up in DC but didn't stay for the show. I tried to see him, but his entourage had encircled him, so I didn't even glimpse the hem of his garment. I told people I'd seen him, though. I did see Elizabeth Taylor — who looked beautiful. Big hair. And Alice Cooper — he spoke to me backstage. Asked me where I got my banana boots; I think he was jealous.

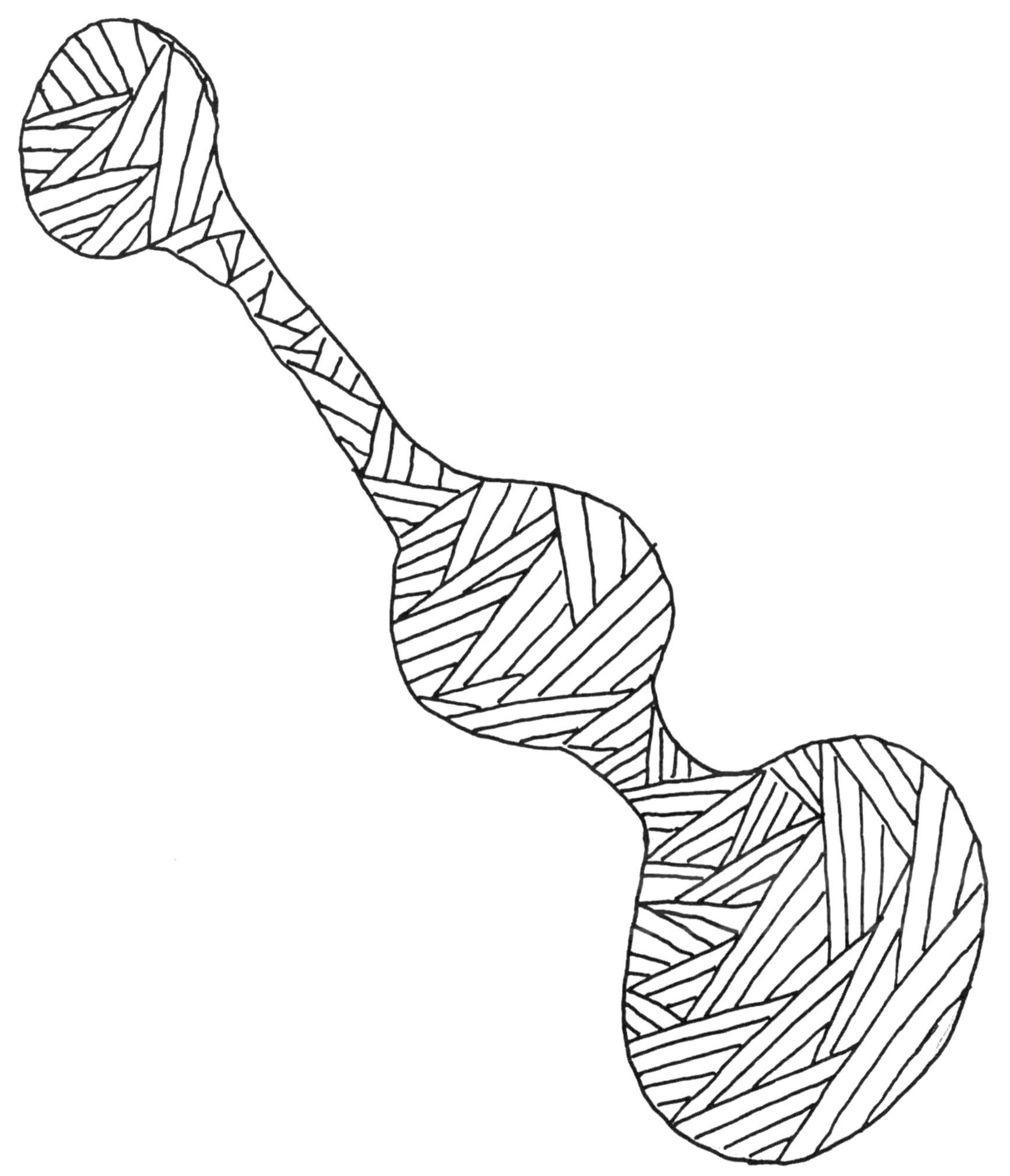

Complex Banjo, 2019

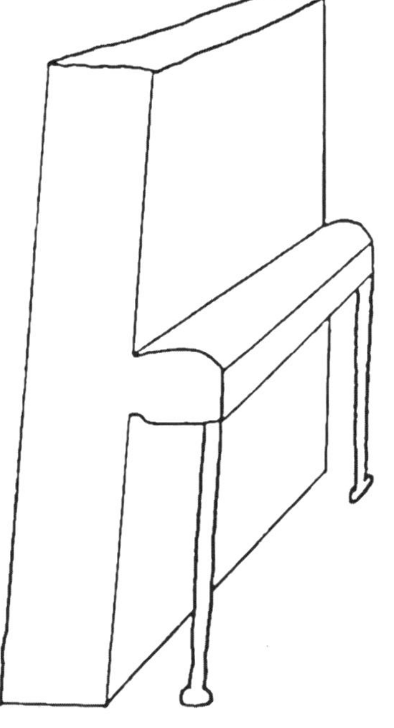

Big Man And Wee Piano, 2017

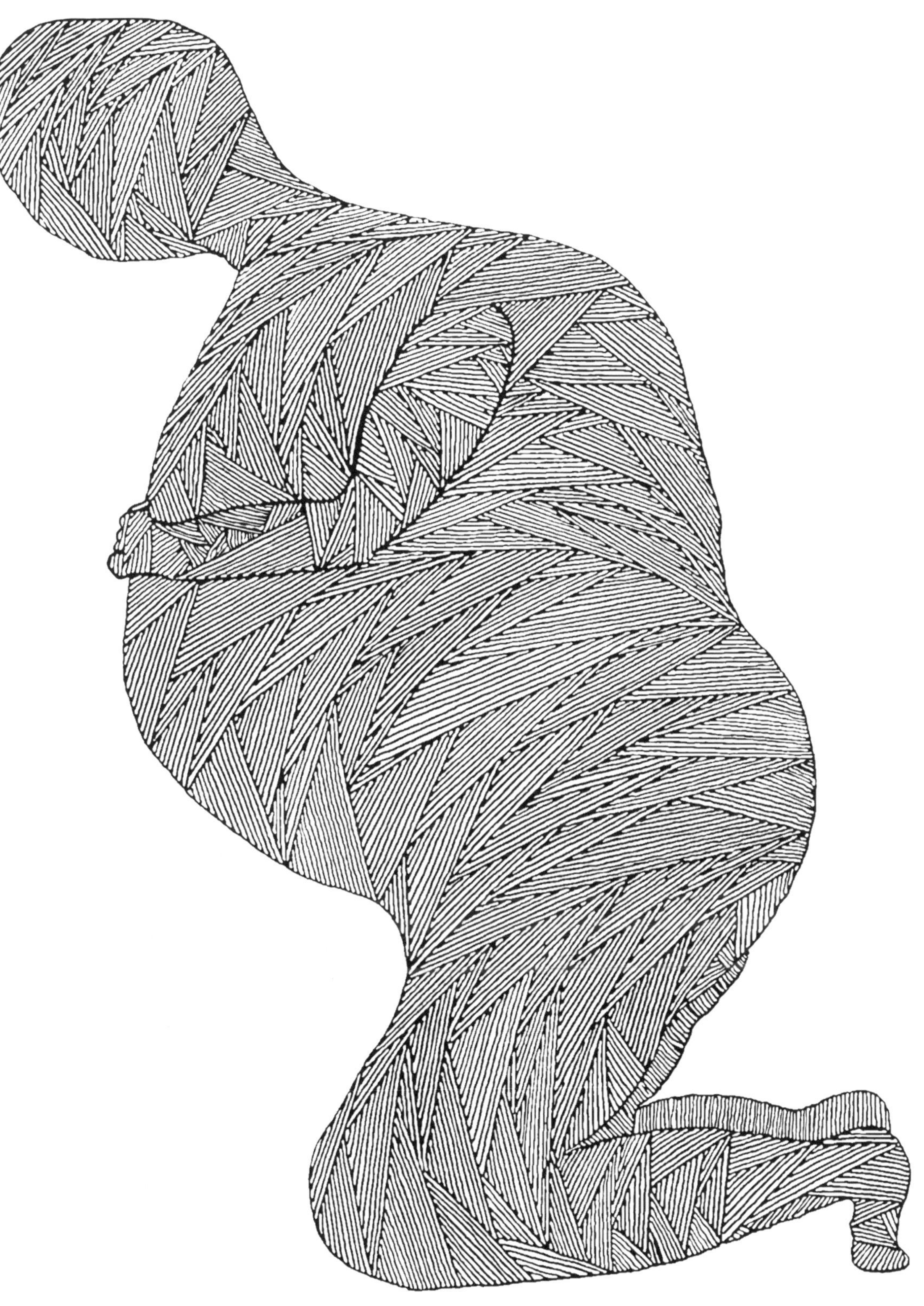

I used to be a folk
singer but I was
dreadful. I had a
voice like a goose
farting in the fog.

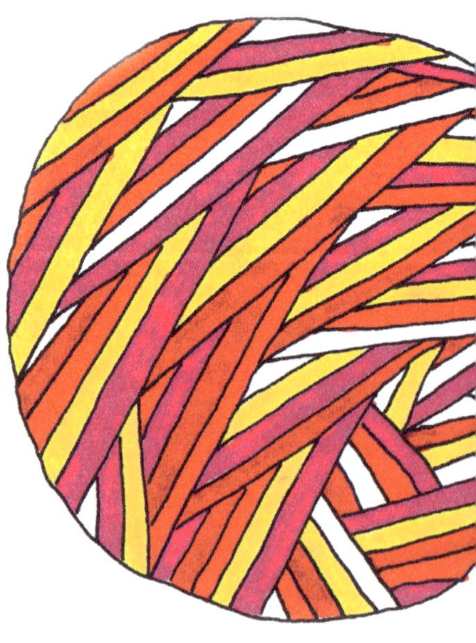

Tambourine Man, 2019

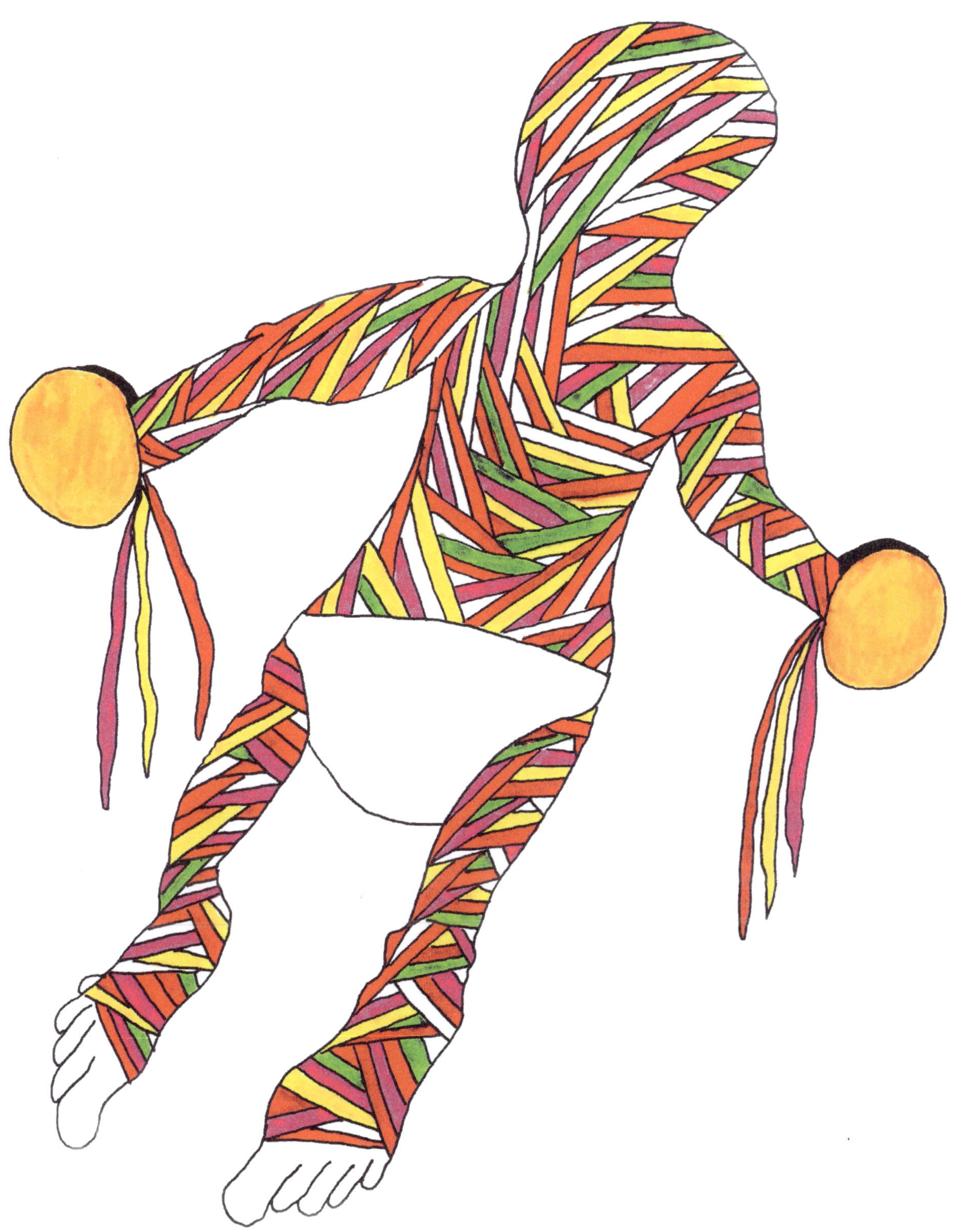

Early on in my comedy career, I knew I could become well known nationally – even internationally – but many people thought that was unlikely with my Glaswegian accent. Then it happened; Michael Parkinson was advised by Jimmy Reid that I'd be a great guest on his show. So, I got the call.

I didn't prepare what I was going to say on the show. In the car on the way to the studio Frank, my manager, said, 'Whatever you do, don't tell that joke about the wife and the bicycle.' Big mistake. If someone tells me not to say something, it remains trapped in my mind until the pressure becomes too much, and I just have to let it out. So halfway through the interview, in front of the live audience, I thought, 'Fuck it!' and just blurted it out. I said, 'I hope I can get away with this. It's a beauty:

This man, he says, "How's the wife?"

The other one says, "Ah, she's dead."

He says, "Wha?"

The other one says, "Dead. In the ground. I murdered her. Pffft. I'll show you if you want."

He says, "Aye, yeah, show me."

So, they go up to his tenement building, through the close – that's the entrance to the tenement …'

At this point I glanced sideways at Michael. He still seemed interested, so I continued.

'And sure enough there's a big mound of earth. With a bum sticking out of it. He says, "Is that her?"

"Aye."

He says, "Why did you leave her bum sticking out?"

He says, "I need somewhere to park ma bike!"'

I imagine Frank was shitting himself, but he shouldn't have worried. The place was in an uproar — in fact, the next day the whole country seemed to be talking about it. When I arrived back in Glasgow, people in the airport started applauding.

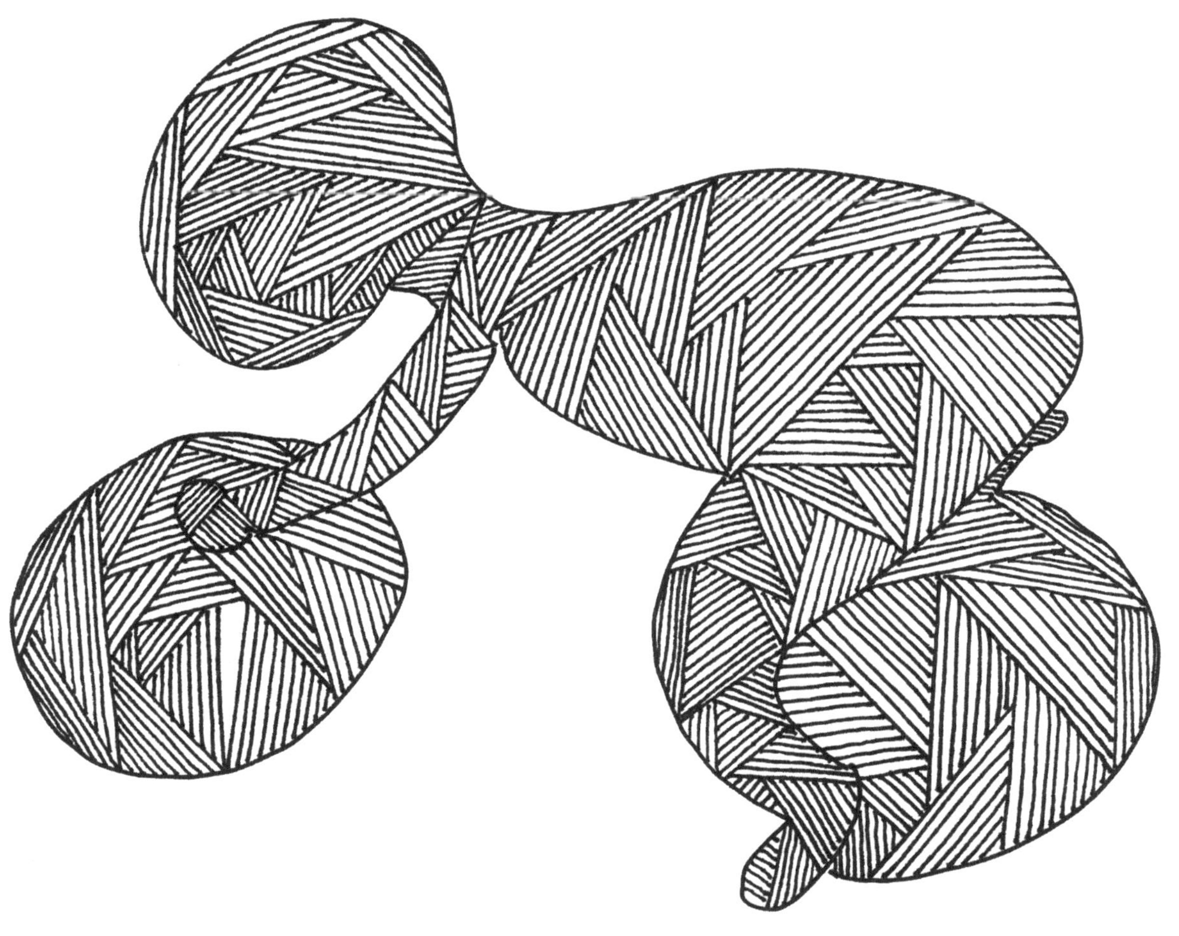

Early Bicycle, 2012

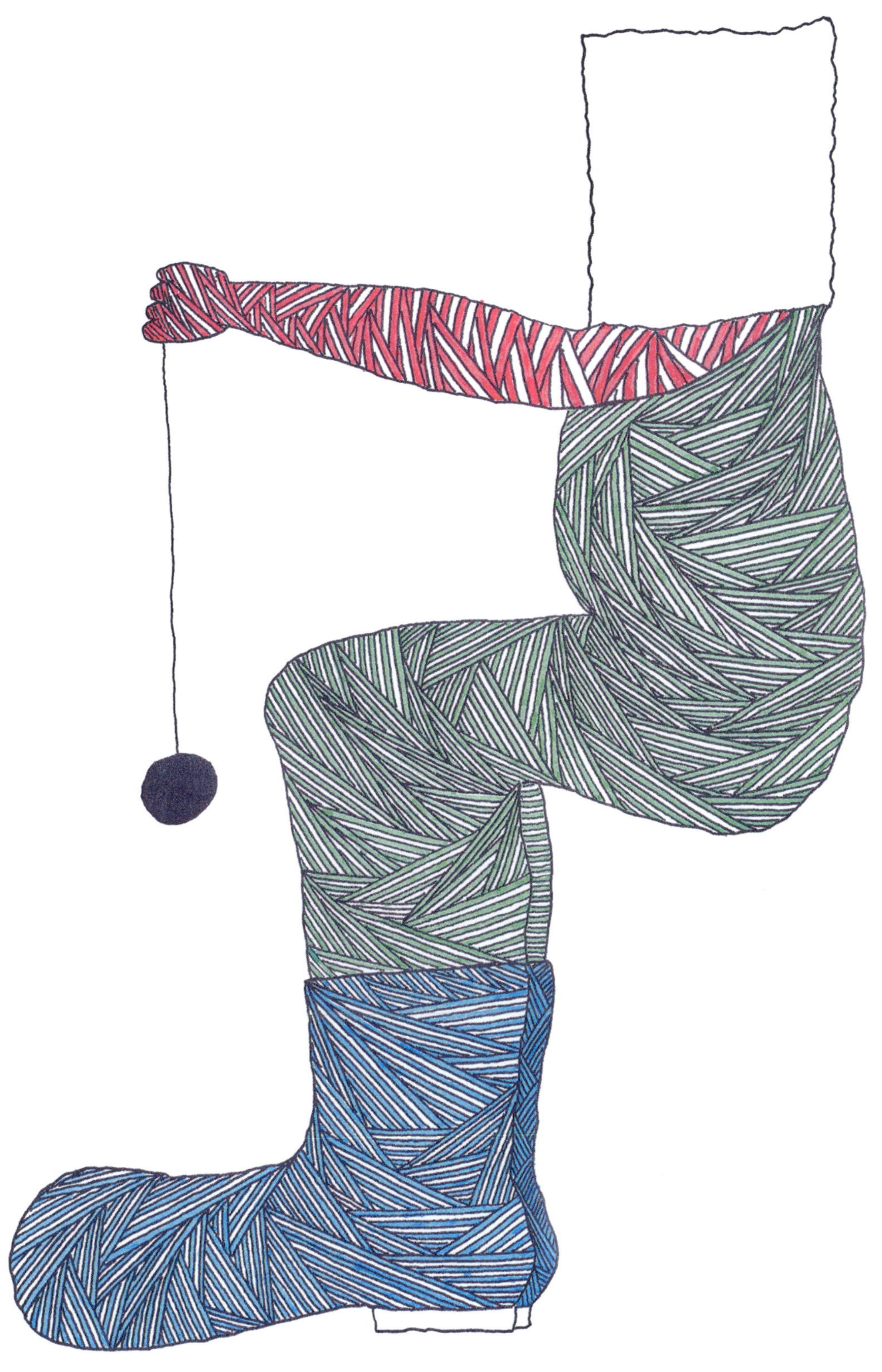

An Act Of Balance – Baghead, 2021

Wellies they are wonderful,
oh wellies they are swell,
'Cause they keep out the water,
and they keep in the smell!

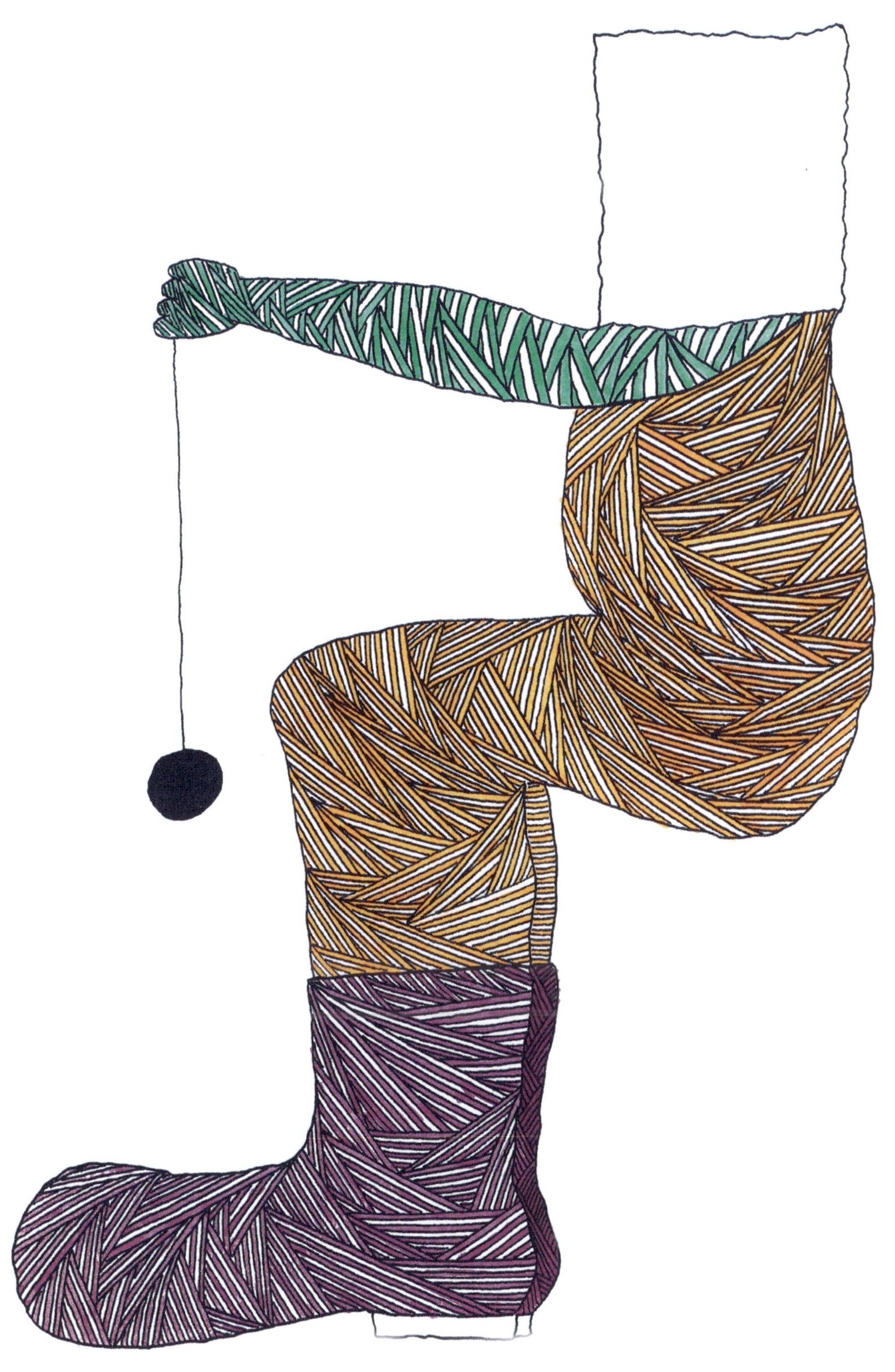

An Act Of Balance — Yo Yo Man, 2021

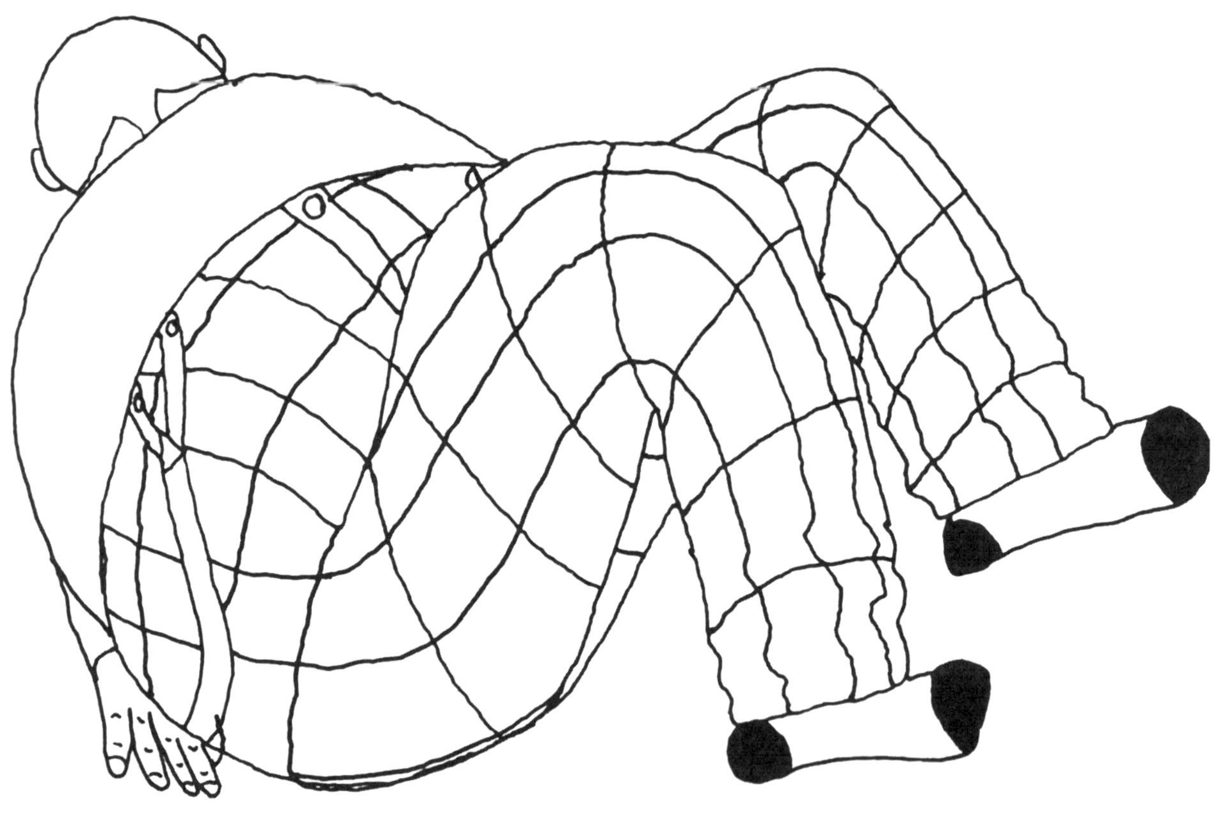

Wilkie Tumbler, 2019

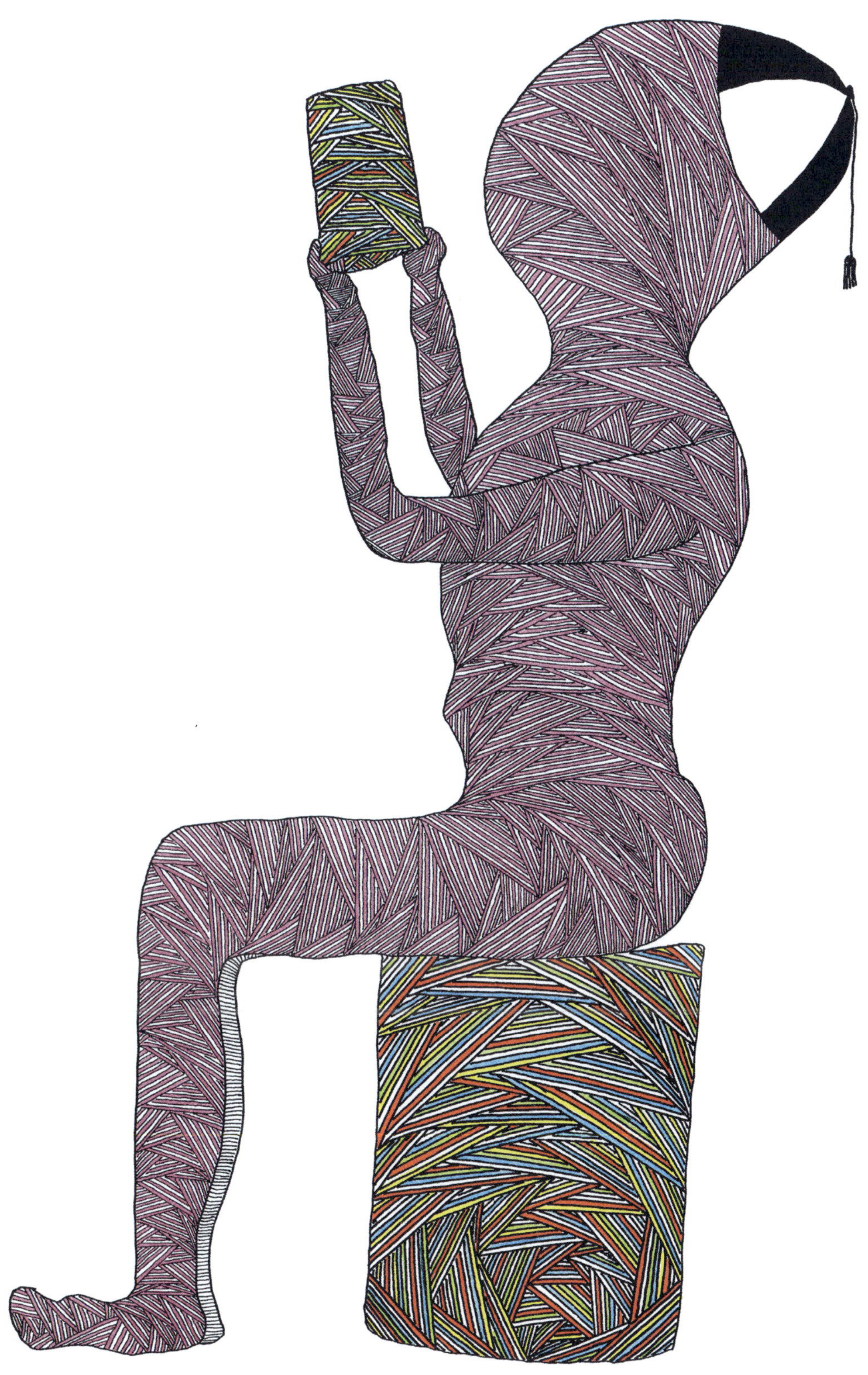

Big Close Up, 2024

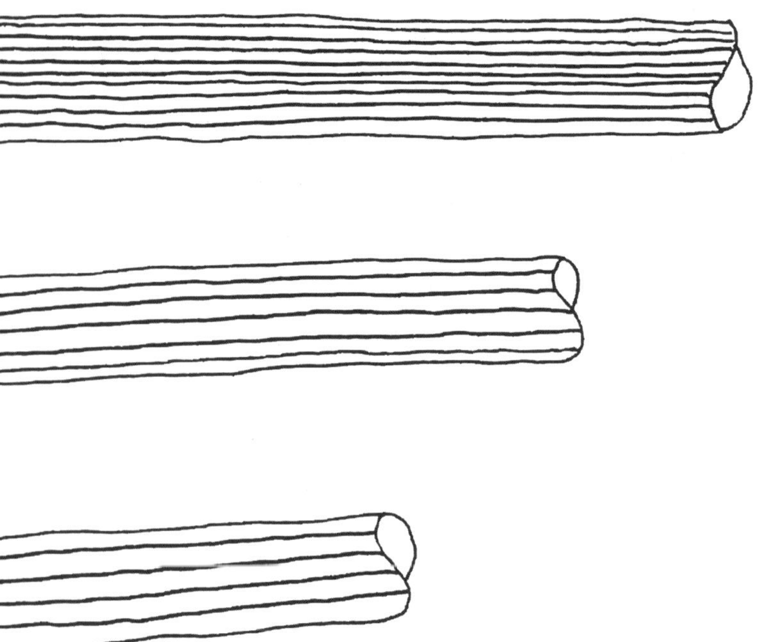

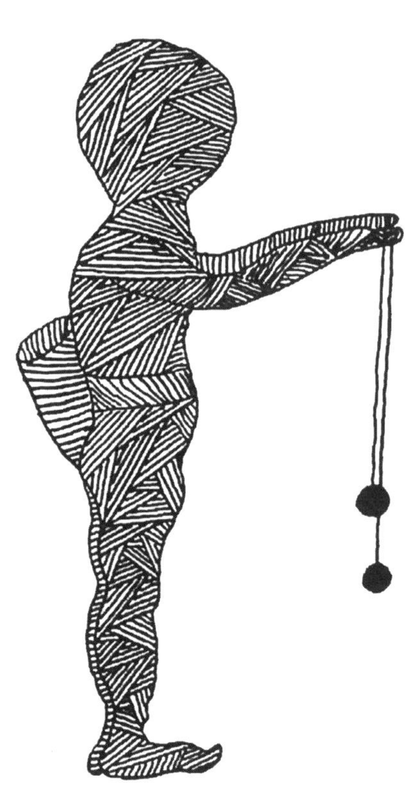

The Game, 2017

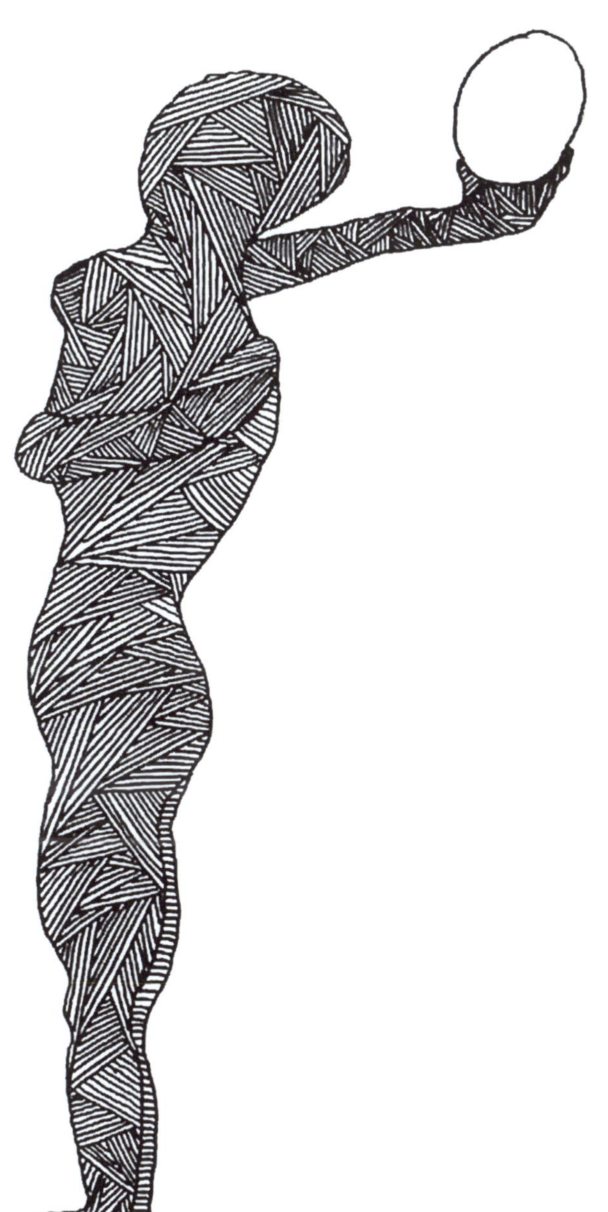

Chic Murray was a Scottish comedian who really inspired me. He used to say:

'I was at the Olympic Games and a man came along carrying a big thing on his shoulder.

I said, "Are you a pole vaulter?"

He said, "No – I'm a German. How'd you know my name was Walter?"'

That kind of nonsense really makes me laugh.

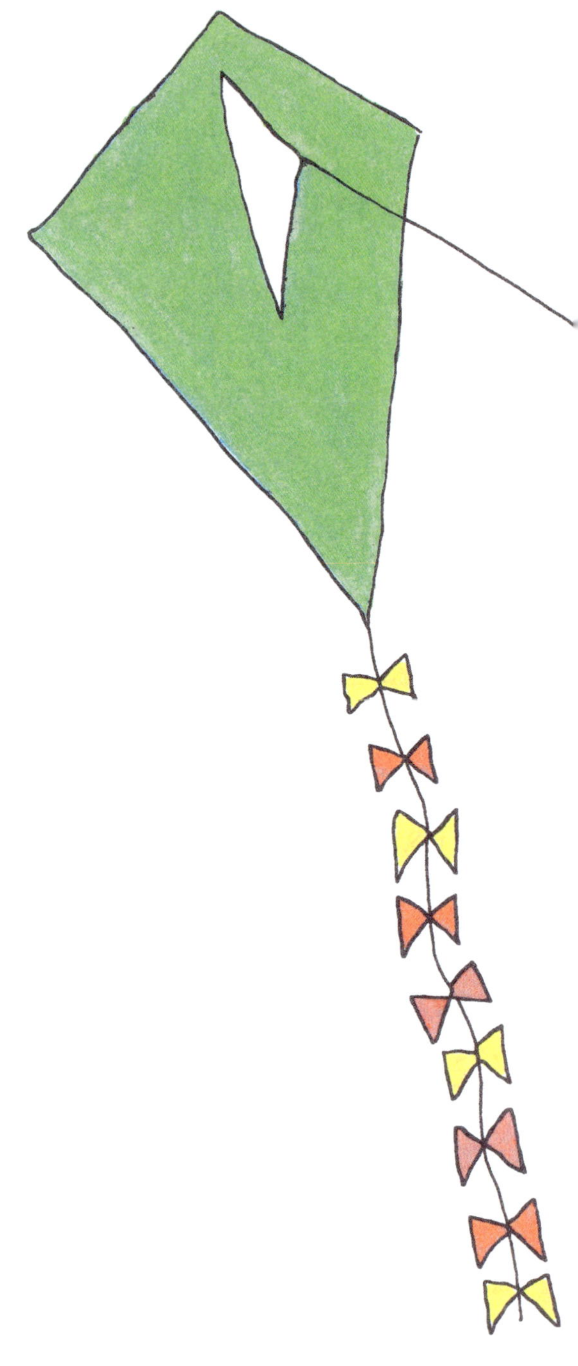

By all means grow old, but
don't mature. Remain childlike,
retain wonder, the ability to be
flabbergasted by something.

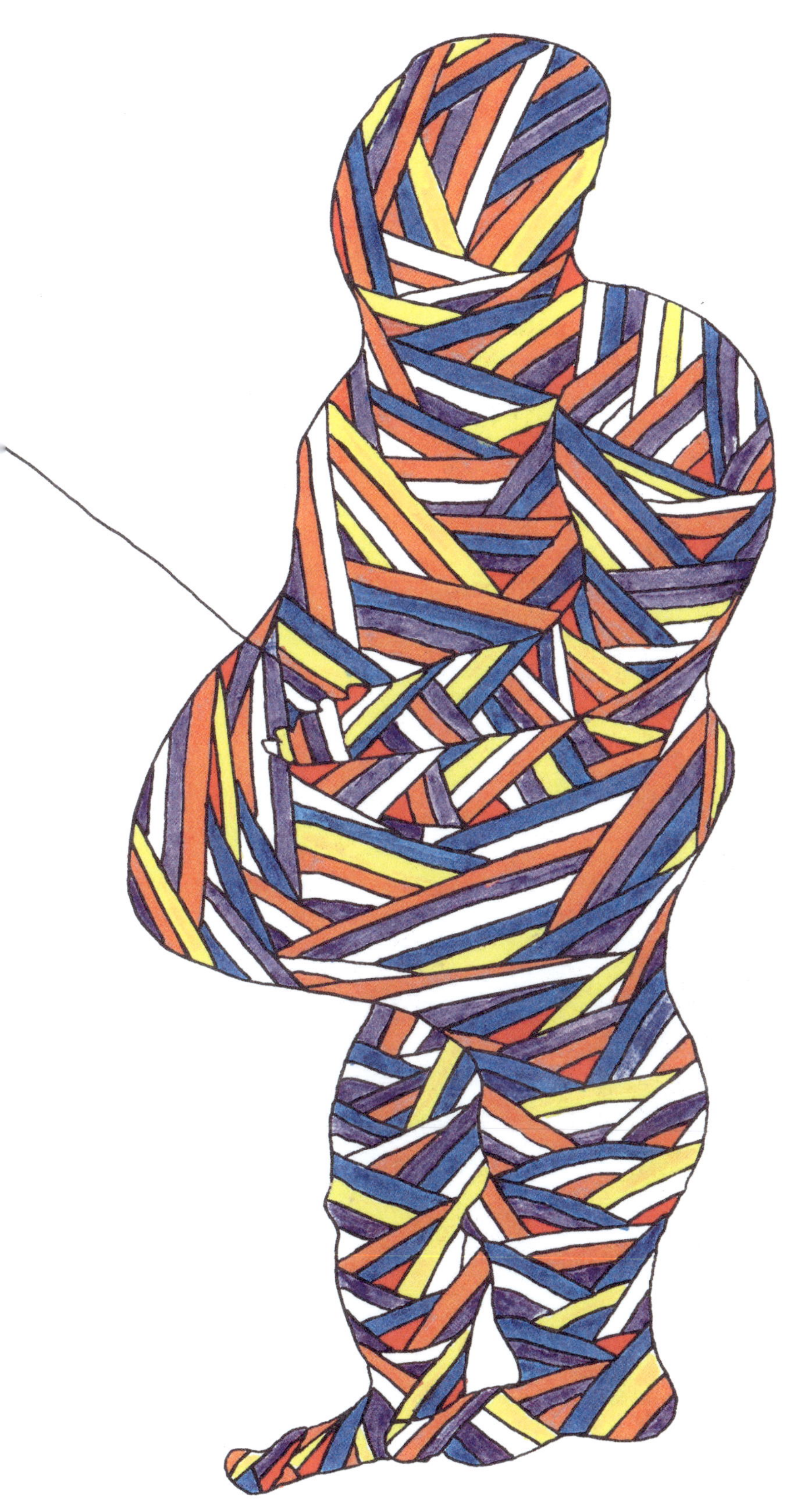

Malkie's Day Off, 2019

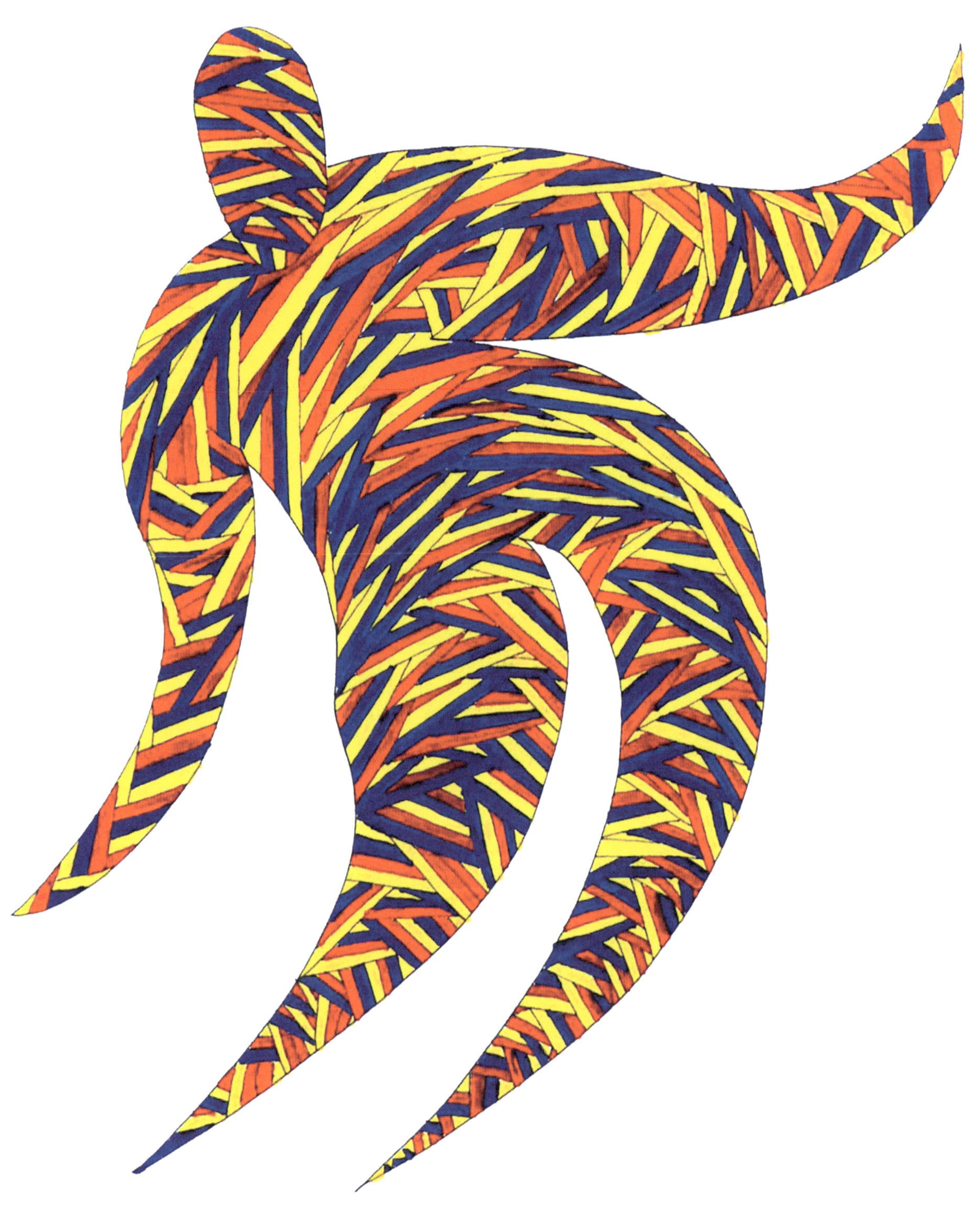

The Point, 2019

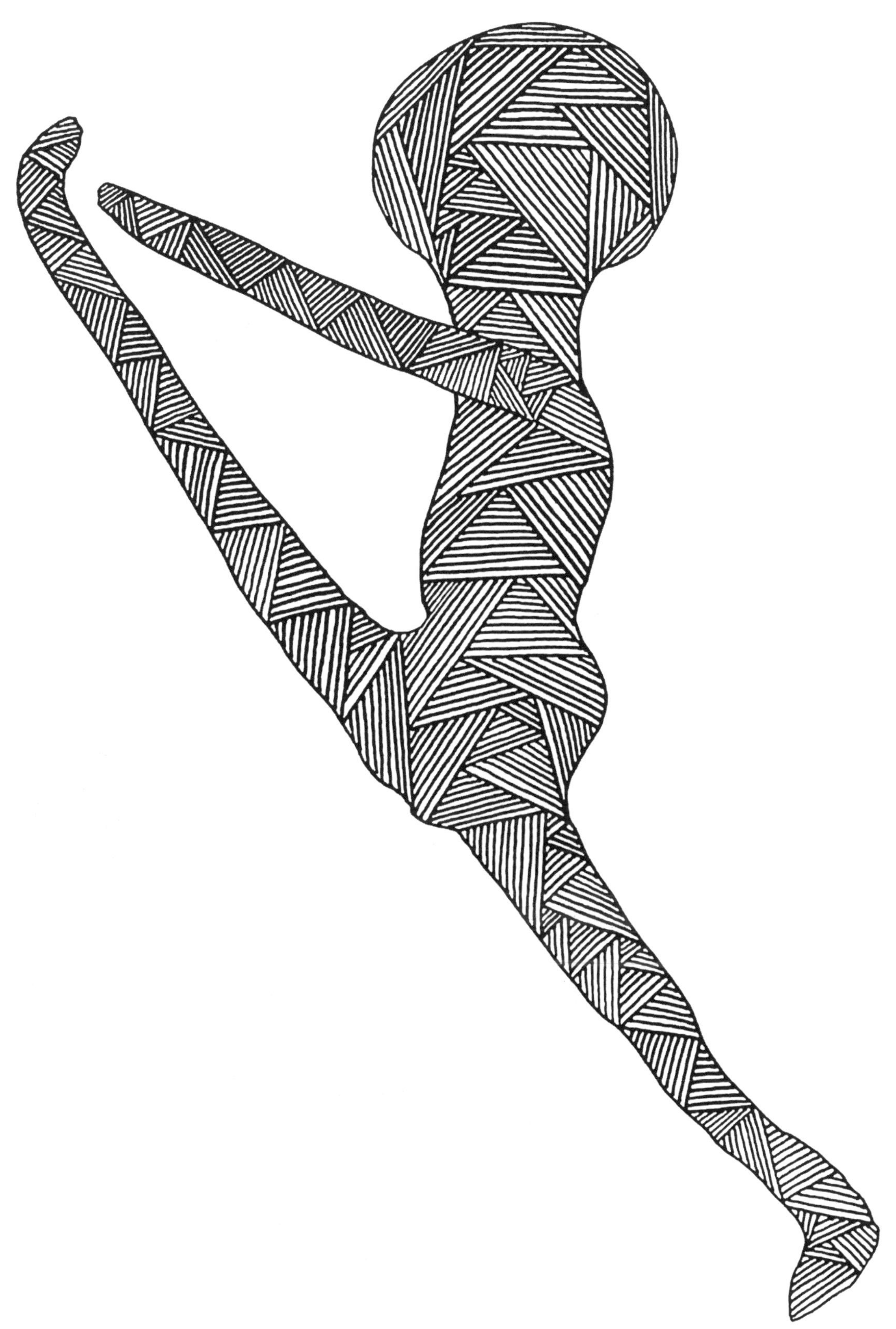

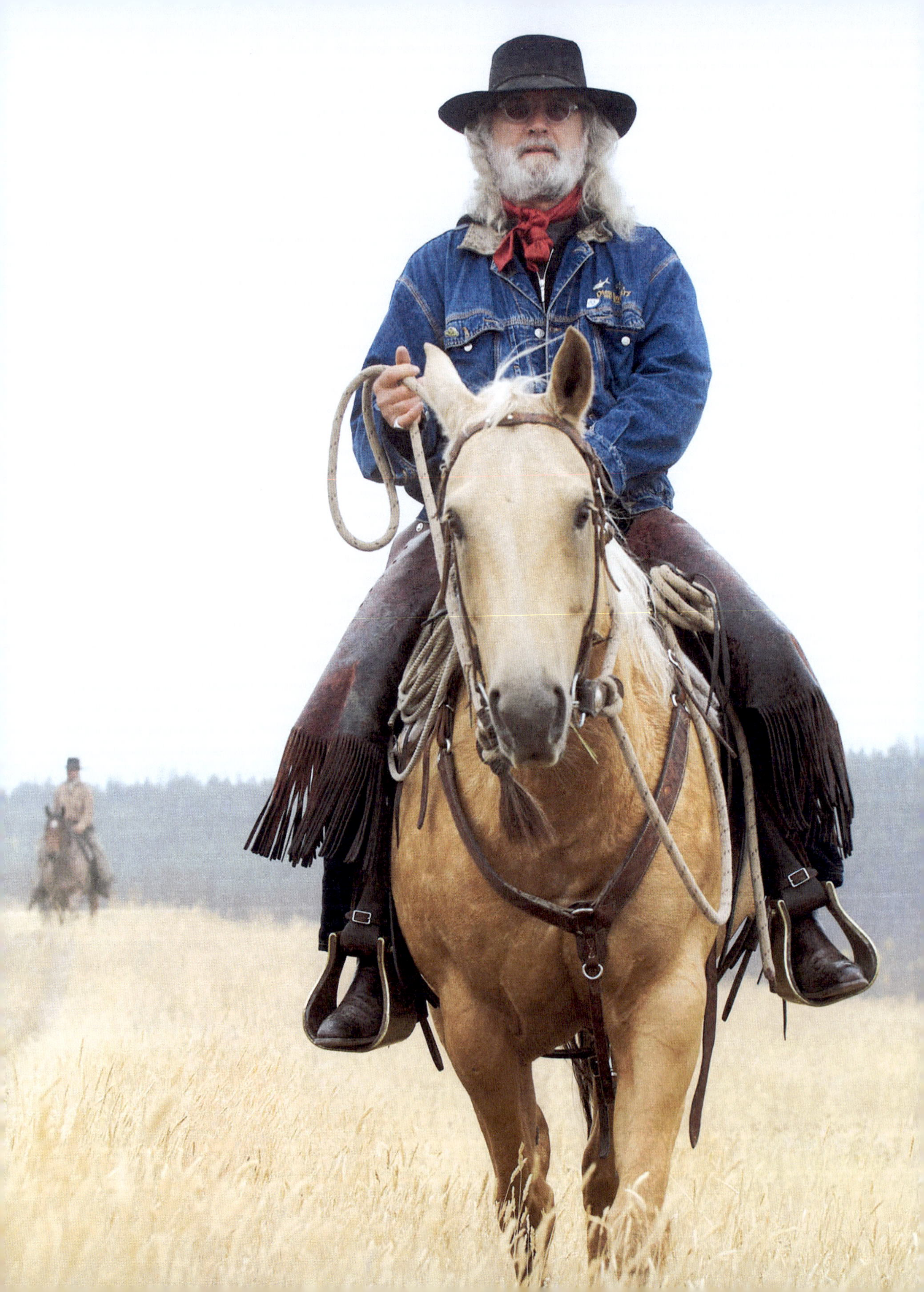

Wildlife

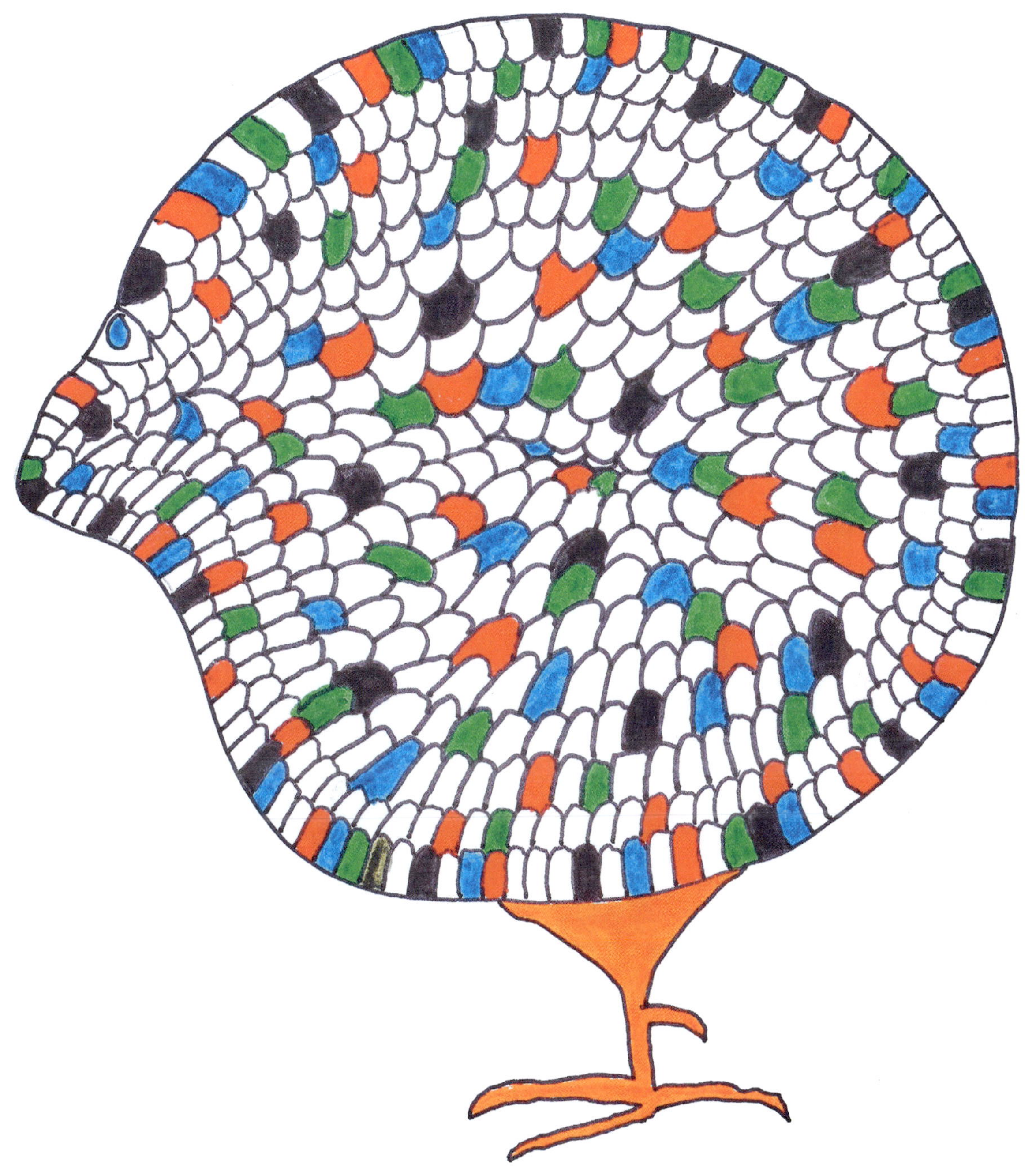

Blunt Porcupine, 2021

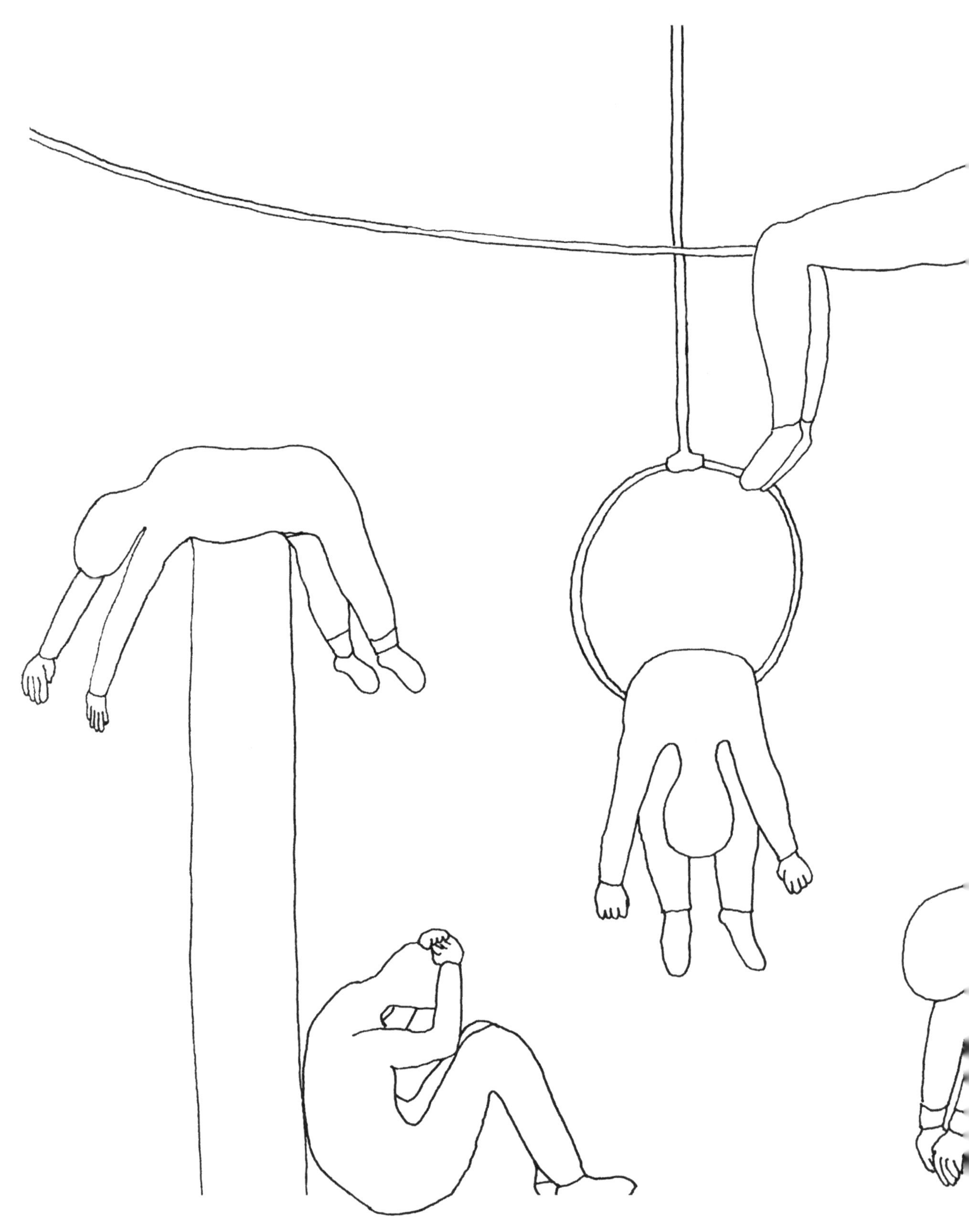

Down Wind Of The Elephant, 2016

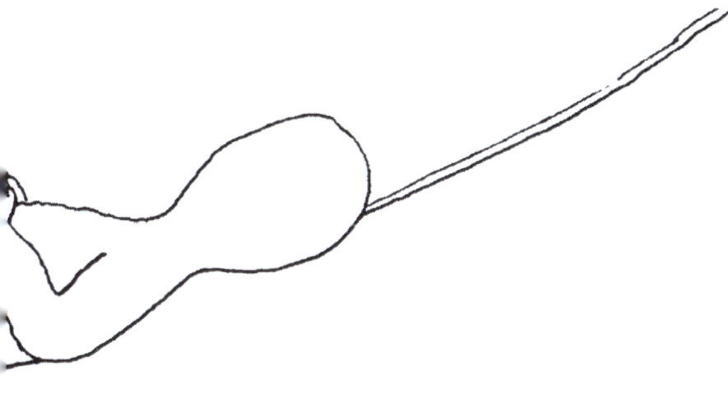

My parents used to
take me to the pet
department and tell
me it was a zoo.

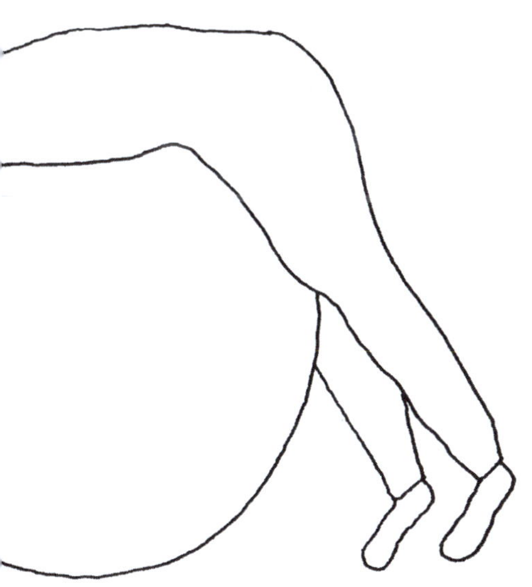

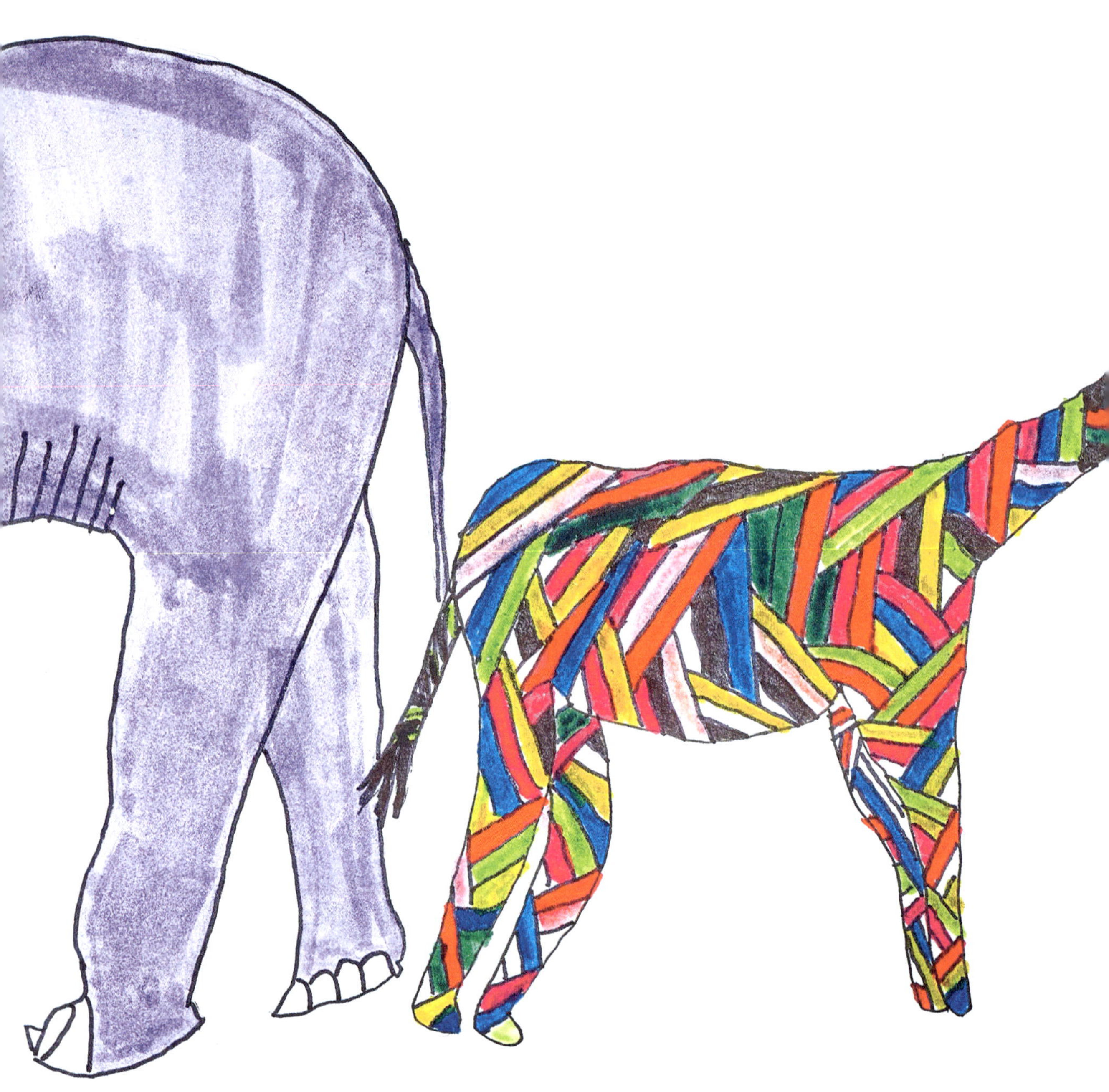

The Elephant In The Room, 2021

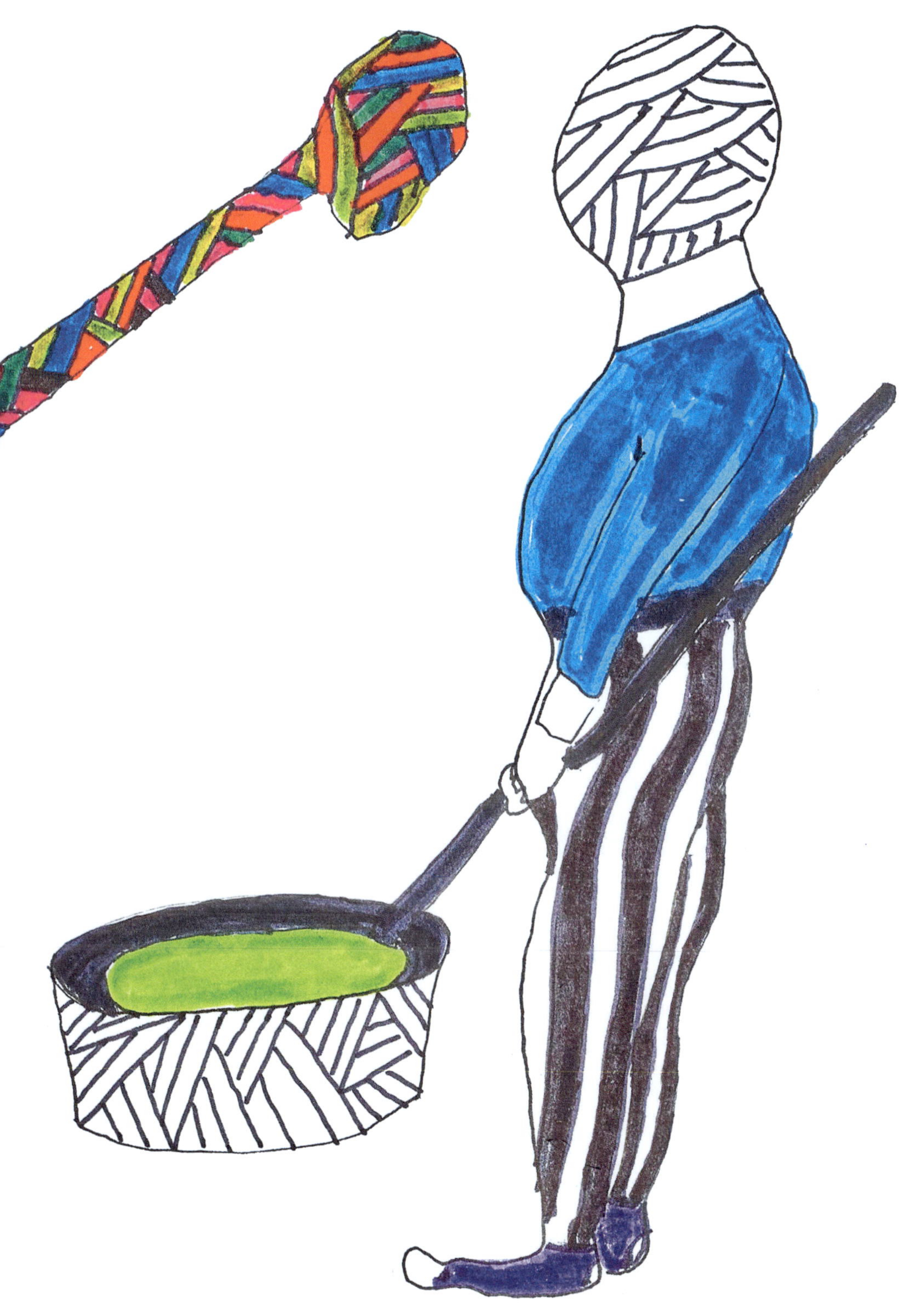

I have little interest in polo, but when my manager said, 'How would you like to go to Nepal and play polo on an elephant?' I said, 'I was just about to ask you if I could do that.' He laughed, and then I said, 'What are you fucking talking about?' He said, 'It has come up. Someone has dropped out – would you like to step in?' I said, 'I'd love to go to Nepal.' When I arrived at the famous hotel called Tiger Tops, I found that, although we were supposed to have been supplied with polo gear, there was none for me, and my luggage had been stolen in India, so I had nothing. Everyone else was in smart breeches and high polo boots, but I was stuck with khaki pants and a pair of desert boots.

Next day we went to the polo field. It was in the foothills of the Himalayas, with stunningly beautiful scenery all around. I remember being flabbergasted. I looked at one of the mountains and I said to one of the guys who knew what he was talking about: 'Look at that! It's right beside us!' He said: 'It's many miles away.' By the sheer size of it, I thought it was just a few steps away.

The celebrity team was me, Ringo Starr and his wife Barbara Bach, Steve Strange and Max Boyce – what a weird collection of people! The other team was made up of proper polo players, Nepalese guys who worked for King Mahendra, the king of Nepal. It was he who hosted the game – sponsored by Cartier. I think he just liked to hold celebrity matches for no reason at all. The elephants were his. Understandably, the other team all hated us novices because we knew nothing about polo and even less about handling elephants.

I was told to get on my elephant, but nobody showed me how, so I just improvised. I ran at it from behind, jumped on and put my feet behind its head – I knew you did that last bit. But then the guy in charge of my elephant – the mahut – hit the elephant in the head with a file. I said, 'Hey, no more. Don't fucking hit it with that!' Then one of the guys in charge came over and mumbled something. He was probably saying, 'He's a townie. He knows fuck all about it.' But I did know you don't hit animals in the head with files. Later on, I was on my elephant, and a guy was collecting my elephant's shit in a big sheet, and he said to me, 'It's a normal job here.' I said, 'No, it's a nail-biting cure.' They liked me from then on and I liked them. A bit of humour can always break the ice.

We got beaten in the end. Well, of course we did – none of us knew what we were doing. Nobody really showed us. They just said, 'That's your pole. That's the ball. Use the pole to hit the ball towards the goal. The elephants will get very excited but don't panic. They'll rise up on their hind legs and make an enormous din, but you'll get to love it.' It was true. The elephants were bellowing 'Bahoooooo!! Bahooooo!!' when they were running for the ball. My elephant would rear up on its hind legs like the old circus elephants, but I was well and truly tied on by a rope going over my lap, under my thighs and round its belly. The mahut was in front of me, further up the elephant's neck, and I had to tell him which way to go. He did the steering. At the end, we got big fancy prizes. I got a beautiful ashtray. And that was it.

The day after the match they took us out into the jungle, but we'd not been travelling for long when the guide suddenly stopped. 'I can smell a female tiger. She is near.' I said: 'Well, why the fuck are we still here?' We retreated sharpish. Later that day I saw a baby rhinoceros. It was just magnificent, walking behind its mother through the elephant grass. Then, we got off the elephants and we were having a cup of tea, and I saw a rabbit. I said: 'Oh God, look, a rabbit! At last, something that won't eat you.' But as I walked over to it, it scuttled off and I went: 'Fucking hell! That ain't no rabbit!' Its legs were like my fingers. It was the biggest, scariest spider I'd ever seen.

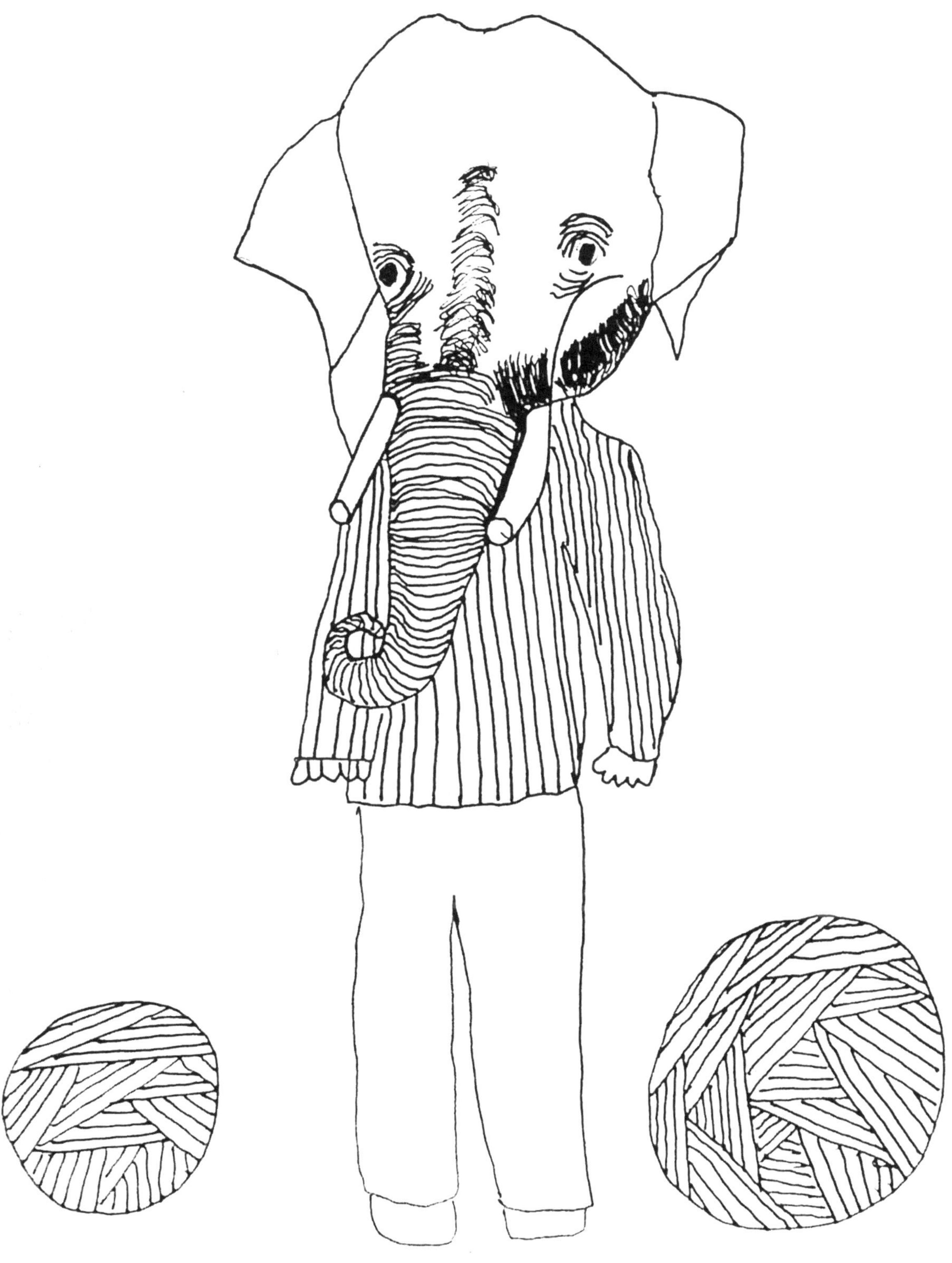

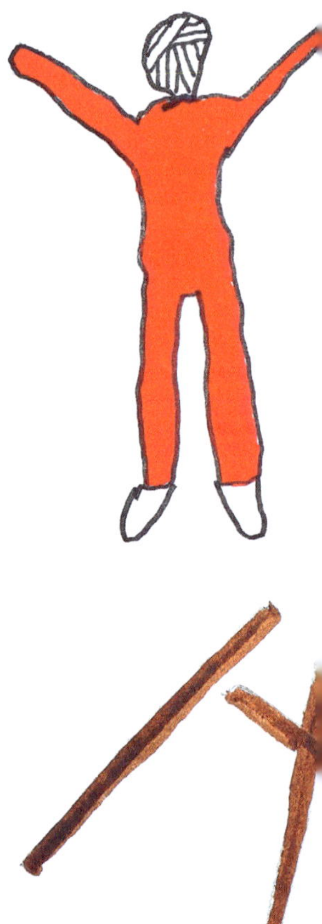

The Greatest Show On Earth, 2021

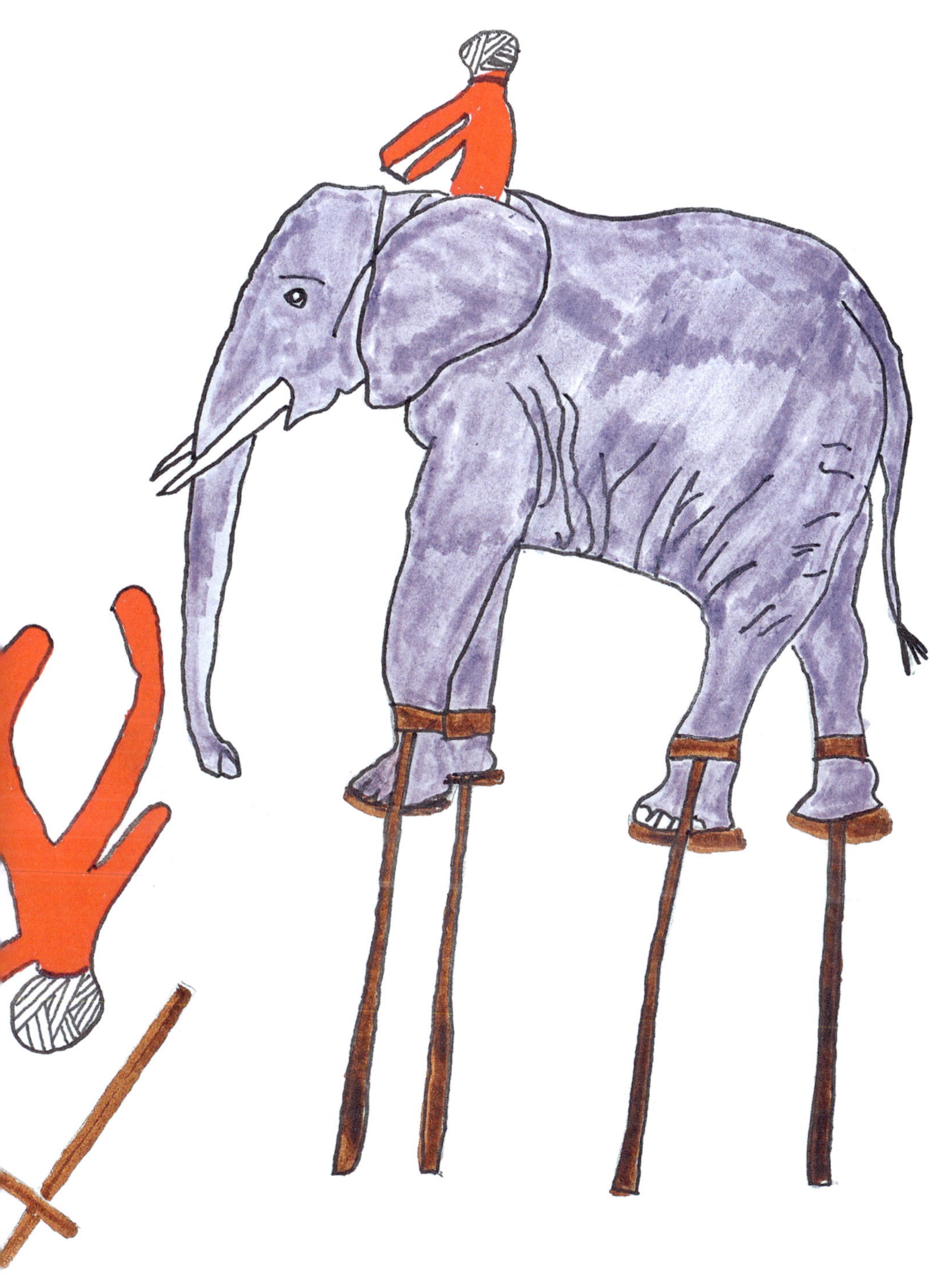

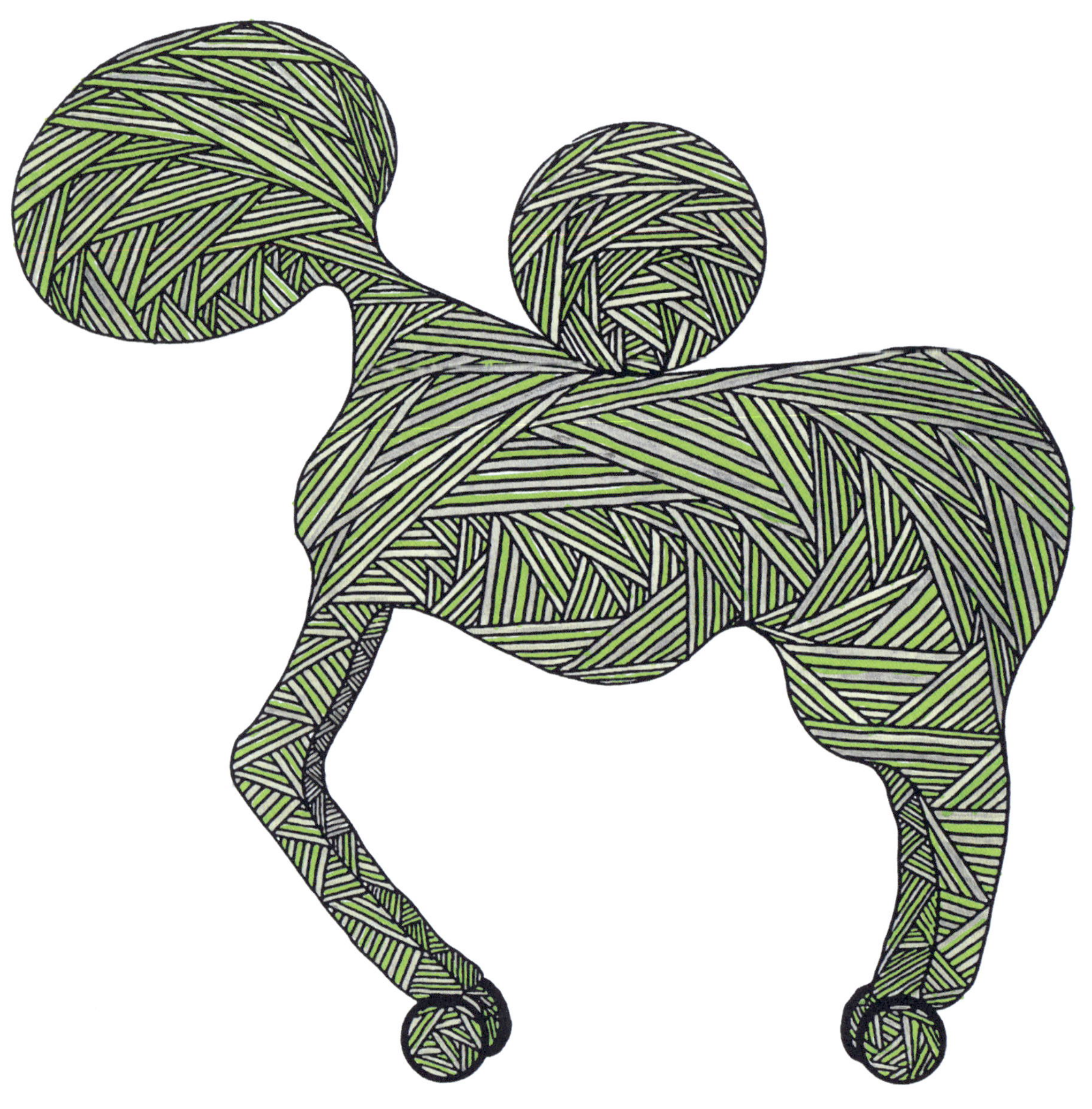

Hobby Horse, 2021

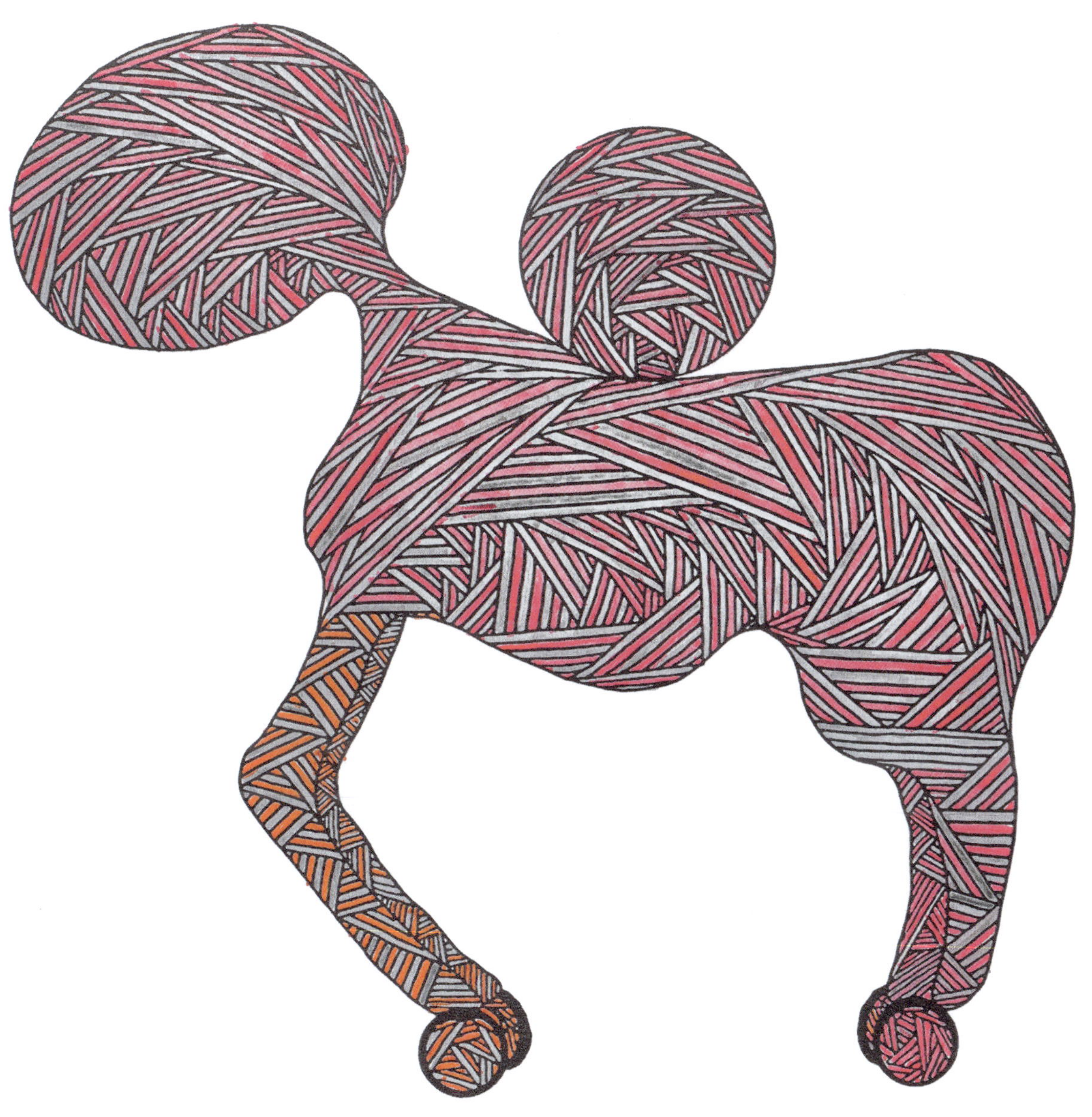

Horse Of A Different Colour, 2021

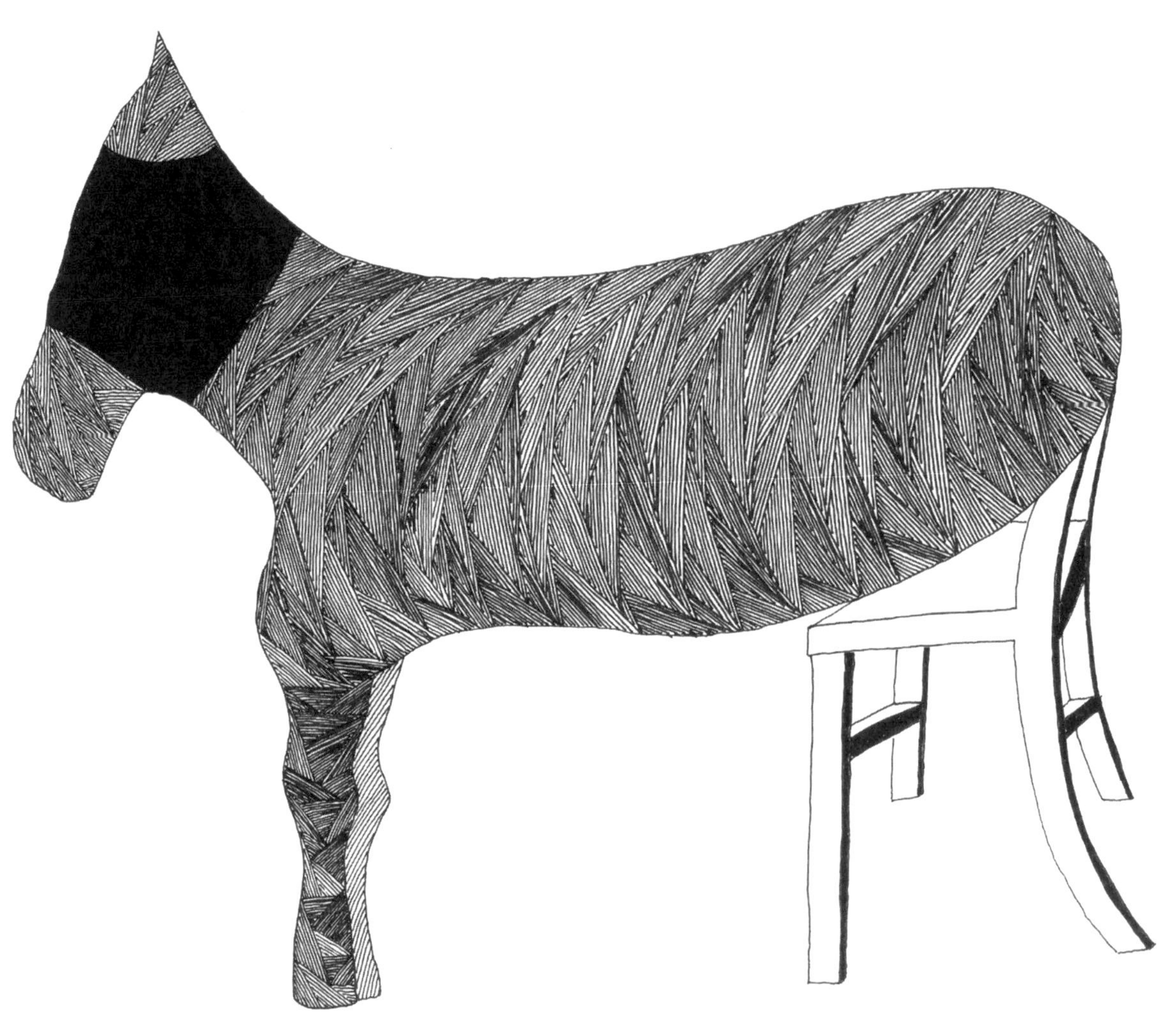

Back Seat Driver, 2013

The first time I rode a horse for real was for a TV show where famous people were taught to do new things they hadn't been capable of before. One guy learned to hang-glide, and I learned to ride a horse. I went to some posh stables in Kingston upon Thames. On the first day, the horse stood on my foot. Fucking painful — I'll never forget it. I had no idea how near or far you could stand from a horse. She was a lovely horse, a tremendous-looking gold-coloured mare, but I think she could spot a rookie. She bit me one day. I was standing outside her door — you know those half doors? And she leaned over and apropos of nothing just bit my shoulder. I went, 'Get out of it!' very sternly and she never came near me again in a malicious way.

The first time I sat on the horse it was indoors in the riding school while my trainer led us round in a circle. Eventually I graduated to riding round the park and crossing the pond. The water was up to her knees. Then we did a few jumps. That was hard because I couldn't control my bum properly. When you're jumping and airborne, you're supposed to stick your bum out backwards. At first it felt really awkward, but eventually I got the hang of it.

I slapped the horse's neck one day. The trainer said: 'We don't slap horses' necks in here. That's what cowboys do in cowboy films. You can pat her if you want.'

What I remember most was just walking through the woods, and there'd be squirrels on a tree just looking at you — they didn't run away cos you were a horse, you weren't a guy. It was great.

When I'd learned to trot and canter through the park, I was considered ready to be on film, so a crew came to capture me riding through the New Forest National Park near Southampton. It's a place where they train wild forest ponies. Some of them become working ponies, while others just stay in the forest eating grass and fucking about. It's very different from the Kingston stables. The people who look after them are called agisters. I was stood talking to my horse one day and she bit me. Second horse, second fucking nip. One of the agisters came over and said, 'Don't let her do that!' and punched the horse right in the face. I thought, 'Oh, this isn't Kingston.' The horse went, 'Oh fuck.' Took the lesson seriously.

The agister said, 'Get on.' I mounted the horse. He said: 'What have you done?' I said, 'I've trotted and cantered, jumped a bit. Not much.' He said, 'Come on, we'll see.' And he slapped the horse on the neck from his horse and we shot up a hill together. It was exhilarating. Through the trees to the top of the hill and along the top. He went 'Swishhhh!' and hit it again. That's when my horse went cylinder-shaped. I crossed my legs underneath her. I felt like I was on a wild rocket ship. We rode along to where the other horses started to appear, and by the time we got close to the end of the park there were horses everywhere — about forty of them. They started running along the fence beside us: 'Ayeeeghhh! Ayeeeghhh!' Neighing loudly and making quite a racket. I was truly living a rambling cowboy fantasy. We were going like a fucking train. Then we cut down a hill, and as we picked up speed I could see a branch coming towards us about the horse's height. They had told me to watch out for that at the riding school so I just laid back on the horse's bum and went under the branch, and the people from Kingston went 'Whoohooo!!' I felt like a rufty-tufty stuntman.

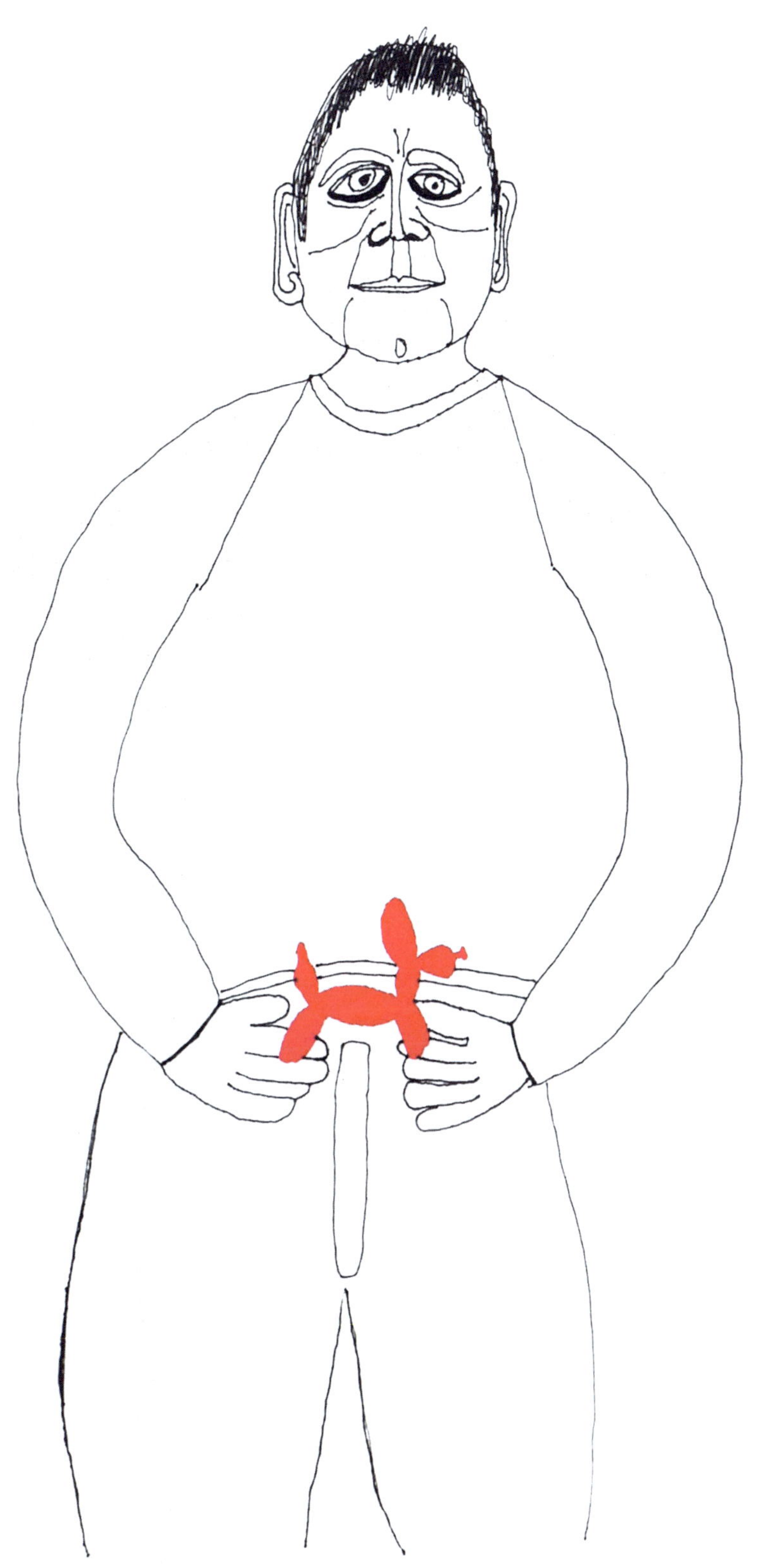

The Hoarse Whisperer, 2019

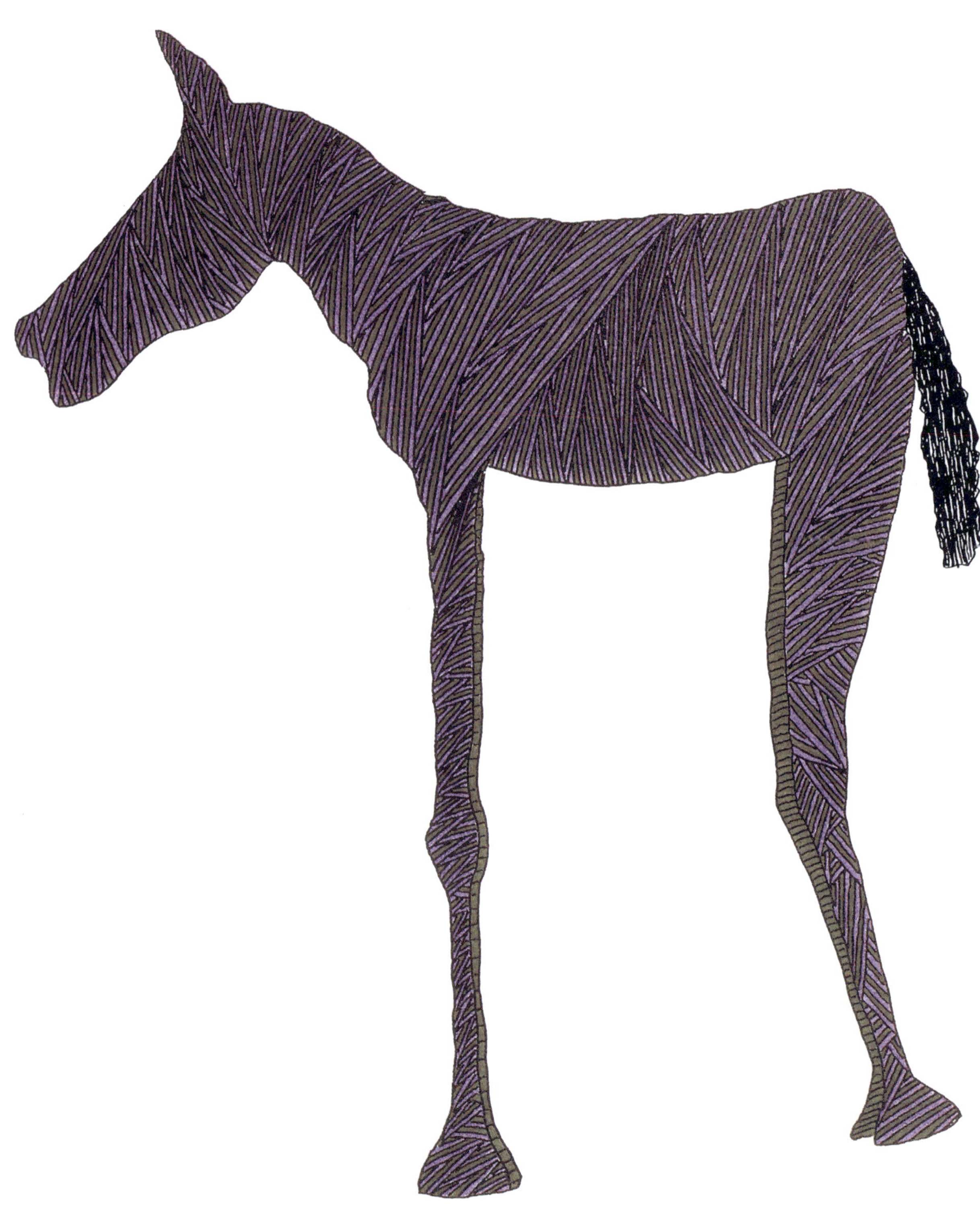

Self Portrait With High Horse, 2023

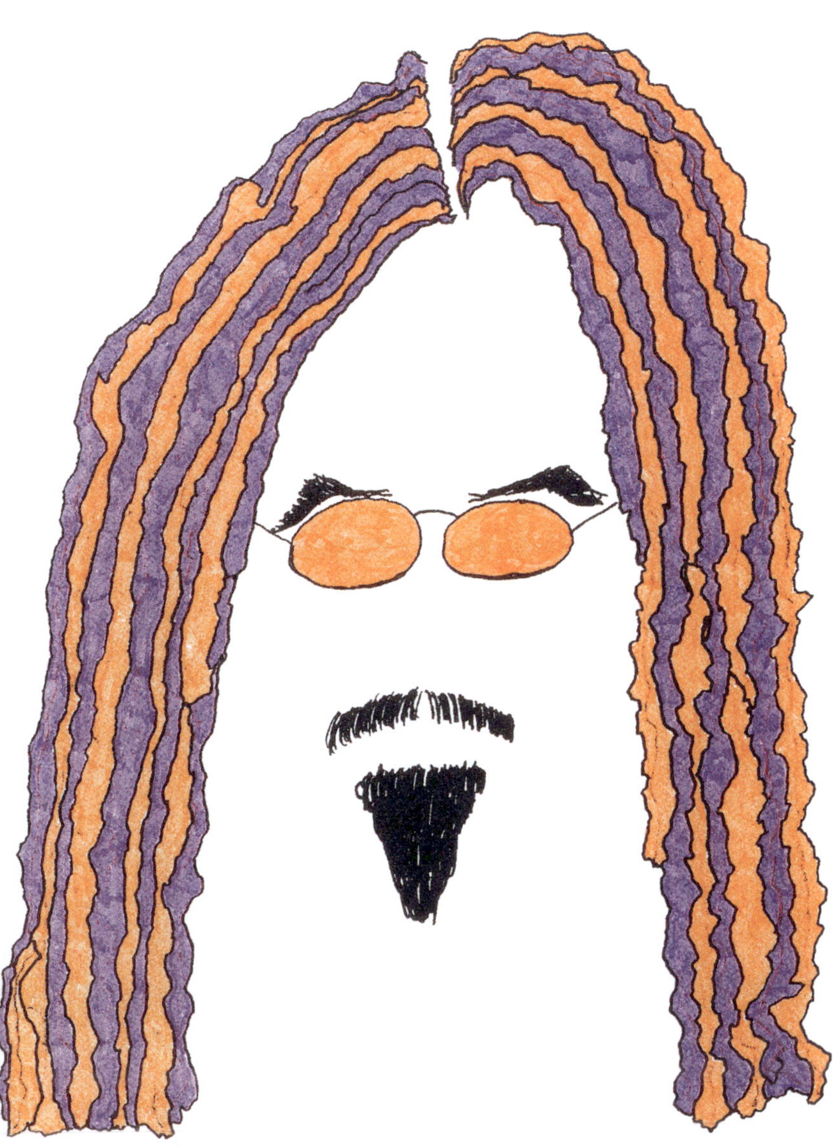

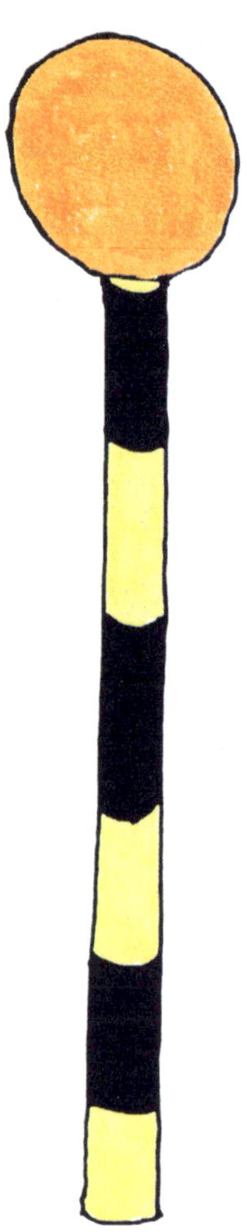

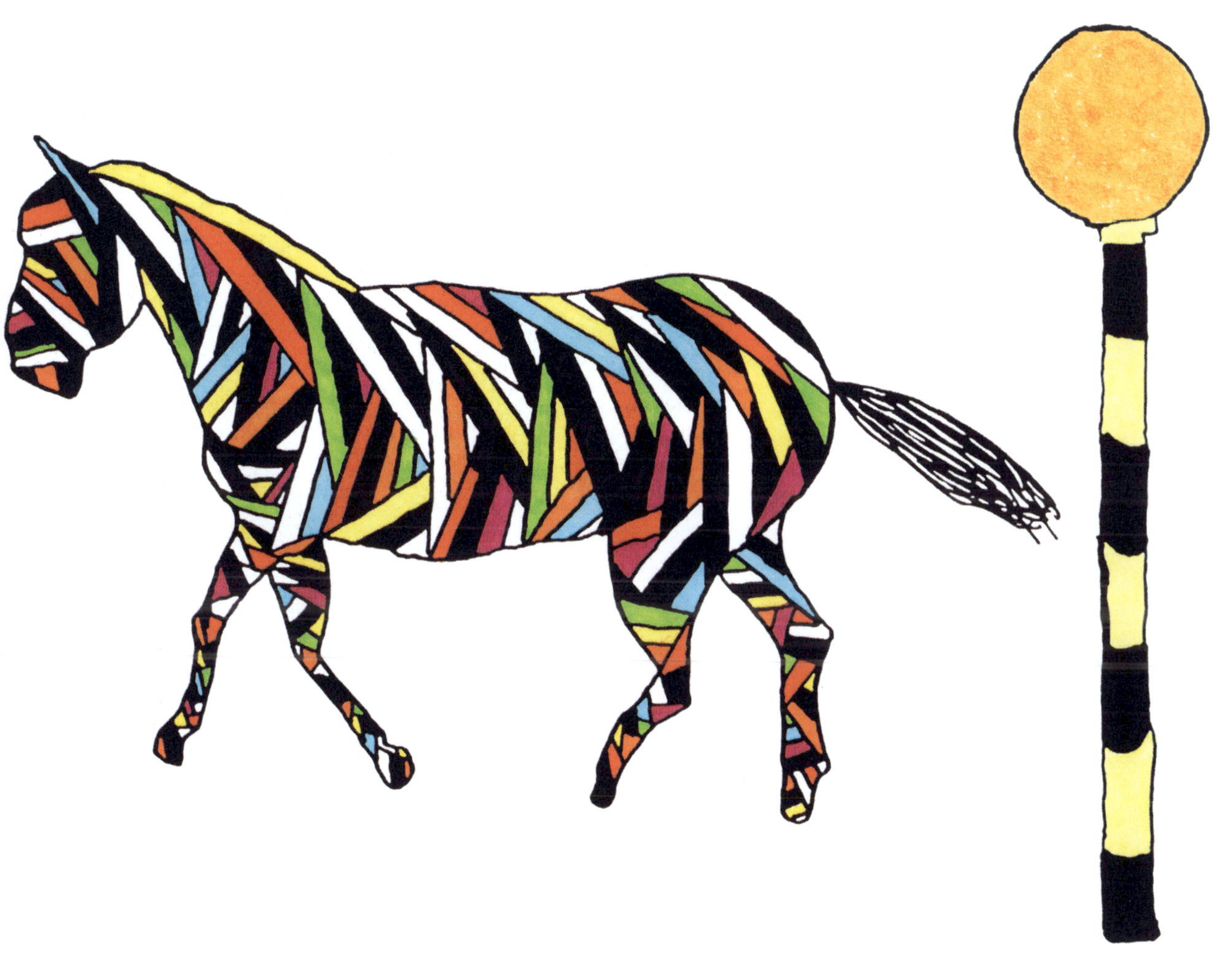

Zebra Crossing, 2023

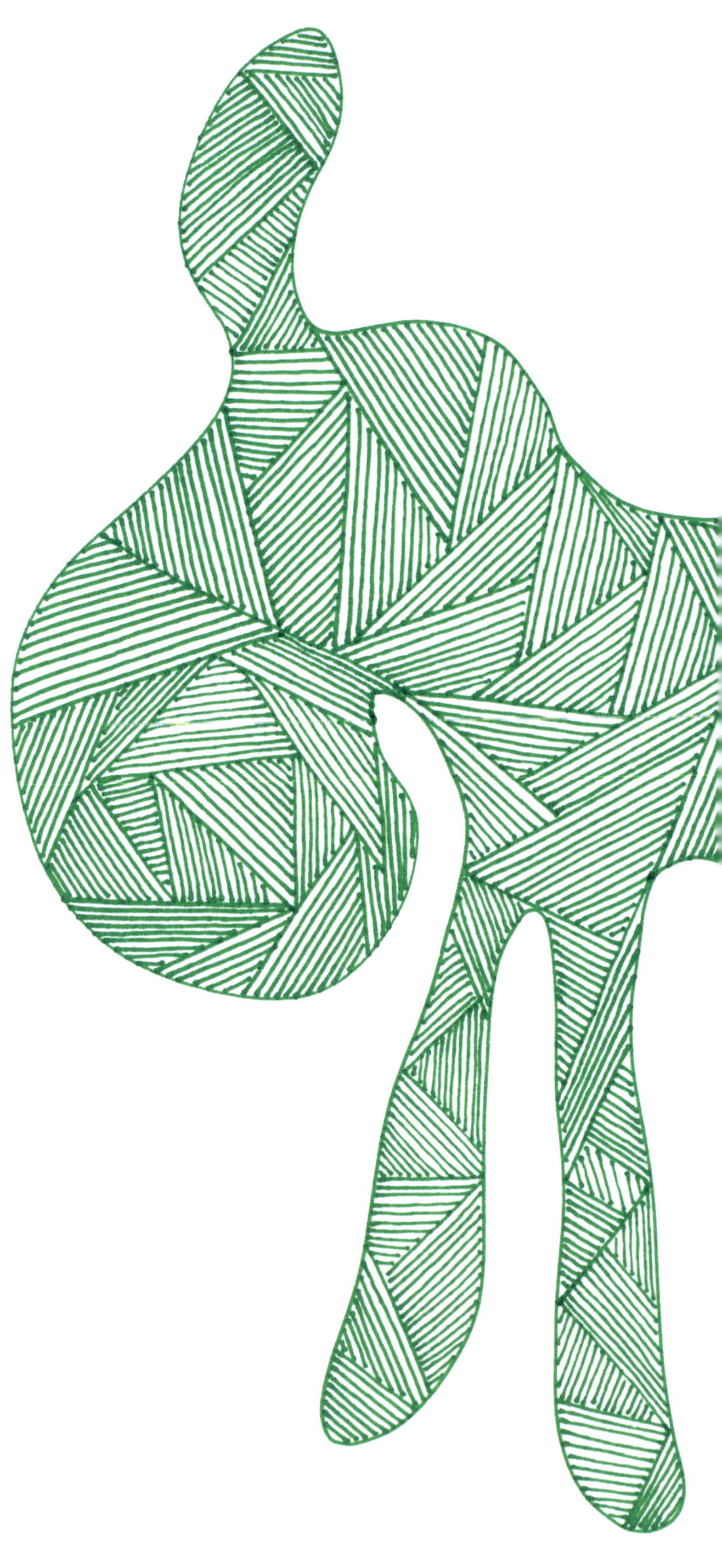

Drunk Donkey, 2012

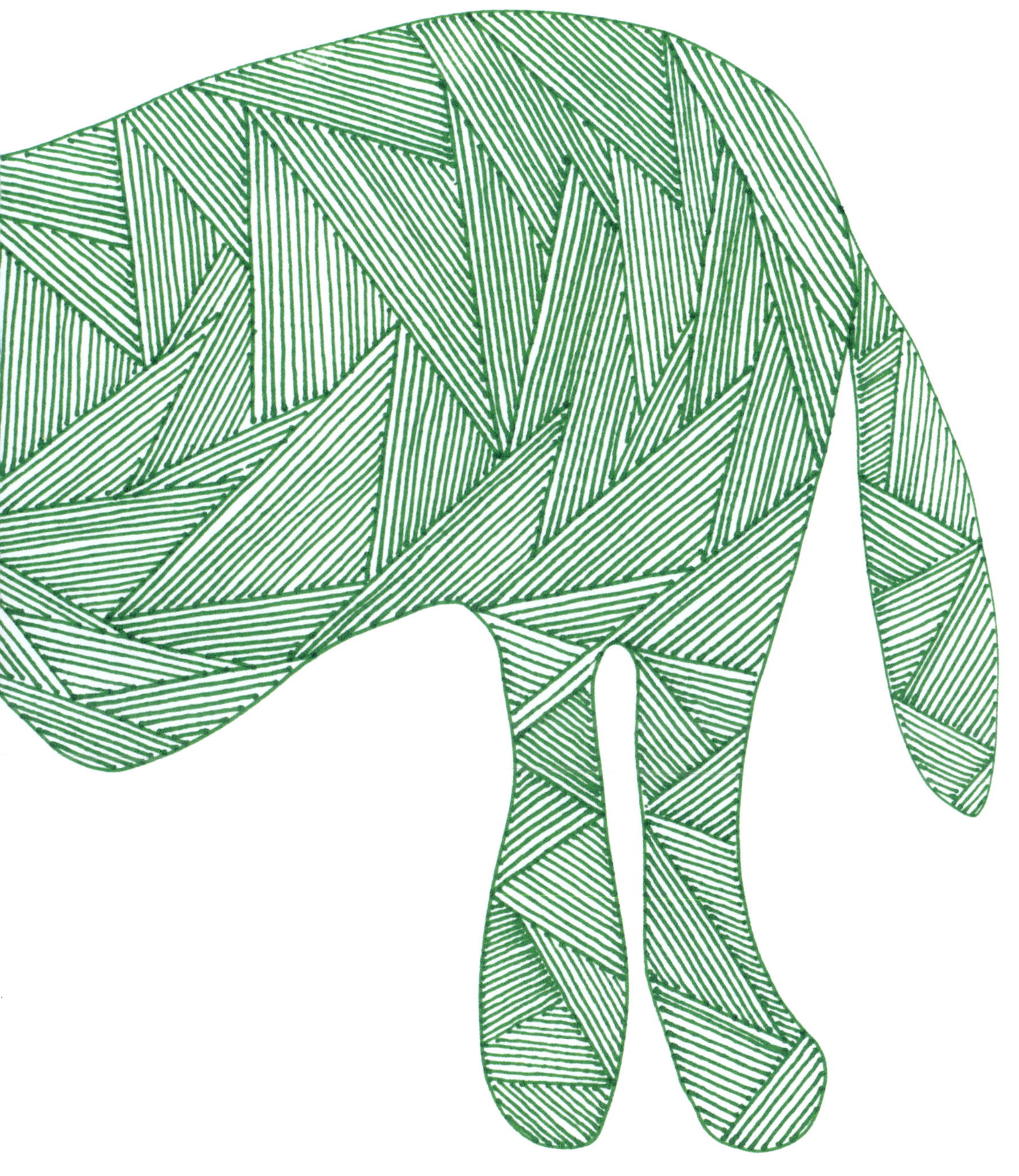

A bird in the hand invariably
shits on your wrist.

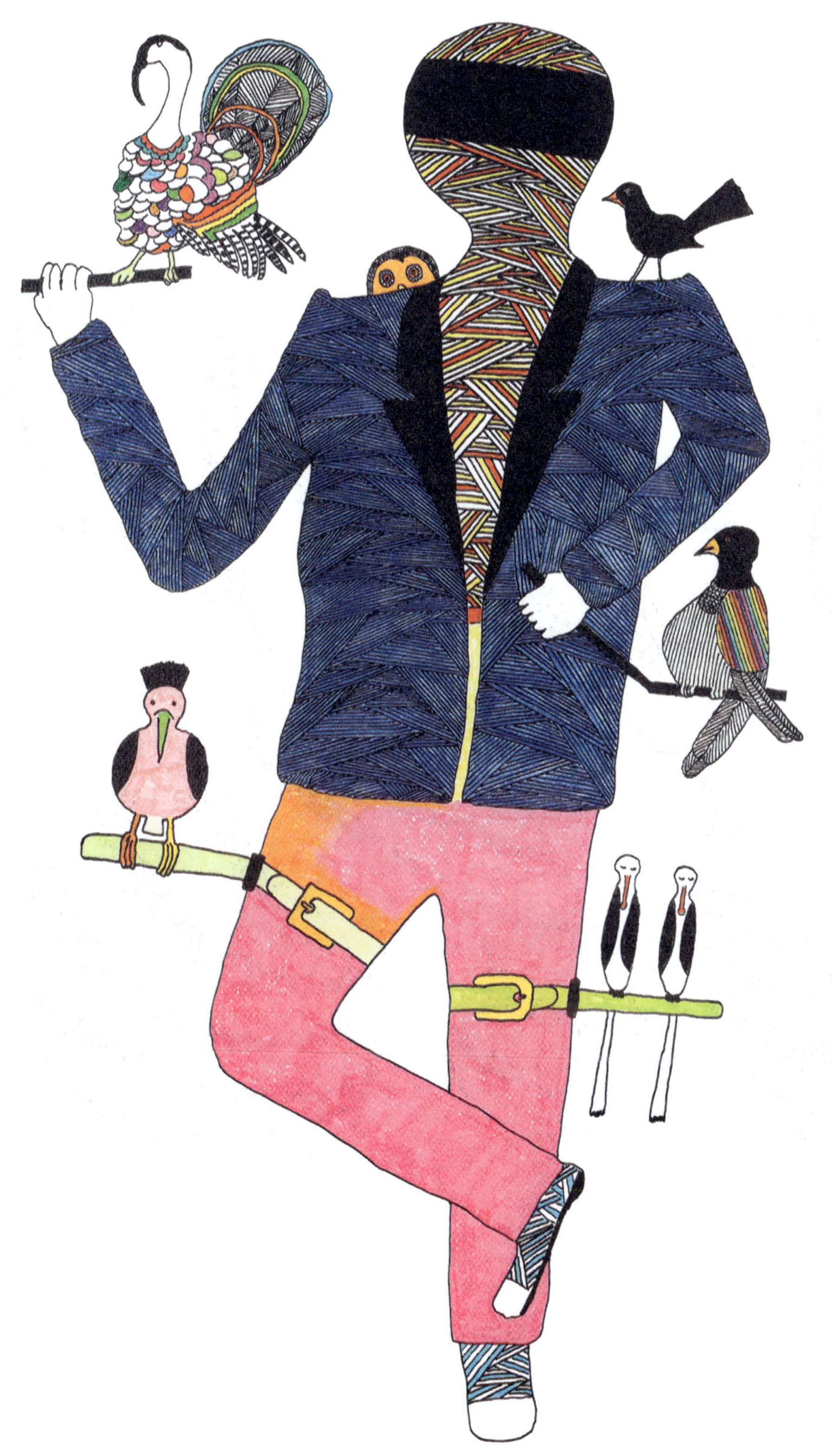

Fly Away Peter, 2023

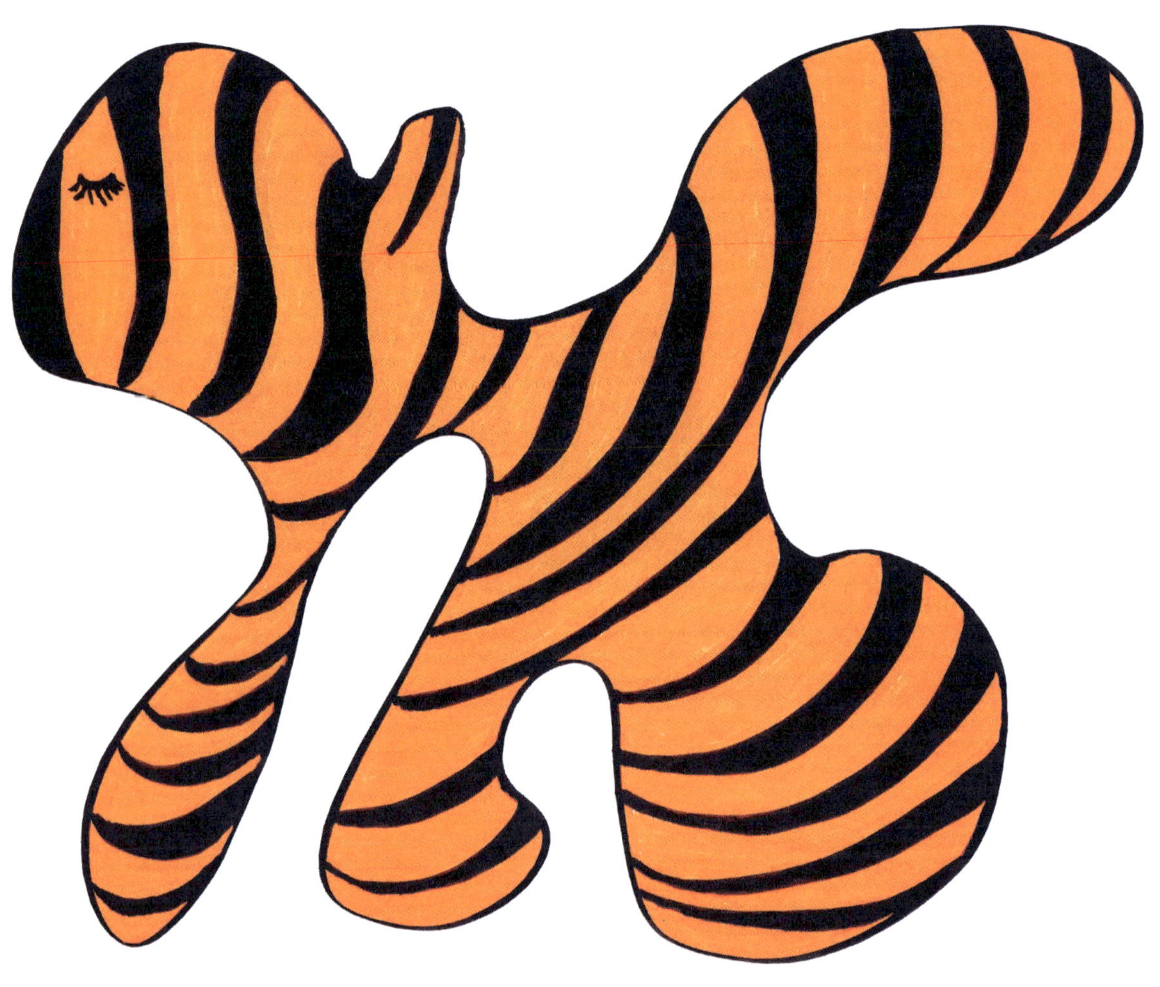

Silence In The Undergrowth Is Key, 2010

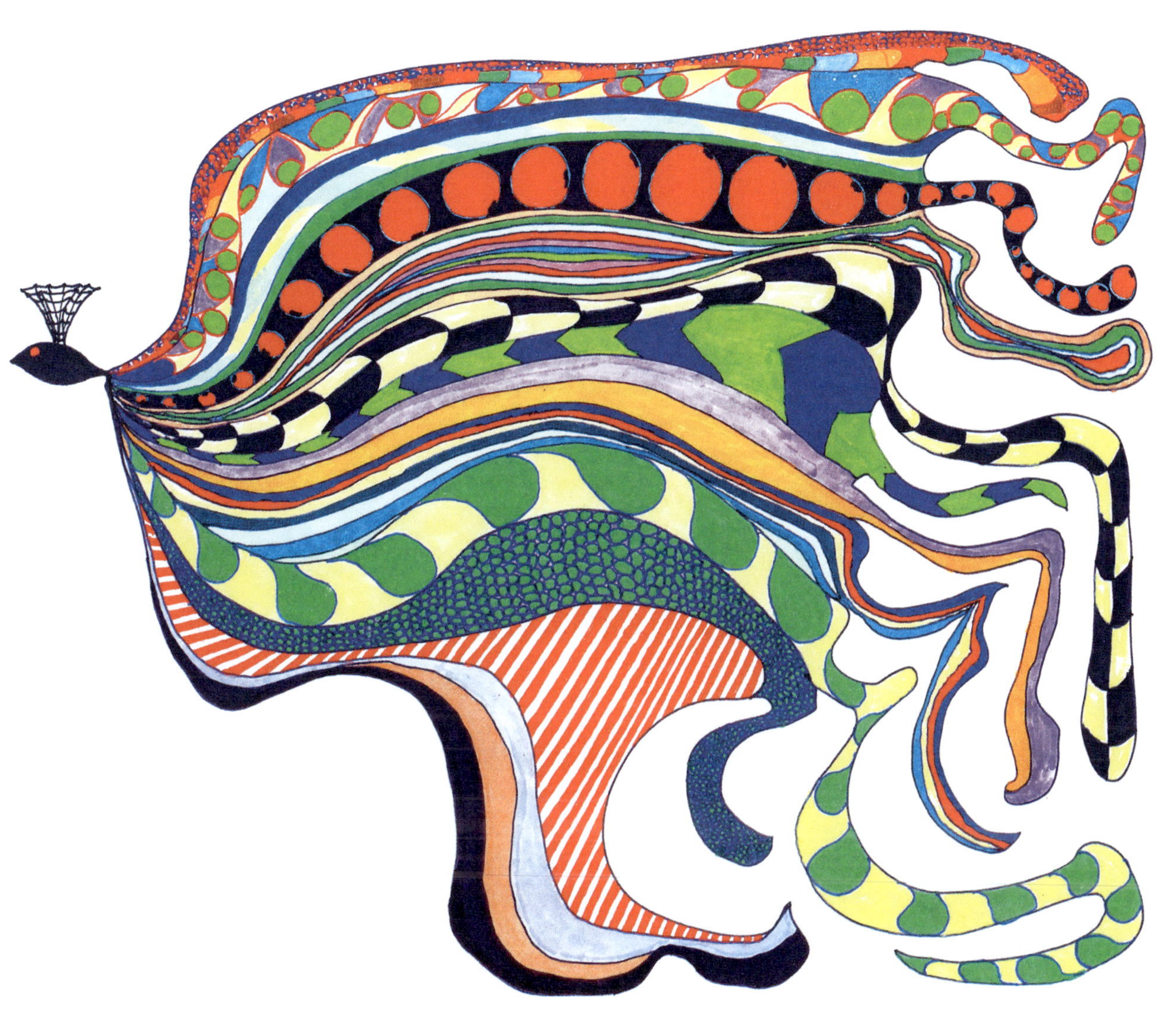

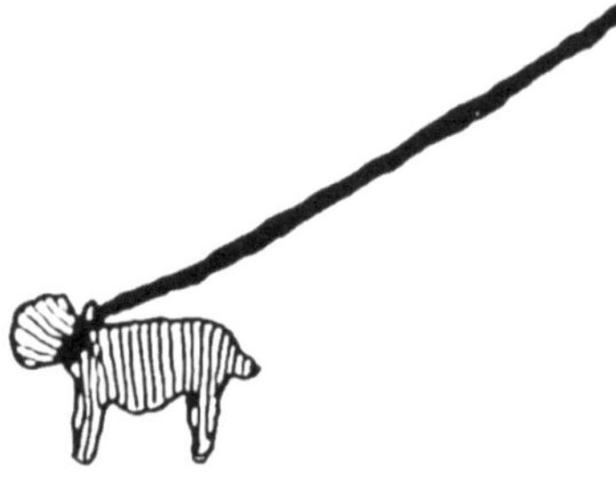

A Man And His Tiger, 2012

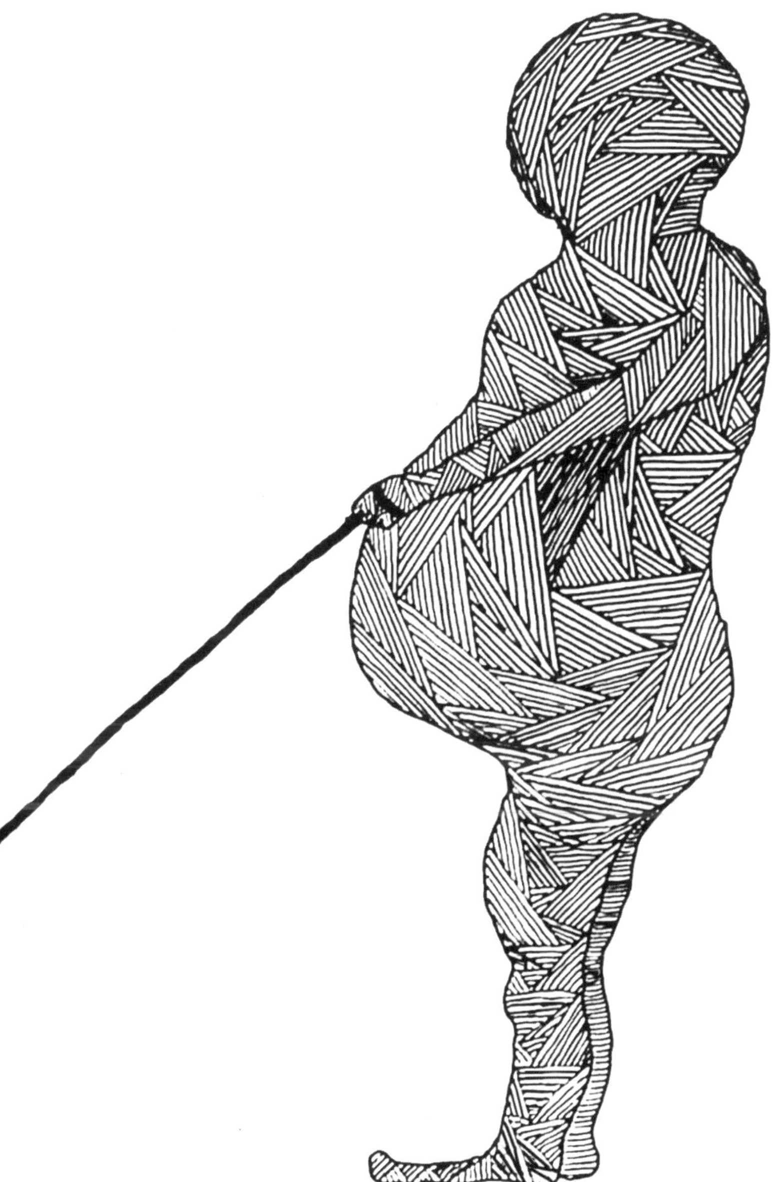

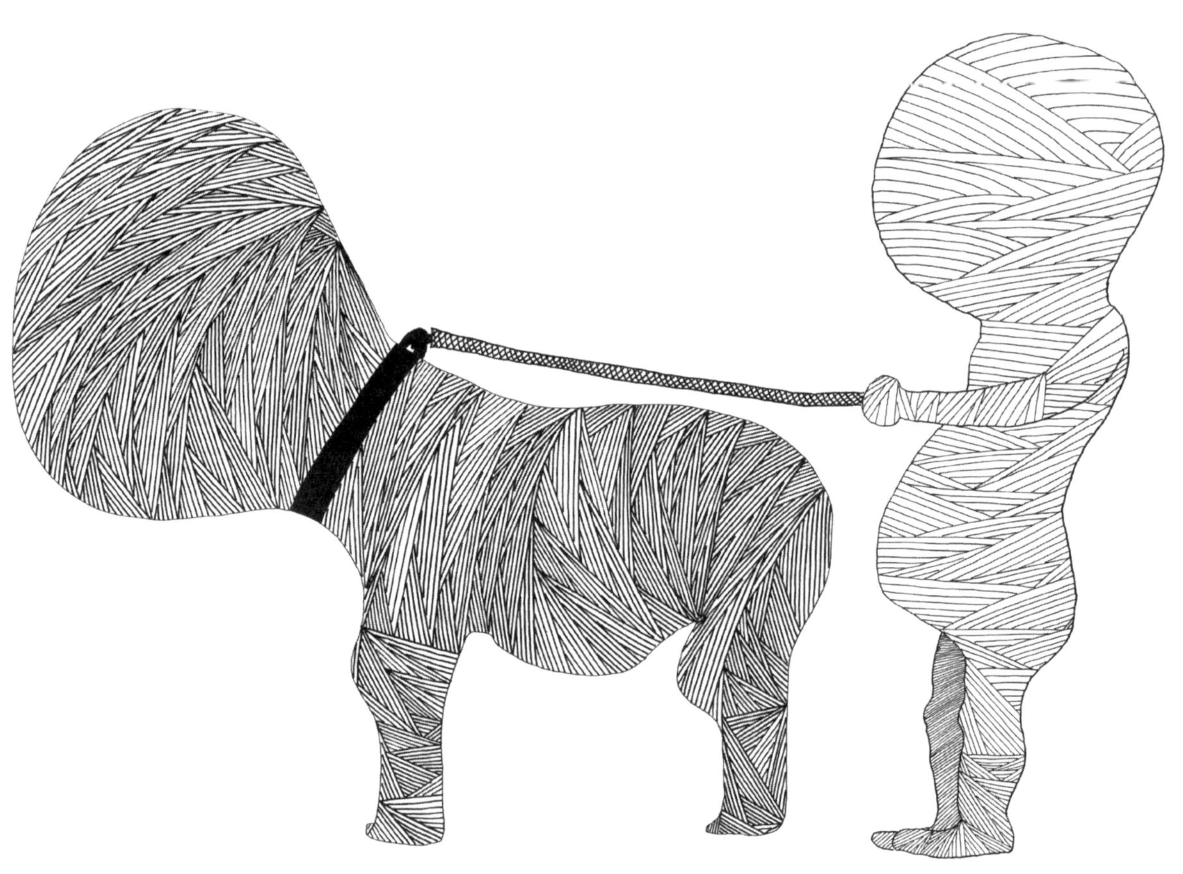

Walkies, 2012

I'm a doggie kind of guy, myself. I like doggies. I bought all those books telling you how to train them. There's these monks in New York — the Monks of New Skete — who breed dogs, they've written two very good books on that. They're really into teaching the humans as well as the dogs, and building the relationship between the two. It's fascinating stuff. I learned a lot from them.

My dogs were OK at sitting and staying and how to come around on one side of me or the other side of me, and running and stopping and all of that. They're fine. But no book I've ever bought teaches you how to stop them sniffing people's crotches. That's what I'd really like to learn how to make them stop doing, but I've never found any helpful advice. My dogs are forever going up to people and doing that: sniff-sniff-sniff!

'Oh for goodness' sake! I'm so sorry! I guess they're pleased to see you!' It's so embarrassing.

In Scotland they're up people's kilts at the back. A big wet nose suddenly pressed up against the inside of a bare thigh. It's a terrible habit. And you stand there and go: 'Oh, I'm awful sorry about that!' And people laugh and say: 'It can probably smell my dog!' Which makes you think: 'Oh? Oh! Oh, OK. Fair enough. Live and let live. We'll draw a discreet veil over that. And you can trust me never to tell a soul.'

But dogs are nice. My dogs are nice, and they're very clever, too. As a matter of fact, all dogs are clever. When did you last see a dog stepping on a human shit? I rest my case.

They're good things. And they have some great attitudes. I envy some doggy things. Like sex. Dogs have a season. And I think that would be good for us. You see, when they're not in season, they just get on with it.

It's a weird life: 'Sit! Stand up! Go for a walk! Sit! Stand up! Eat your dinner! Lie down! Sit over there! Come here! Go for a fucking walk again! Have a piss! Go for a walk! Catch the ball! Lie down! Stand up! Catch the ball! Eat your dinner! Go over there! Lie down! Try not to fart!' Their life's all planned, and they're happy with that.

And then one day: sniff … sniff-sniff … sniff-sniff-sniff …

Doinnng! The penis is up like an antenna!

'Sit!'

'Fuck you!'

This power emerges from somewhere. It changes them. Now, I would like that. I wish we were like that. Because I was never ever any good at chatting women up. I don't know if I was lousy at it and saying the wrong things, or being too funny or silly, but I couldn't read the signs. I didn't know when it was working. When a woman was on my case, I didn't see it. I couldn't get the message. My friends used to tell me: 'She's fuckin' mad for you!' 'Who?' 'That one over there!' 'What one??'

You see, everybody lied about sex and I believed everything they said. 'Hey, Billy, I'll tell you what you do: you blow into their ear and their knickers fall off!' I'm at the movies, arm round a girl: phhh-hooooo! 'What the fuck are you doing?' Have a look at the floor: nothing. 'Lying bastard!'

A season would be a good thing for us all. For the chatting-up inept department.

It would be hard, though. You'd maybe have to spray your wife, and the doorstep, because the garden's full of guys going, 'Aaa-ooooooooooh!' 'Go on, get out of here!' You've got your daughter locked in a room upstairs. Guys at the door – ding-dong – 'Hullo, is ya daughter in?' 'Fuck off!'

But for the single guys it would be such a godsend. You see, it's not easy being a man. Men are under pressure. With a dog's sex life, they just grab the first one that's passing: 'Yeah, you'll do!'

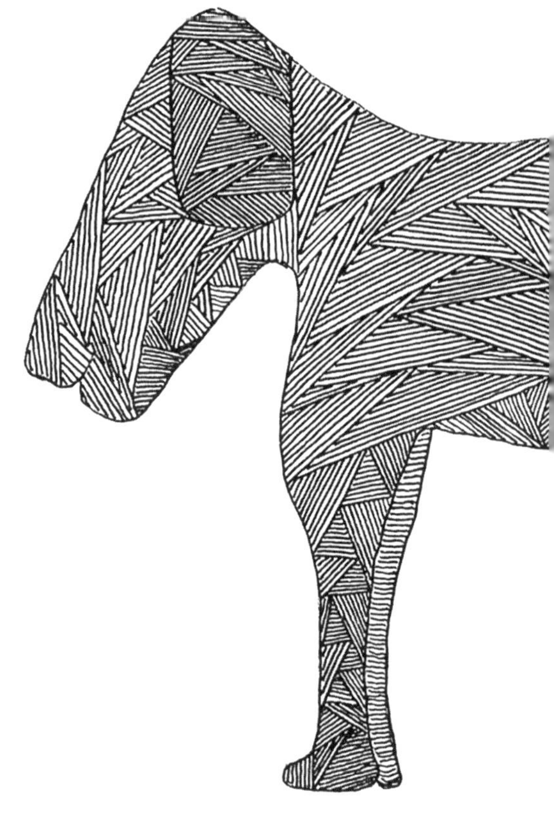

Support Your Friends, 2018

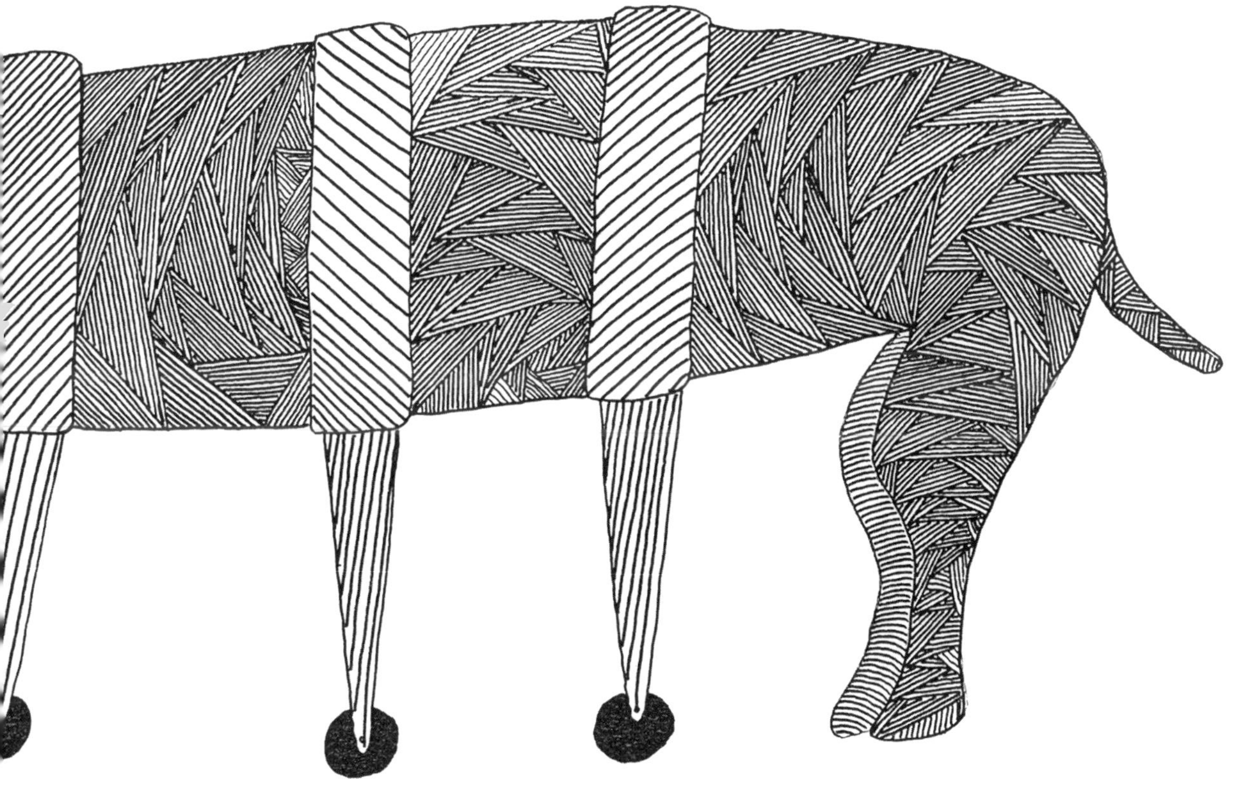

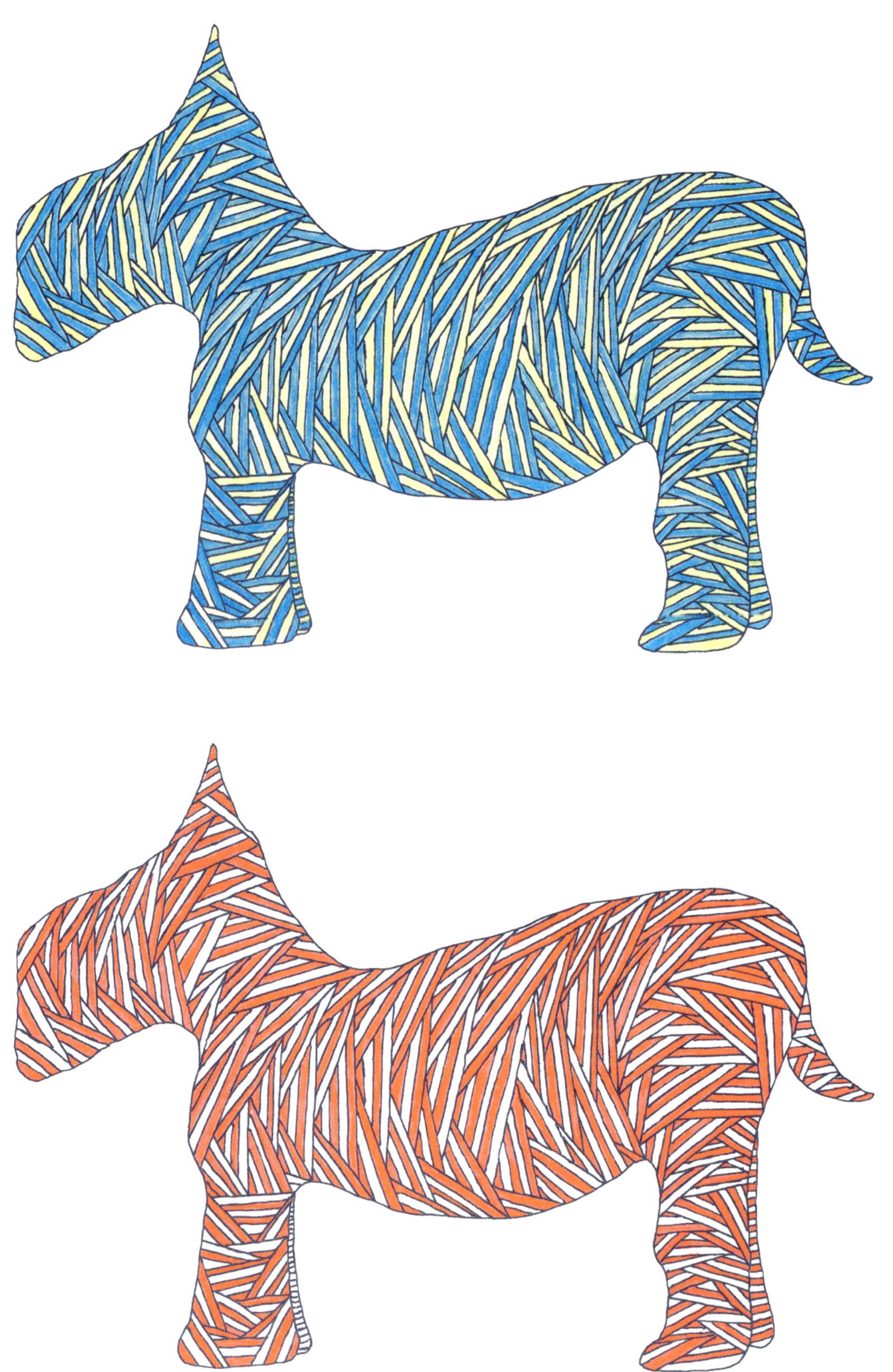

Scotty Poser / Scotty Poser, 2022

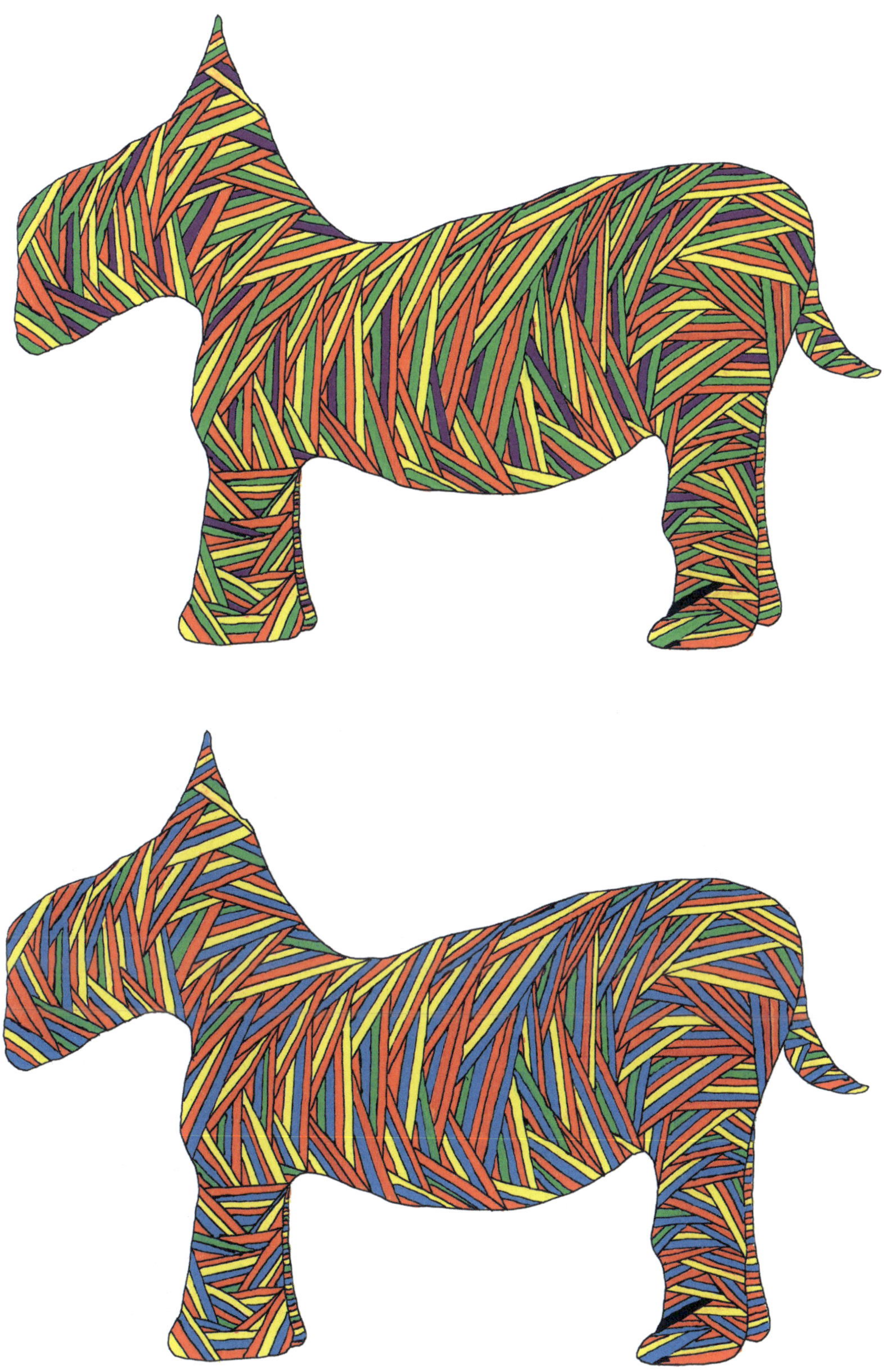

Scotty Poser I / Scotty Poser II, 2021

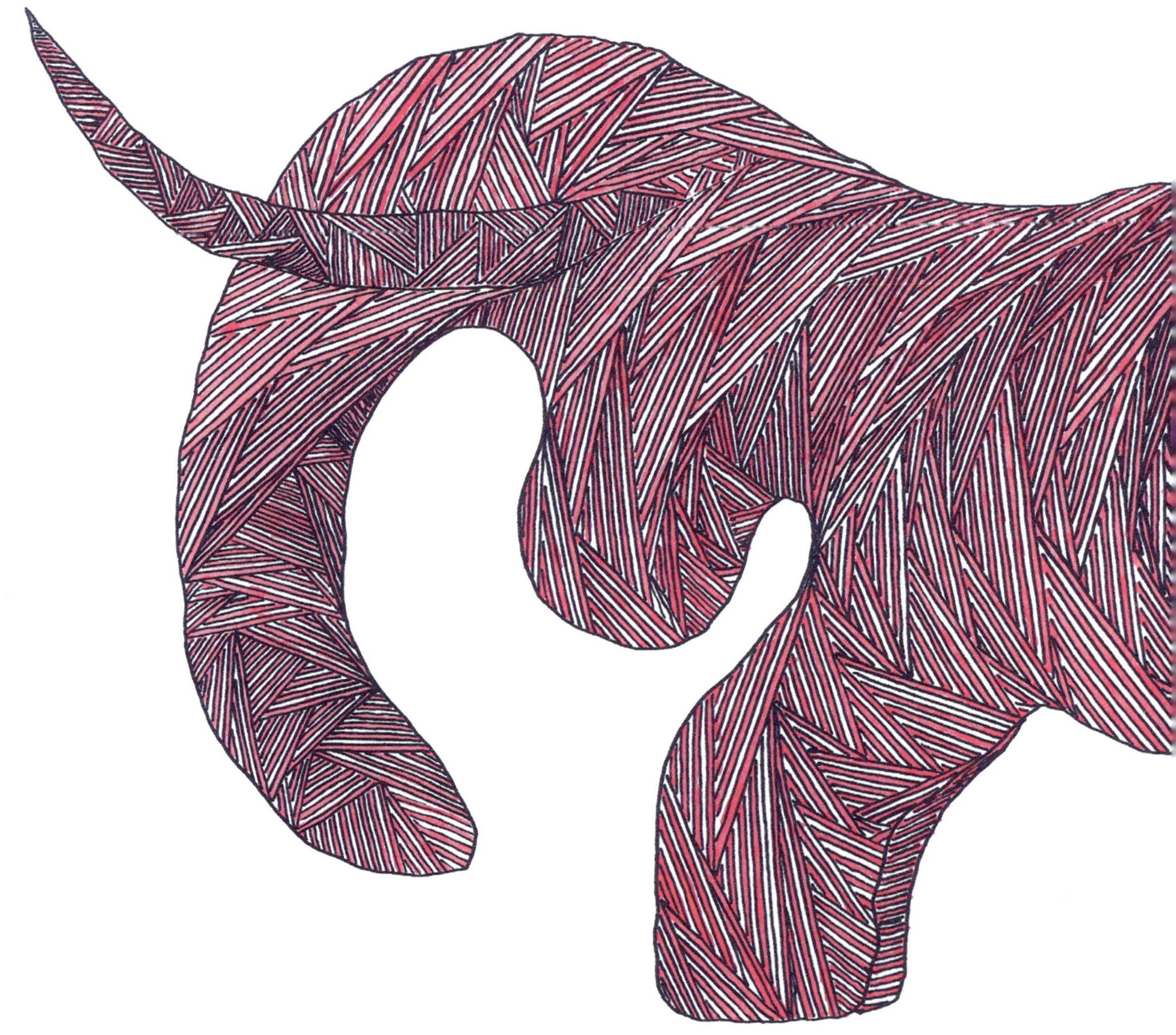

The Unuphant — An Invented Animal — Purple People Eater, 2021

Who discovered we
could get milk from
cows, and what did he
think he was doing at
the time?

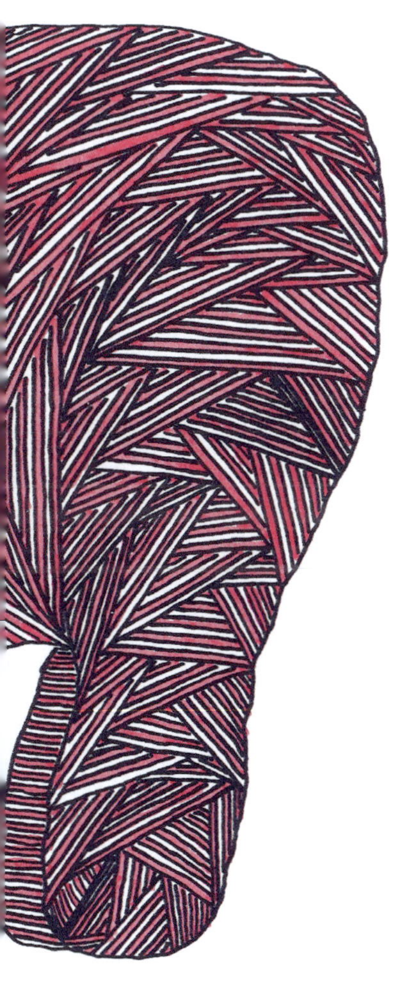

157

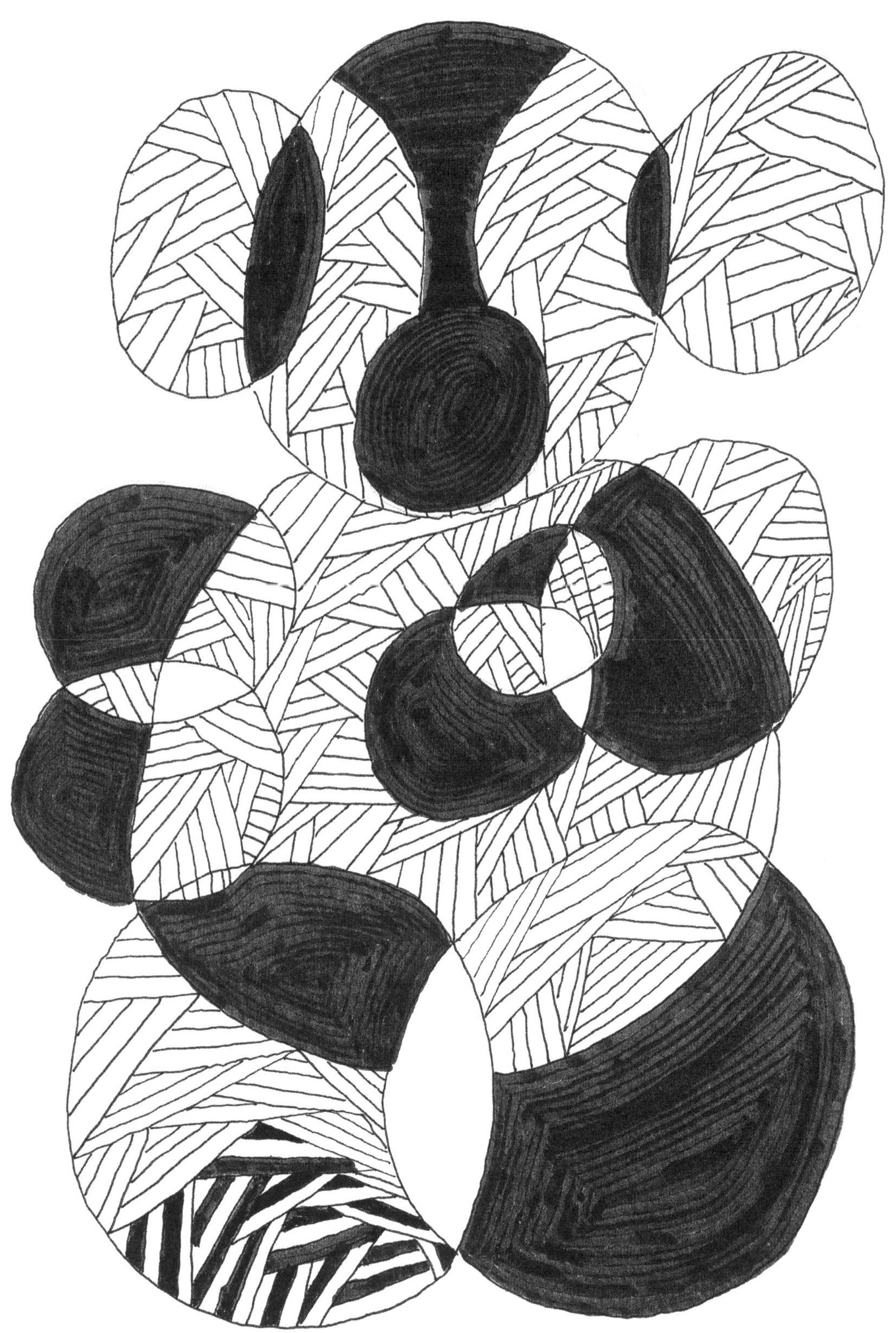

Lunar Koala, 2020

I love Australian animals, especially the bigger ones – kangaroos and koalas. They're beautiful and, apparently, they taste good. Not the koala. I saw kangaroos in the outback when I was travelling to Iron Knob. We were driving along, and kangaroos just started hopping along beside us. I don't know why. It was like dolphins following your boat, or the wild horses that once followed our car when I was travelling in Montana. Maybe the kangaroos thought we'd feed them, like the monkeys that used to climb on your car and rip off your windscreen wipers at Windsor Safari Park. Anyway, whatever they wanted I thought it was amazing to see that. It was the first time I saw a live kangaroo.

My favourite animal in the whole world is the wombat. I first saw a wombat on a TV programme. He was a hairy-nosed wombat and I thought that was the nicest name for a creature I'd ever heard. Later, I met some people in Australia who told me they had a wombat as a pet and that he was a downright nuisance. He dug huge holes in the garden, which made them furious because he wouldn't come back through the same hole – he'd always dig a different one. Their backyard was just a mess of underground warrens. But the contrariness of the creature really appealed to me. Wombats have a wee pocket just like kangaroos but it's the other way round – the opening is near their legs – so it doesn't fill up with stuff when they dig. The first live wombat I saw was in a TV studio with his zookeeper and I was allowed to pat him. He was like a big mouse. I never saw one in the wild, but I had a toy stuffed wombat called Wally. I saw a few in the zoo, and I really wanted to get closer to this one they called 'Digger', but they said he was a vicious bugger. Another smaller guy was called 'Not So' because he was not so hairy as the others. Really? They must stay awake all night thinking up these names.

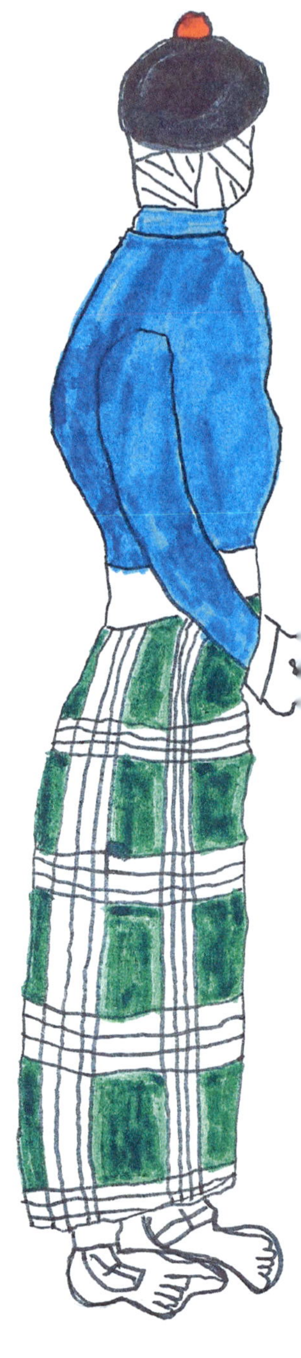

Oz Walkies, 2021

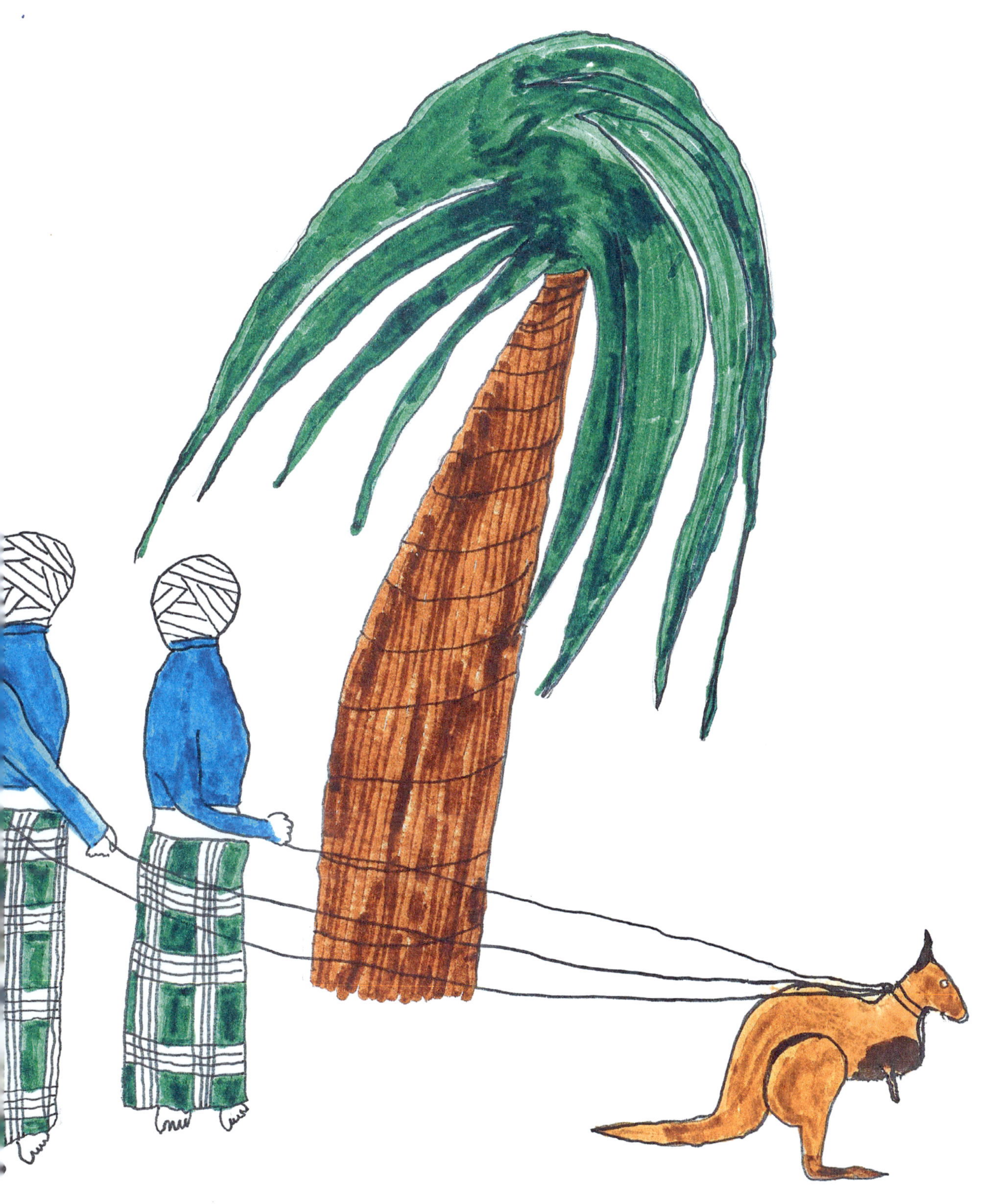

like platypuses too because they are creatures with features that normally shouldn't go together. It seems like a design flaw. A beast that lays eggs, fights with his claws and has poison on his back? I've never seen one in the wild though. Nowadays I like to draw weird creatures; maybe they're inspired by the platypus. I invented the Gozunder Fish that has a unicorn horn and a kind of platypus-tail-shaped leg.

Some Australians catch worms using fish as bait. Now, that's one for the trivia quizzes: 'When would fish be used for catching worms?' Answer: in parts of Australia, they mash up dead fish, put them in the leg of a woman's nylon stocking, then dangle it over incoming waves to lure the worms, which are six to twelve inches long. Once one of them pops its head up above the water, you use a credit card to trap its head against your fingernail to pull it out of the water. I loved fishing in Darwin, in northern Australia. One part of the sky was blue with white fluffy clouds, but in another part a huge storm loomed on the horizon. It was a dramatic and beautiful thing — nature showing you how insignificant you are, which is very, very good for you. Between the sun and the storm, I caught a little barramundi. It was a perfect frying-pan size. Barramundi is probably my favourite fish in the world. It's every bit as good-looking as salmon but it tastes better. It tastes even better than haddock, and that takes a bit of saying. While I was fishing for the barramundi, a red dragonfly landed beside me. I didn't move a muscle. I didn't flinch, I didn't cry or run for cover. I didn't even wet my trousers. Because that's what I'm made of.

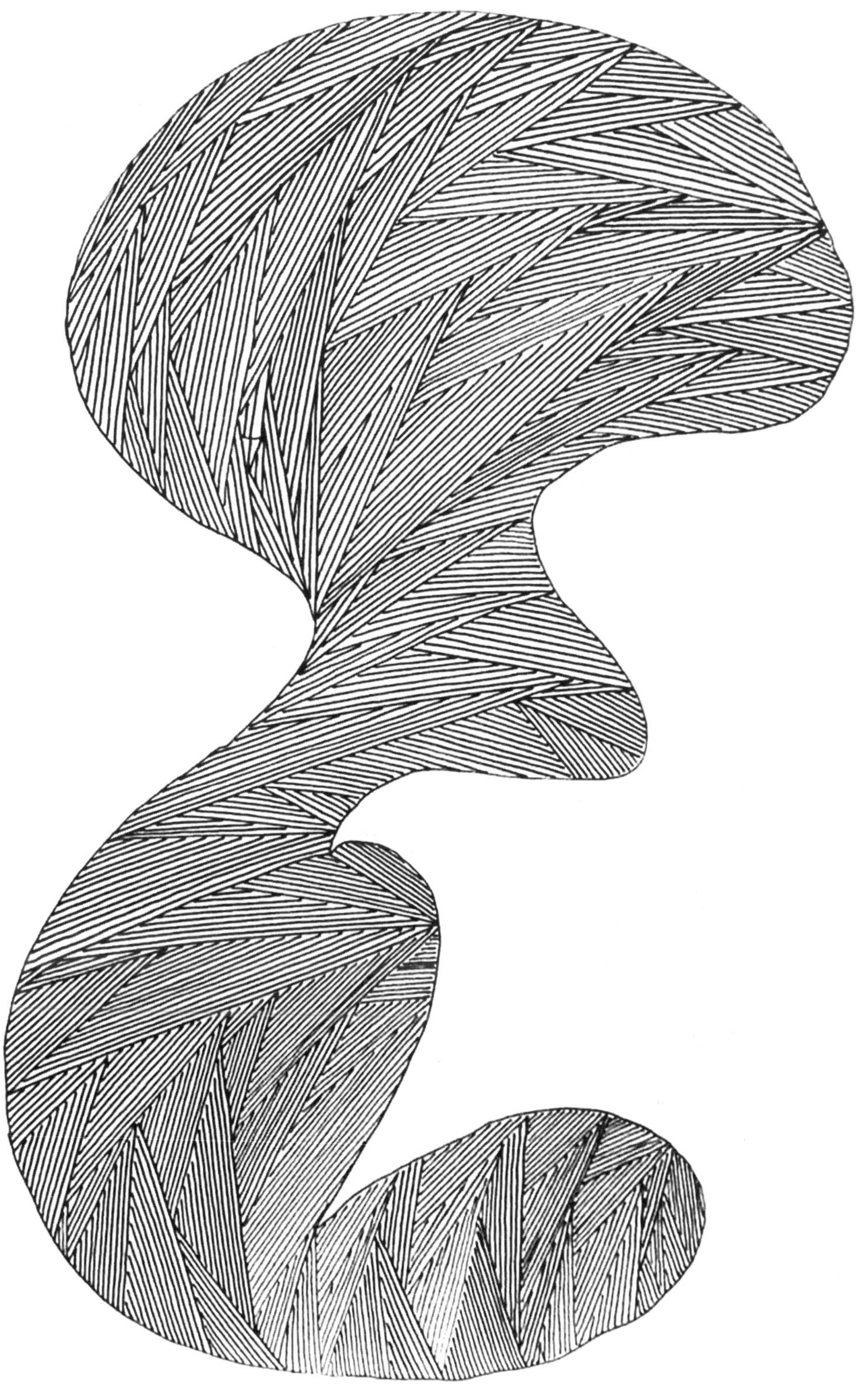

Extinct Scottish Marsupial, 2012

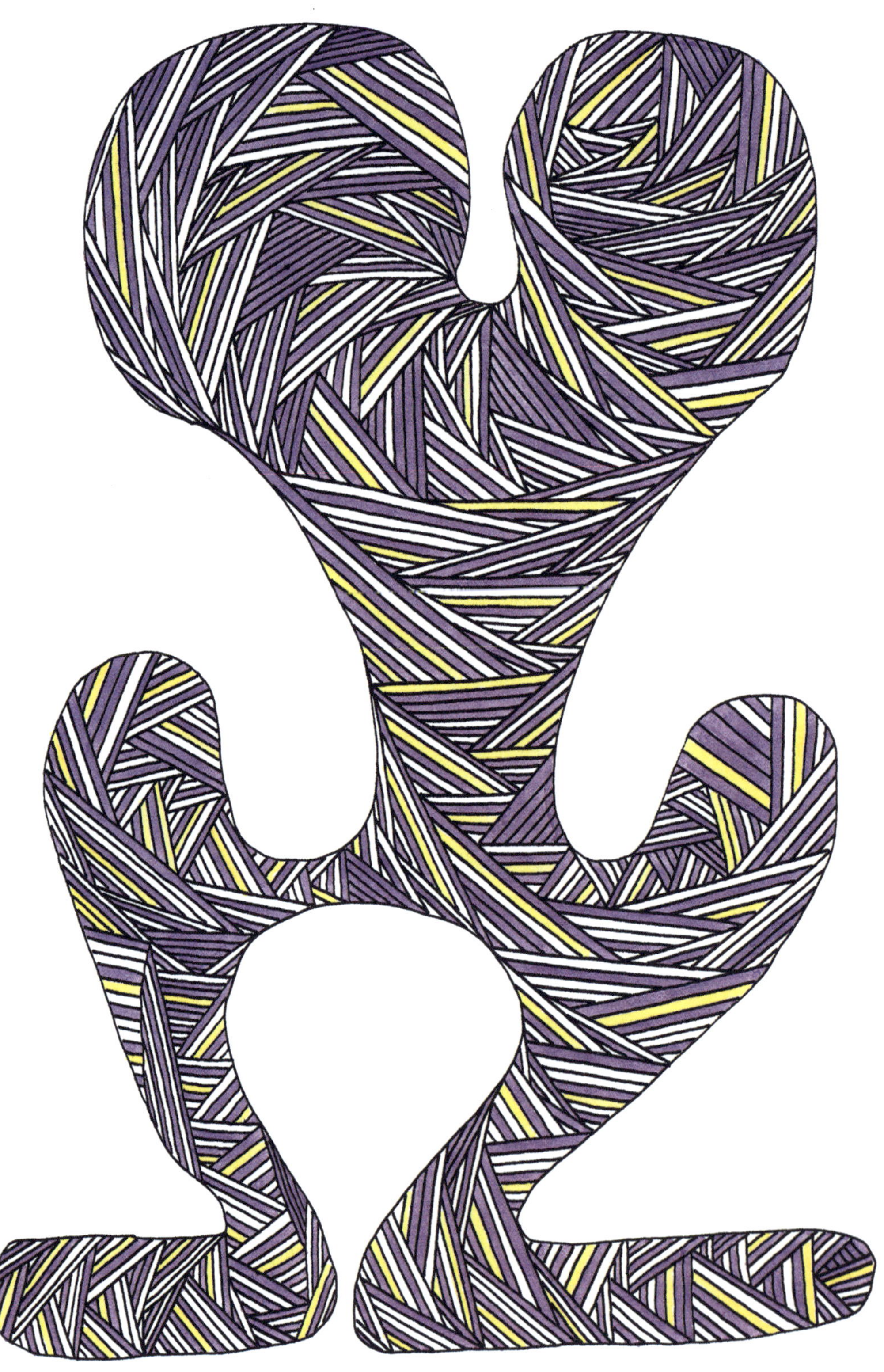

Extinct Scottish Amphibian, 2024

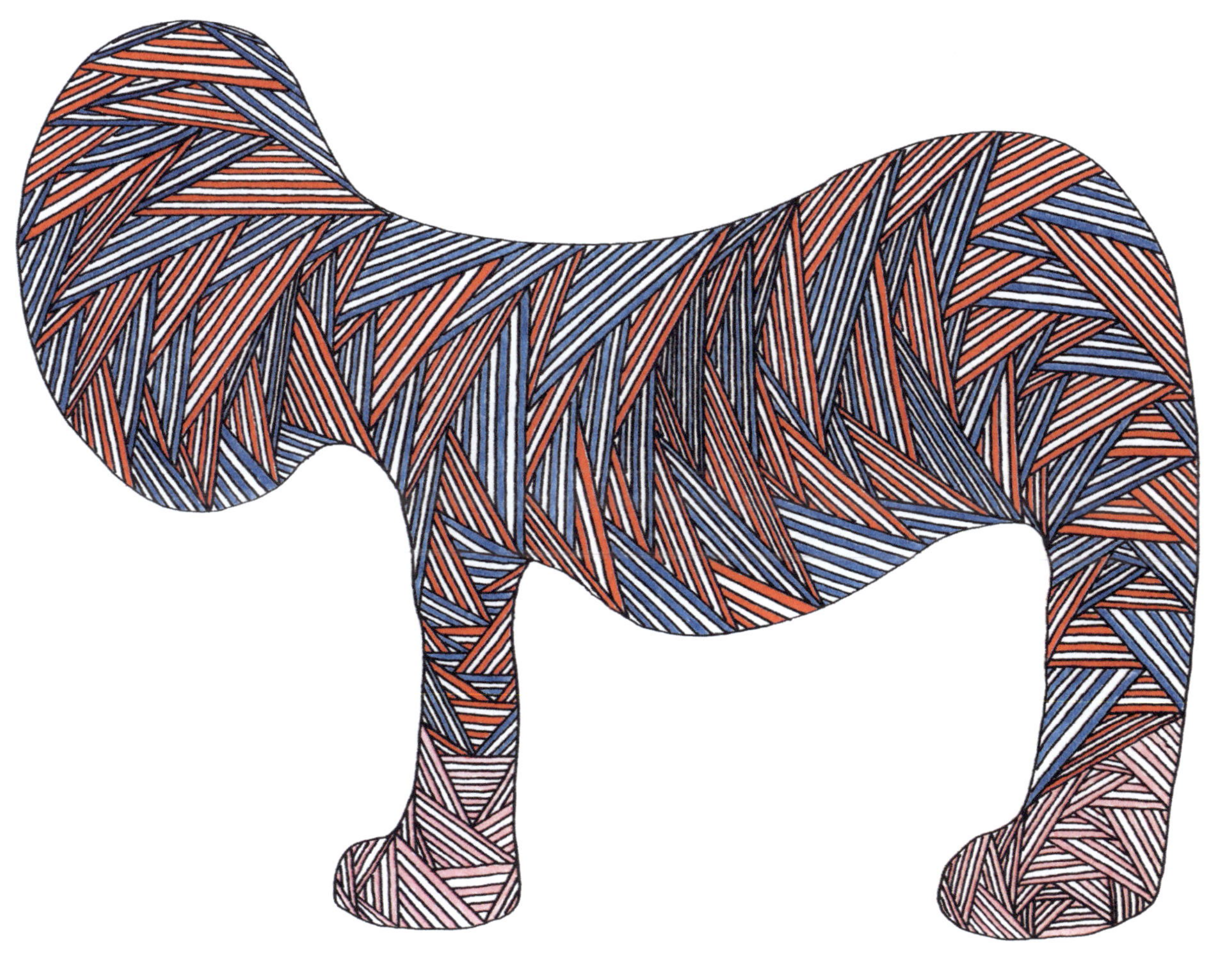

Extinct Scottish Cat, 2023

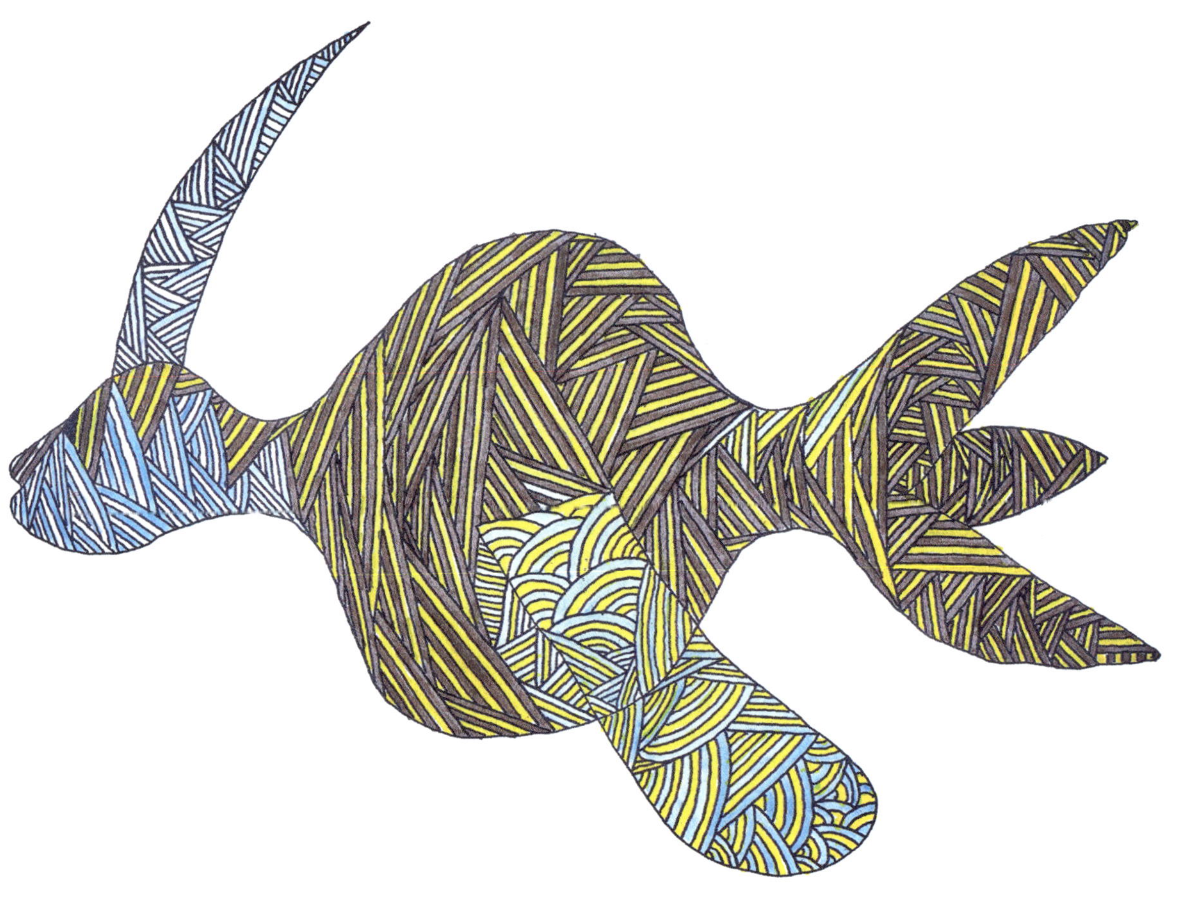

GoZunder Fish, 2021

I like all the wildlife here in Florida Keys — all the feral chickens, the six-toed cats you see at Hemingway's house, and the enormous green and orange iguanas that most locals hate. I love the tiny indigenous deer, and the roosters. You forget how beautiful roosters are till you see their feathers glinting in the sunlight. You see them out strolling in the main street with their babies, and when the sun hits them, they're spectacular-looking creatures. We were in town the other day and a chicken was crossing the road with twelve or so baby chickadees. It was the most beautiful scene. People were slowing down to let it cross. Why do the Florida Keys chickens cross the road? To annoy drivers. And you see road signs in south Florida that are just pictures of crocodiles or alligators. You get no more information than that. But it would be useful to know if those reptiles like to take a wee stroll thereabouts — or are they hunting for lost motorists? There are harmless nurse sharks, barracuda, snowy ibis and huge pelicans. The manatees are a good reason for coming here. I just love them. Some bastard wrote 'Trump' on the back of one in 2020; luckily, it was written in algae, not scored into the flesh. Many of them have scars from running into propellers. They are endangered creatures. I think it's because they're so sociable. They like people and get too close.

Manatees seem familiar to me. The first time I went to Bally-conneely in west Connemara where my ancestors came from, I went into the local bar and ordered a drink. There was a man sleeping at a table in the corner, and the barman tried to wake him. 'Arthur! Arthur!' The guy looked up suspiciously.

'Arthur! Look who's here! — Billy Connolly!' Arthur stuck his head up and gave me a very old-fashioned look. 'Connolly?! … Yous came from the sea and yous'll fucking go back again.' In Irish mythology, the Conneelys were creatures a bit like seals that came ashore and shed their skin to become people. Such mytho-logical creatures are called silkies. I really like the idea.

I'm all for being a silkie. I was thinking about it the other day when I was sitting on my deck in Florida and a big manatee came swimming up. I was thinking, 'That's my family!' It's probably just my imagination, but those manatees seem to know me. They come to see me all the time. I love them. Big peaceful vegetar-ians, sauntering about in the water and checking me out. They lie on their backs flapping their flippers and guzzle the fresh water that runs off our deck after it rains. They're the hippies of the sea. Make me feel great. 'Hoila Noila Noila' — that's what you're sup-posed to sing to silkies. I think I'll try it with the manatees.

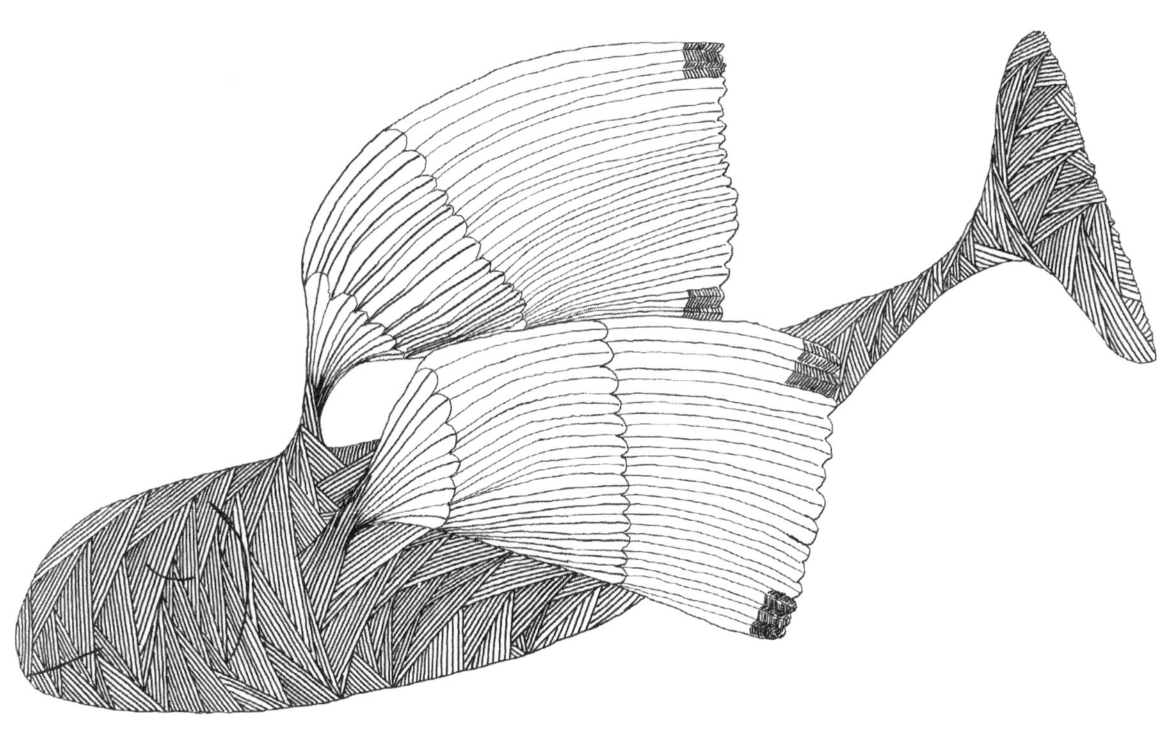

Flying Fish, 2017

Sea creatures are smart beasties. Once at an aquarium in Auckland, the people in charge told me they'd had some crayfish in a tank across from this octopus's tank and they were mysteriously disappearing. They tried many ways to find out what the hell was going on and eventually discovered that this canny octopus was sneaking out of his tank at night and octopussing his way into the crayfish tank and eating them. He looked very satisfied the following day. Apparently, an octopus can squeeze through a hole the size of a twenty-pence piece. Don't you love them though? The most extraordinary creatures. An octopus has three hearts. You can break his heart and he'll still be in love with you again — twice! And eight tentacles. I thought it was testicles when I was a boy. I thought, 'Them buggers must have a scrotum like a bag of potatoes.' And they have suckers you can't escape from. They can drag you into a cave and shag you senseless.

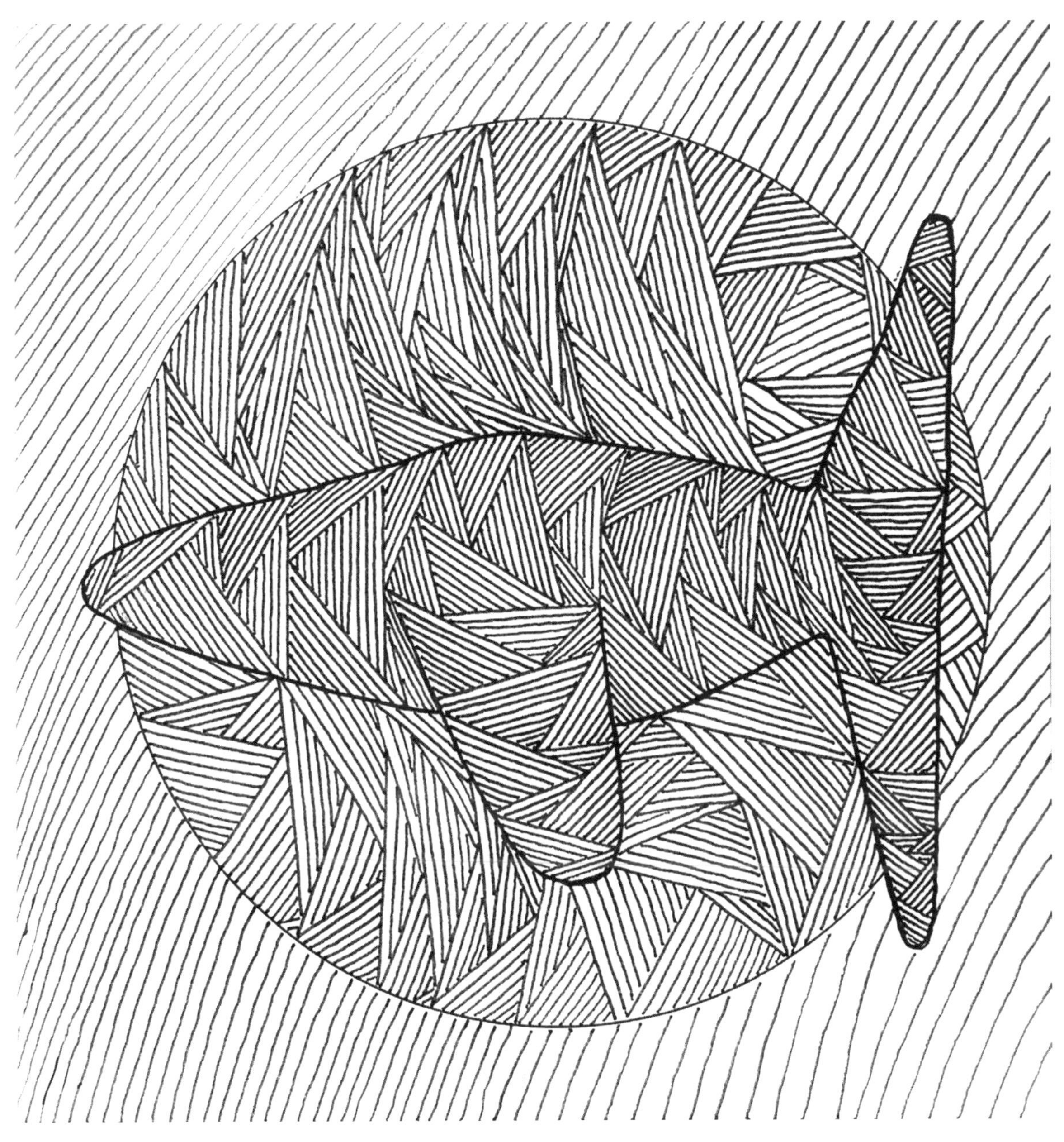

Wooly Fish, 2018

There's a constant battle between man and sea-beast. For example: the stonefish looks like a stone, lying there in the sand saying, 'Stand on me – I'm just a wee stone.' But if you stand on this thing, they say you'll feel the worst pain known to humans. How they know that I'll never know. Maybe they have a pain-ometer. Some kind of meter that goes from 'Ouch' to 'WTF?' From 'Jesus Christ!' to 'Sweet Mother of Jesus' to 'Agony' to 'Worst Pain Known to Man?' 'Fuck! It's right off the scale!'

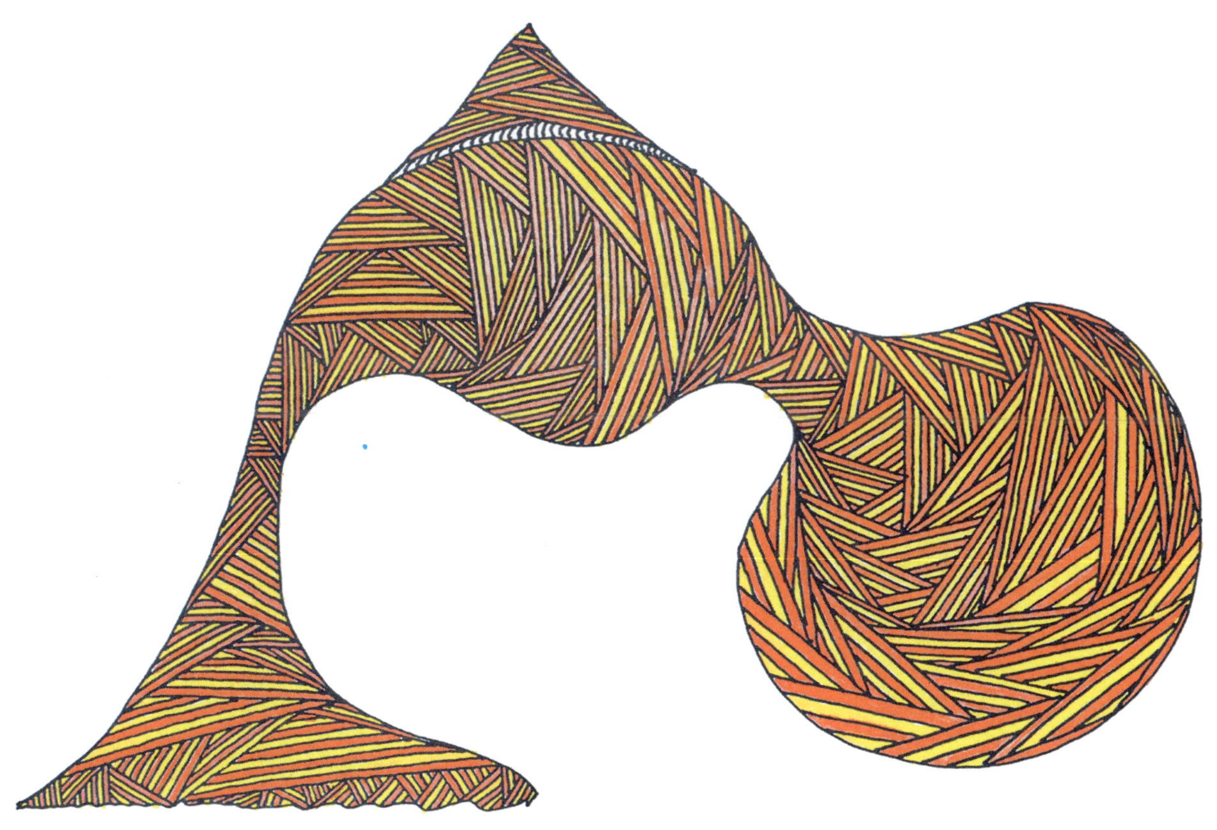

Very Humble Goldfish, 2021

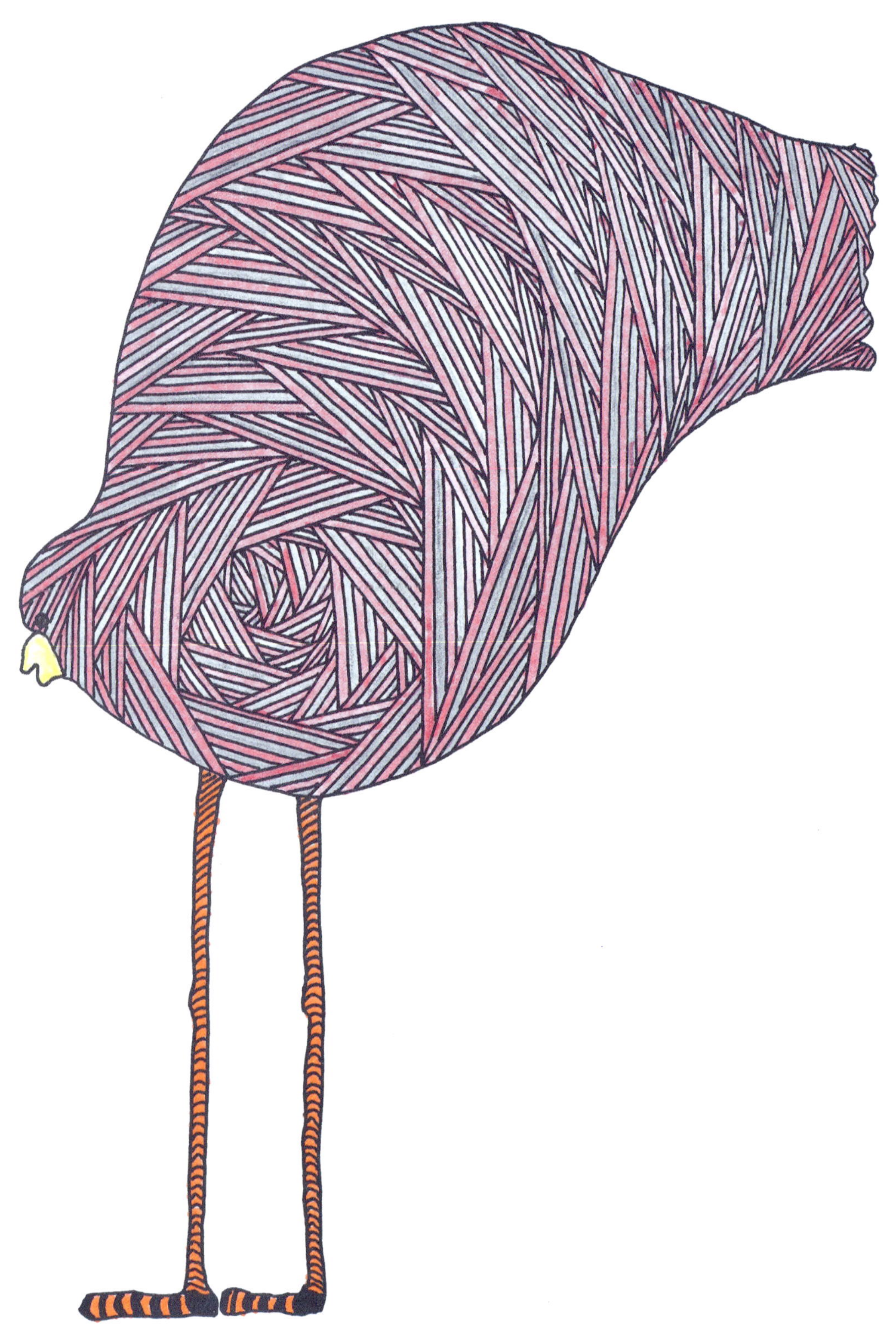

Wading Bird, 2021

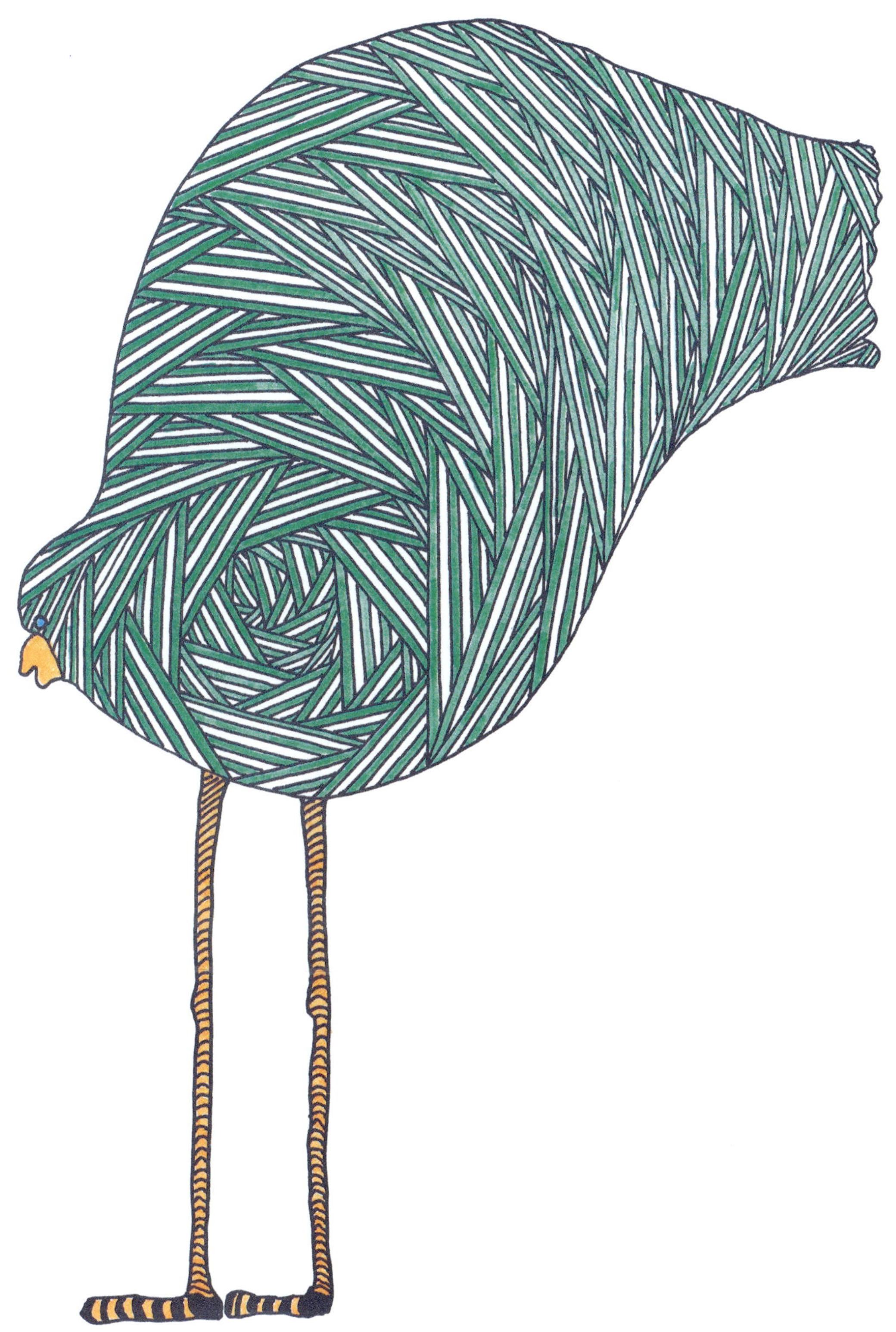

Wading Bird, 2021

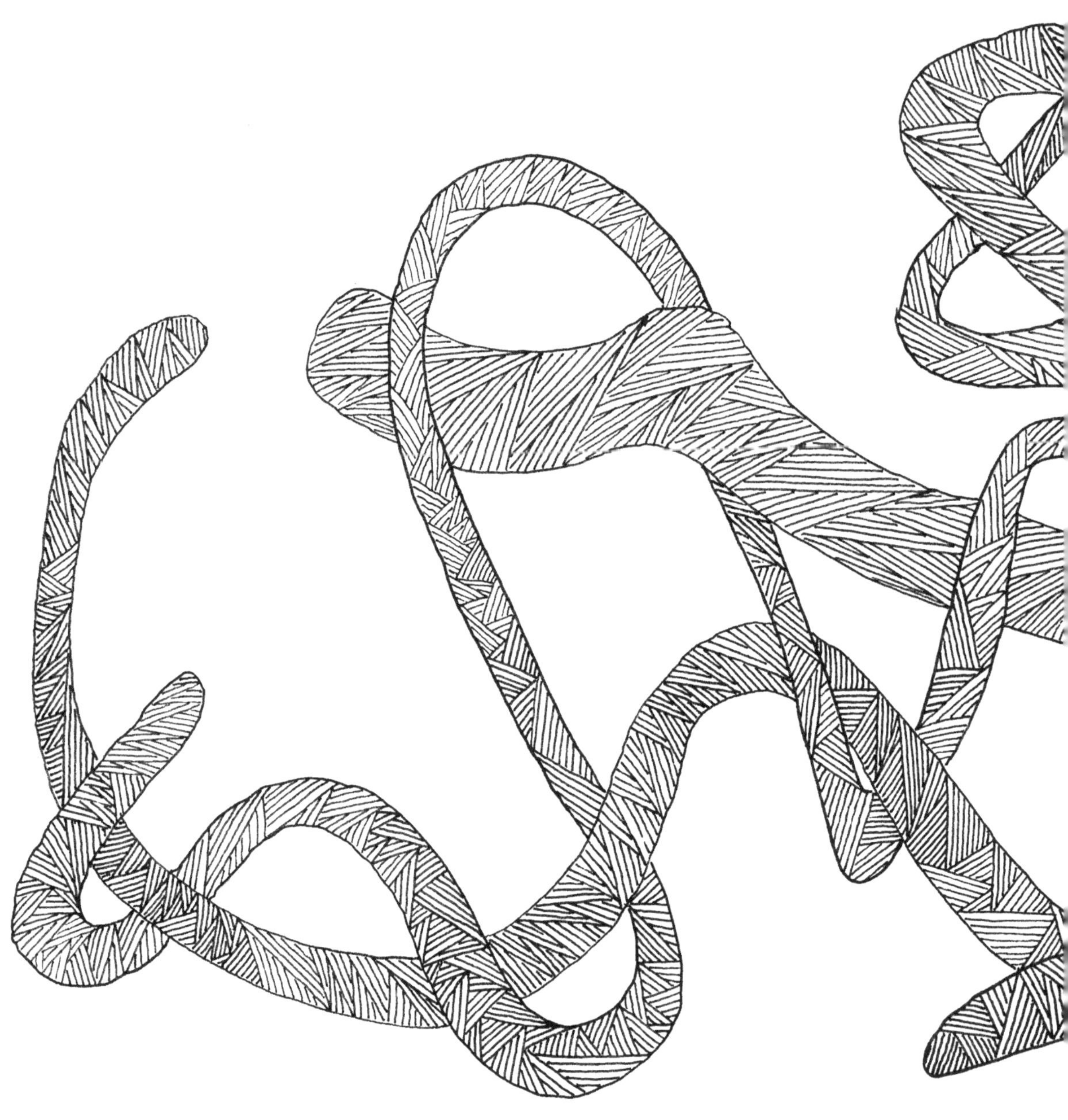

Live Bait, 2012

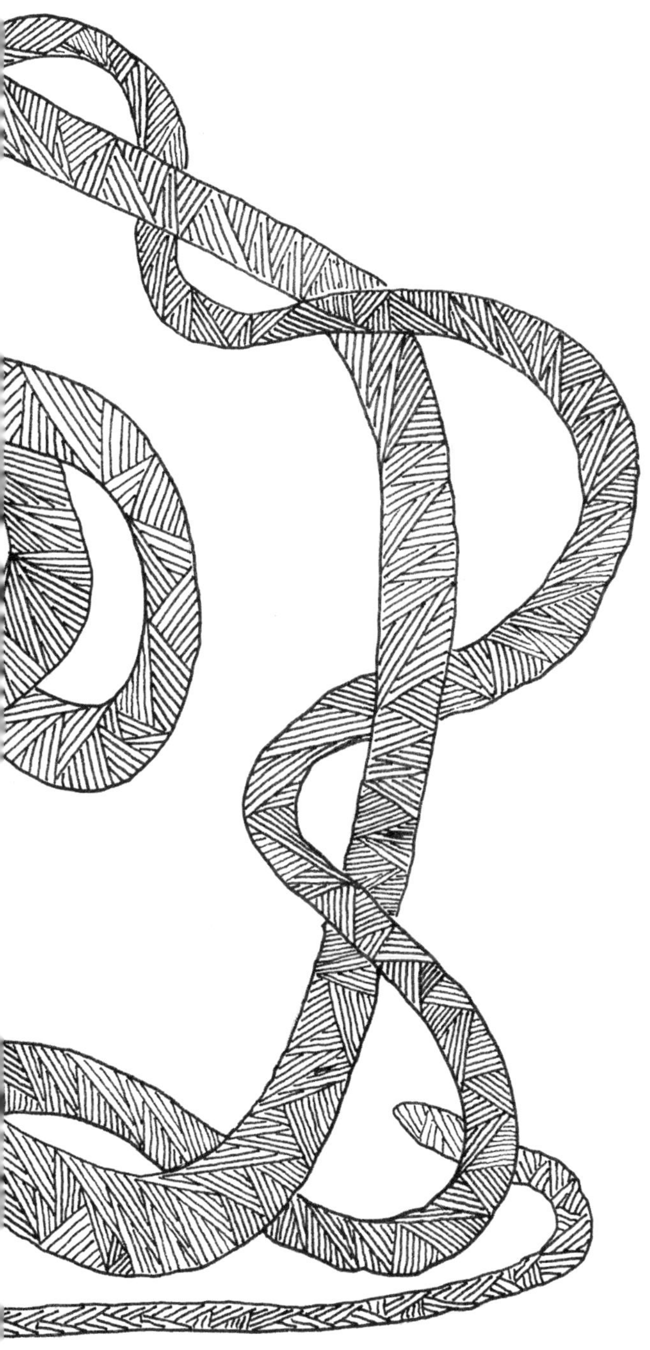

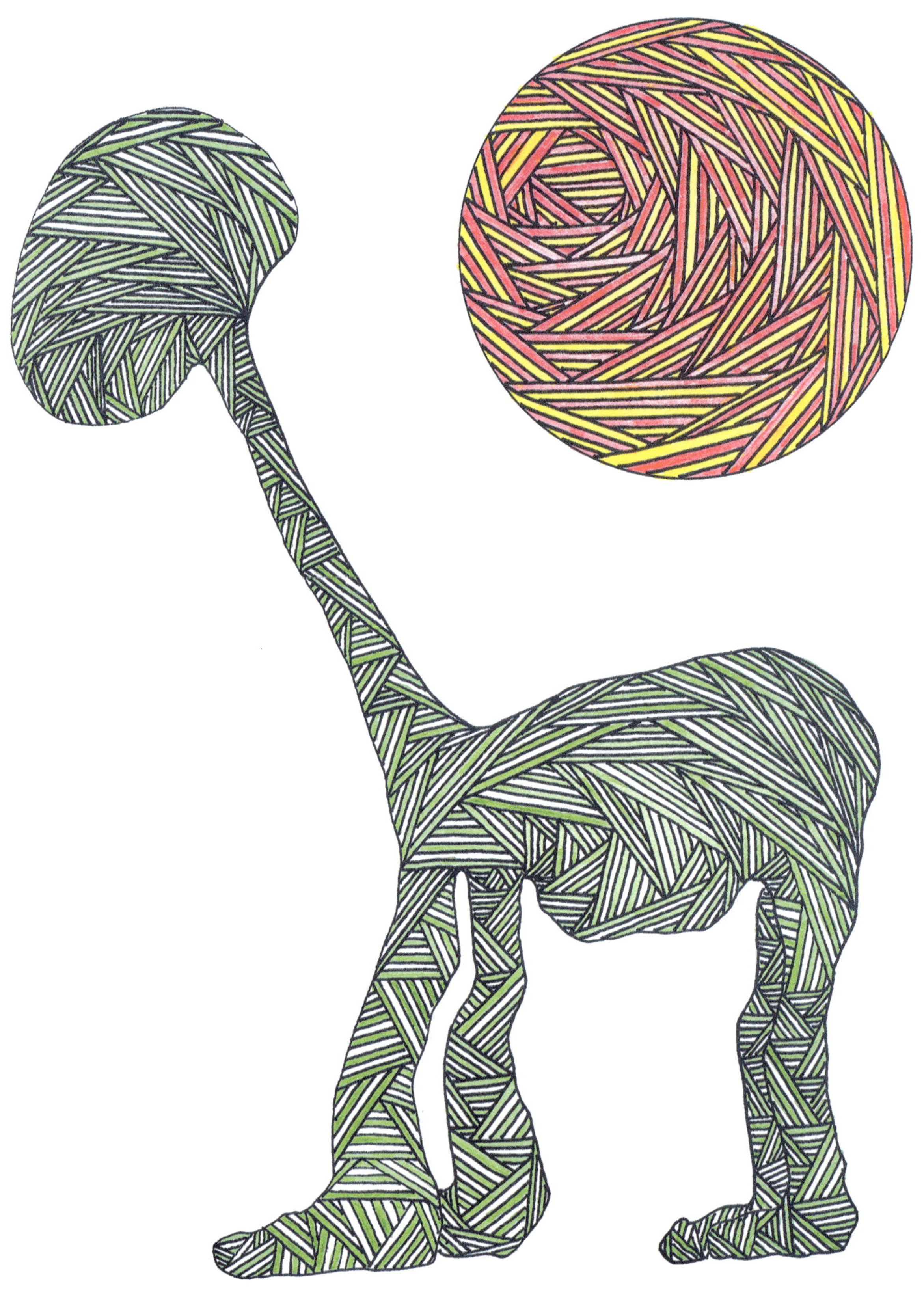

Gironkey, 2021

I get that we are asking for trouble when we enter an animal's habitat, but many animals seem to think they can come into ours no problem. I was once in an AIDS ward in Mozambique, Africa, filming for Comic Relief. I was visiting a guy whom we had filmed a couple of days earlier and I went back to see how he was getting on. While I was talking to him a goat came in and pissed against his bedside table, then walked out again. And I saw a giraffe at Nairobi Airport. The park is adjacent to the airport. I said to the taxi driver: 'Look! A giraffe!!' He just gave a disinterested 'Yeah?' like I'd pointed out a pigeon.

I never liked pigs. I find them rather vicious. I was bitten by a pig once, when I was just trying to be nice to it … although I was in its pen. I have become immensely fond of some animals, though. I love my wee dogs at home. And I adored Ralph McTell's parrot. His name was Albert, and he was the best talking parrot I've ever come across. 'Hello, Bill!' If you rattled your keys he'd say: 'Is that you away, then?' And if the atmosphere was quiet, he'd say: 'What d'you have to do to get a drink round here?' Ralph became really worried when Albert developed a cough. It was a deathly rattle, so Ralph took him to the vet. The vet examined Albert, then said: 'I hate to tell you, Ralph, but that's YOUR cough! He's parroting you. Your parrot is perfectly healthy, but you're going to have to do something about your own cough …'

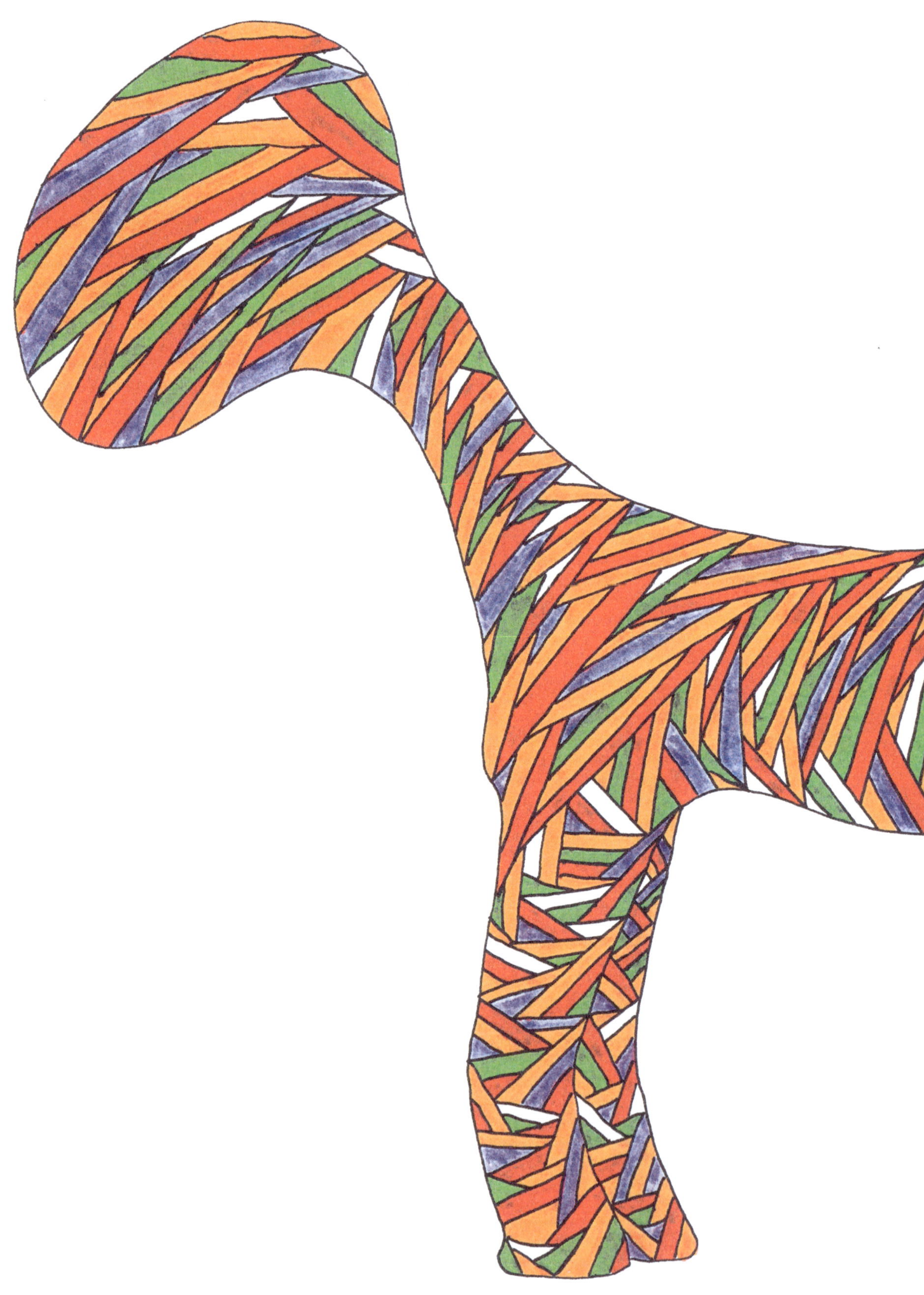

Brahmarama Llama, 2019

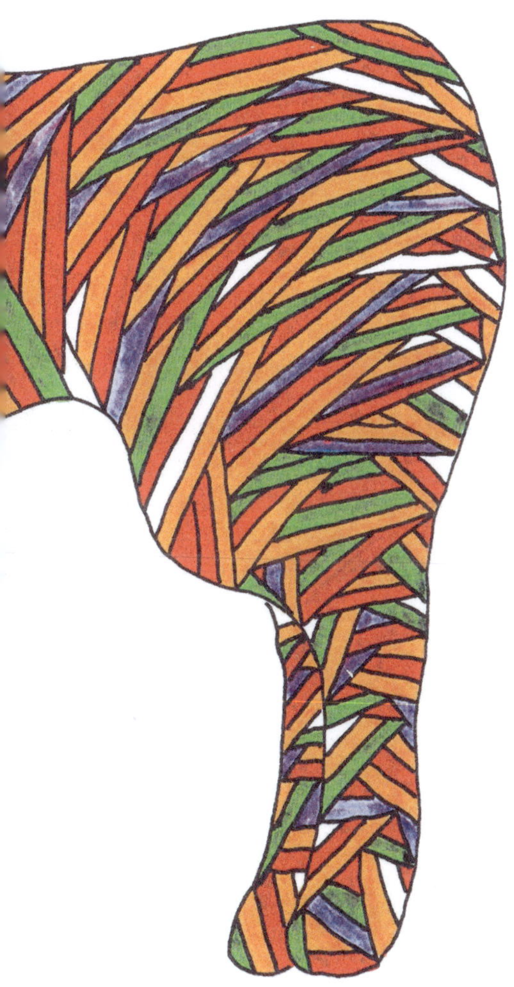

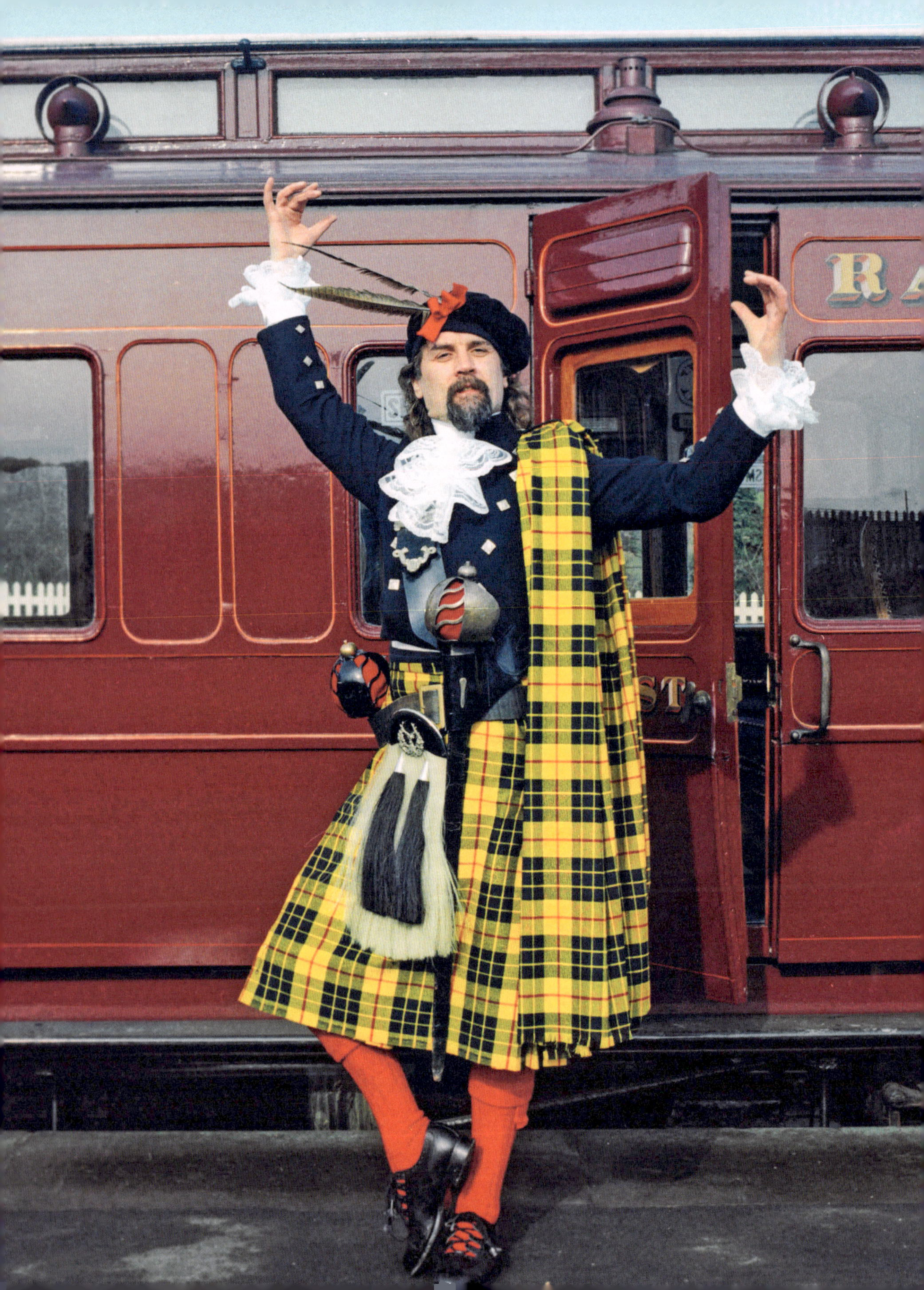

Heritage

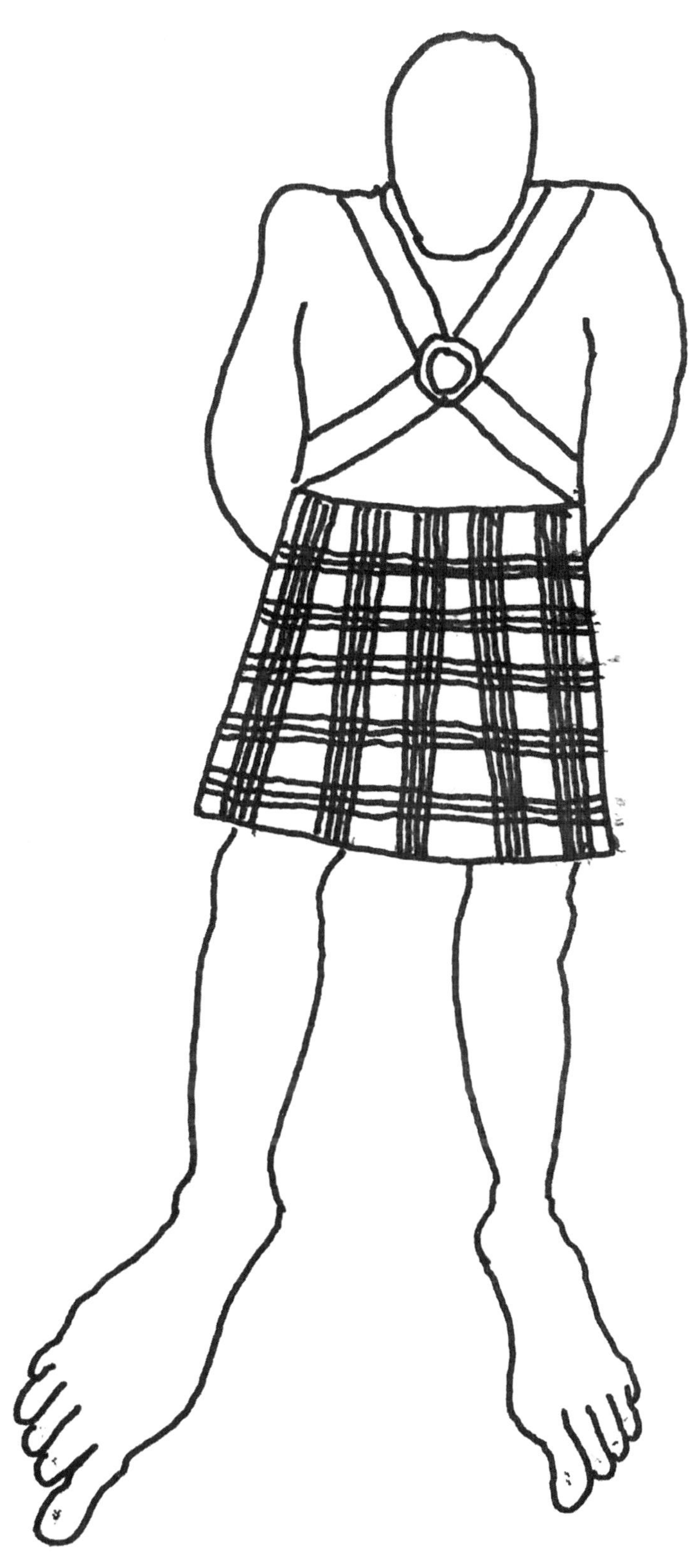

At Ease, 2015

You should go to Scotland. I'm sick and tired of meeting English people who say: 'You know, I've been everywhere, but I've never been to Scotland,' as if I should be fucking delighted to hear it. Go — it's a lovely place. And don't just go to the usual places. You know, people go to look at Edinburgh Castle, and then they go to look at a couple of mountains, and then they come back. Go further afield for a change. Go to Fife and Dundee and Aberdeen and Glasgow — you'll love it, there are lots of nice places. And don't do what people always come to me and do. They say, 'Oh, I went up to Scotland once and it was raining.' Of course it was fucking raining! Where do you think Scotland is — the fucking Pyrenees? Take a raincoat, you stupid fucker! The mountain rescue are sick of it — going up and down Ben Nevis and saving people in fucking khaki shorts and sandshoes. Where do they think they've gone, Benidorm?

Anyway, let me tell you about Fife, where metal is located. It's opposite Edinburgh. It's the other side of the River Forth. It sits between the River Forth and the River Tay. The River Tay is at Dundee, Edinburgh down below and that sticky-out bit on the right-hand side is the Kingdom of Fife. And it's a great place. If you go across the Forth Bridge from Edinburgh, you're into Fife. If you come the other way, you're back in Edinburgh. You can go two ways on the Forth Bridge. Yeah, it saved us building two fuck-ing bridges, didn't it? Because we're very mean. You've probably heard that before. There's a nasty rumour that copper wire was invented by two Scotsmen fighting over a penny. My father once dropped fifty pence, bent down to pick it up and it hit him on the back of the neck. He used to wake up at night to see if he'd lost any sleep. Yes, and we've the most crowded taxis in the world: 'What? Four pence for seven miles? You fuckin' highway robber!' No, Fife's a great place, you would like Fife. Everybody likes Fife,

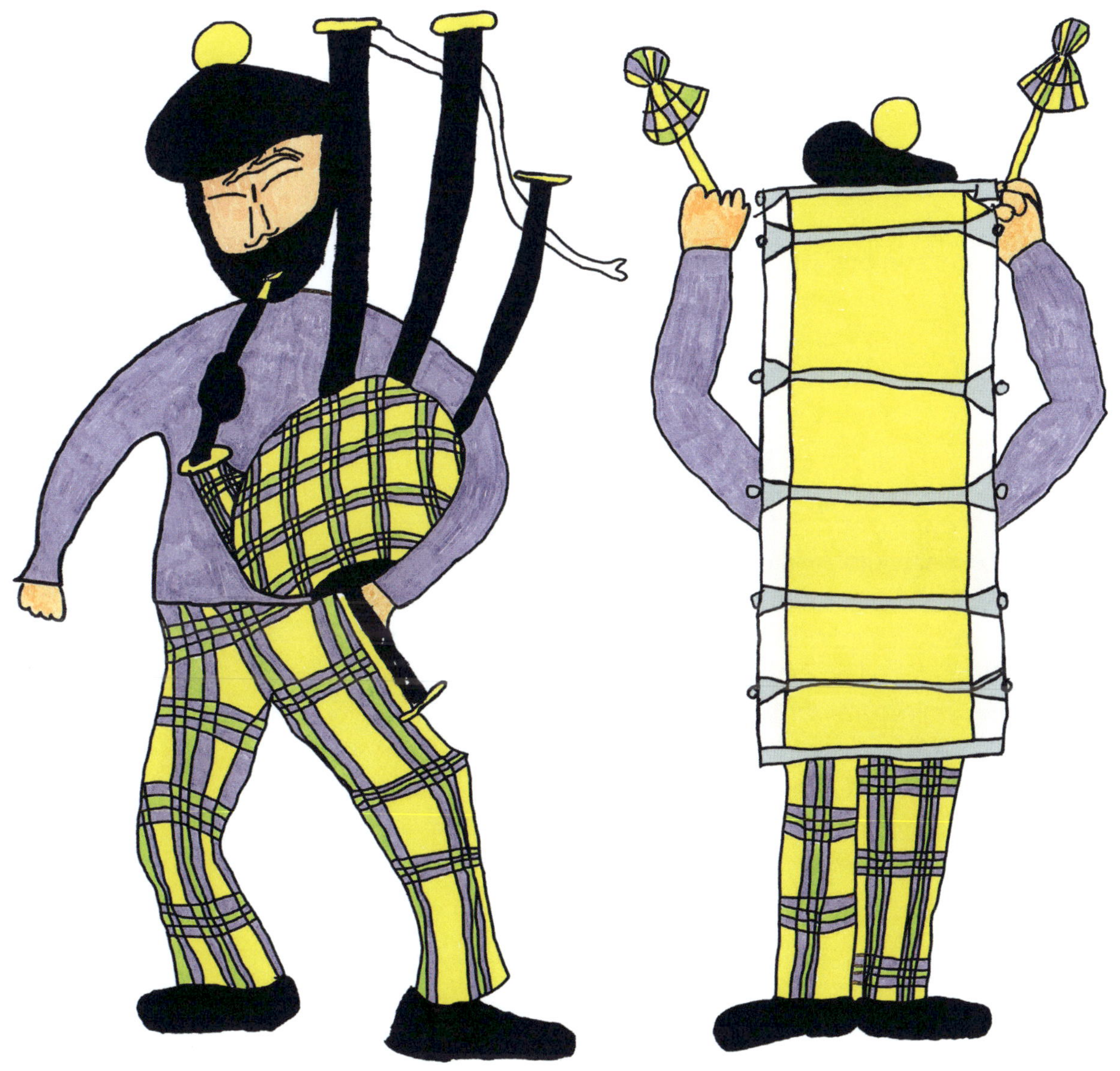

The Gloaming, 2023

it's great. St Andrews is in the north. St Andrews is kind of posh and it's got the golf and all that, and a university. It's full of posh folk. A lot of them are called Alisdair. Alisdairs always spell it for you: 'Could you sign it "To Alisdair" – d- a- i- r. Alisdair.' 'Alisdair? Have you seen Farquhar?' 'Oh, yes. Farquhar is over there with Finlay. Finlay and Anderson – they're talking to Campbell.' 'Are they really?' 'Yes. Campbell is talking to Robertson, and Robertson is talking to Farquhar and Farquhar is talking to Fettes. There's nobody with first names round here any more.' And it's nice agricultural land up there. It's really pretty. Seasidey places, nice fishing. You should go. Pittenweem and all those nice wee villages, you go in and get pissed on the coffee – they put whisky in their coffee and you get totally trousered. Come down and there's Dunfermline, and Kirkcaldy – fabulous town, where they used to make linoleum, great place! Making linoleum is a kind of smelly thing; they were going to change the name of Kirkcaldy to Whatsthatfuckingsmell. It's the first thing people said when they got off the train. Now, the linoleum industry went down the pan, and they've got a million reasons for that. My personal one is that no one could pronounce 'linoleum'. They used to go into shops and say: 'Hello, can I have a roll of linoliment, thank you.' 'I'm sorry, what was that?' 'A roll of linominint.' 'A romint and only one?? We don't sell romints.' 'I never asked for a fucking romint! I said a roll of limo-minum!' 'Look, I think I'm going to have to ask you again, at the risk of appearing rude. I'm awful sorry about this.' 'God knows it's simple enough: a romaminomium!' 'You've got me there.' 'For God's sake! A romum… oh, fuck it – give us a carpet!' And that's what happened.

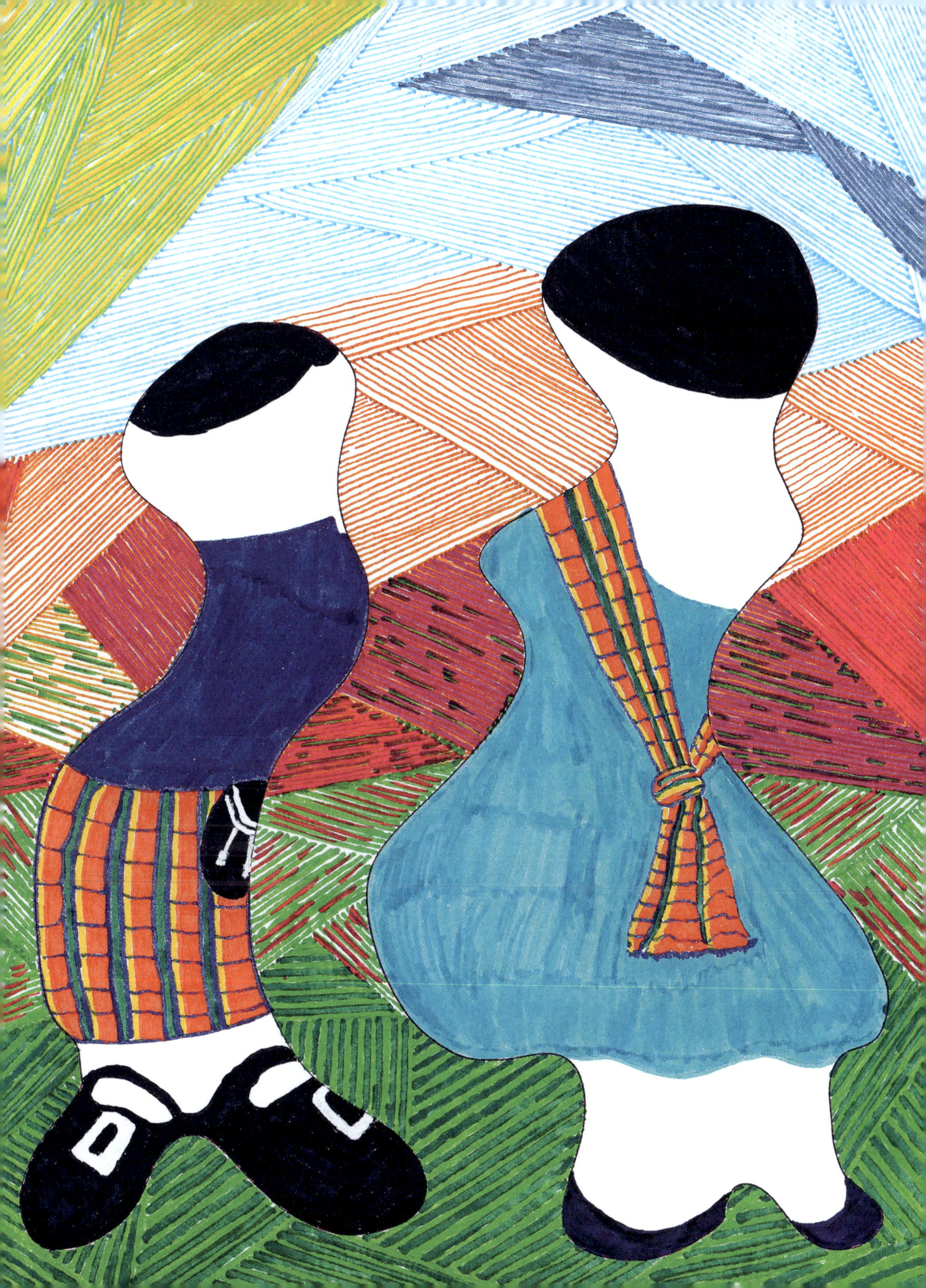

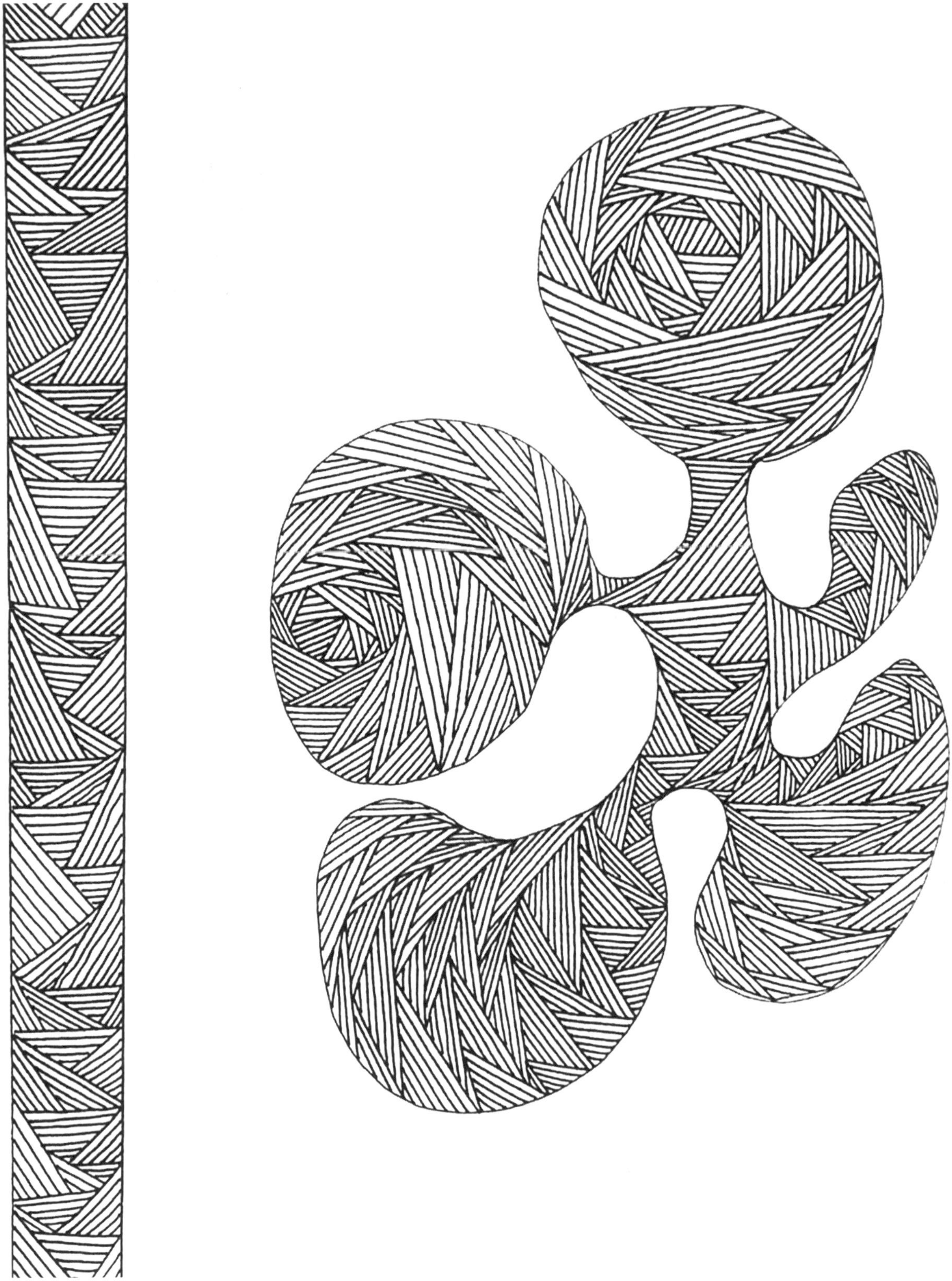

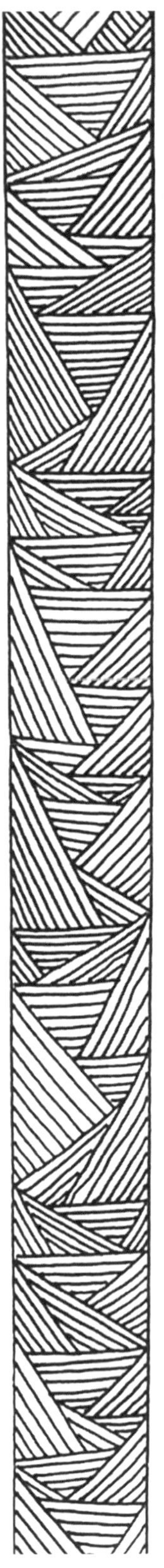

Wee Warrior With Targe, 2011

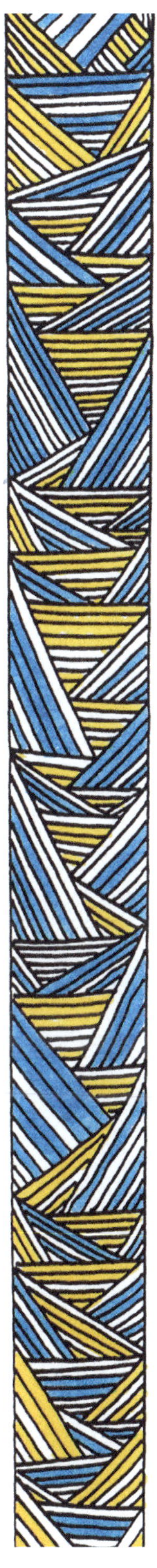

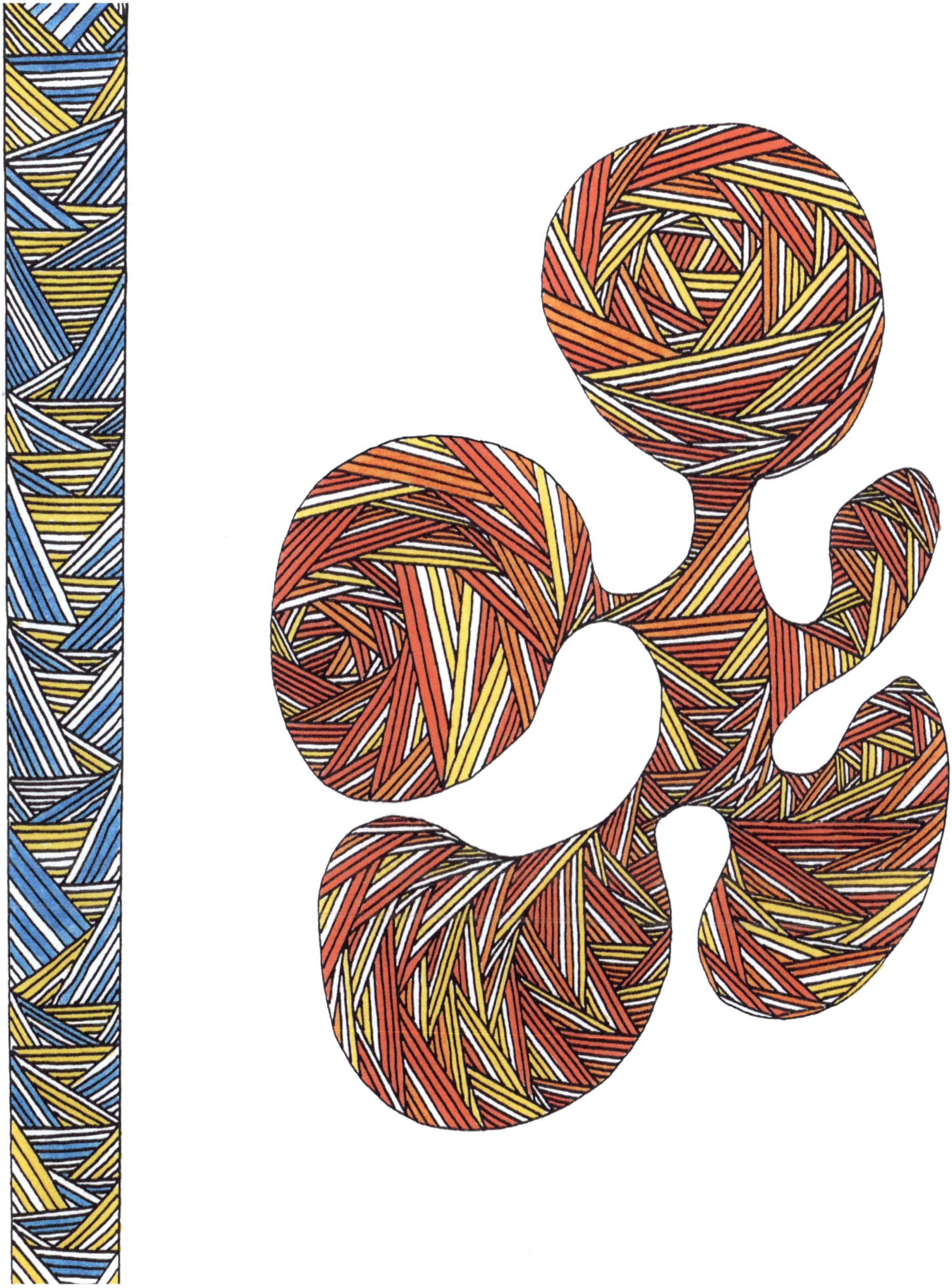

Wee Warrior With Targe, 2023

I'm actually pale
blue: it takes me a
week of sunbathing
to turn white.

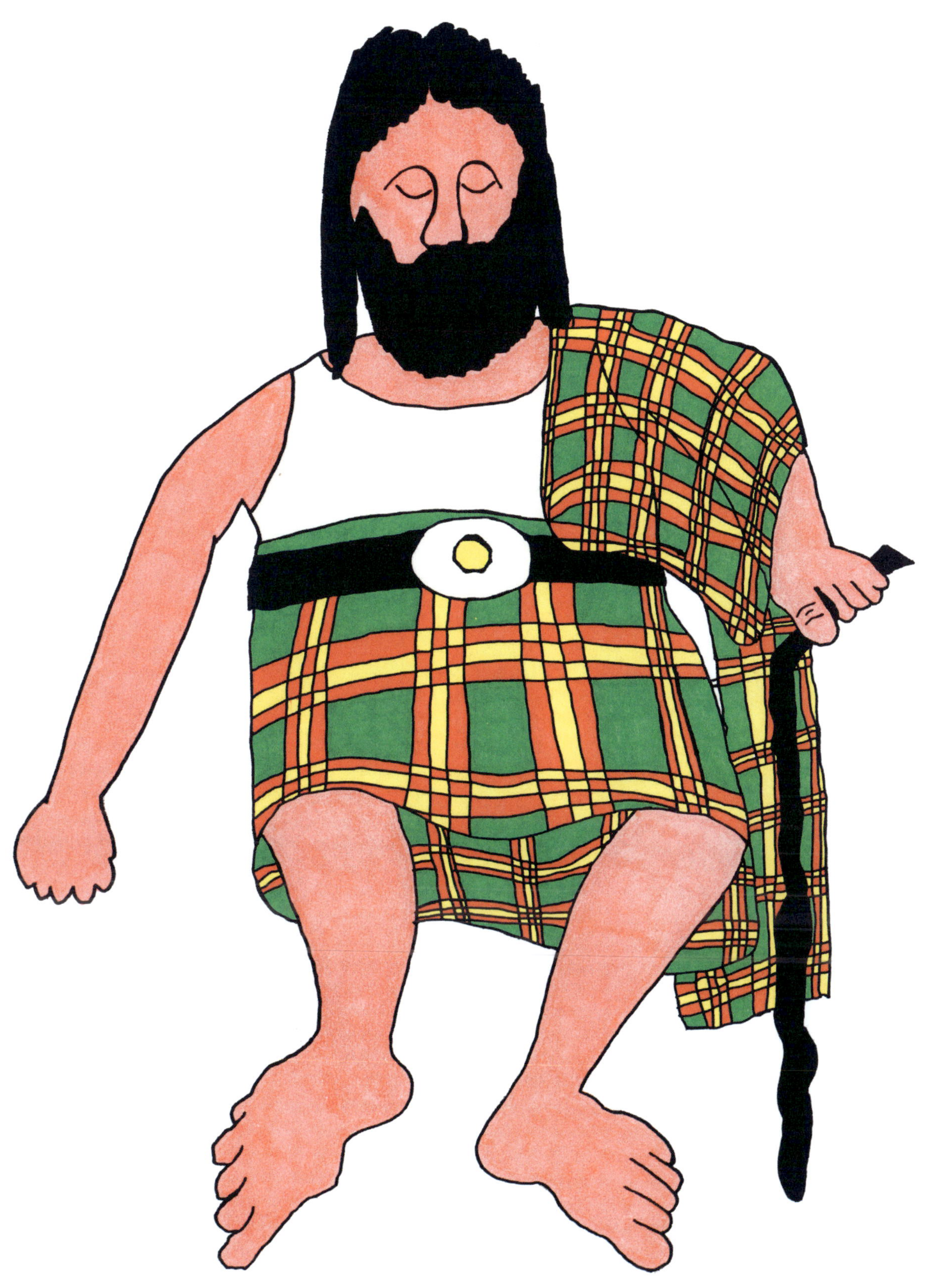

Sunburned, 2022

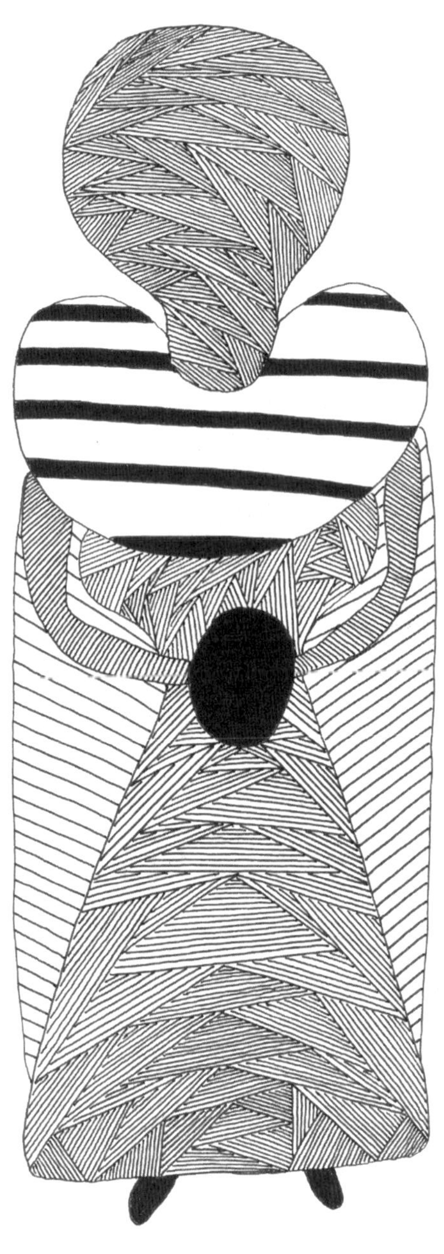
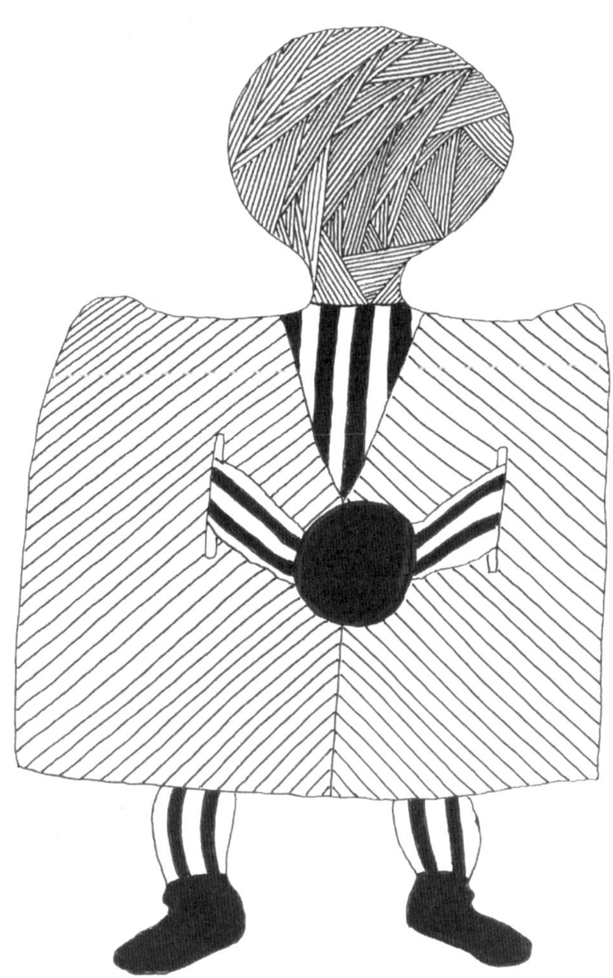

Mixed Marriage, 2013

A few years ago, I was summoned to the Office of Births, Deaths and Marriages in Edinburgh. And I happily attended. They wanted to talk to me because they were doing an exhibition to encourage people to come and look into their family backgrounds and to use their facilities to do it. They'd got ten famous Scottish people and they had researched their backgrounds, and you could go there and look at it and see what you thought.

Ten famous Scots. There was Sean Connery, me, and eight other guys. I just say that to irritate Ewan McGregor. And Brian Cox — how do you fucking like that?

No, of course, there are lots of other famous Scottish people.

One of them is Alan Cumming.

I once did a gig in Hollywood for BAFTA — the British Film and TV Academy — presenting Britannia Awards to Americans who'd been in British movies. It was a nice night; it went very well. And the following year they got Alan Cumming to do it, so I had to show up and hand over to him — that's the way they do it. And I'd always been dying to meet him anyway, because I think he's amazing. Plus, he comes from Carnoustie on the east coast of Scotland, and I had a holiday there when I was ten and I was dying to tell him. Not only that, but Carnoustie is also very close to Arbroath, and I lost my virginity in Arbroath, and I was dying to tell him that as well. So, I met him and we got on like a house on fire. And as we were chatting away, I said, 'I believe you come from Carnoustie?' He said, 'Yeah.' I said, 'I had a holiday there when I was ten and I had a lovely time.' He said, 'That's nice.' Then I said, 'And I lost my virginity in Arbroath.' And his answer to that will go to my grave with me. He said, 'I passed my driving test there.' I said: 'I think I won.'

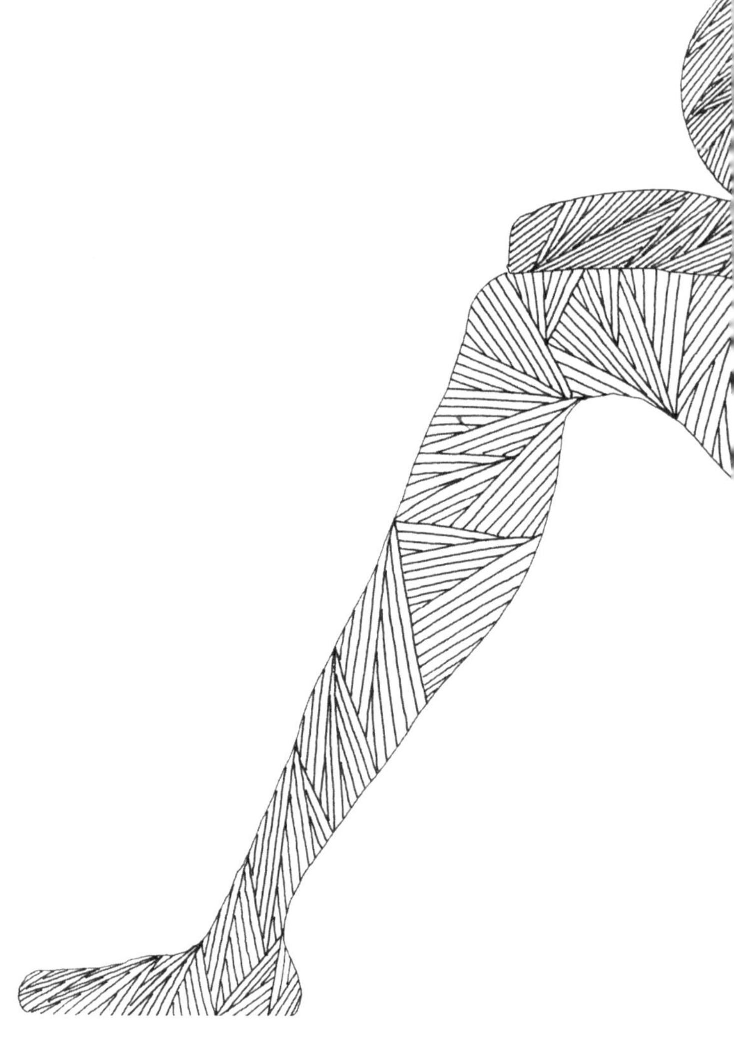

Birth Ball, 2012

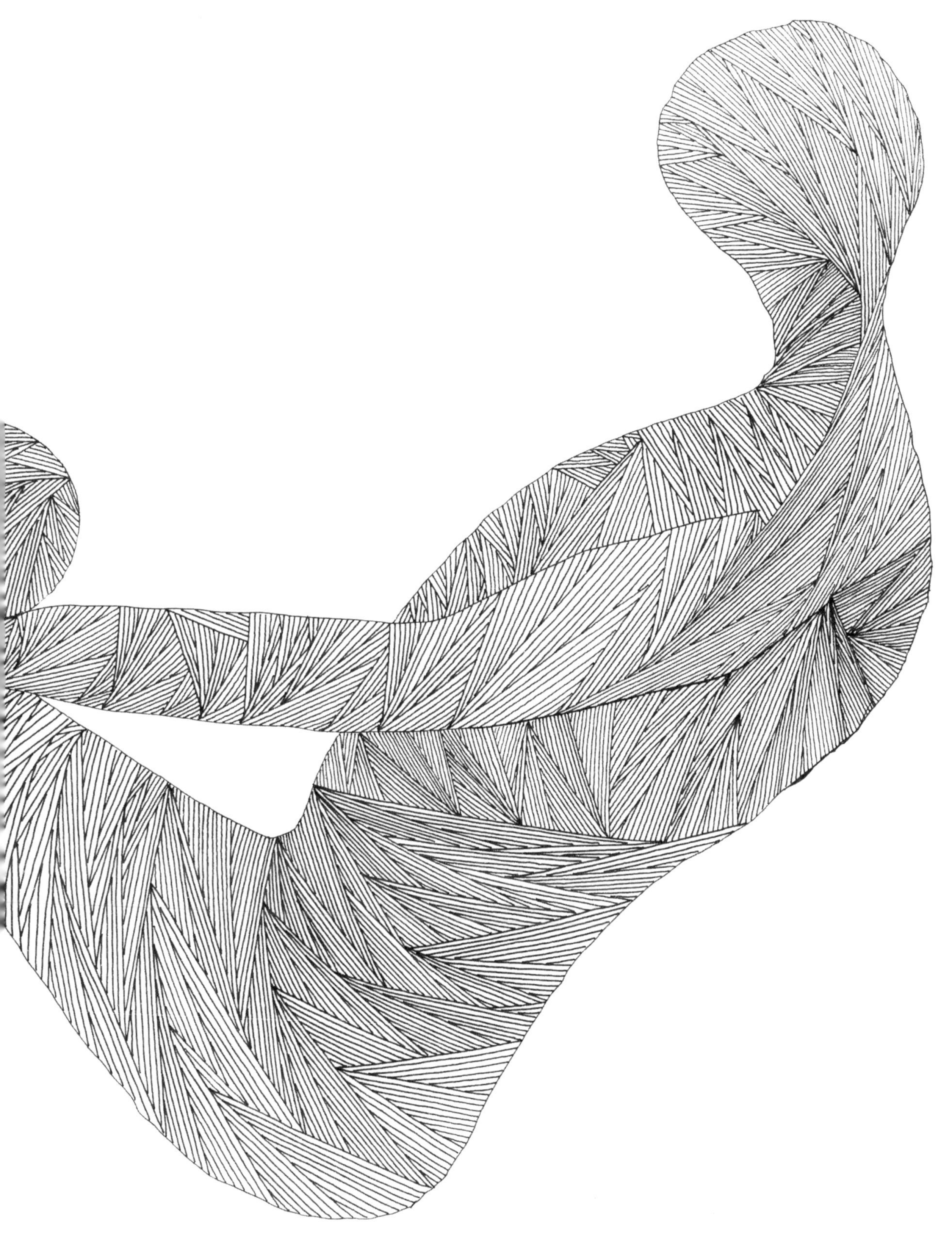

But the Births, Deaths and Marriages was great. They'd charted our lives and our ancestors, and they'd made a great job of it. There was a woman called Morrison, I think it was, who was the historian there, and she took me through the history of my family, from Galway and the Isle of Mull and all of that, and it was all very interesting. And at the end of it she said, 'What do you think?' I said, 'I'm delighted.' She said, 'You're not disappointed?' I said, 'Why would I be disappointed?' She said, 'Well, some people, when they realise their whole family are peasants, they get disappointed.' I said, 'I'm delighted about that. I love peasant stuff. I love peasant food, music, literature. There's no reason why I'd be disappointed about that.' She said, 'That's a very refreshing attitude.' I said, 'I'm a very refreshing kind of person, Mrs Morrison.'

I said, 'I can't believe people get disappointed.' She said, 'Oh, last week we had a big fat middle-class woman in here' — she just said 'a woman', I added those other bits; there's a bitchy side of me I'm going to have to do something about — 'and she was really disappointed to find out that her great-great-granny's name was Fanny Kissing.' I said, 'Why was she disappointed? It's my hobby!'

But if you ever get a chance you should go to that place — the Office of Births, Deaths and Marriages — because it's brilliant. It's got brilliant stuff.

The historian changed into white gloves at one point. I thought she was going to do an Al Jolson impersonation, but it was to go and get this incredibly rare certificate. It was the birth certificate of Mary, Queen of Scots. I actually got to hold it in my hand.

I was trembling, it was a magnificent thing. I couldn't believe it. She was executed just around the corner from where I was standing. It was extraordinary.

And then she went and got another one. Rob Roy MacGregor. What a prick. He was a spy for the English against the Scots, and a spy for the Scots against the English. He was a murderer and a thief, he was almost seven feet tall, and it's said he could tie his bootlaces standing up. He must have been the most peculiar shape.

Now, I dislike him especially because of the movie *Rob Roy*.

If you've seen it, you'll remember a scene where someone has stolen his cattle and he and his men are up in the hills looking for them. And one of them jumps over a fence into a field and says: 'Ah, there's nae cows here, Robert … Wait a minute.' He finds a cow shit, and he picks it up and takes a big bite out of it, spits it out, and says: 'They've been gone two hours, Rob!'

I am here to inform you: the people of Scotland do not tell the time by eating shit! My grandfather lived to the age of ninety-six; I never once saw him reaching into his waistcoat pocket, pulling out a piece of dog shit, having a bite, and saying, 'Fuck, is that the time already?'

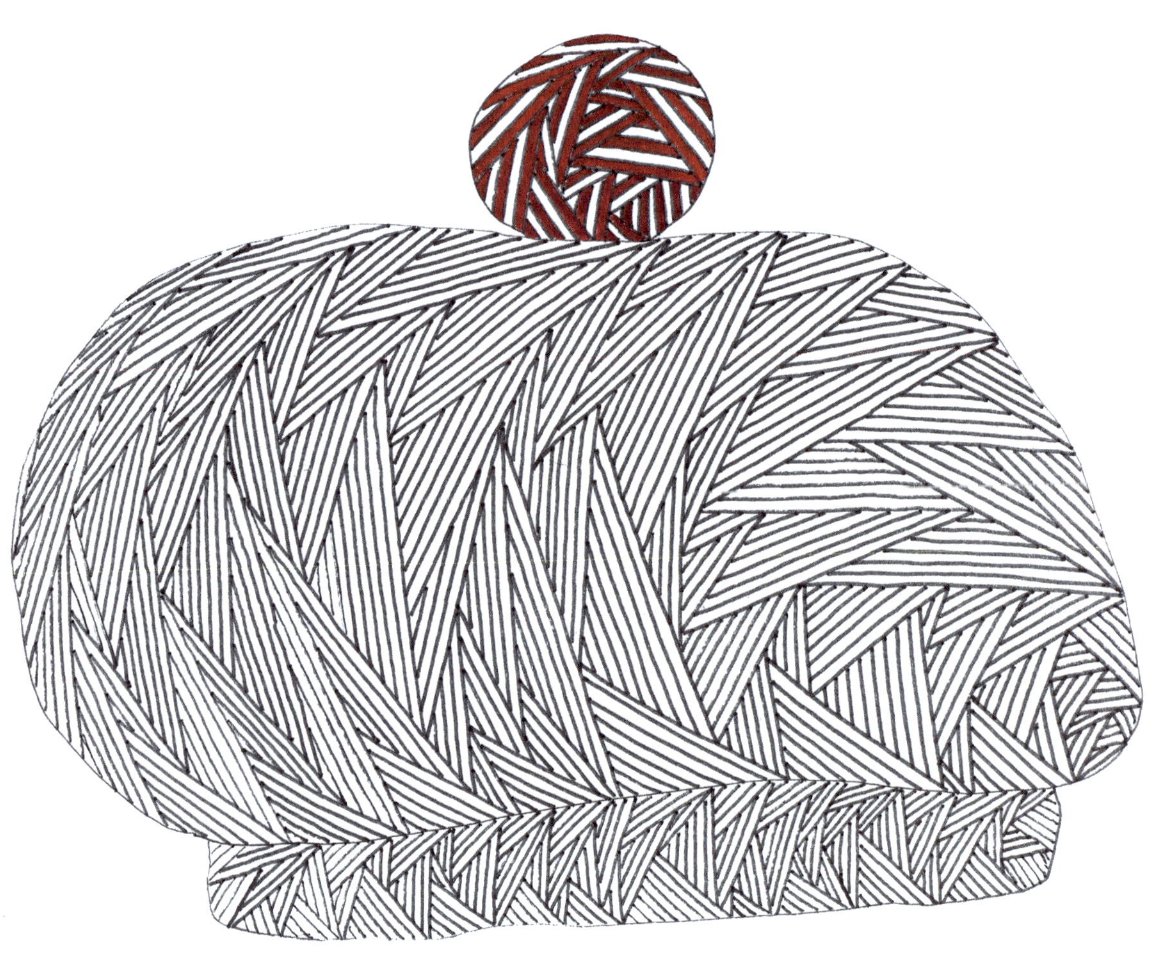

A Tammy, 2012

In Scotland there are
only two seasons …
June and winter!

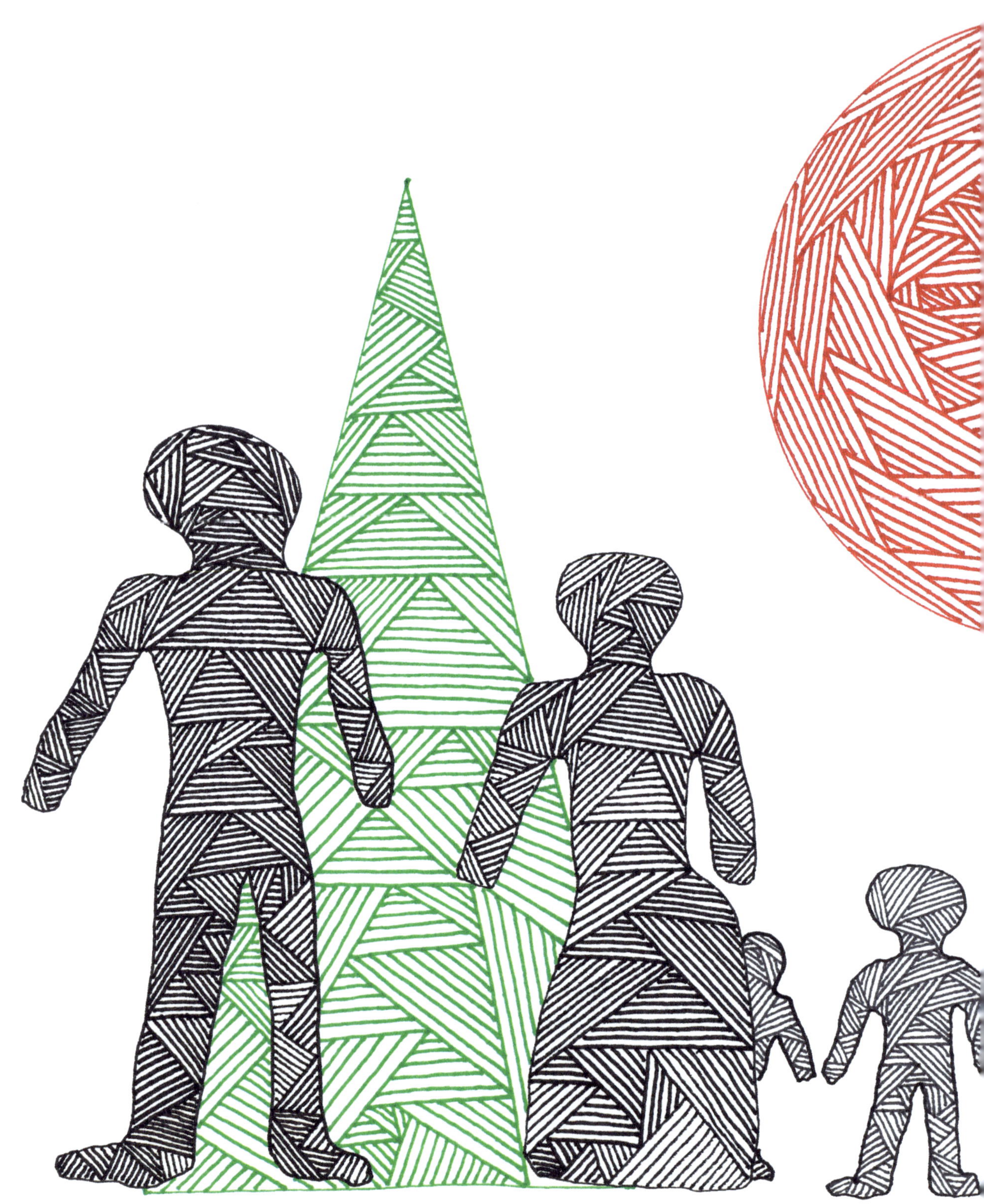

Christmas Tree, 2012

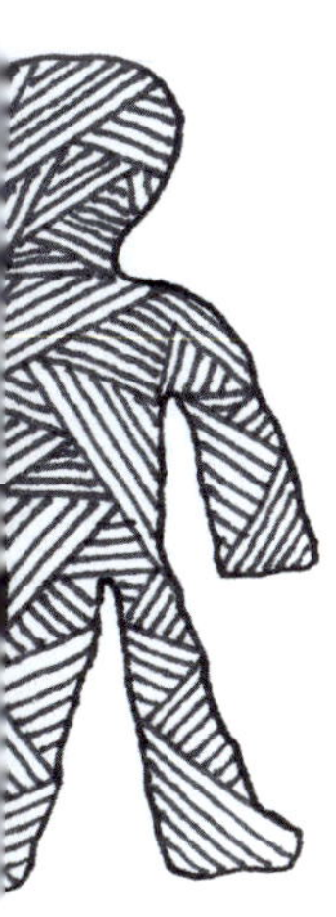

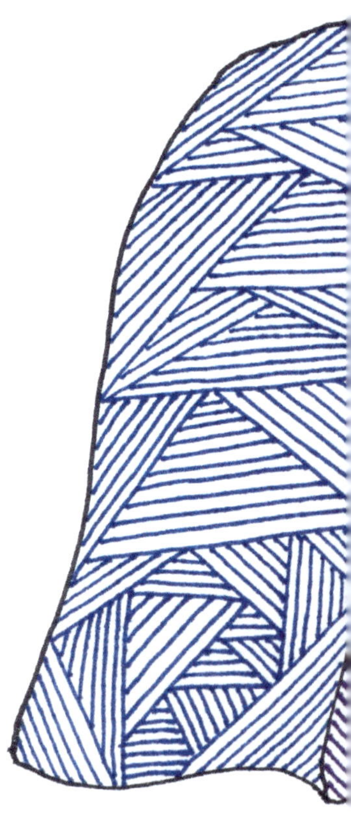

The Find, 2013

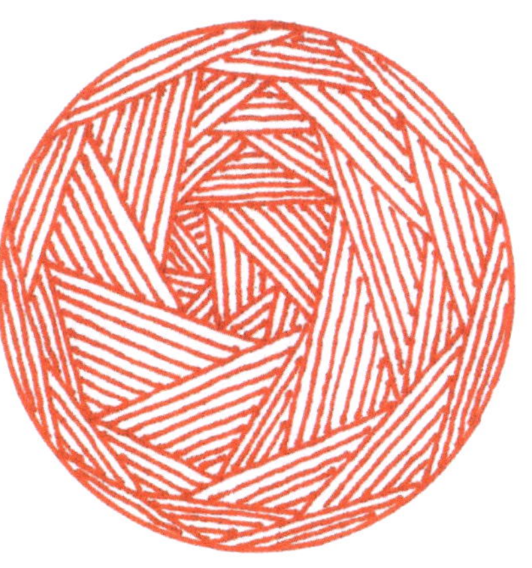

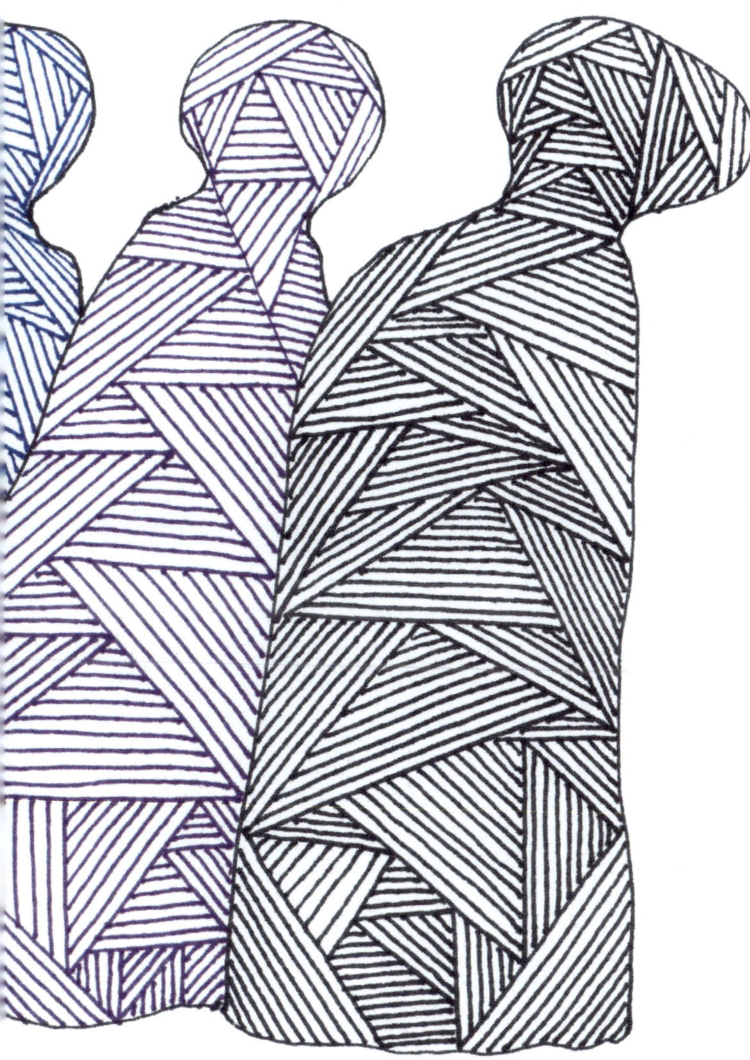

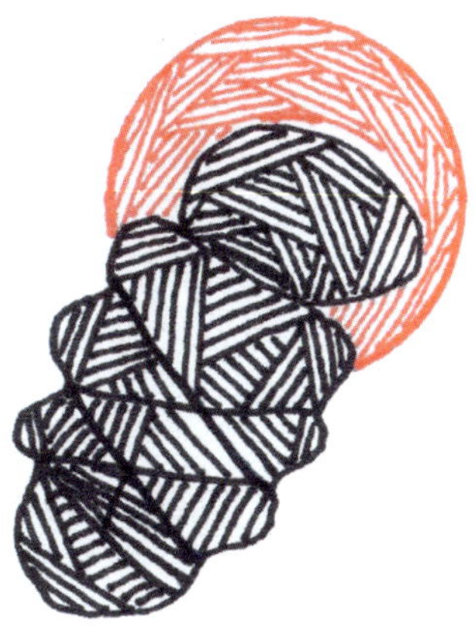

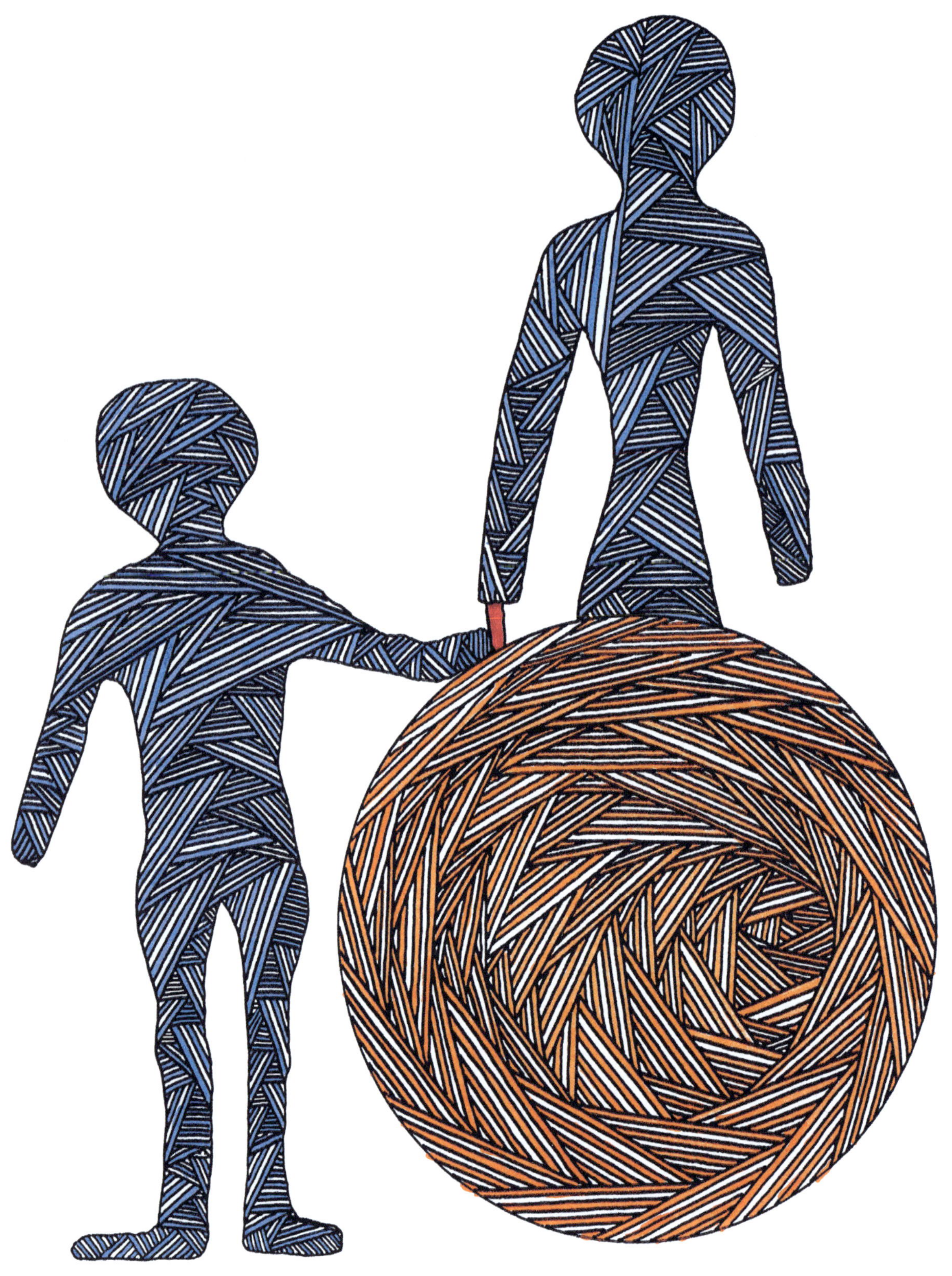

Helping Mummy With Twine, 2021

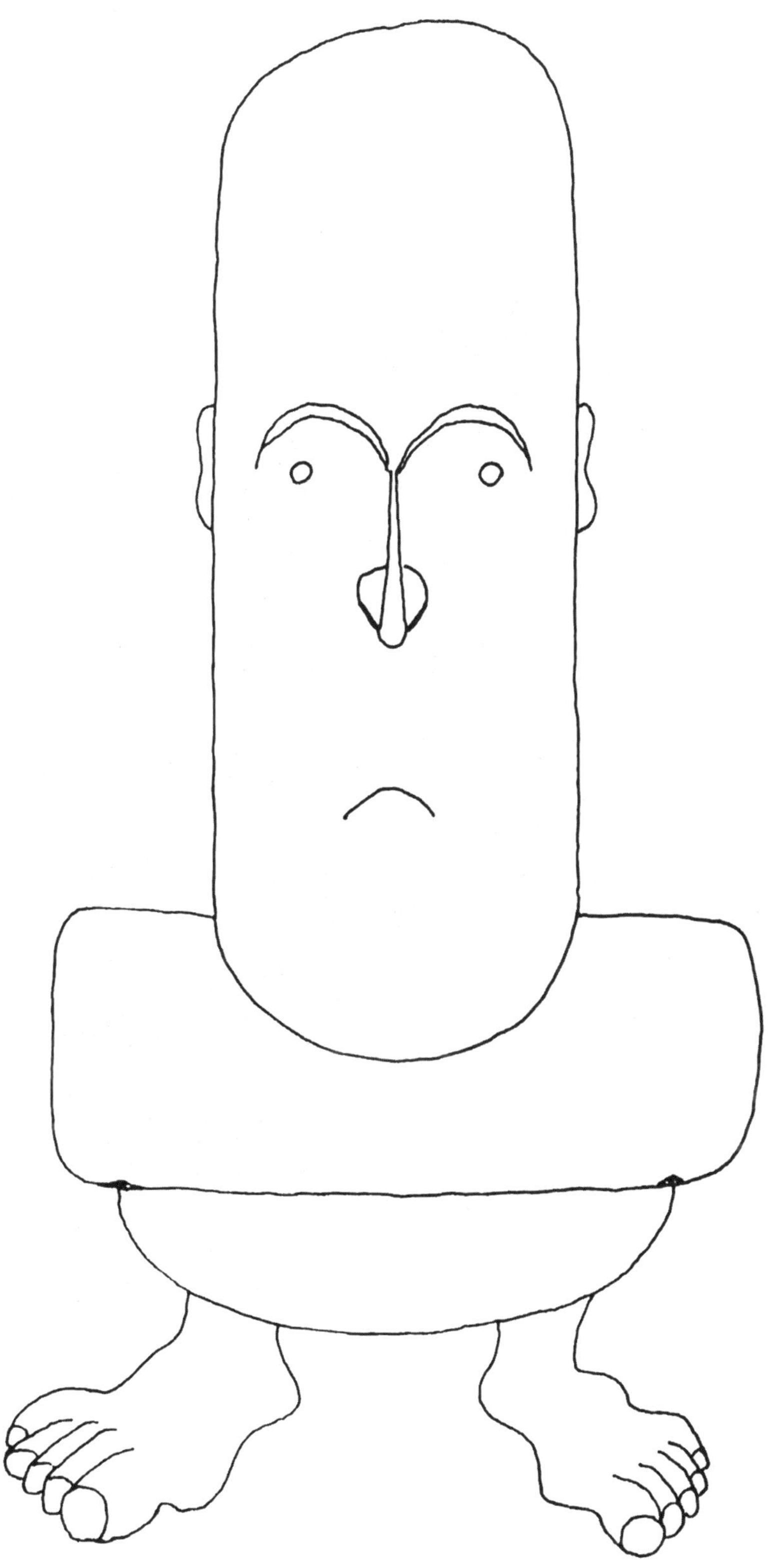

Nasty Little Bastard, 2018

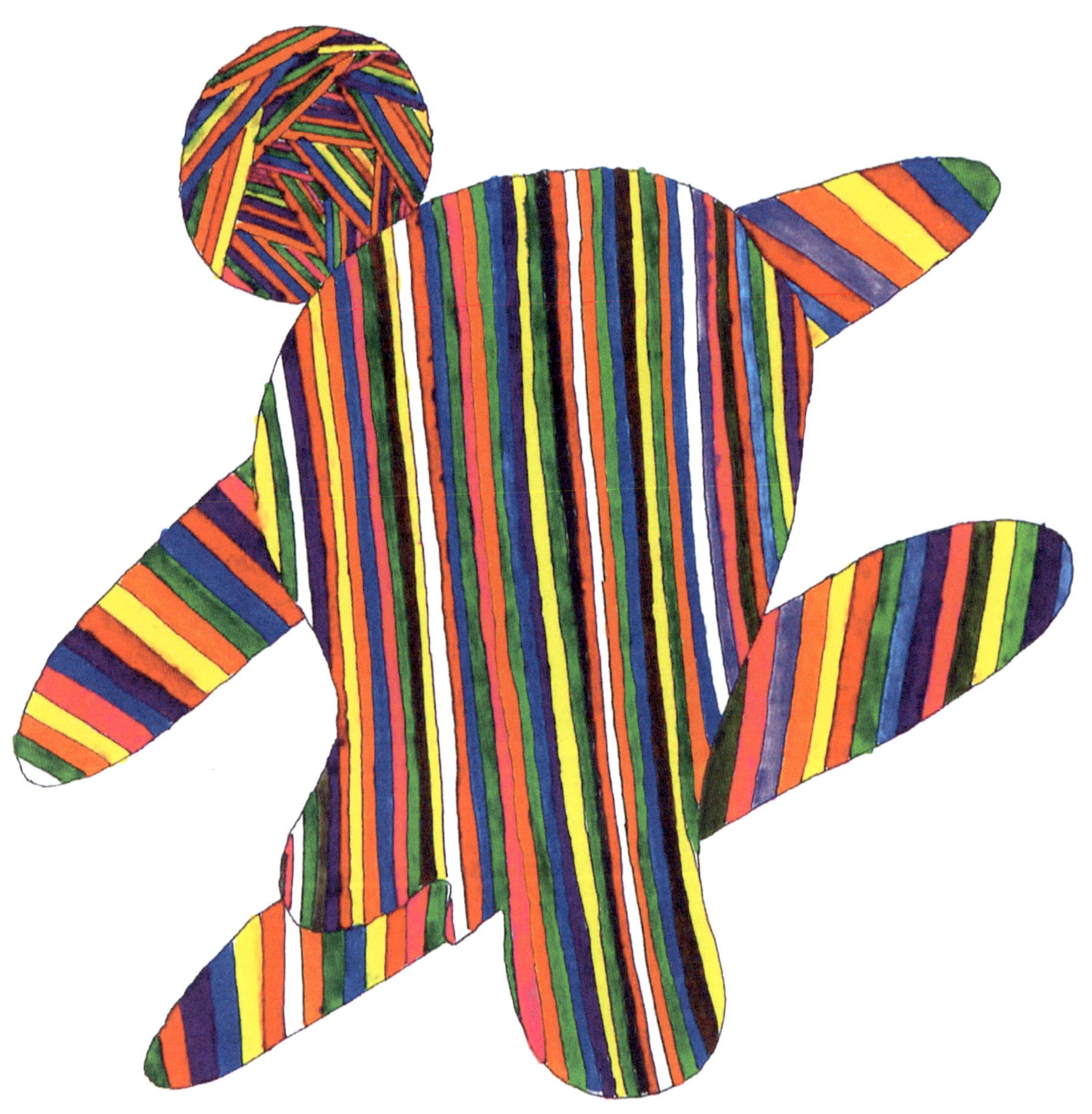

Dancing Thing, 2019

I first learned dancing at school. They taught us Scottish country dances – the Gay Gordons and Strip the Willow, which I have continued to enjoy – plus really rotten jiving. There was a school dance in the gymnasium every year. We never normally got to mix with the girls at St Gerard's, but at Christmas they opened up the dividing wall of the gym and held a dance for everyone. You weren't allowed to go to the Christmas dance until the third year. It was awful being a little third-year guy at your first dance, because you'd quickly learn that those dances they'd taught us in class were useless. Instead, the older boys would put on records and do some serious moves you just wished you could do. I desperately wanted to cut a serious dash but that was not to be. I was a dead loss.

I asked Rena Connell if she would come with me to the third-year school dance. When she said 'Yes' I was so surprised I just stood there, not knowing what to say next. I hadn't practised any follow-up line. As the dance drew closer, my anxiety mounted. I couldn't remember whether I'd agreed to meet Rena somewhere first, but it eventually came back to me that I'd mentioned the subway. To my surprise she actually showed up there, and I walked her along to the school. She was beautiful in her dress. I was in my school uniform – I didn't have a suit – and on the way I tripped and fell on my face. I guess Rena thought that was a long way from a suave move, because when we got to the school, she shot inside to join her trendier friends and avoided me for the rest of the night. I didn't even get to dance with her.

Rena Connell ended up marrying a policeman.

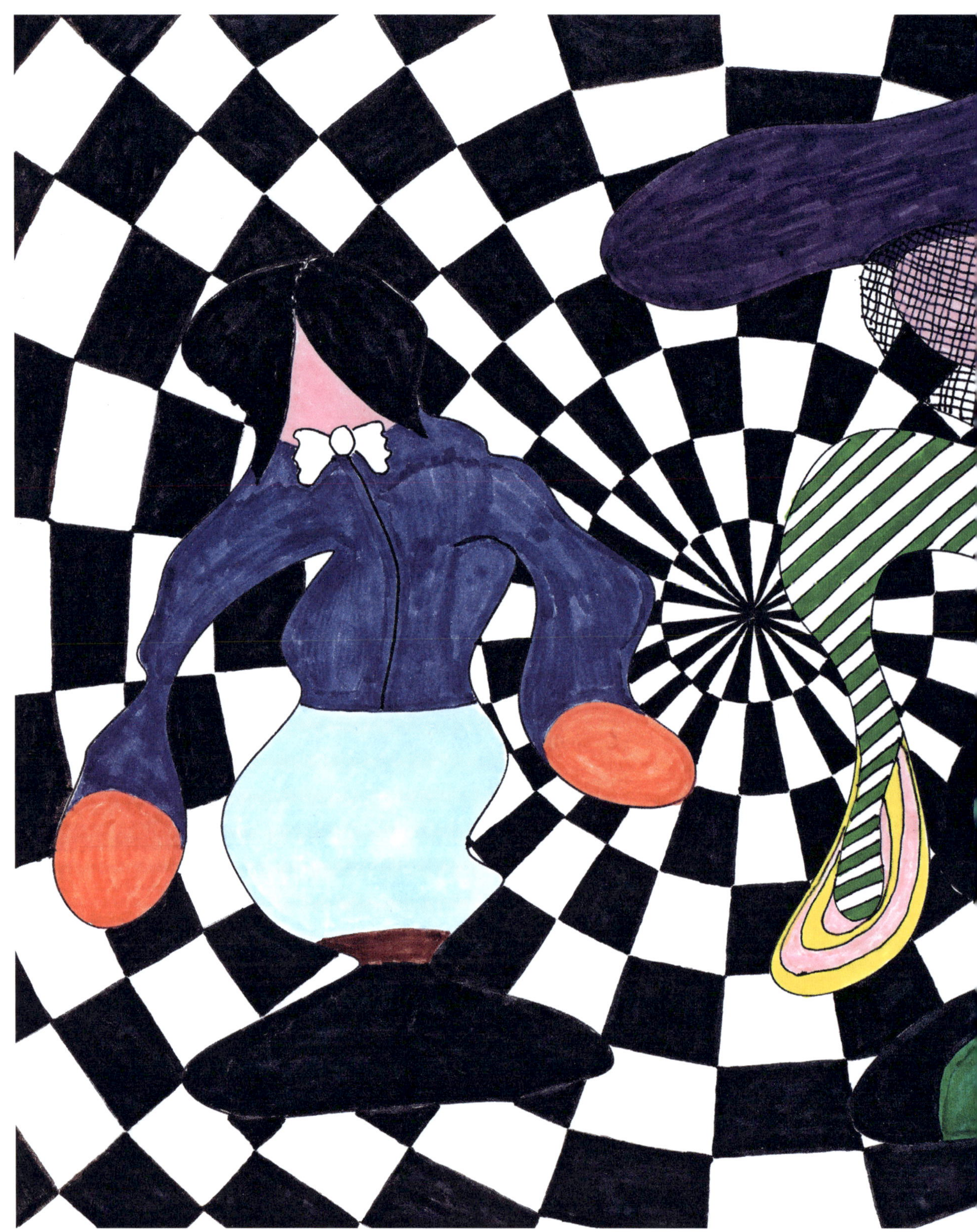

Robert Burns And Mary Of Argyll, 2010

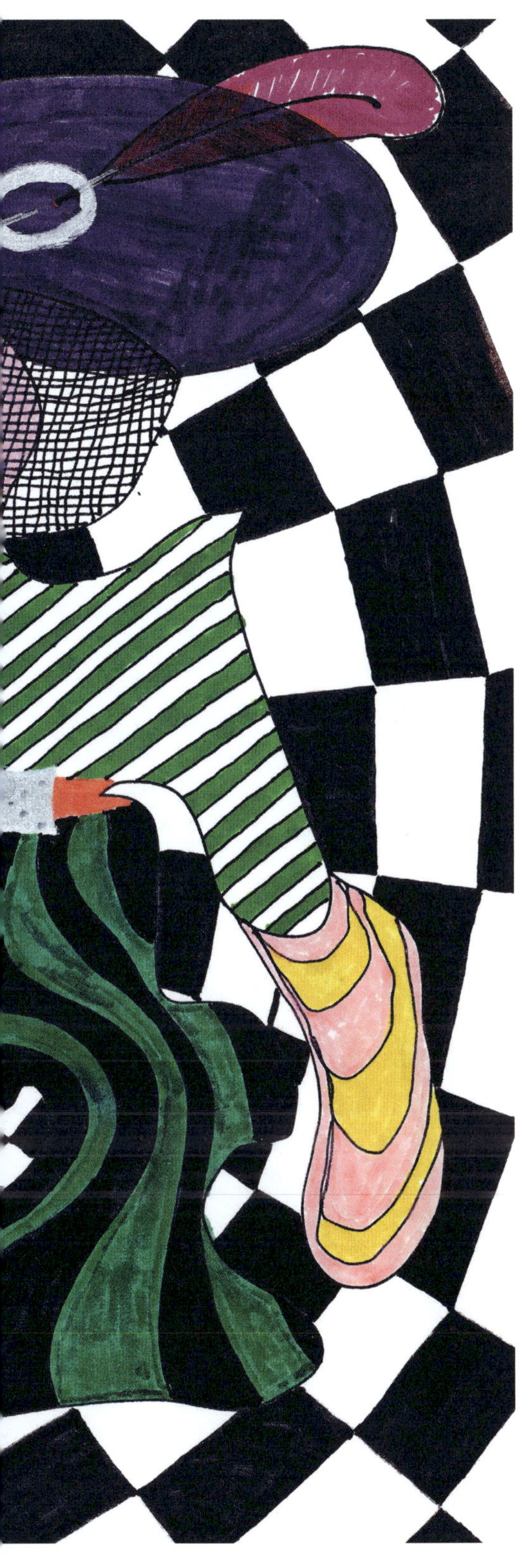

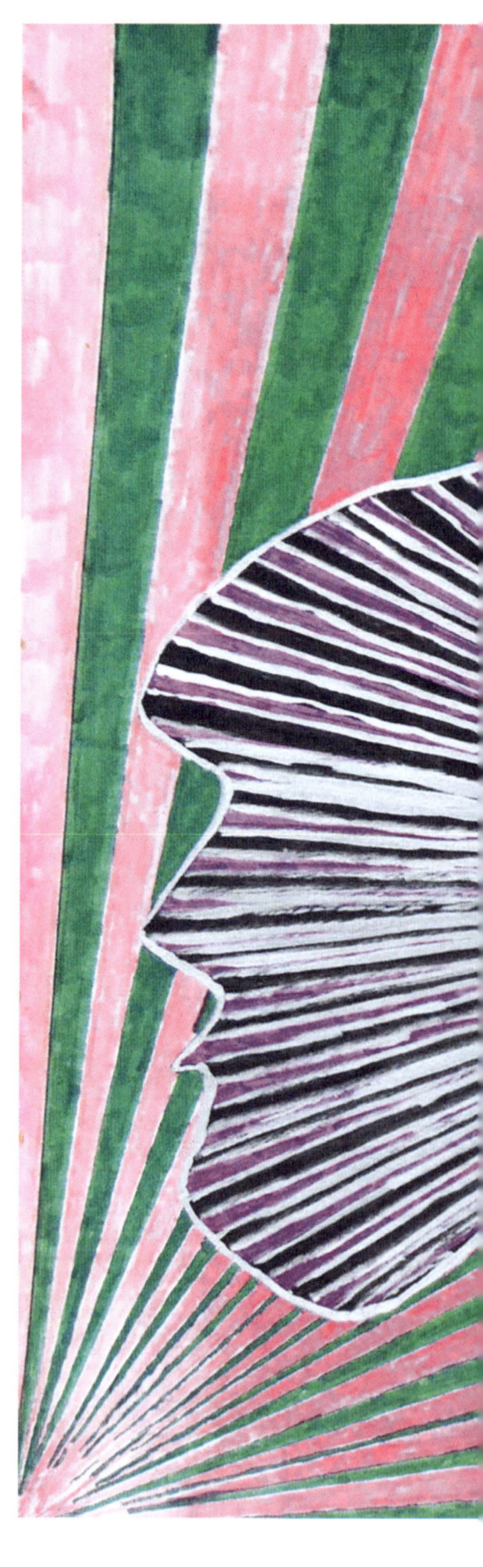

Cousin John, 2010

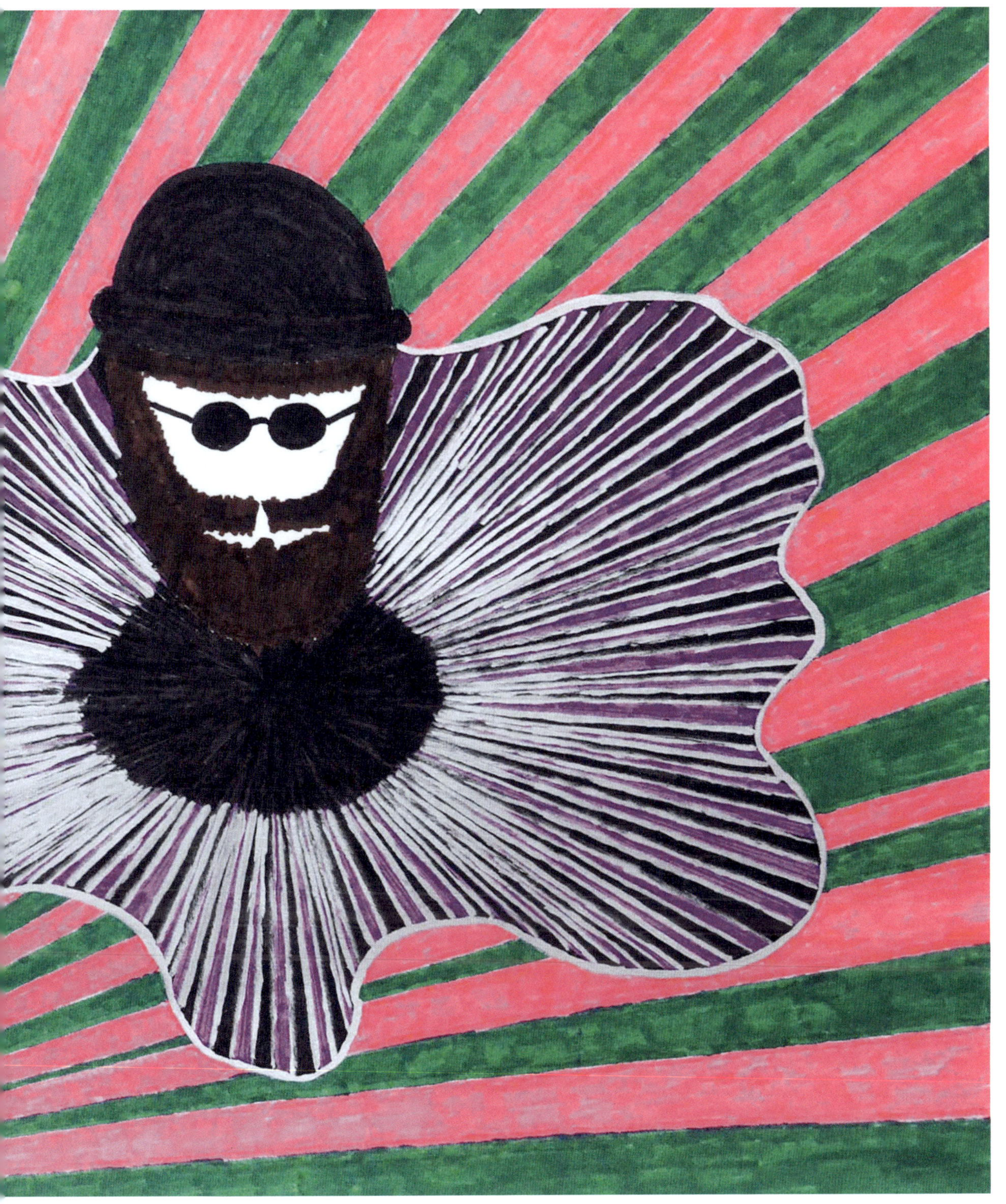

You would have loved my cousin John. He was lovely. He's dead now. You wouldn't like him now. But you would have loved him then.

He was one of those guys that people liked to call a loony, you know? He was a bit of a nutter. But I'm always suspicious when people do that: 'Oh, you'll love him, he's a loony!' You go: 'Oh, fuck.' But he was a great guy — very bright, very funny.

I'll give you an example. He could be quite frightening. Do you re-member — most of you will be too young — there was a campaign in petrol stations: 'Put a tiger in your tank'? Well, just after that, there were other campaigns: 'Make your car look like a racing car.' There were numbers and things you stuck on. And one that never quite took off was: Bullet Holes. You peeled them off a card and stuck them on your car. You looked like you'd just driven past Al Capone, you know?

John had them. On his glasses.

He used to quite frighten people. 'This is my cousin John.' 'Oh, Jesus Christ!' But he was a lovely guy.

He taught me so much. Useless stuff. Like, he taught me how to slice up a banana inside the skin. I've had endless fun with that.

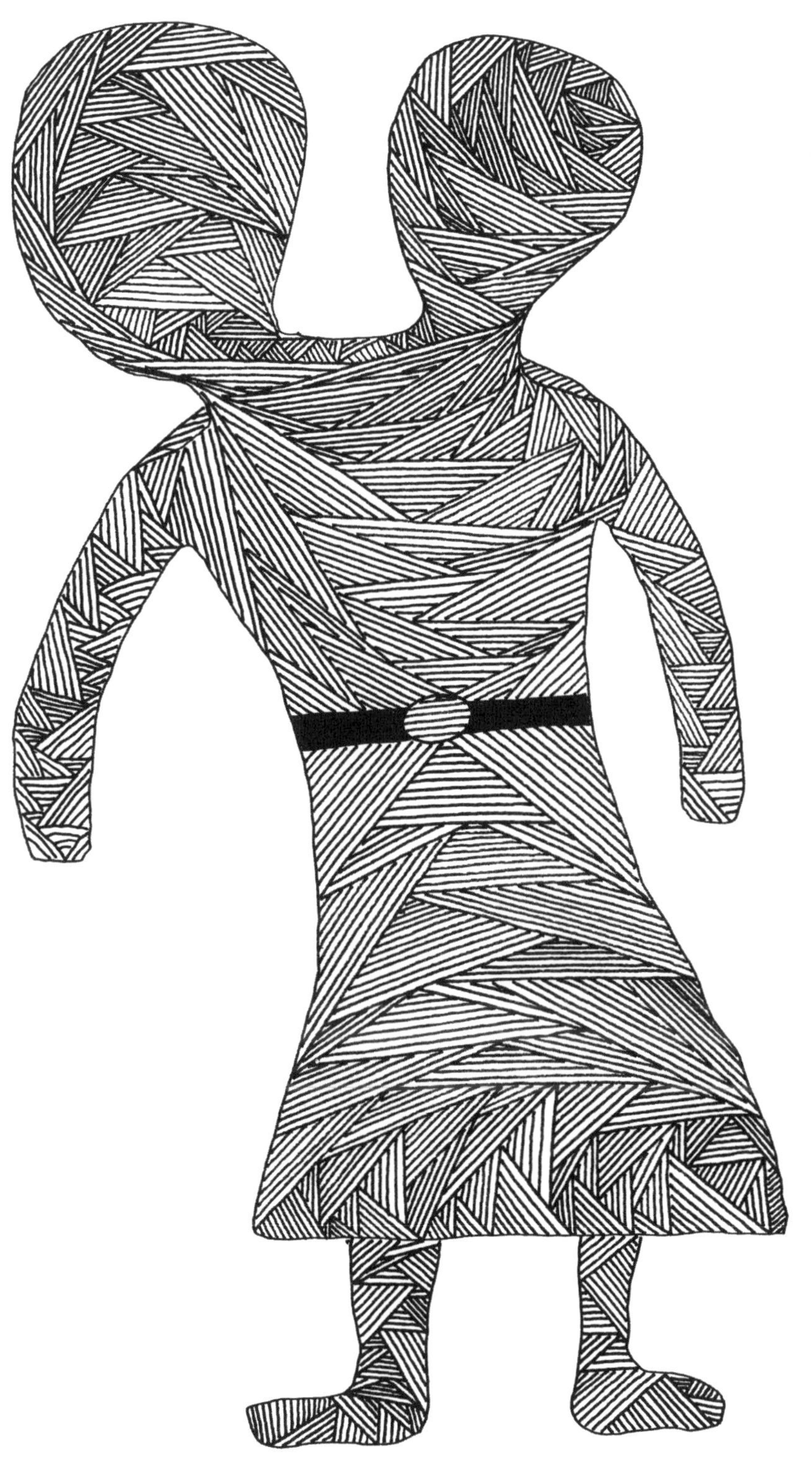

I remember when Cousin John and I toured in France, hitch-hiking. We were living in a youth hostel in Dunkirk and when you had food you'd keep it in these cubicles in the kitchen that were open to everybody. You could just steal stuff. We'd steal a banana and he'd get a sewing needle. And he would hold the banana as vertically as you can hold a banana, and he'd come down an inch and push the needle in and — swish-swish-swish — across, horizontally, and then he'd pull it out, then down half an inch and he'd do it again, then down half an inch and do it again, until you got to the bottom. Then you put it back where you got it.

And you'd wait for the owner to show up. Which he eventually did. And as soon as he'd lift the banana and went to peel it you'd turn away, and he'd do that: plun-plun-plun-plun-plun! 'Fuck's sake!' And you'd say, 'What is it?' 'The banana was sliced inside its skin!!' And he spends the rest of his life trying to prove it to you.

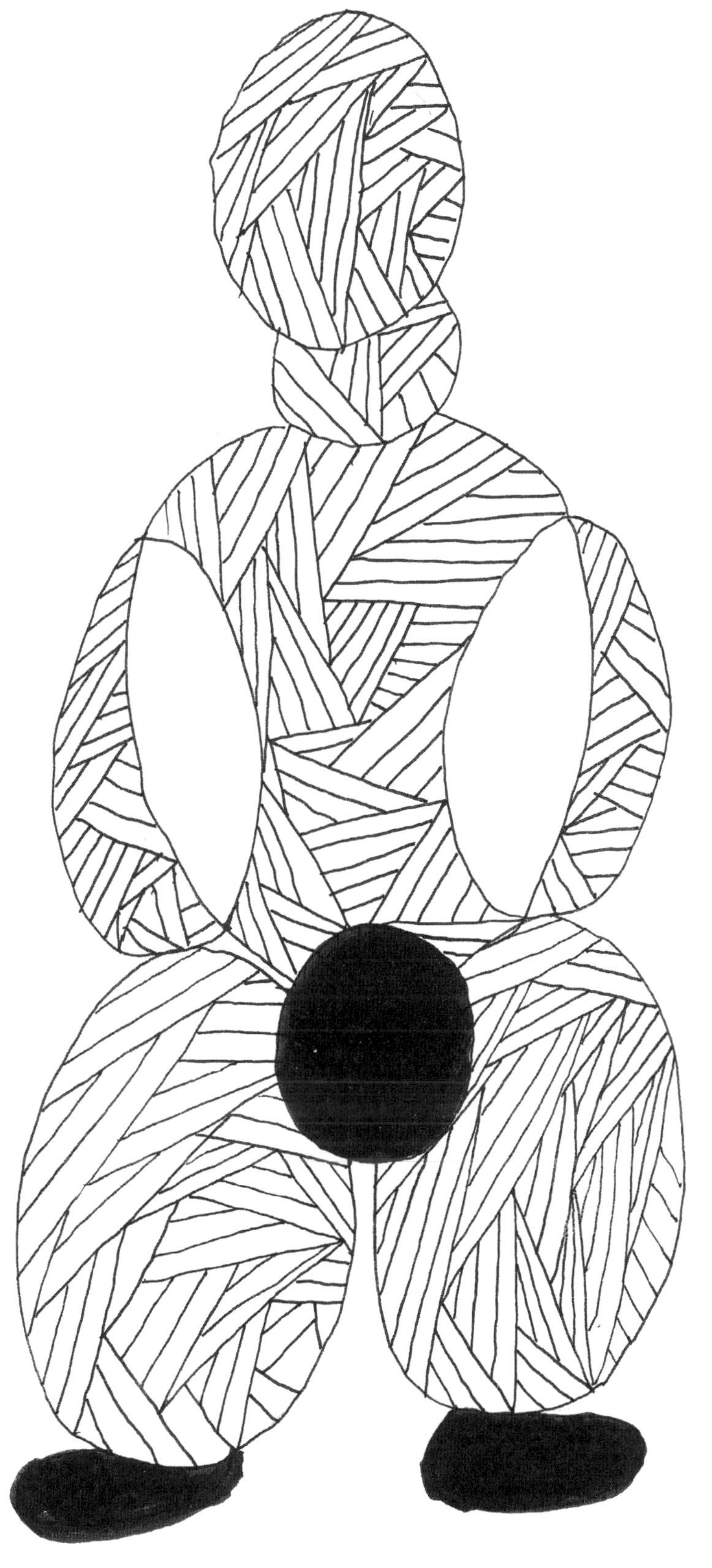

Boy With A Sporran, 2011

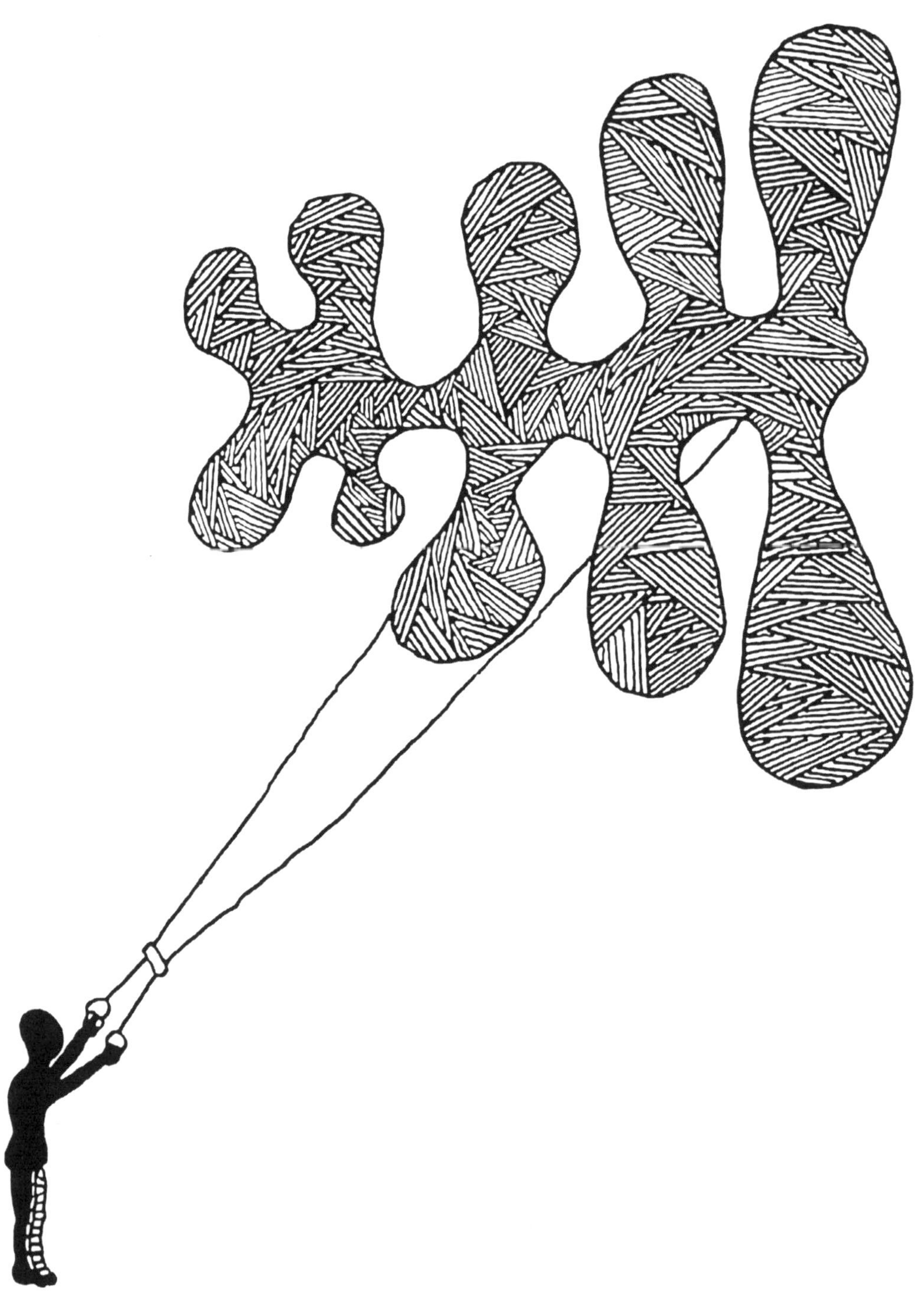

Go Fly A Kite, 2015

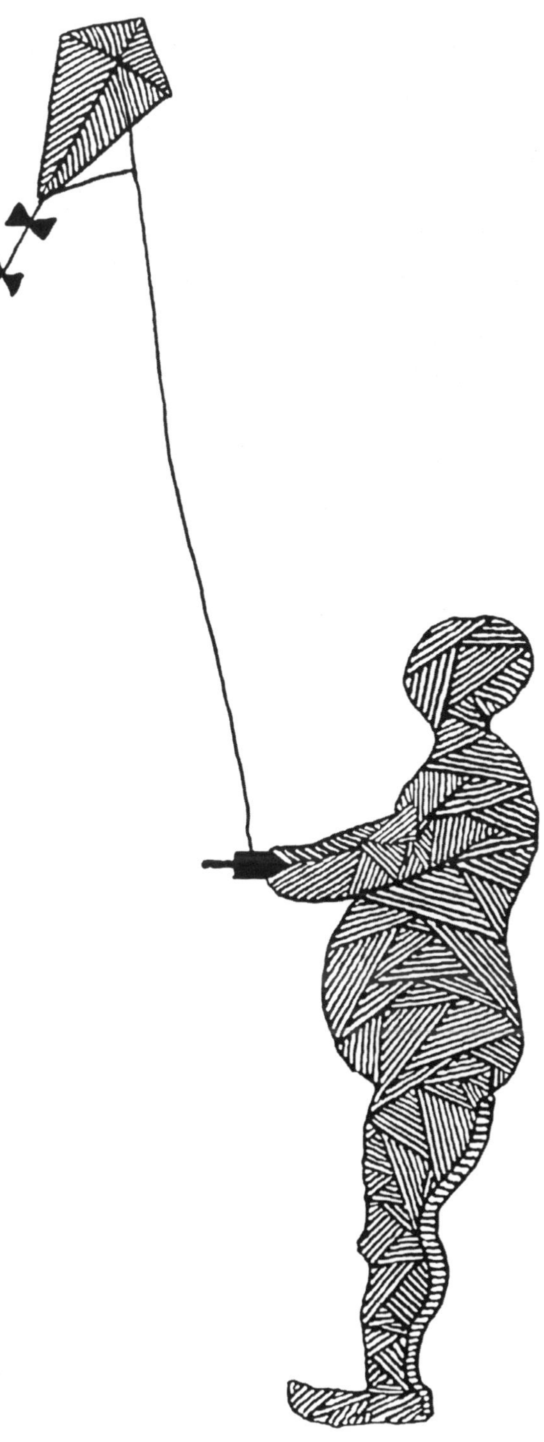

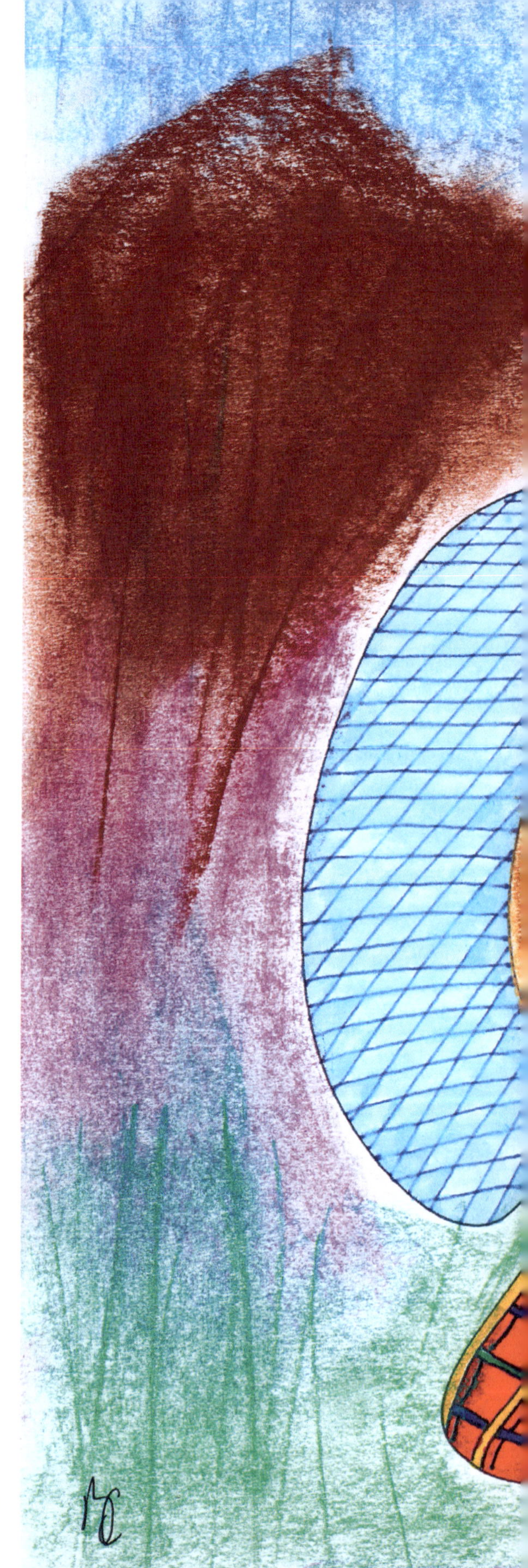

Hamish's Big Stone, 2010

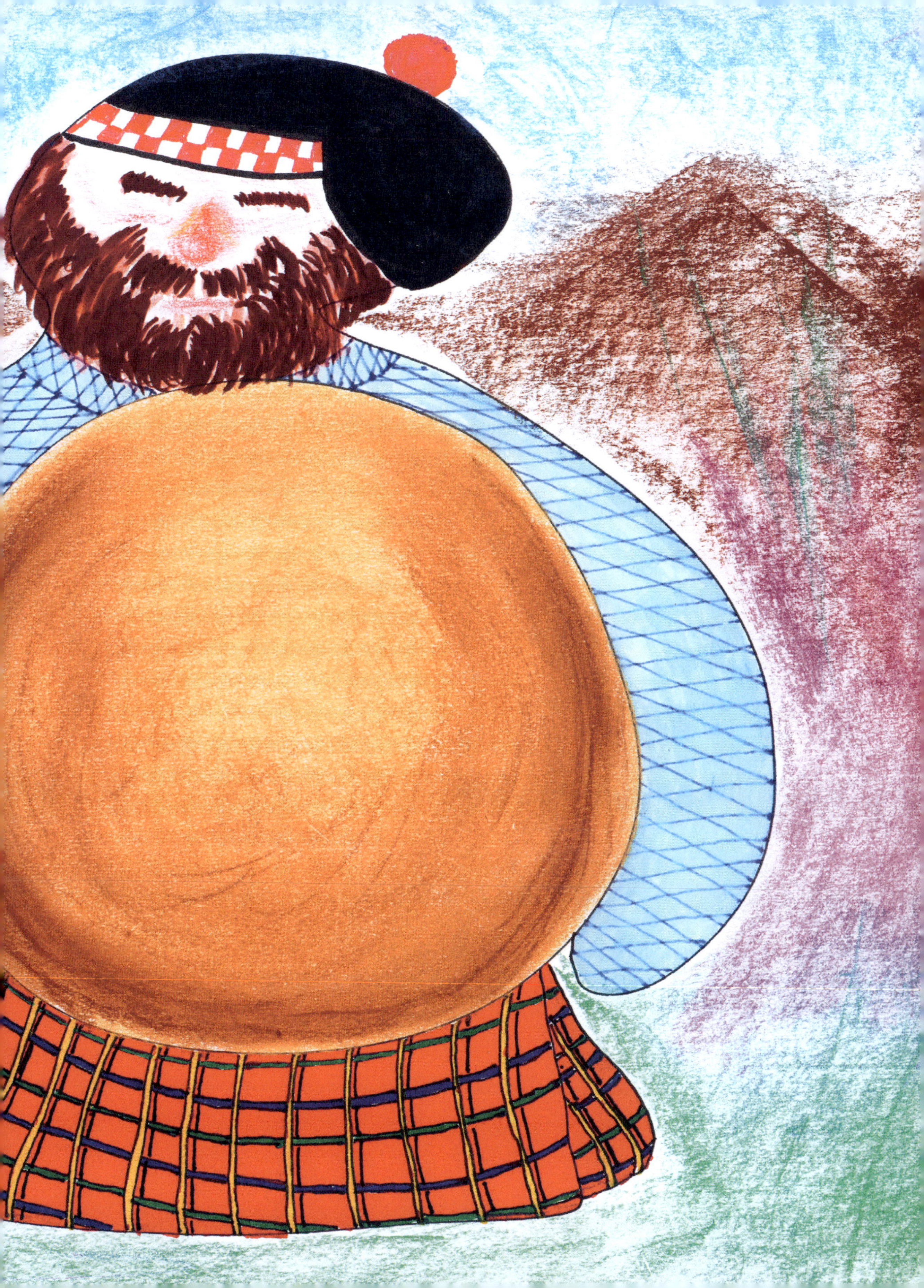

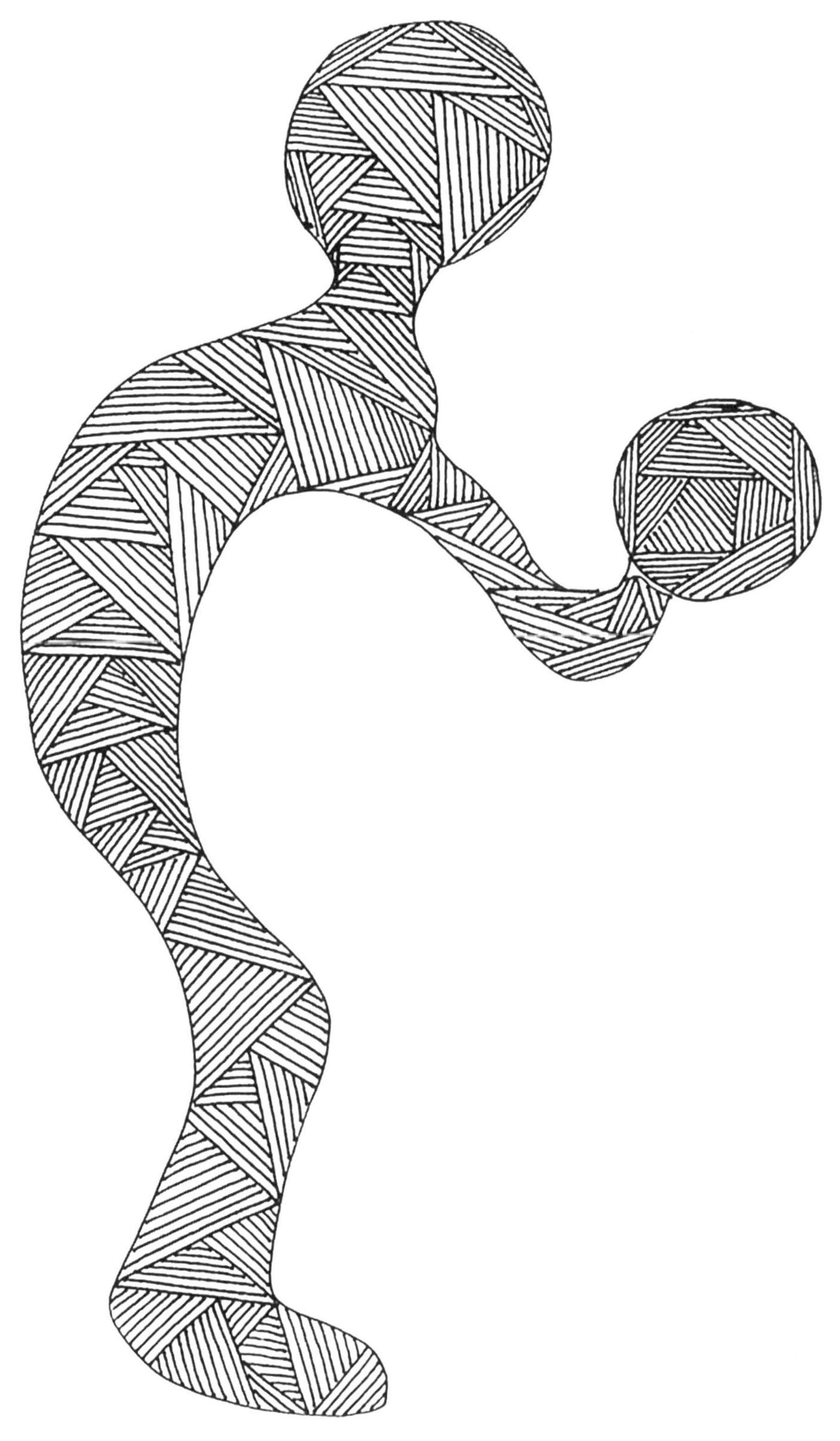

Night At The Bools, 2012

Another thing John used to do, which I found great: he would steal an egg and he'd get the same needle, or one very like it, and he'd put a hole in the top of the egg. And a hole in the bum. Then he would blow the egg into a frying pan. Phhhhhhhhhh. Then he would get a sheet of toilet paper — you know that hard stuff that hurts your arse? — and he would write on it, 'Sorry, I was starving!' Then he'd roll it up real tight, shove it inside the egg, and put it back where he got it. But maybe my favourite … For some reason he had a dislike of people who went to bed with their socks on. And you know in these hostels you sleep in dormitories? Well, we would lie there waiting, watching people going to bed, and eventually he would see somebody and go, 'Billy, nine o'clock, blue socks …' 'Right, OK.' We'd wait until the guy was sleeping, we'd creep up and roll the sheets back from his feet, to expose the socks, take one sock off, and put it on top of the other one.

You'd see the guy in the morning, looking for his sock. 'What the fu—? Has anybody seen a blue sock?' Eventually he puts on his hiking boots with one bare foot and one not. And he hobbled off.

I've always wondered how he got on when he got home and was undressing. 'Jesus Christ! How did that get on there?'

John was great. He was a funny man.

He had a French phrasebook that he'd got from his father, who fought in France during the war. You never saw women like it, the bewildered expressions, when he whispered in their ear, 'We have reason to believe there are Germans hiding in your cellar.'

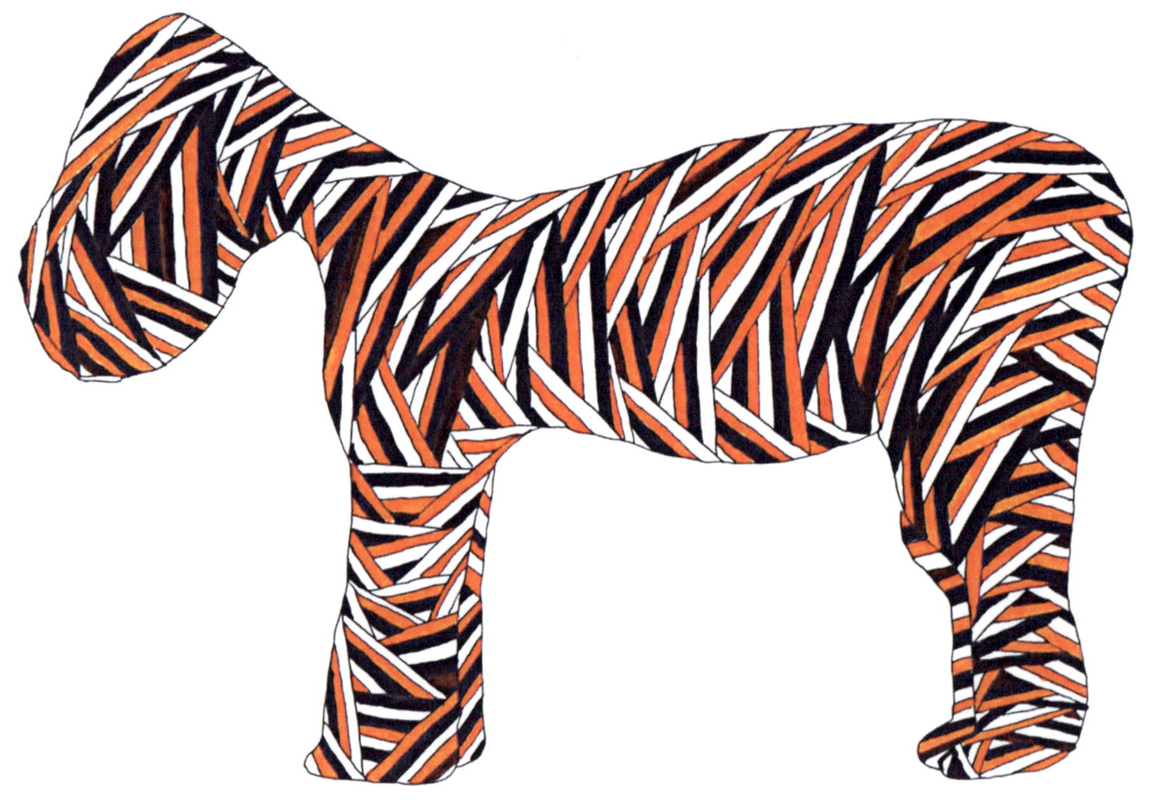

Glaswegian Dog, 2019

like the rain. If you're born in Scotland or Ireland, you have to like the rain, because it's there whether you want it to be or not. I mean, these two countries: they didn't get green by mistake.

It pelts down there. And that's sort of a good thing. It makes your skin lovely, and you have a bad hair day every day of your life — so that's another thing not to worry about any more. You just get yourself a sexy raincoat and get on with it — you get on with life.

I had a campaign a while ago — it obviously didn't work very well — to get the weather people in Britain to stop calling rainy weather 'bad weather'. Because if it rains every day, and they say it's 'bad' weather, you're going to be seriously pissed off most of your life. 'Sorry, ladies and gentlemen, it's going to be yet another crap day tomorrow.' You know, that can seriously affect the national psyche. When people are setting off each day to earn their living, or, even worse, setting off for a nice leisurely day out with the family, they really don't need these characters telling them it's going to be shite out there.

But I do like rain. I taught my children to like it too. They were brought up in Los Angeles, but I taught them how to take their shoes and socks off and just walk around in it and experience it. It's part of life. The fishermen in Scotland always say: 'There's no such thing as bad weather, there's only the wrong clothes.' And they're quite right.

I love it when it rains when I go home to Scotland. It feels natural, it feels normal, it feels right. Rain is OK. As they also say in Scotland, 'The graveyard's full of people who would love this weather.' Right again.

You can do all kinds of things in the rain. You can have all sorts of fun. I used to give people electric shocks in the rain.

It happened when I was young, when I worked as a welder in the shipyard in Glasgow. One of my friends at the time, who was called Alex Mosson – he still is called Alex Mosson, actually – who's since been the Lord Provost of Glasgow and all kinds of grand and important things. But back then he was just a nutcase like me. He was a carpenter.

He and I would go on to the deck of a ship and look for puddles in the rain. And if we found a nice big puddle, we'd nod to each other, and I would go down underneath the deck with my electric welding equipment, directly beneath the puddle, and lurk there with my electric welding gear. And he, meanwhile, would stay standing up above, holding a metal rod, and he'd wait until someone walked through the puddle, then he'd quickly knock twice on the deck with this rod, and I'd go – fizzzzzzzzz. And the guy would go flying in the air. 'Aaaagghh!'

We'd do it quite a few times. We'd swap places, take it in turns to electrify the puddle. Up they'd come – knock knock – fizzzzzzz – 'Aaaagghh!' You wondered how high they would actually jump. We were going for world records there.

That was one of the funniest things you'll ever see, certainly in the rain.

So, don't despair when it rains. Embrace it. And use your imagination – have some fun in it. It's an opportunity.

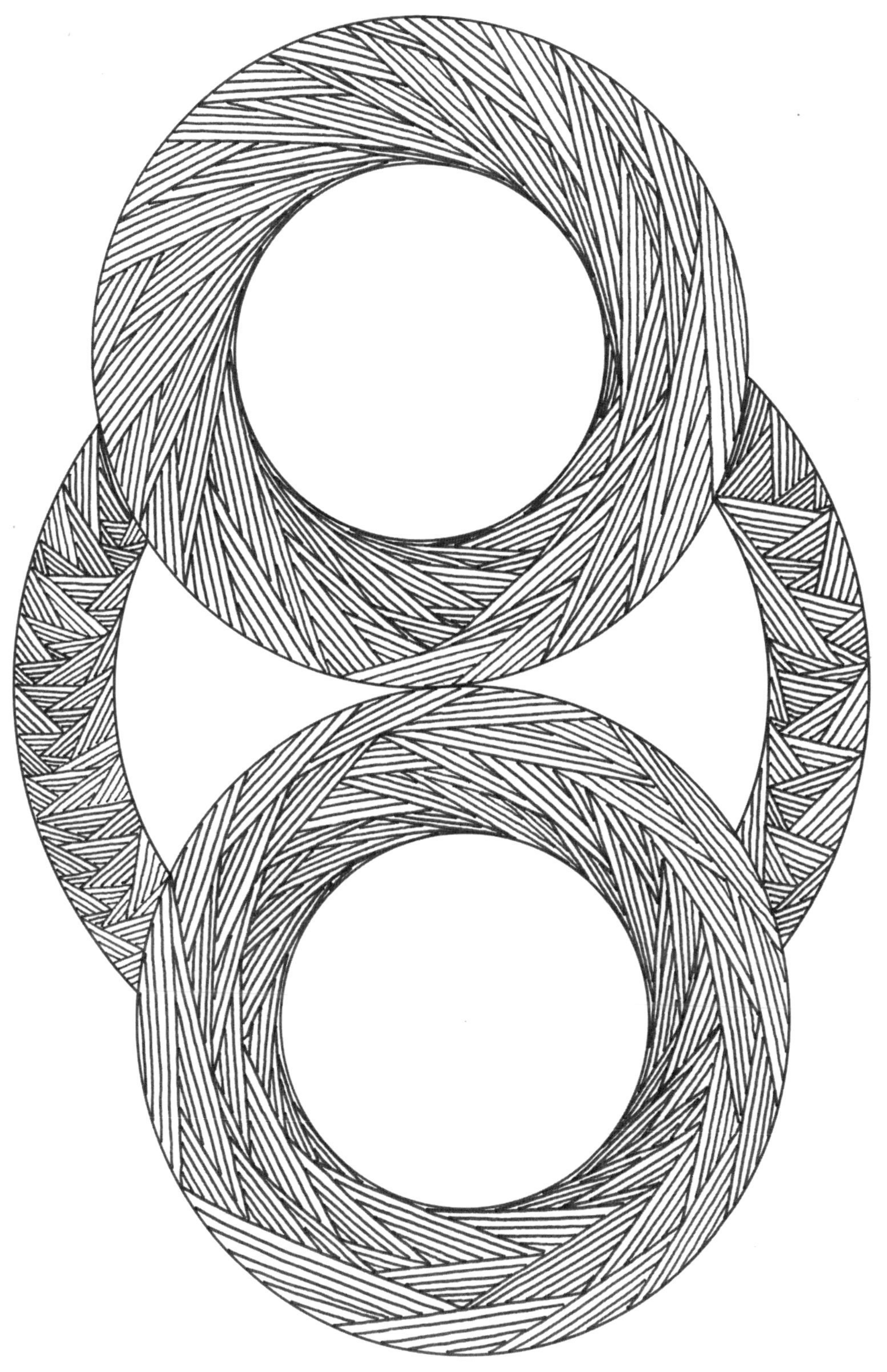

Celtic Bling, 2012

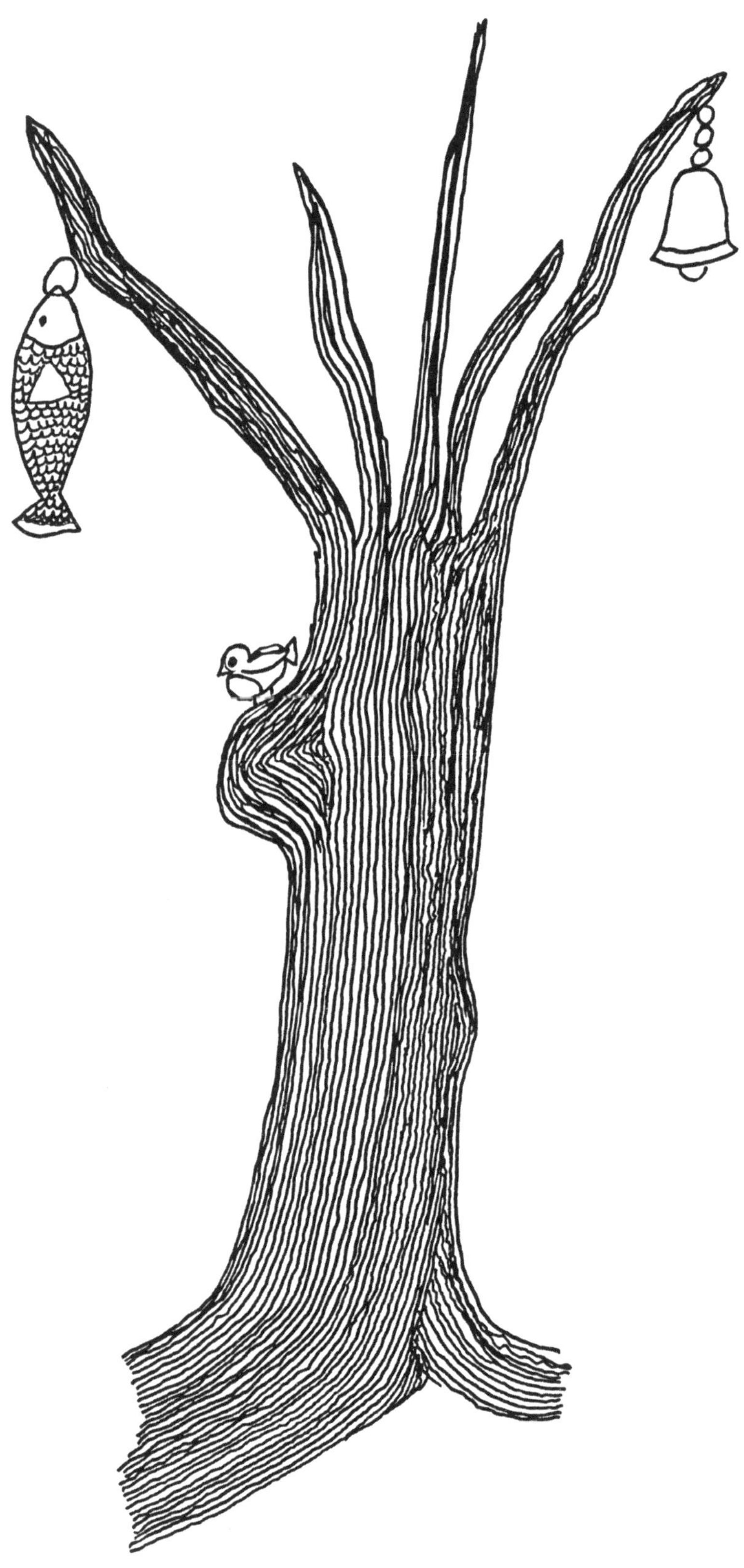

Glasgow, 2019

Oh I wish I was in Glasgow
With some good old friends of mine,
Some good old rough companions
And some good old smooth red wine.
We could talk about the old days
And the old town's sad decline
And drink to the boys on the road.

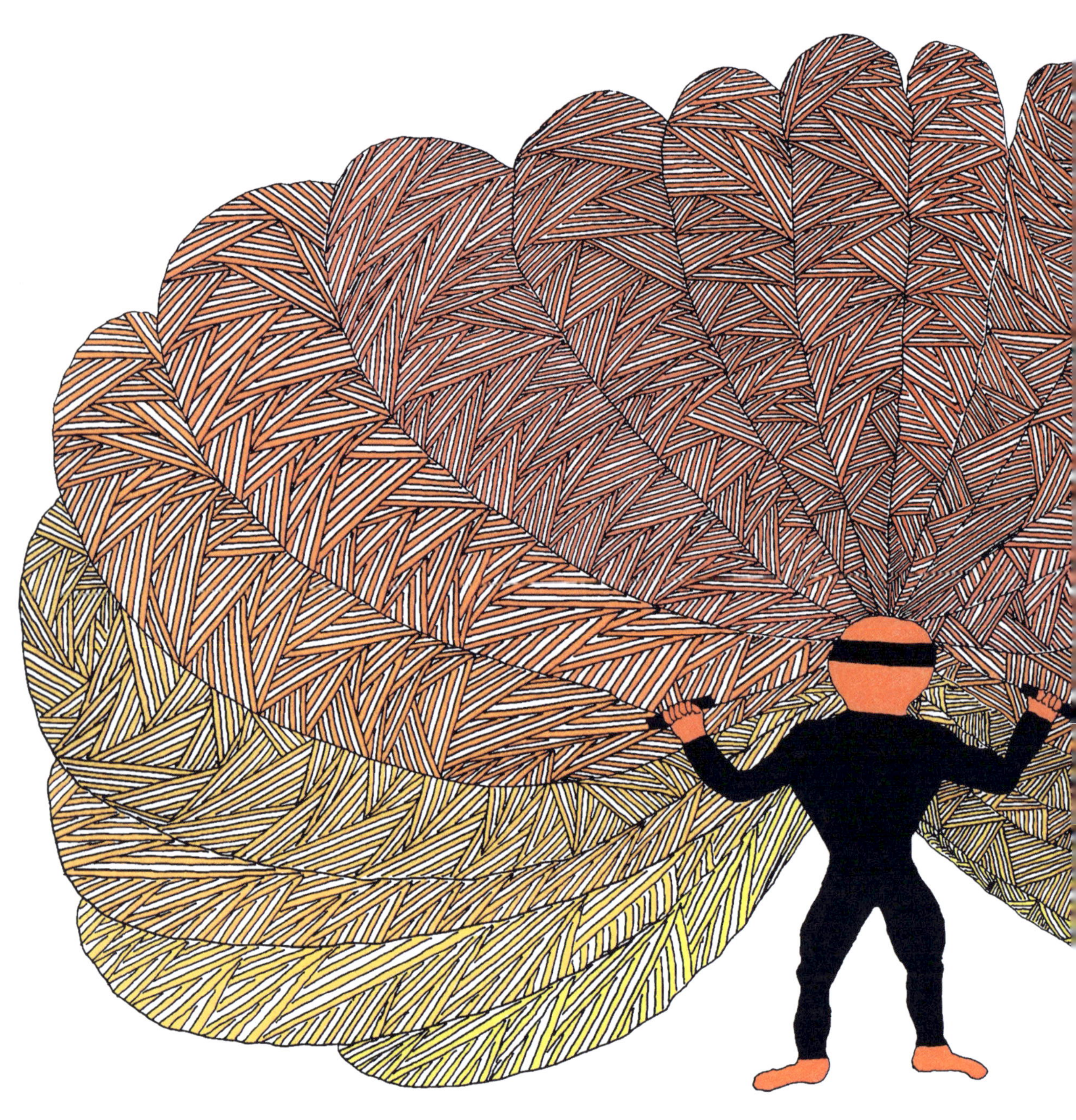

Glaswegian Icarus, 2023

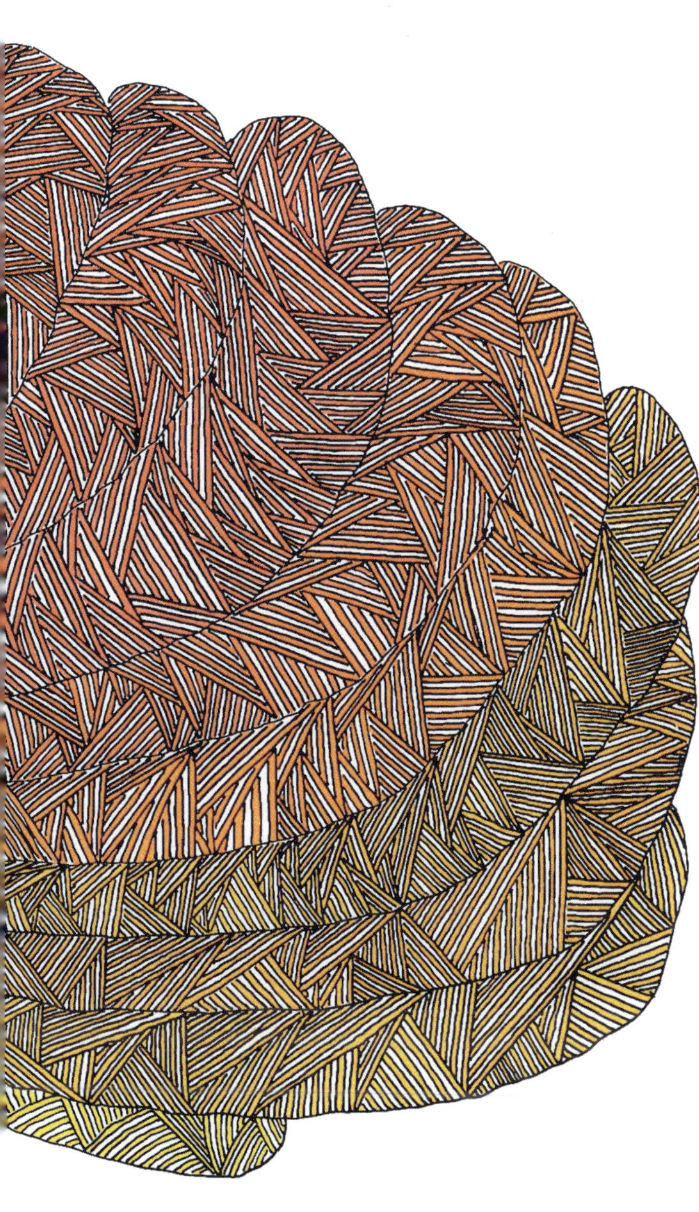

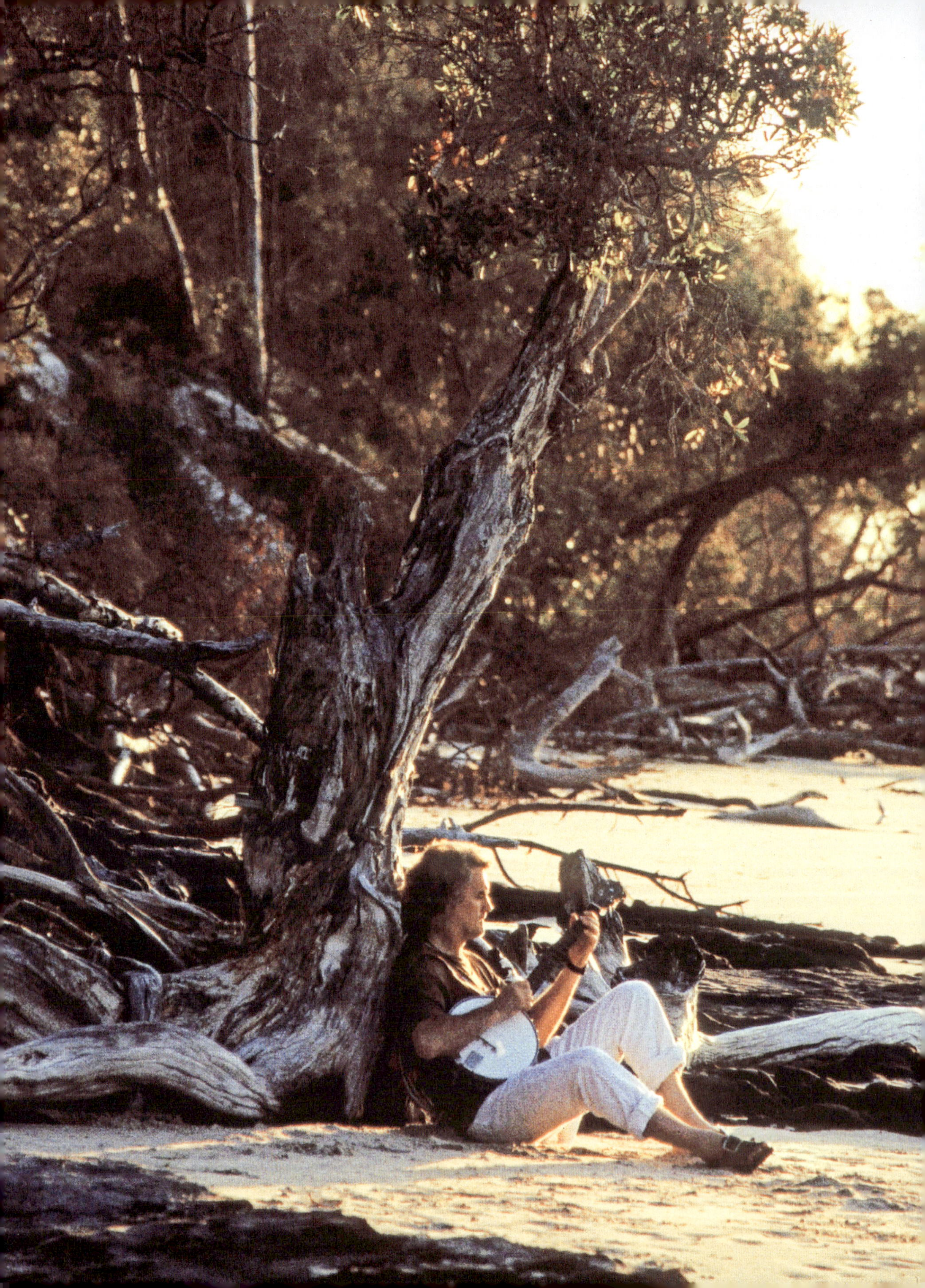

Philosophy

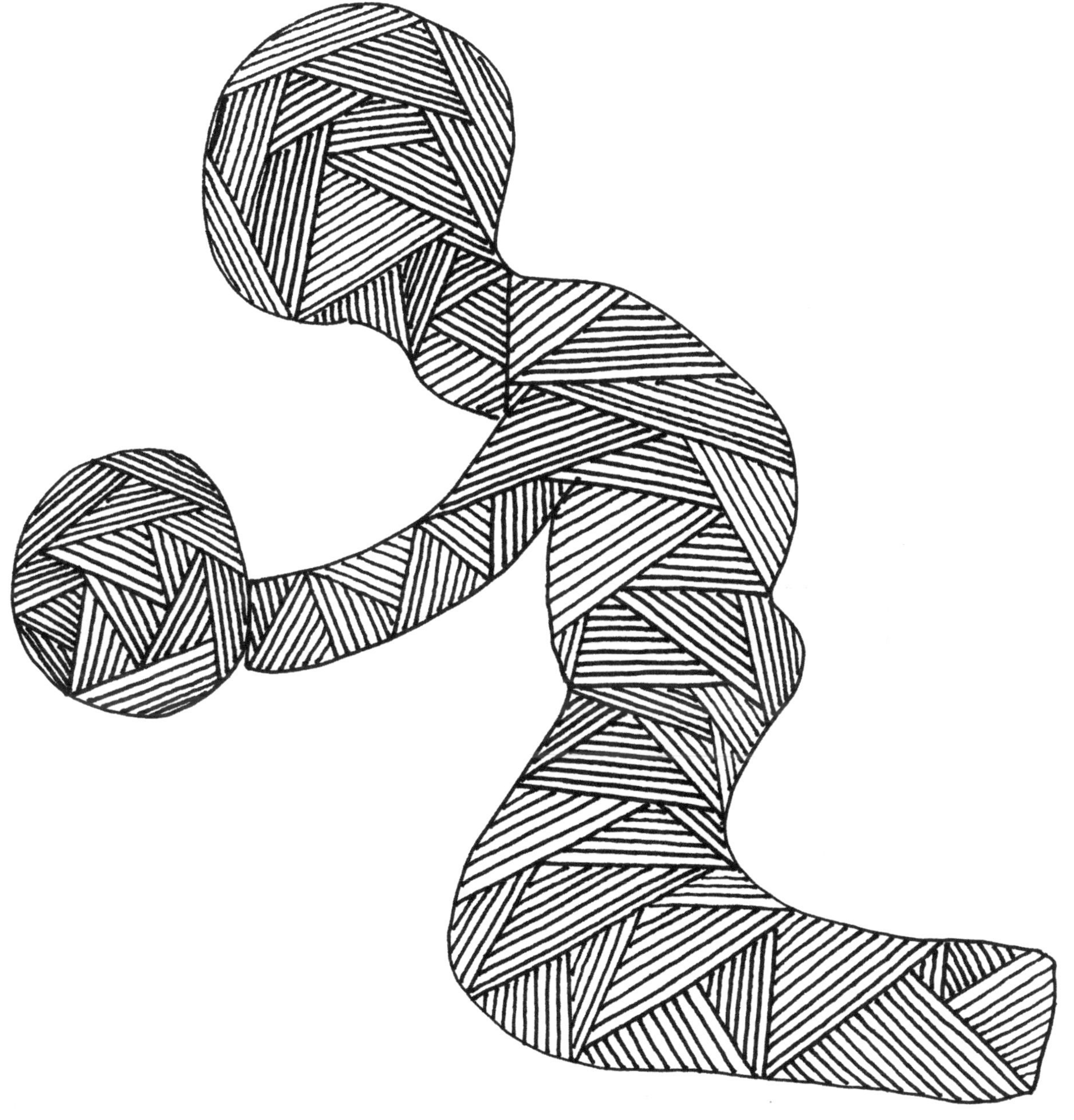

Spiritual Bools, 2012

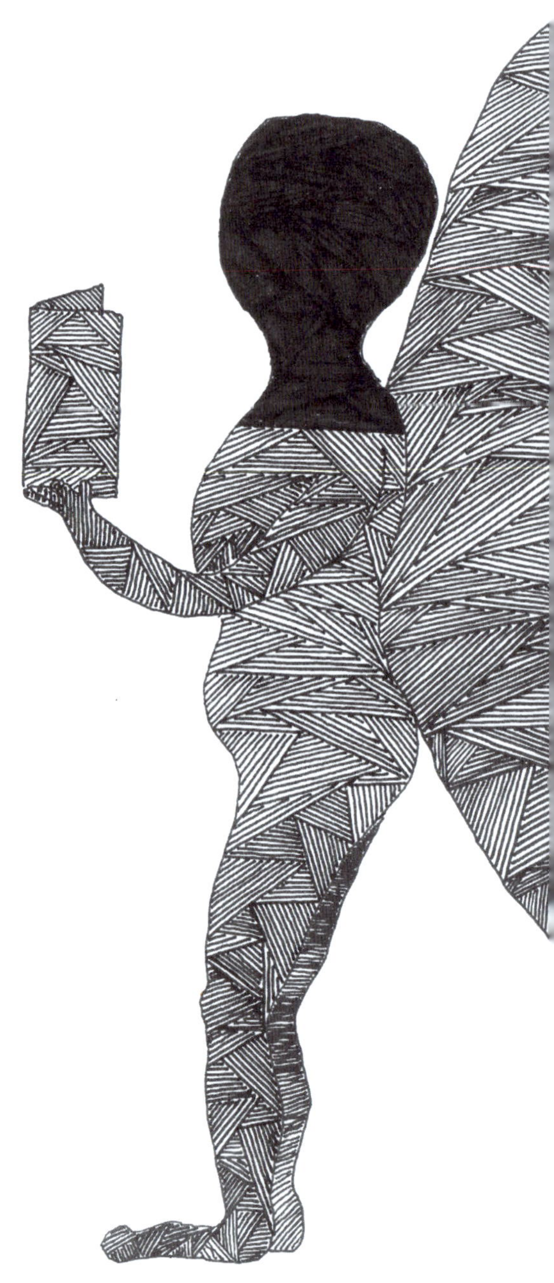

On The Same Hymn Sheet, 2013

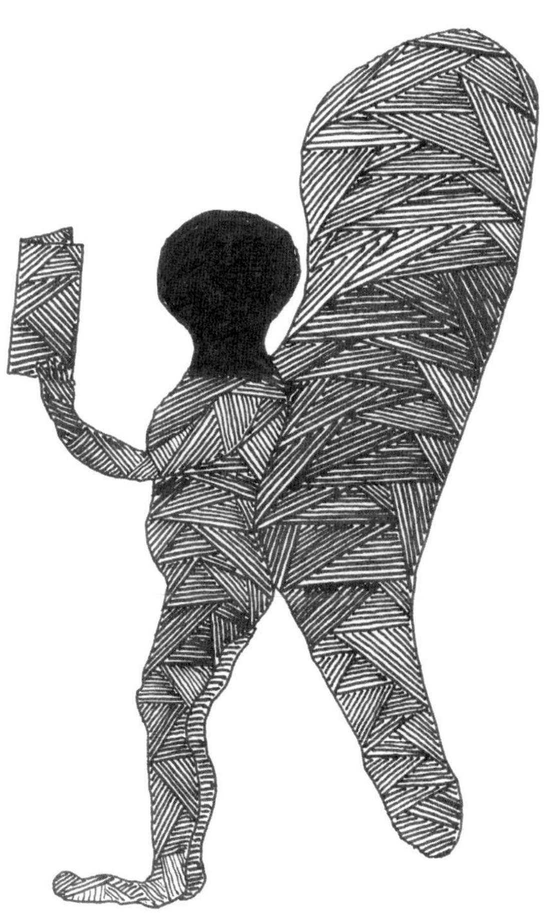
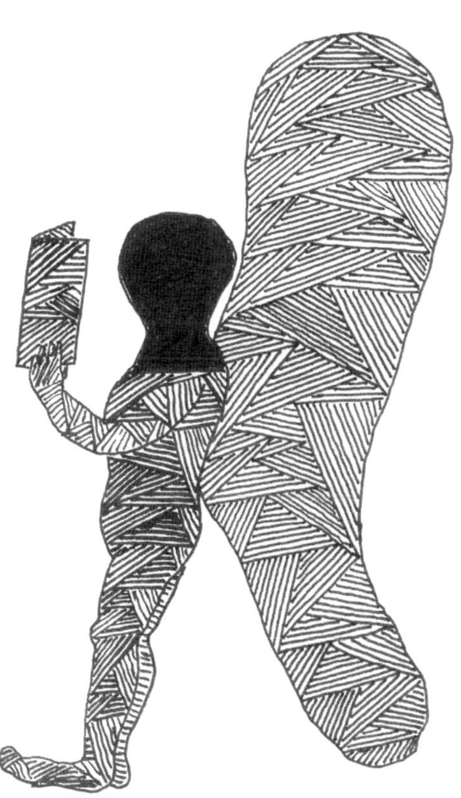

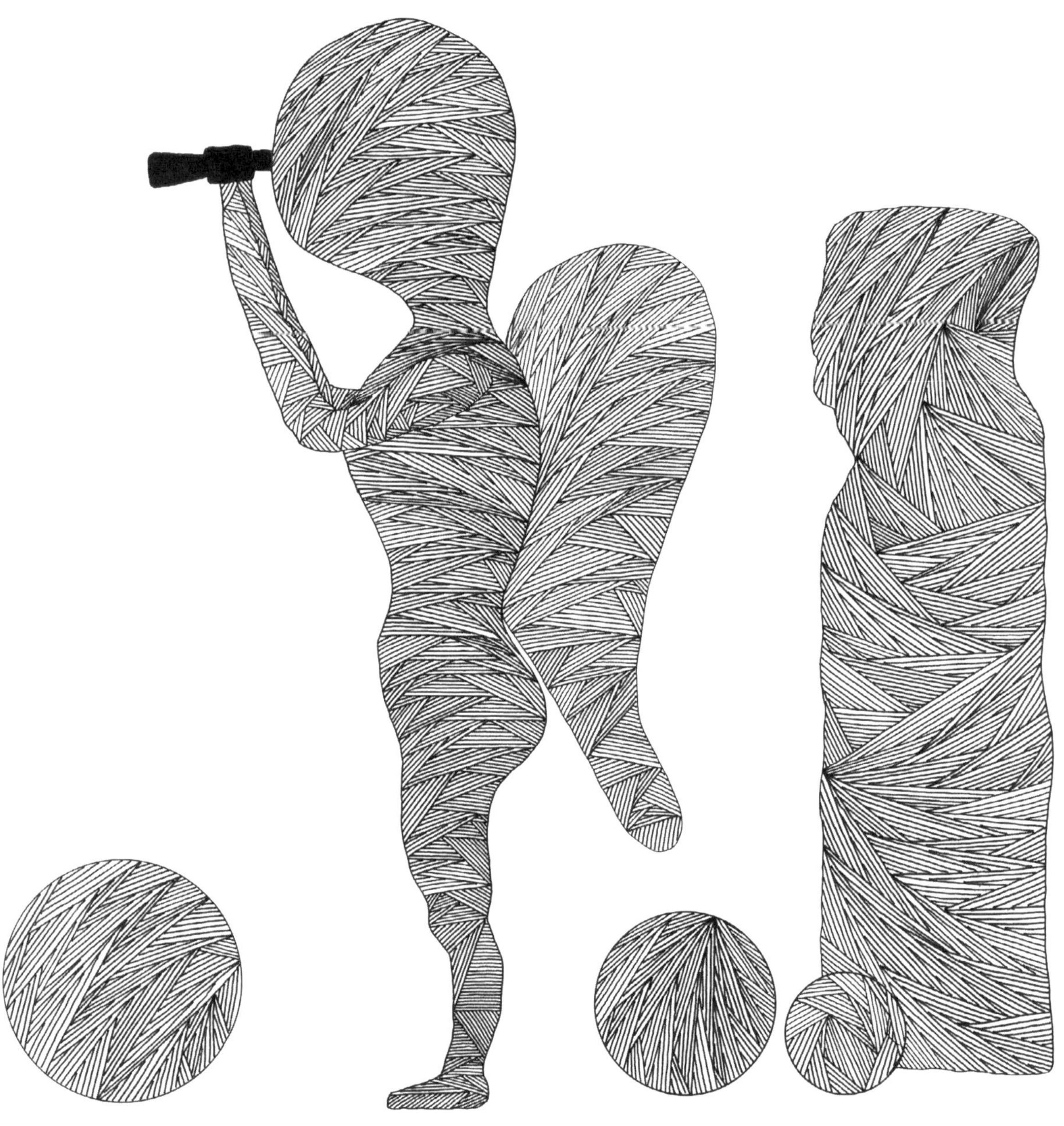

Angel & Pillar Of Salt, 2012

The first piece of art I saw was when I was a boy, and it was a bleeding life-sized statue of Jesus. It scared the crap out of me. I don't believe in organised religion, but I don't believe in dis-organised religion either. When you're an evangelist you can tell people God's talking to you and they'll send you the money. But go up to any psychiatric unit and tell them God's talking to you — they won't even let you home for your fucking pyjamas. I don't get it. Fuckwits coming to your door. I don't care. Fuck off. Fuck-less people. People who've never been fucked. A fuck-free zone. Here's what you can do if you're having trouble with religious nutters coming to your door:

Knockety knockety knock … Don't open the door. You call out: 'Are you here to tell me about God?' 'Yes.'

'Fine. I'll be opening the door in five seconds. I'm naked except for a fireman's helmet. I have an erection. The choice is yours. Five, four, three, two …'

When you open the door, they'll be specks in the distance.

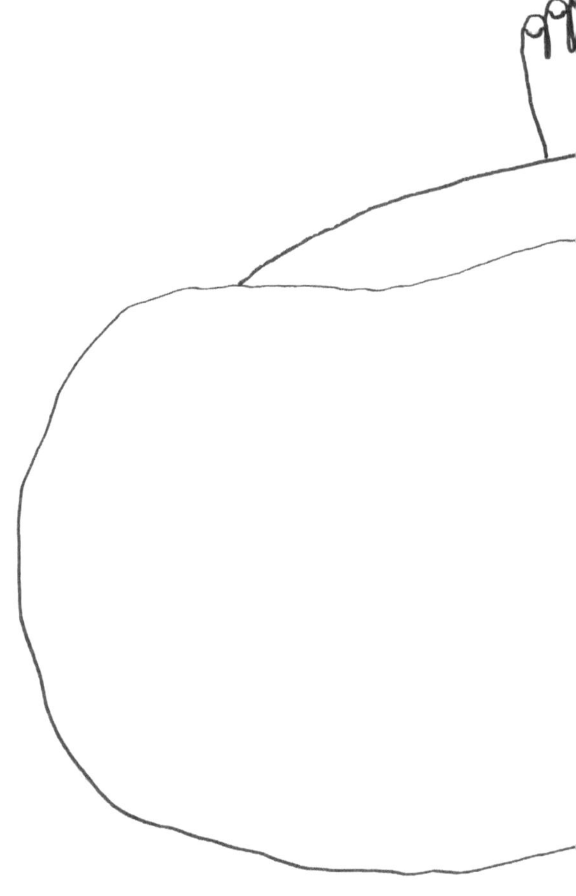

How God Sees Us, 2013

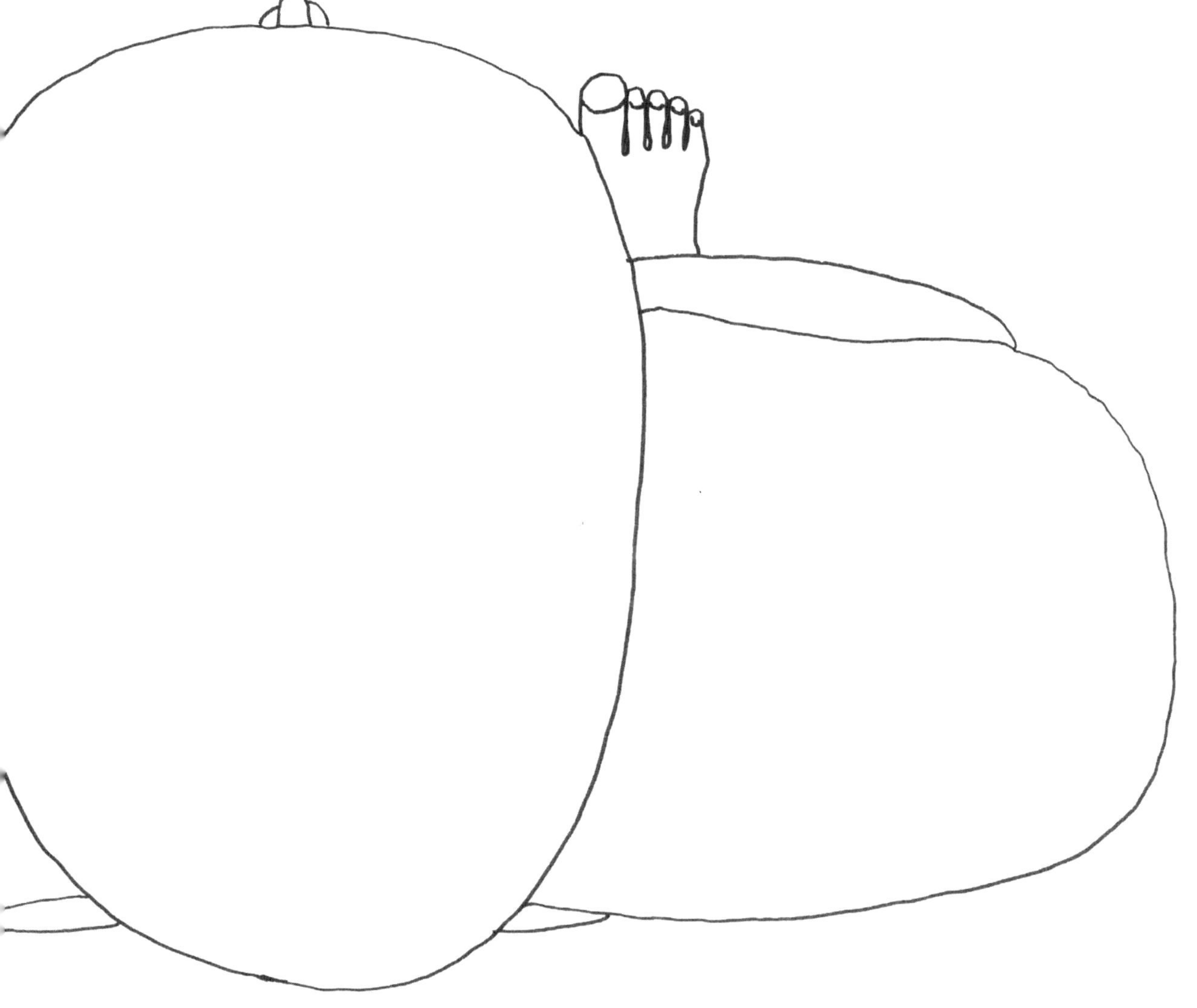

When I was younger, I thought confession was an extraordinary thing. I felt great afterwards. But it wasn't easy, deciding on the right sin for the occasion. My best friend at that time was Joe West. We met in the line to start primary school, and he was my friend for seventy years until he died. When we were eight, we were comparing notes about confession and he came up with a great idea. He said, 'You can make it all up. As long as the last thing you say is "I've been telling lies", you can cancel what you've just said and still be forgiven.' I never tried it, but I think he did. He was braver than me.

It was generally understood that your confession would be confidential. But some priests — like Father Balducci — would throw discretion to the wind and yell, 'WHAT? You're a DISGRACE! That's DISGUSTING!!!' People nearby could hear it. The line outside his door was short compared to the long lines outside the other priests' doors. It was better to go to confession when you weren't in a hurry.

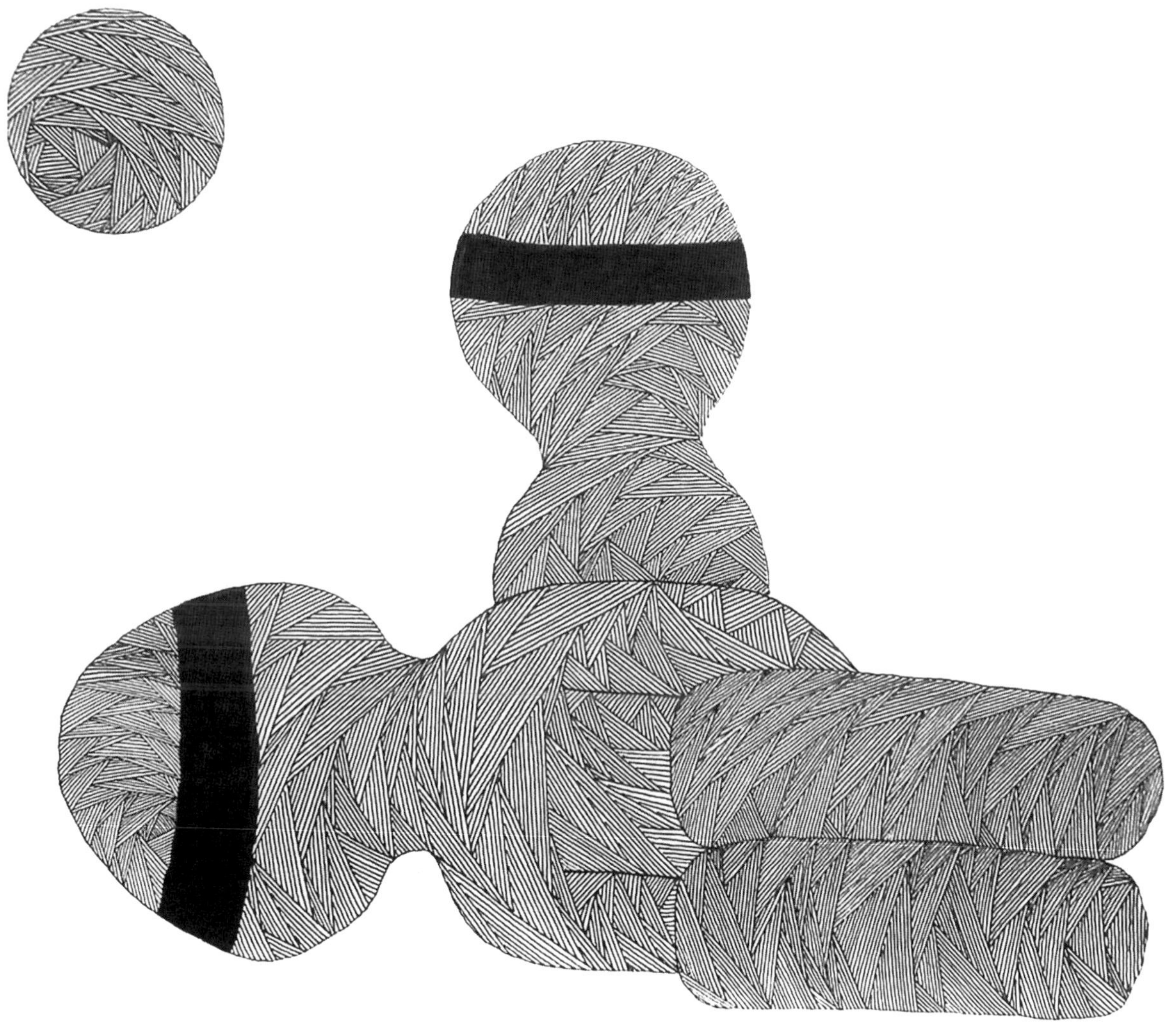

Sharing Secrets, 2012

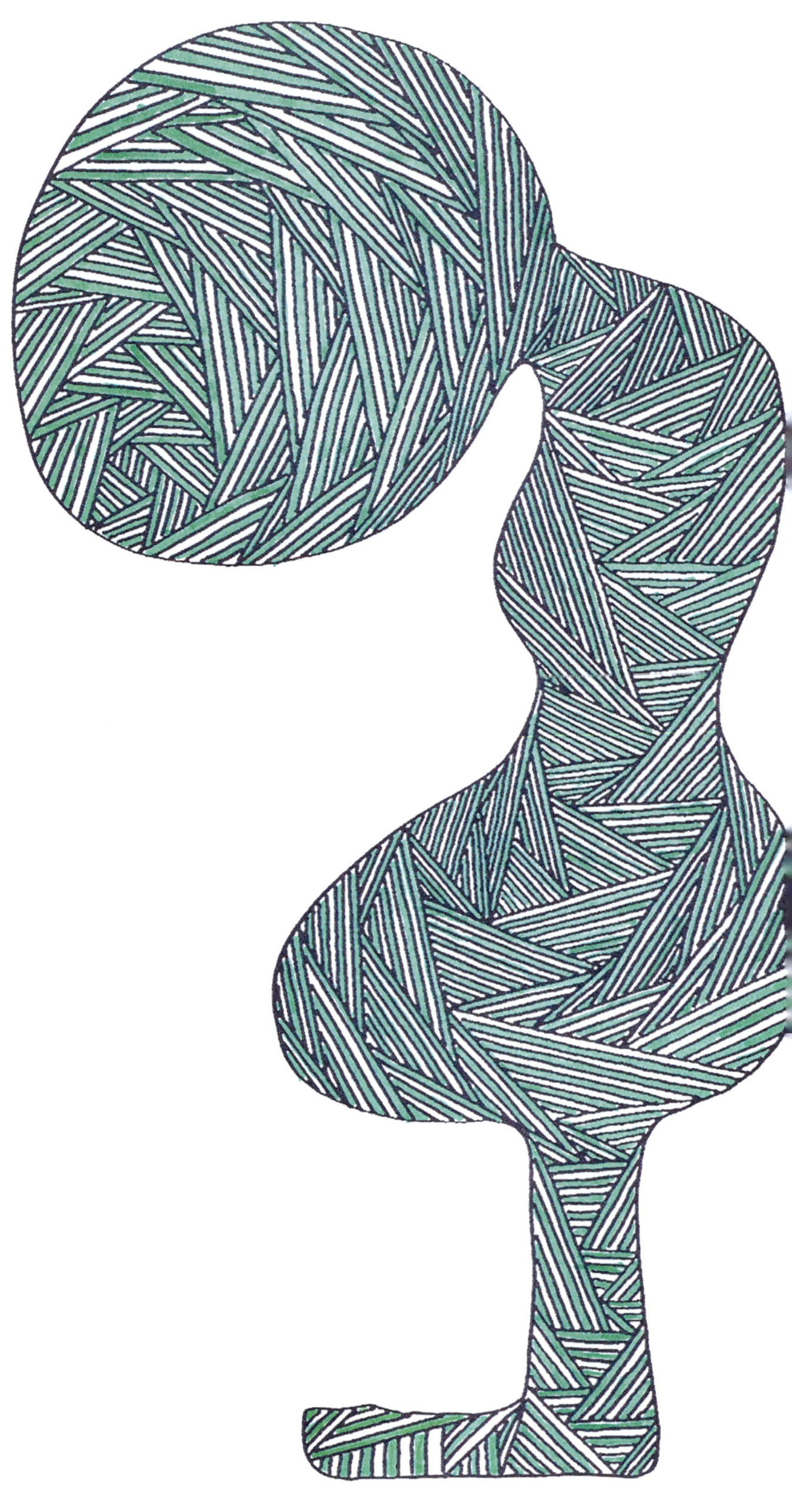

Meditation, 2021

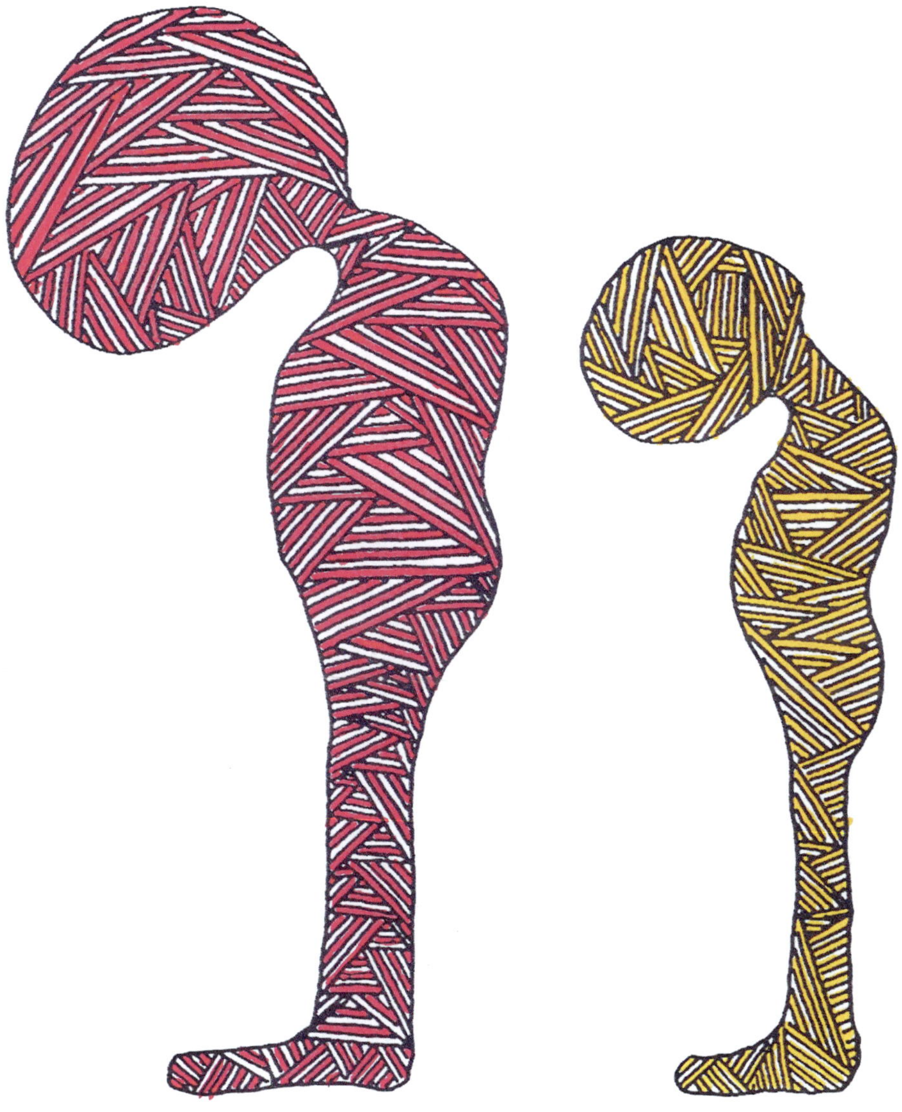

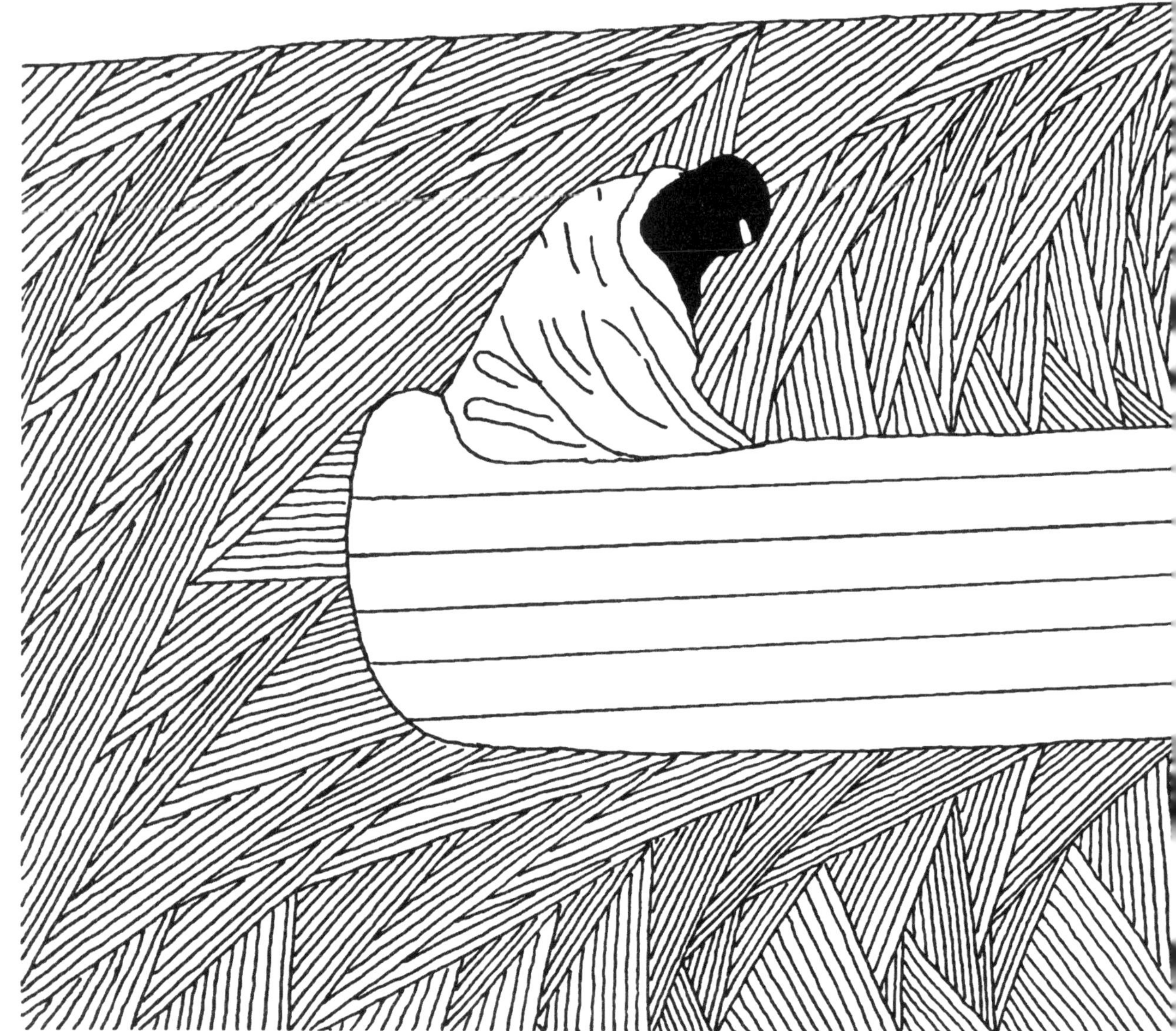

Purgatory, 2018

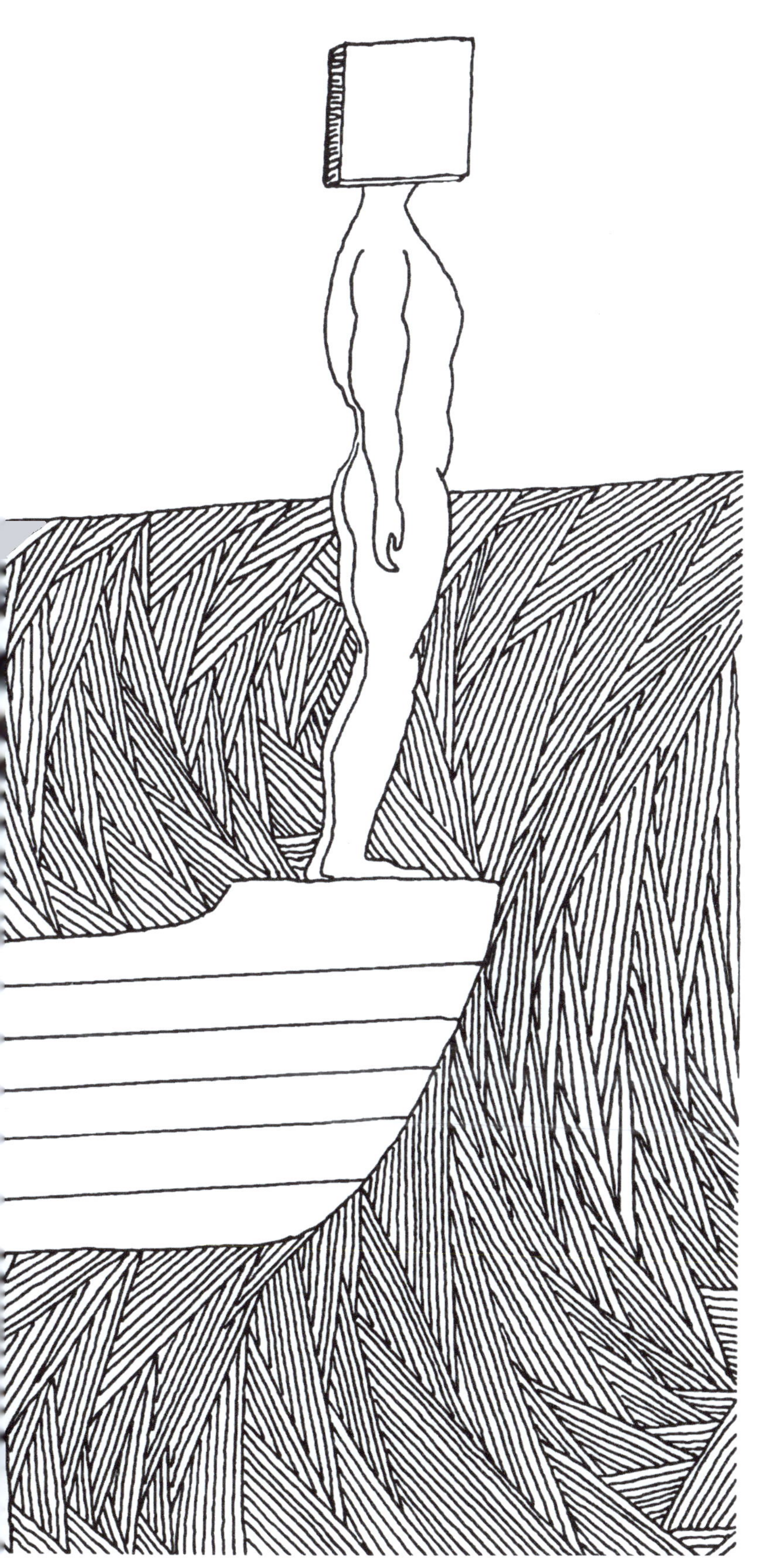

I don't like Born Again Christians. I'm not too keen on Born-the-first-time Christians.

I always wondered why they gave you prayers as a punishment. Wasn't prayer supposed to be a holy and wholesome thing? But back when I was a kid I believed much of what I was told — even when it didn't make any sense — and was happy in the Catholic religion. In fact, I was enraptured by many aspects of the Church. I loved the music and the smells of incense. And the Lenten hymns. It felt good going to communion, and I felt great afterwards. Sometimes I think I'd actually like to go to mass now just to enjoy the service.

I was supposed to be following one narrow religious path, but just down the road in Stewartville Street there was a massive temptation to defect. Abingdon Hall, a bustling centre of evangelical activity, was at number twelve. Unknown to my family, I would sneak into meetings there with my Protestant friends. The leaders were very entertaining. They would tell Bible stories, present slide-shows, and I learned an excellent magic trick there where you fold and tear a piece of paper a certain way, then open it up to reveal the words 'heaven' and 'hell'. Some of the congregation had travelled as missionaries to Africa, and they would tell fascinating stories about villages and tribes. Towards the end of the year, you could put your name down to be given a Christmas present at a community party. They'd have a tinsel-encrusted tree with all the presents under it, and you'd get a jigsaw, a set of watercolour paints, or a toy gun. Best of all, at every meeting we were fed tea and buns. I'd do anything for a sticky bun.

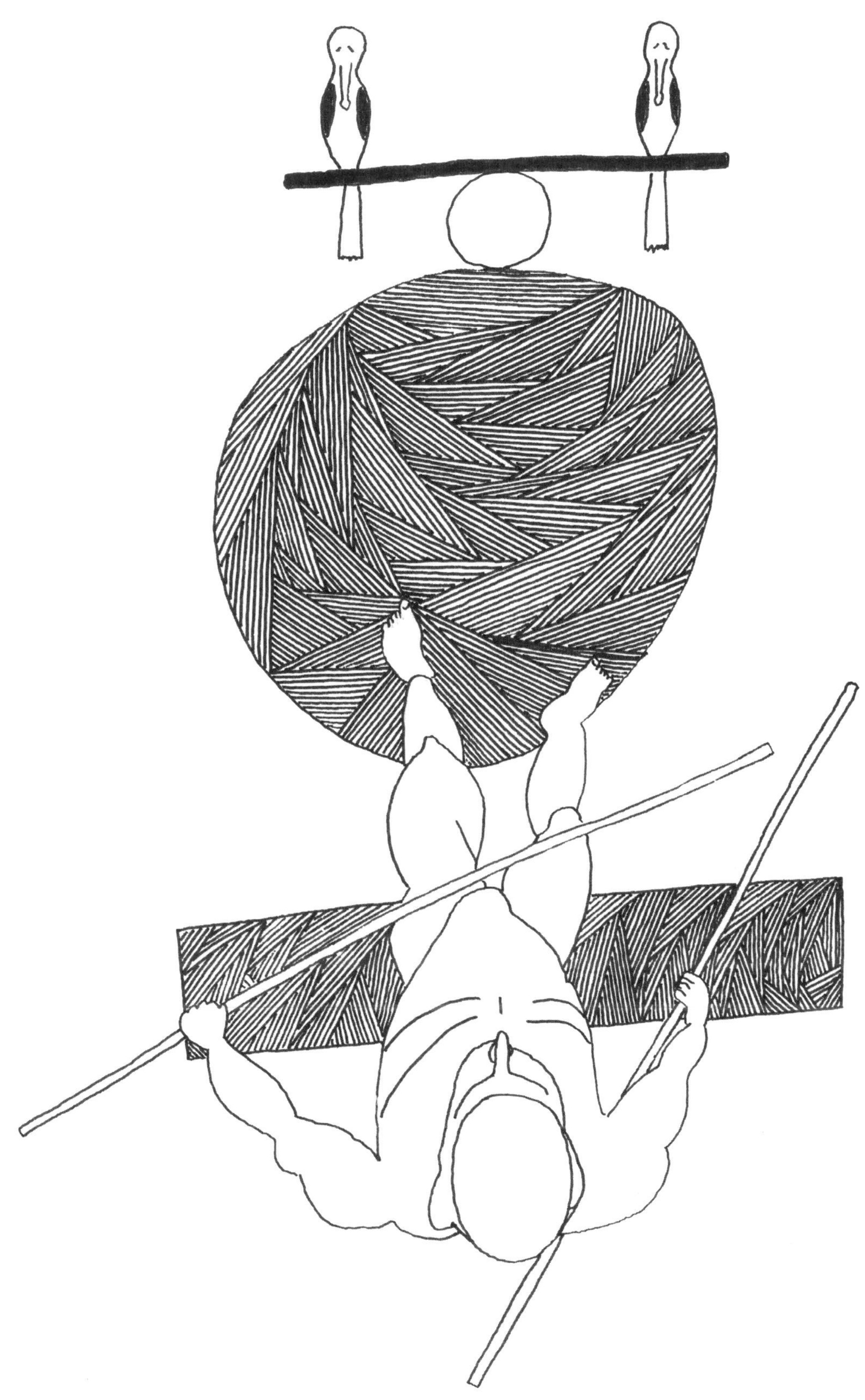

Birds On A Wire, 2018

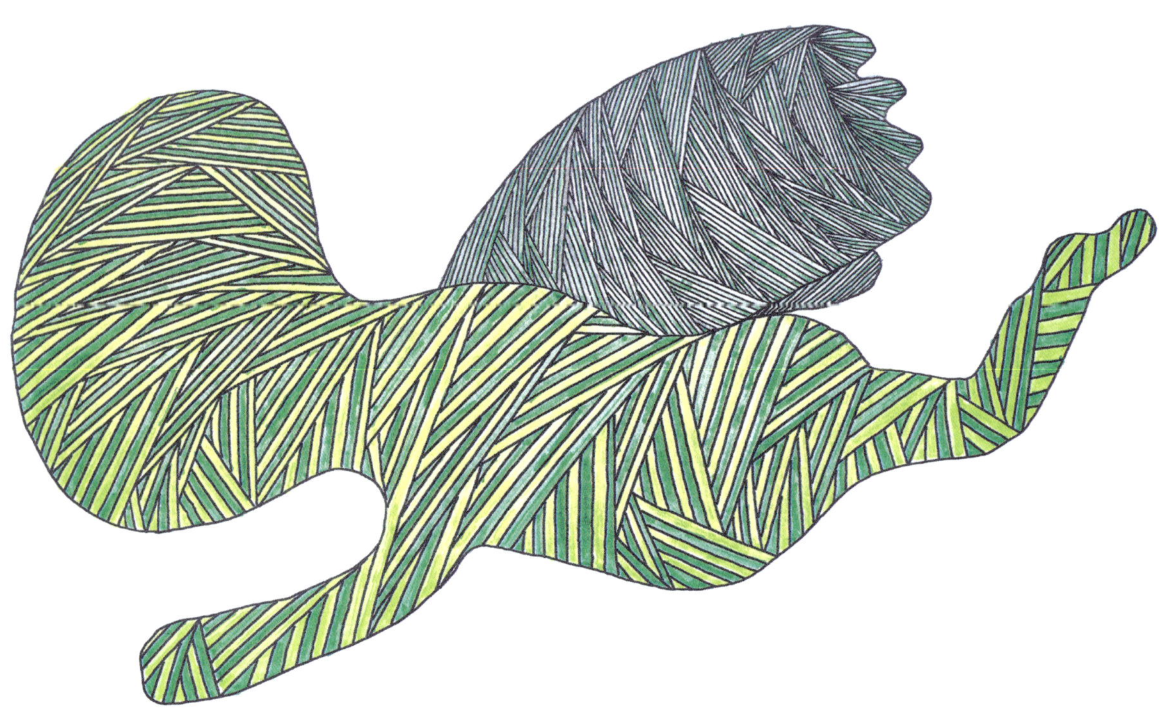

Baby Flier, 2021

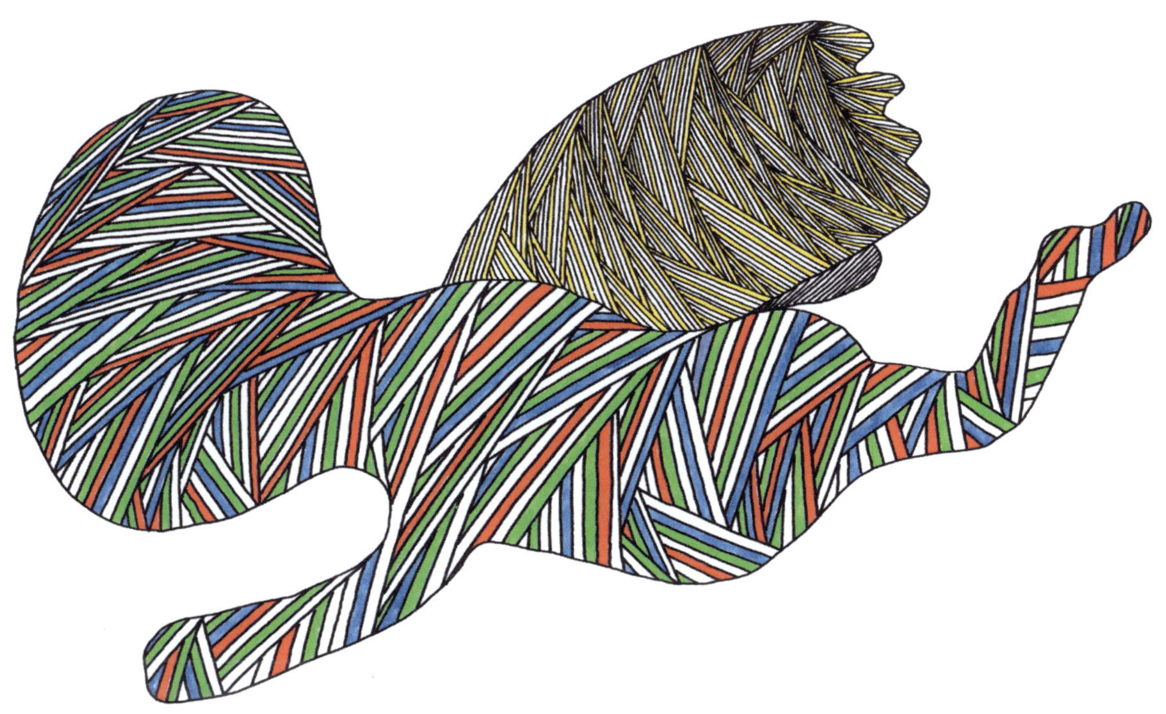

Baby Flier, 2021

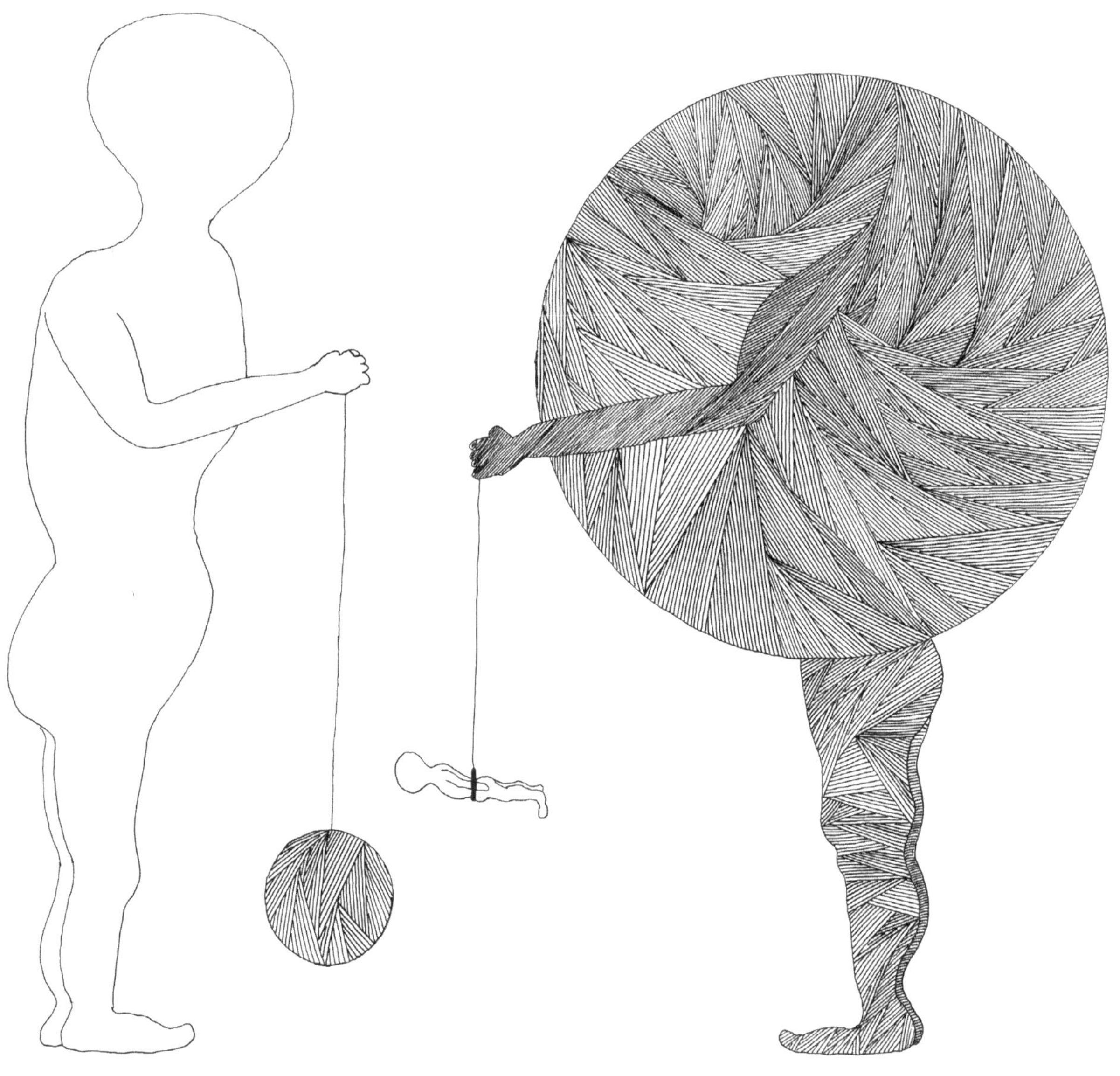

Nightmare, 2012

I've got Parkinson's disease, and I wish he'd fucking kept it to himself. As a matter of fact, I got diagnosed with Parkinson's disease AND prostate cancer the same week. Holy Mother of God. It wasn't too bad, though. I got treated for the cancer and now I seem to be OK. The Parkinson's just rumbles along, doing its thing. It bothered me for a while but when I think about it, I suppose I'm lucky I didn't get something worse. Because I was a welder.

The diseases they talk about now due to welding weren't known when I was in the shipyards. They didn't know about the hazards of asbestos. And men were always dying in accidents too. I was in an accident myself. I fell off the ship into the Clyde. Dropped forty feet into three feet of water and broke my ankle. It was in the newspaper: 'Lucky Bill Falls 40 Feet, Breaks Ankle'. That's what they called me after that: 'Hello Lucky Bill!' It happened when I was pulling on my welding cable. It had joints in it that screwed together to make it longer, but I hadn't fastened them properly. It snapped apart and I catapulted backwards and fell over the side of the ship. Dropped the whole height of the hull, from the deck into the River Clyde. I was exceptionally lucky. I landed in a ten-foot space between two cranes. It was the day before my eighteenth birthday.

I remember the day a guy was killed while painting the anchor well. The anchor is supposed to be secured, but something wasn't in place, so it suddenly whooshed out of the well and drove him into the Clyde. You could see the drips of paint he'd made all the way down the hull to his death. The workplace at the shipyards wasn't like construction workplaces today — not nearly the same consideration for safety. It was a dangerous place to be, and you were constantly told that. But we didn't really care much. A welder would be forty feet up balancing on a narrow beam and we'd go and jump on it. 'Whooooahhhhh!!!'

There were two planks going across the mouth of the deep cargo hold. One day I saw a welder trying to inch his way across with a roll of cable on each shoulder and a bunch of welding rods. Halfway across, the dark visor of his helmet came down so he couldn't see. 'Help!!! Heeeeeelp!!!' We thought it was hilarious. 'Away, you prick, what d'you think you're doing?' He was balanced there, blind. Too scared to move. Someone did help him eventually … once we'd all had a good laugh.

Our humour was dark. Frequently cruel. There was an older guy, a plater-carpenter called Coley. He was really funny. He was in an accident one day in the tank. I'd gone for a piss and was on the way back when I saw that a rescue operation was in full swing. They'd called the ambulance room for help, and responders had come to look after him. I can't remember exactly what had happened — something fell on him, or maybe he'd fallen off something — but when I got there, he was being pulled out with a crane. They'd wrapped him in a swaddling of bamboo mat, and he was being lifted out head-first. Everyone was standing about gawking. As soon as his head appeared out of the tank I said, 'Coley, what happened to you?' He said, 'I was putting the chalk line on the deck and I knelt on my prick.'

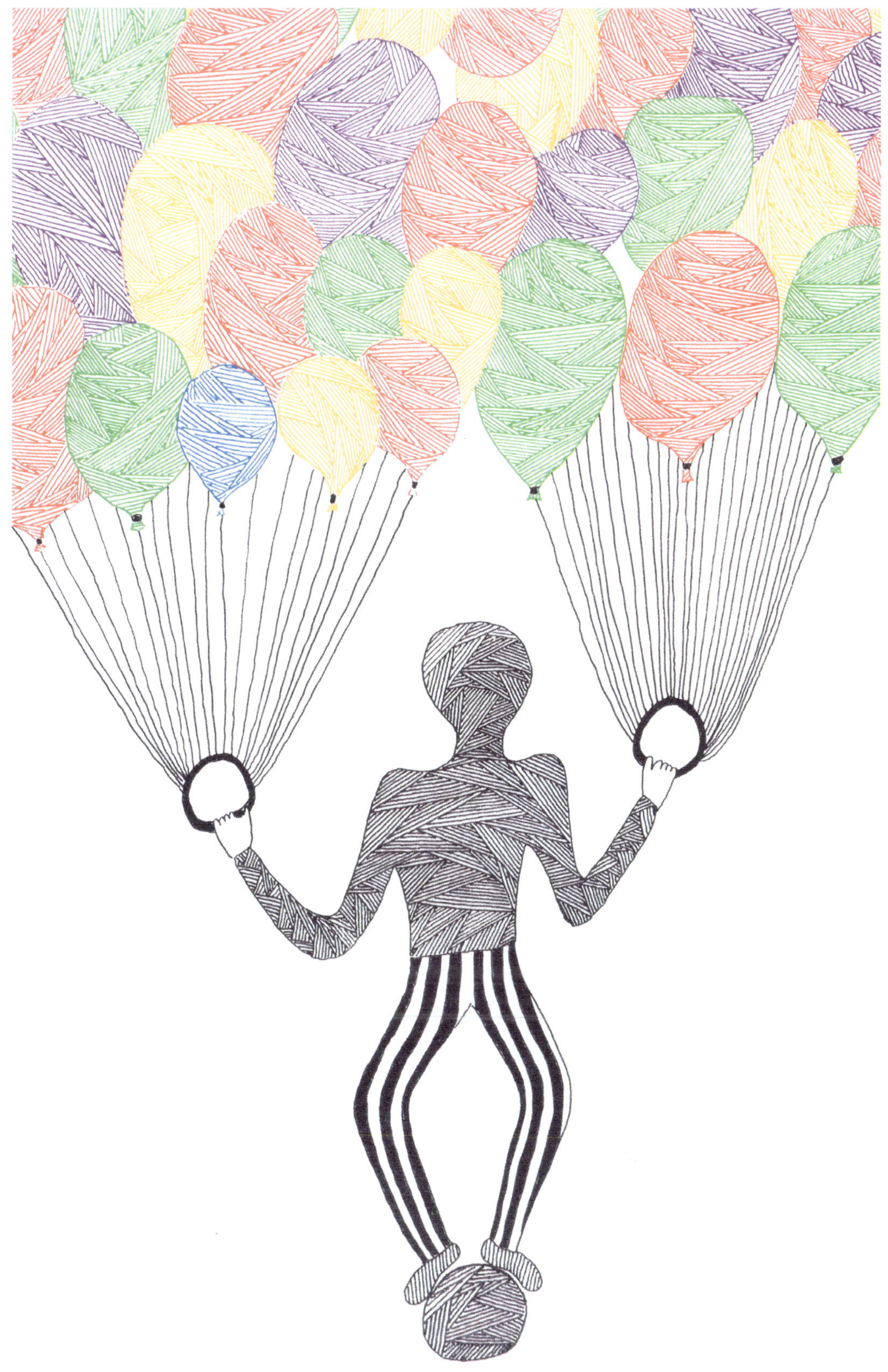

Free Flight Variations, 2020

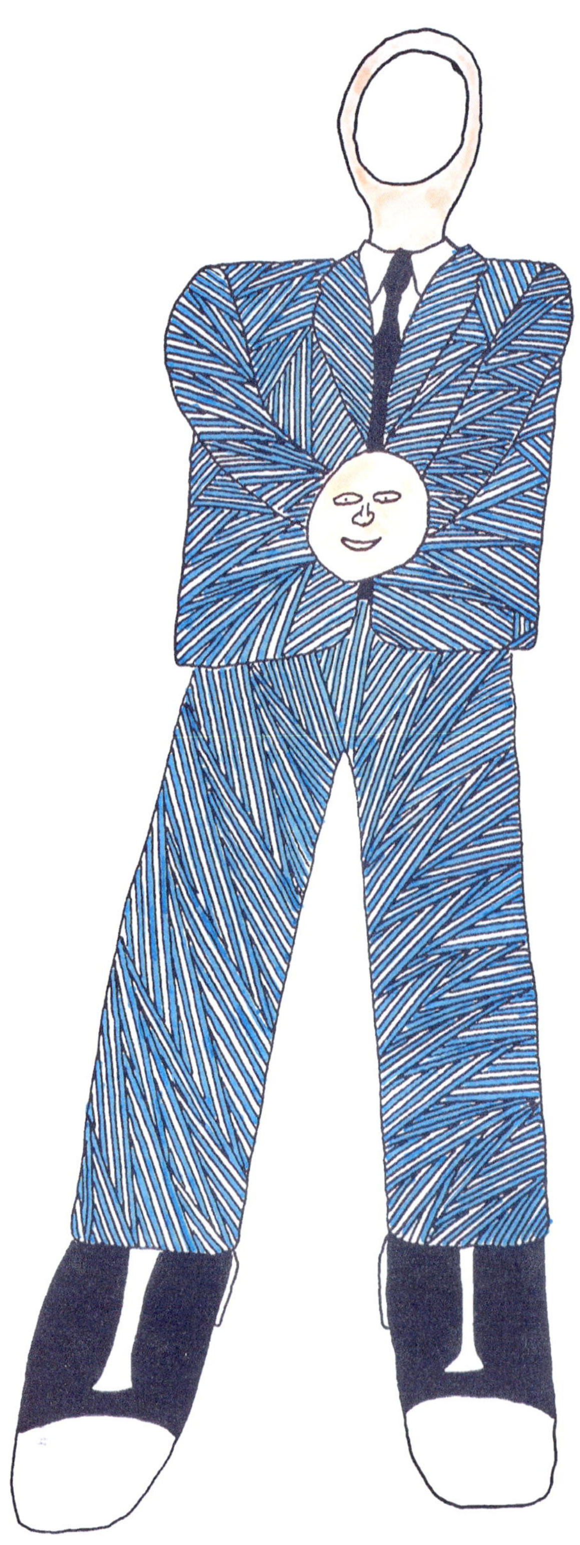

Steal Your Face — Bigfoot, 2021

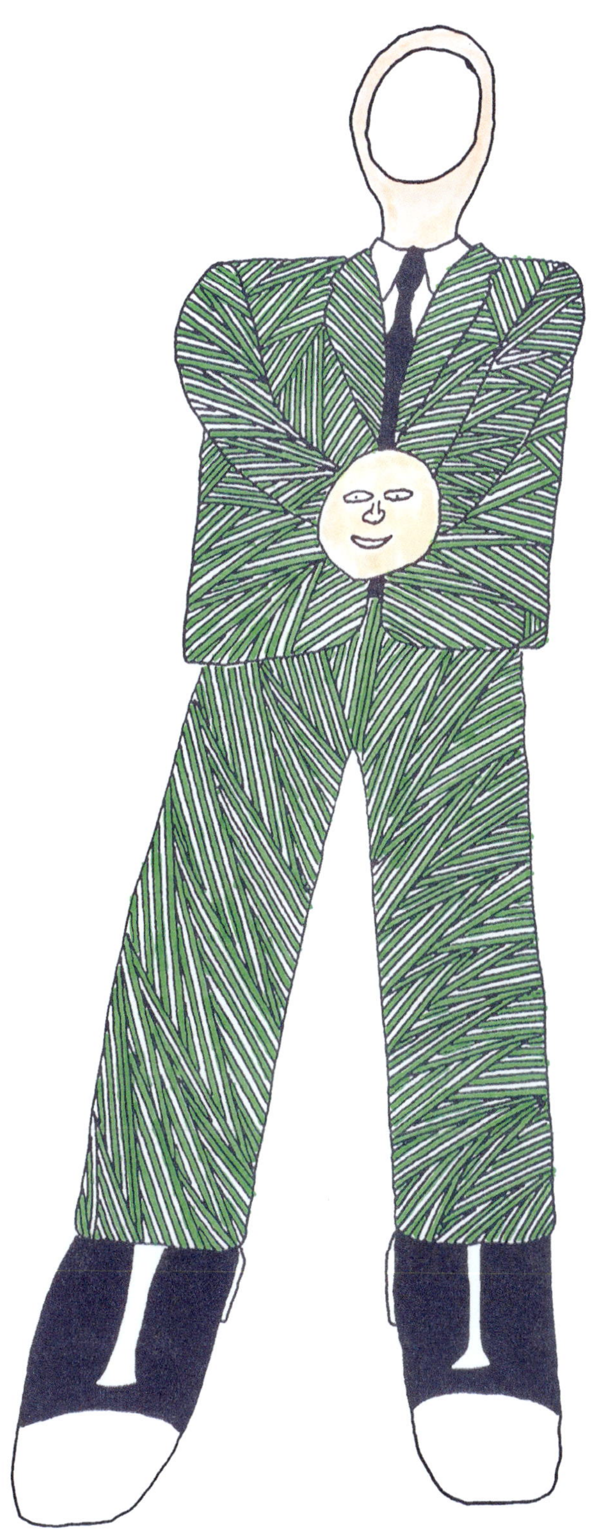

Steal Your Face – Smiler, 2021

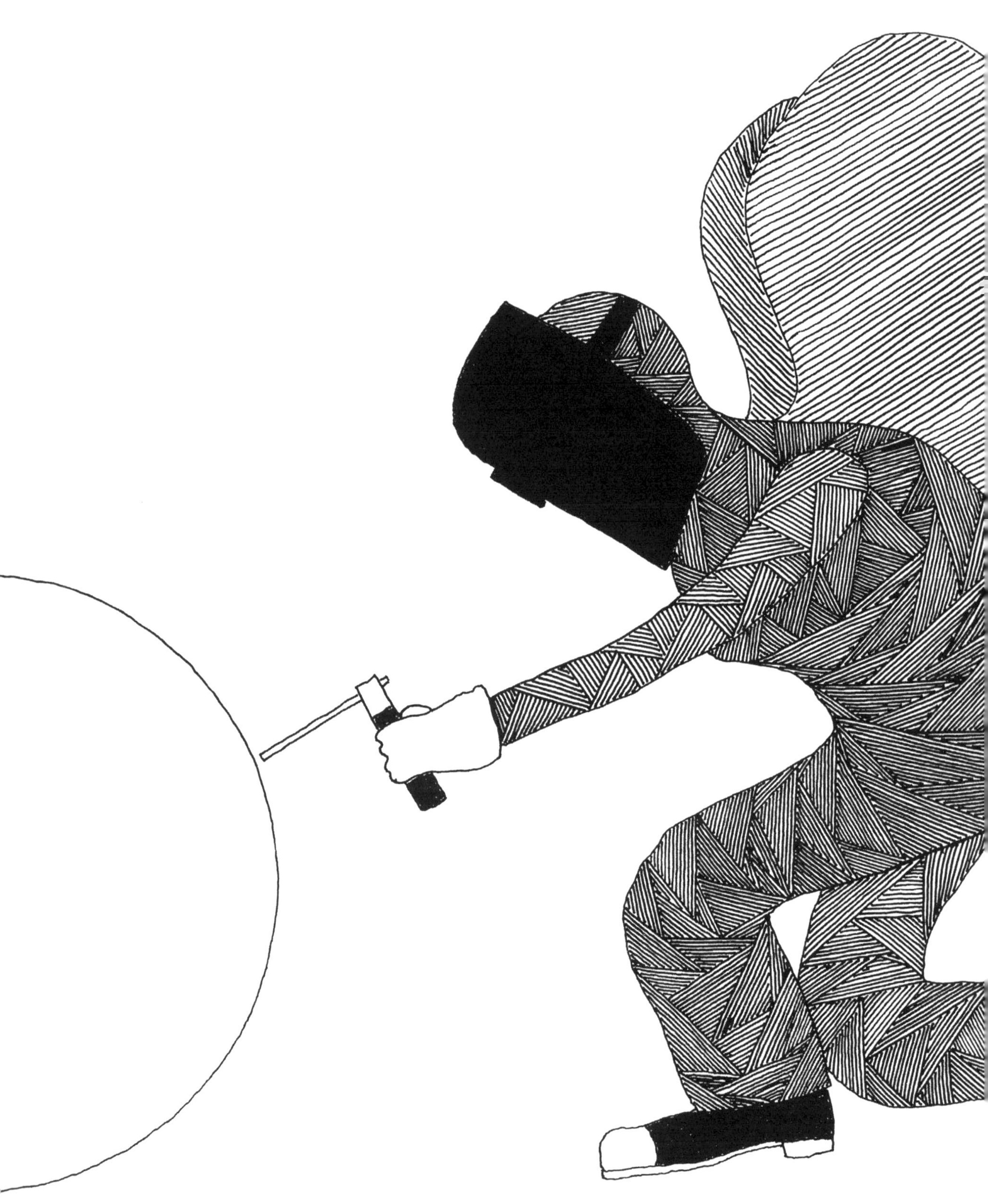

And On Monday, God Made The World, 2012

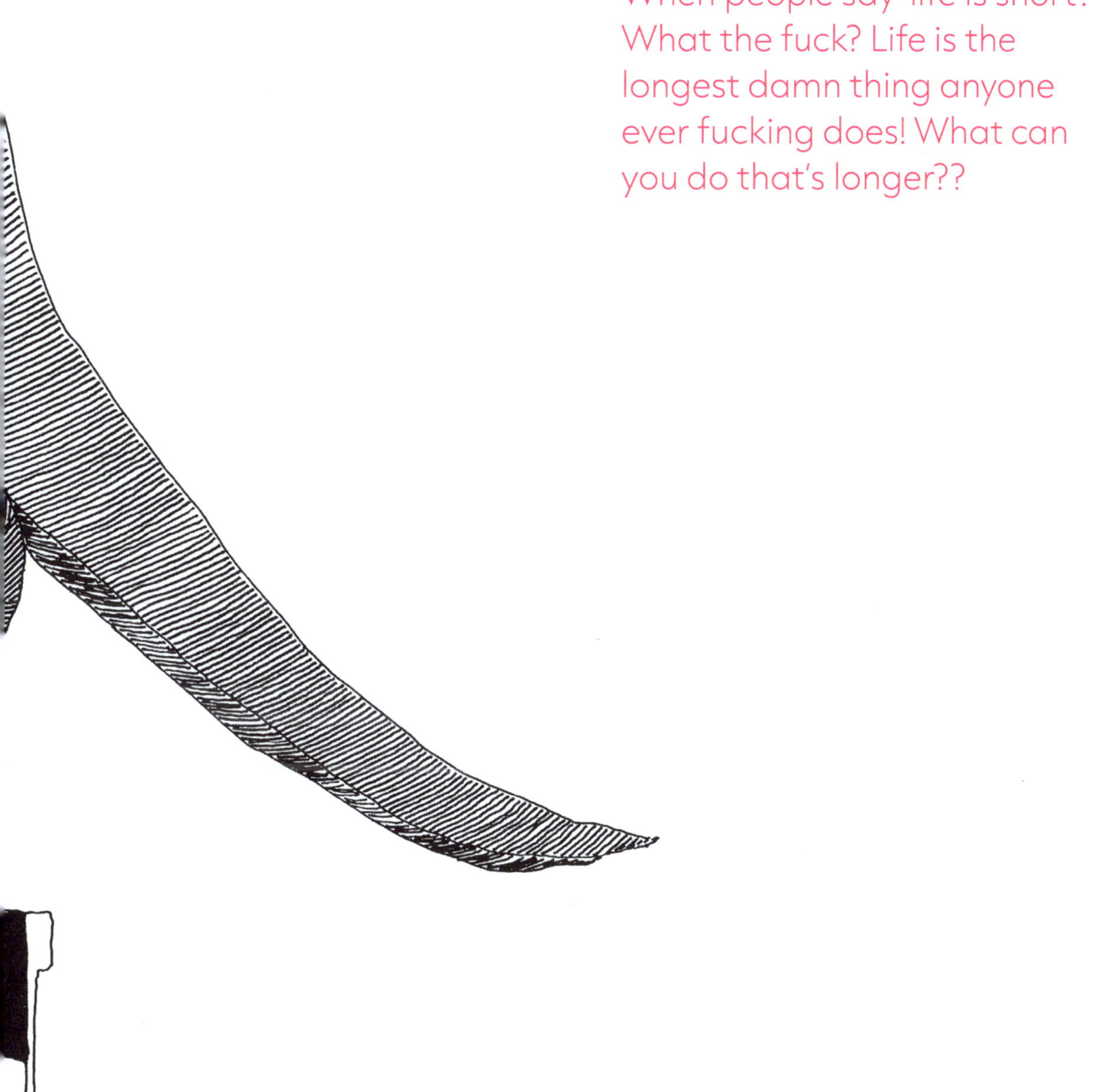

When people say 'life is short'. What the fuck? Life is the longest damn thing anyone ever fucking does! What can you do that's longer??

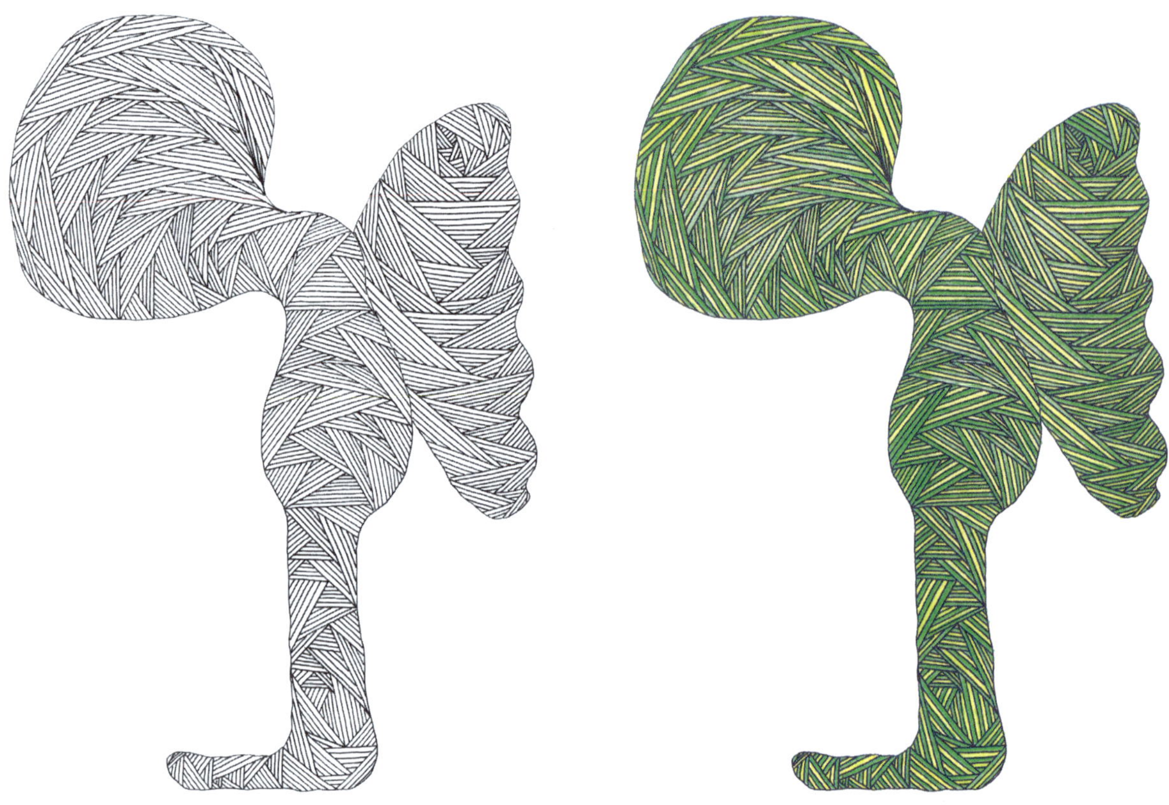

Blue Angel, 2011 / Blue Angel, 2021

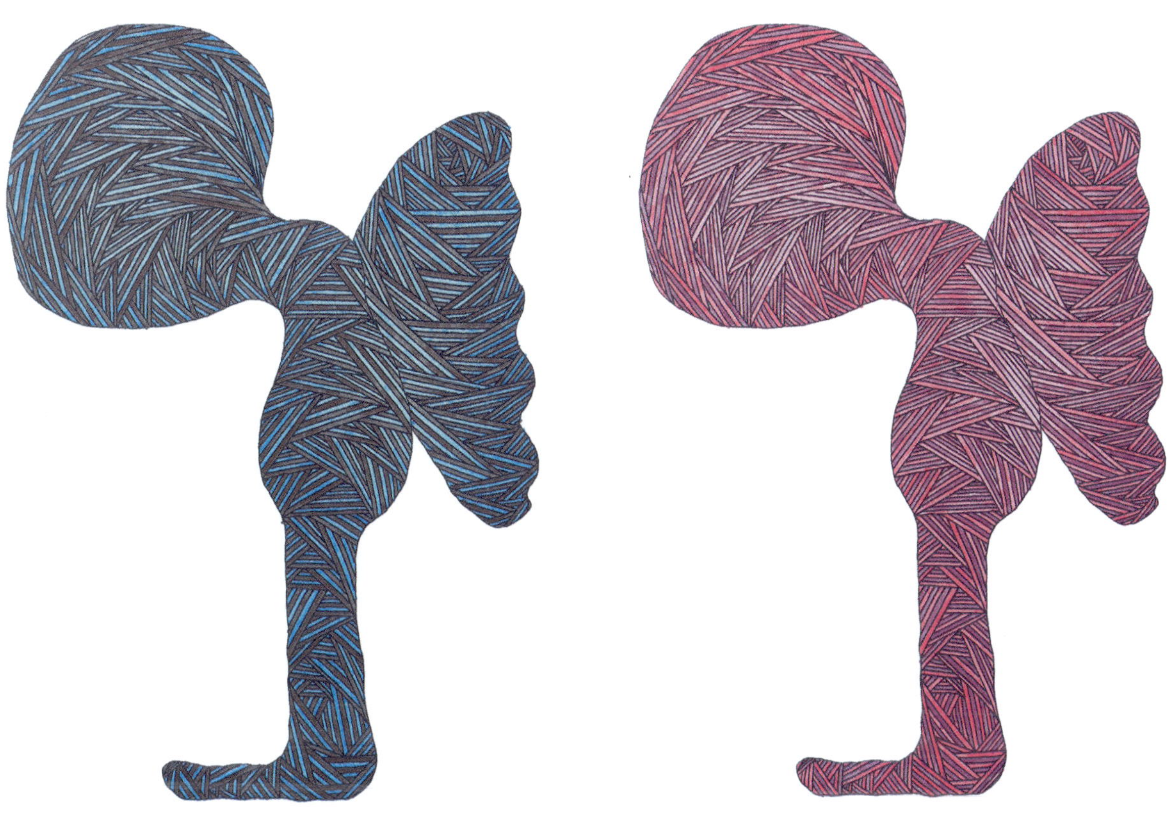

Blue Angel, 2021 / Blue Angel, 2021

once did a whole TV series in the USA about death called *The Big Send Off*. It felt good talking about death and telling the truth about it. You can only lie about it or avoid it for so long. As you learn about the Buddhist way, the Mexican way, the Islamic way of dealing with death, and all these different ways of dying and being buried — you can't kid any more. You have to view death from a practical point of view. There's a great sense of relief about doing that — a feeling of release. Nobody was expecting anything of me when I made the series — just my thoughts — so I found myself being very honest about it. I explored the one certainty in life — that we're going to die.

I'm fascinated by death and how we deal with it. We skirt around the subject of death but it's a 21-billion-dollar-a-year industry in the USA. I visited a pet cemetery where a burial for a guinea pig cost $550 for the plot, $350 for the coffin and $1k for the marble headstone. Then I went to a funeral directors' convention in Texas, where they were promoting embalming fluid party packs, shampoo for dry, lifeless hair, blankets with life-size pictures of the deceased — you can sit with it for a drink or take it to bed with you. They had zombie-proof steel coffins on display, hot-rod hearses, and you could reserve rockets to the moon for your ashes. There was the eco death-suit threaded with mushroom spores; the fungi feed on your decomposing body and take you back to the Earth as human compost. You're of no use to any Earth-dwelling person, so it gets rid of your body in a sensible way without bothering anybody. Not sure how I feel about a mushroom eating me. There's a theory that mushrooms come from space. They came on meteors and stayed. I believe it. They breed unlike any other species on earth. And they look like aliens, not like anything from here. So do octopuses.

There are many choices now when it comes to how you can be buried. The Neptune Society disperses ashes under the Golden Gate Bridge, and no relatives attend, because that's the way the deceased person wanted it. I went along, and thought it was profoundly moving, with the ashes trailing in the water and a wake of flowers following the boat. I'd rather like that for myself. My pal Eric Idle said he wants fireworks and an element of dressing up. Maybe even a cashpoint in his casket so it's a useful visit. His song 'Always Look on the Bright Side of Life' has long been a favourite funeral song.

Some say you only die the last time somebody says your name. The Mexican Day of the Dead is about remembering those who have passed. Some people get memorial tattoos. One woman got a peacock tattoo for her granny because she always had a bunch of peacocks wandering round her property. It was only after she got the tattoo that she found out her granny hated the peacocks and used to shoot them.

There was a point in the past when I thought that maybe I was mentally ill, and so I went and asked some Buddhists – in Lockerbie, of all places – about all this stuff going round and round in my head in such a rapid and chaotic way. And they just said, 'Enjoy it. Sit back and enjoy it. Watch it like a train going past.' So that's what I now do. And that's what I recommend that you do, too.

I met some people who think science is the answer to death and can offer eternal life. There was a whole team of scientists who believe ageing is a disease and therefore curable. In Buddhism, there's a meditation for when you see a dead thing on the road: 'That is the Way of all things, and it will be the Way of me too.' I like that. I met a guy who said he believed in everything – 'That way I can't be wrong!'

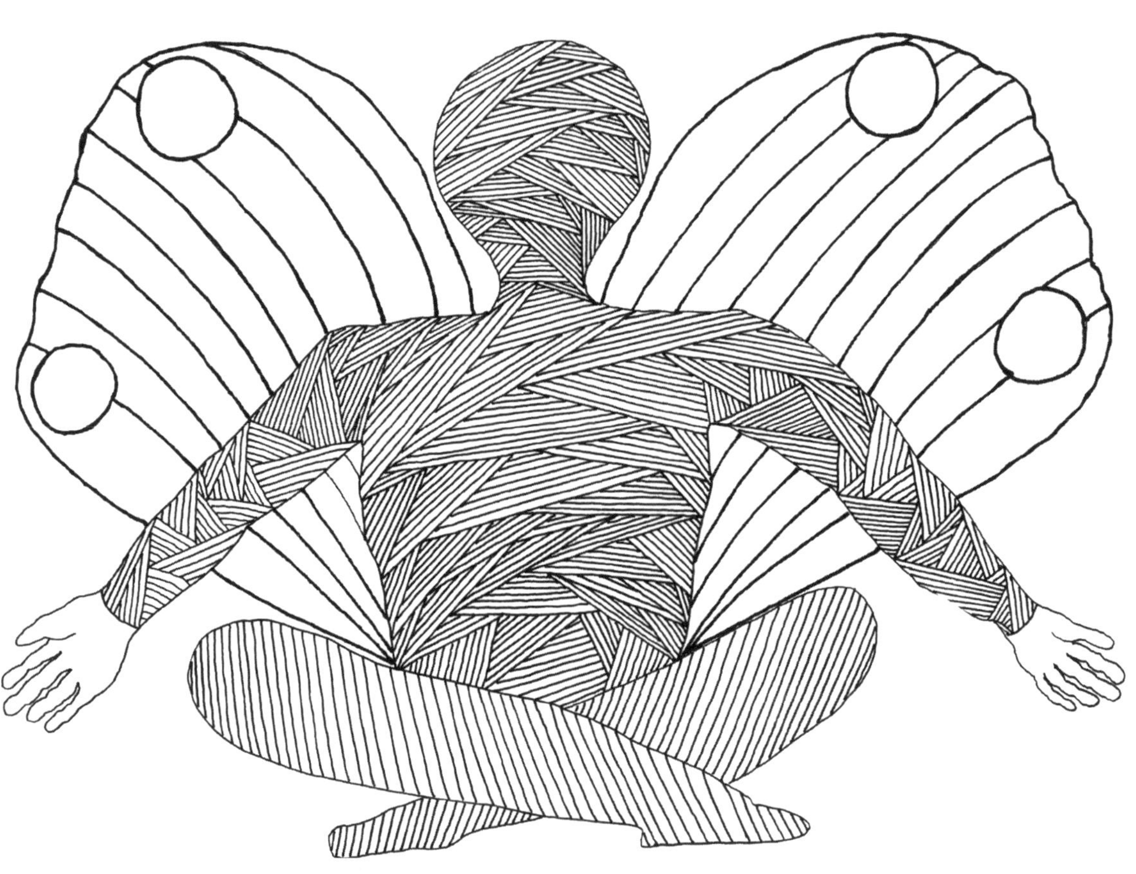

Hang Glider, 2017

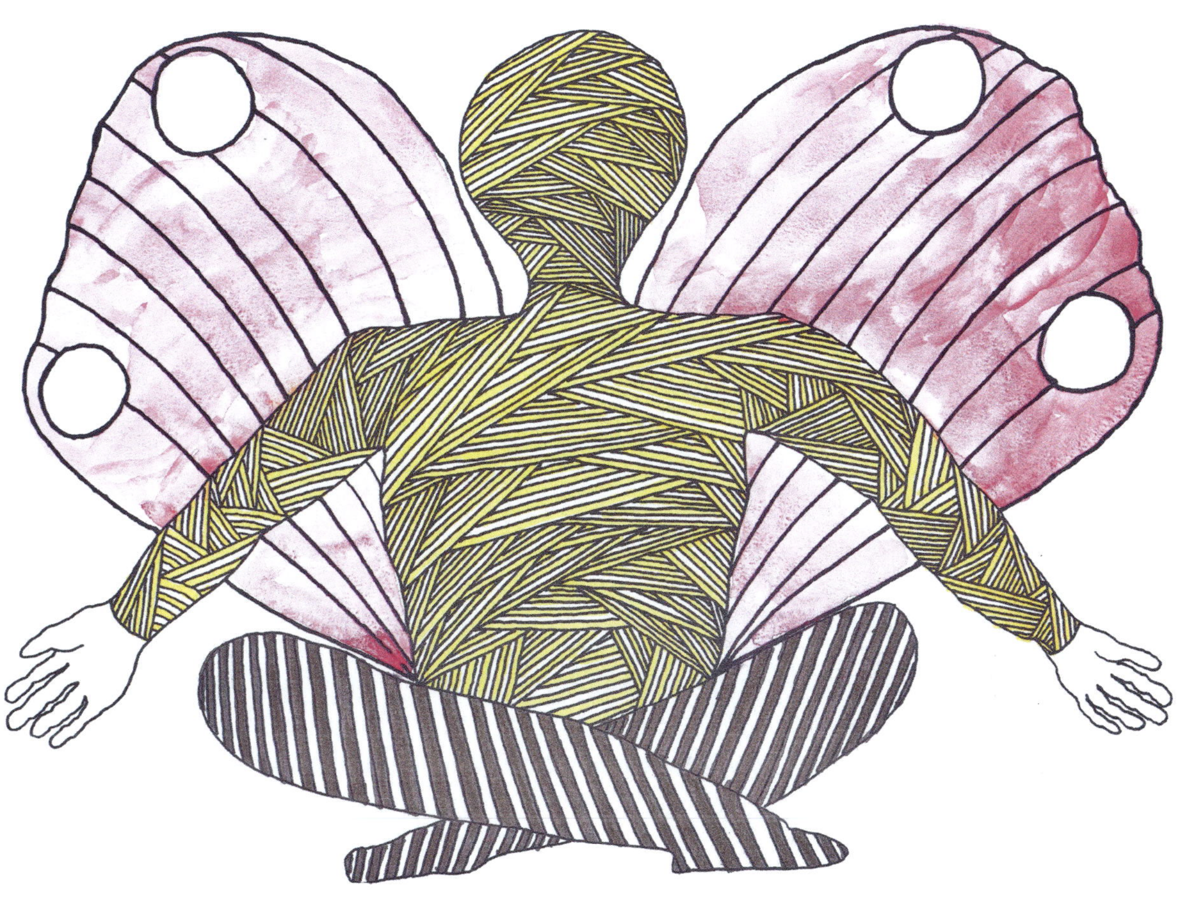

Hang Glider, 2021

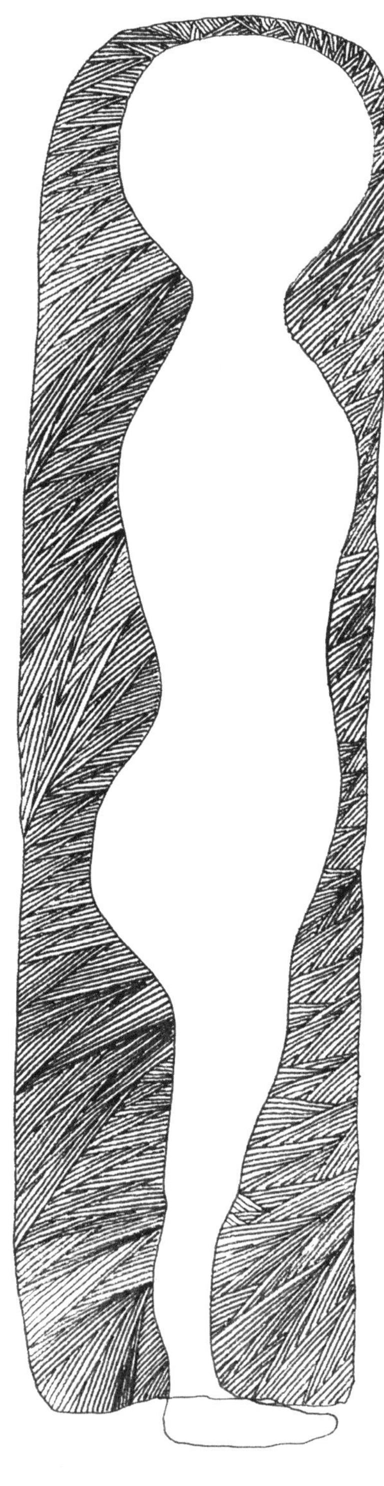

Waiting To Be Discovered, 2012

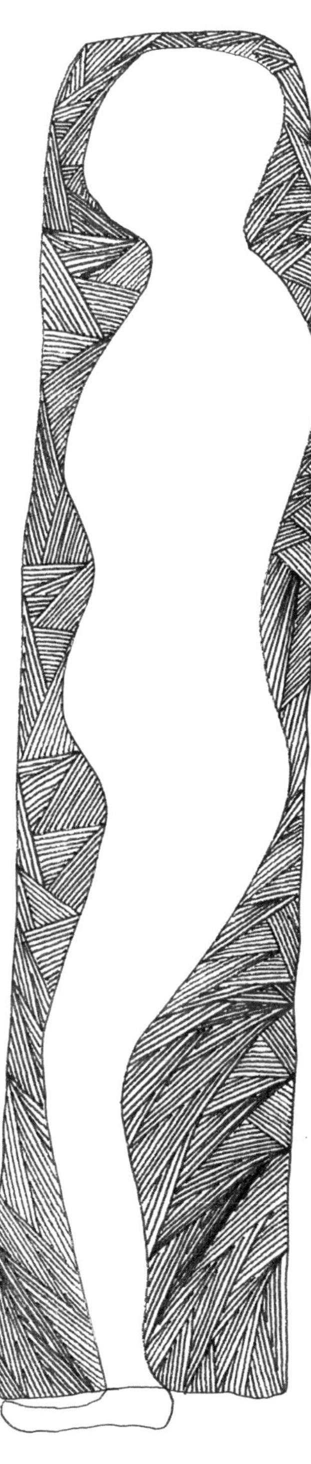

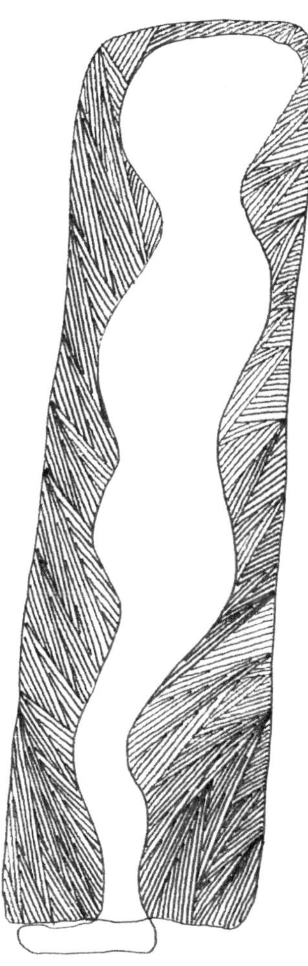

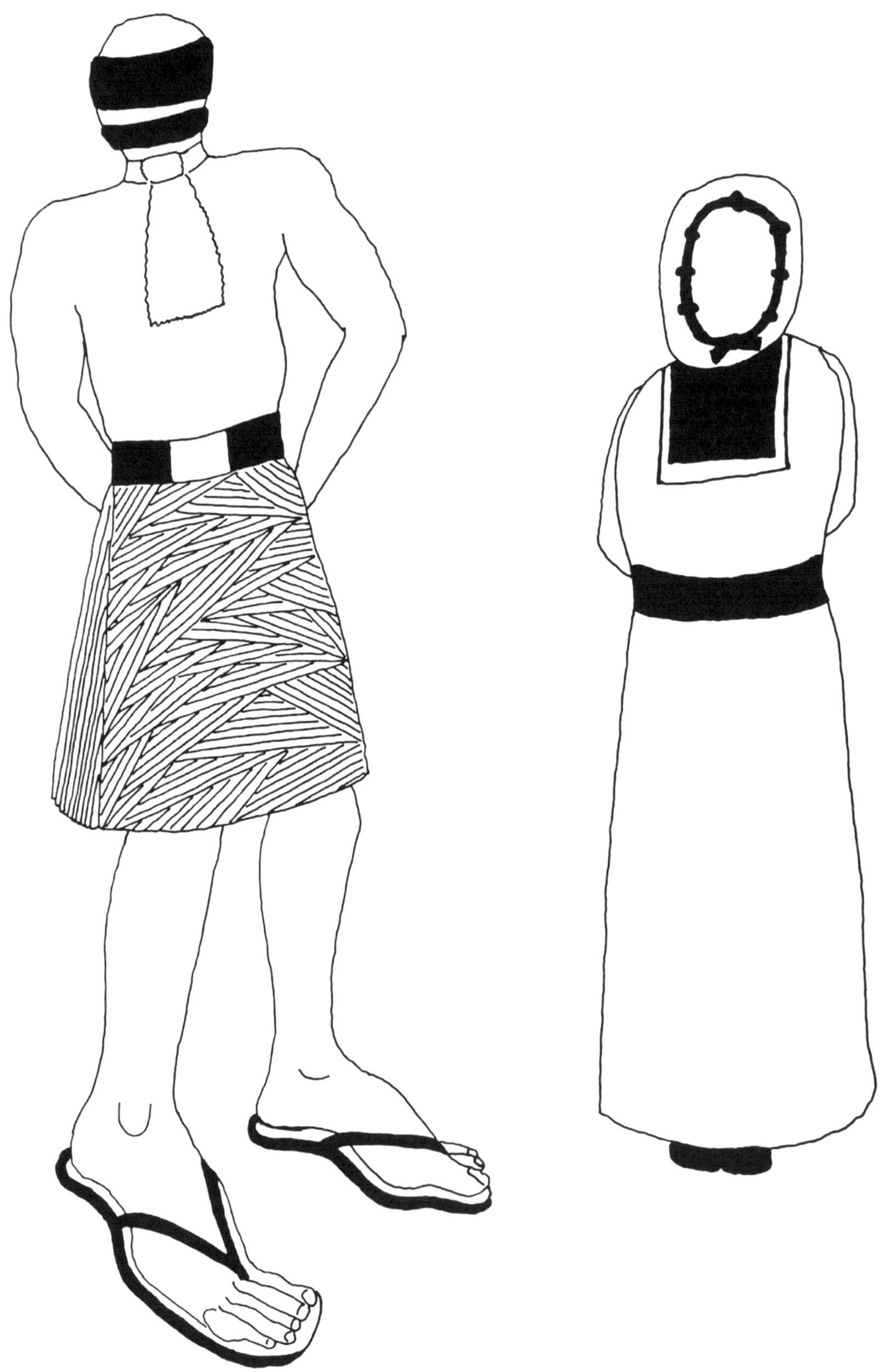

Waiting For The Boatman, 2018

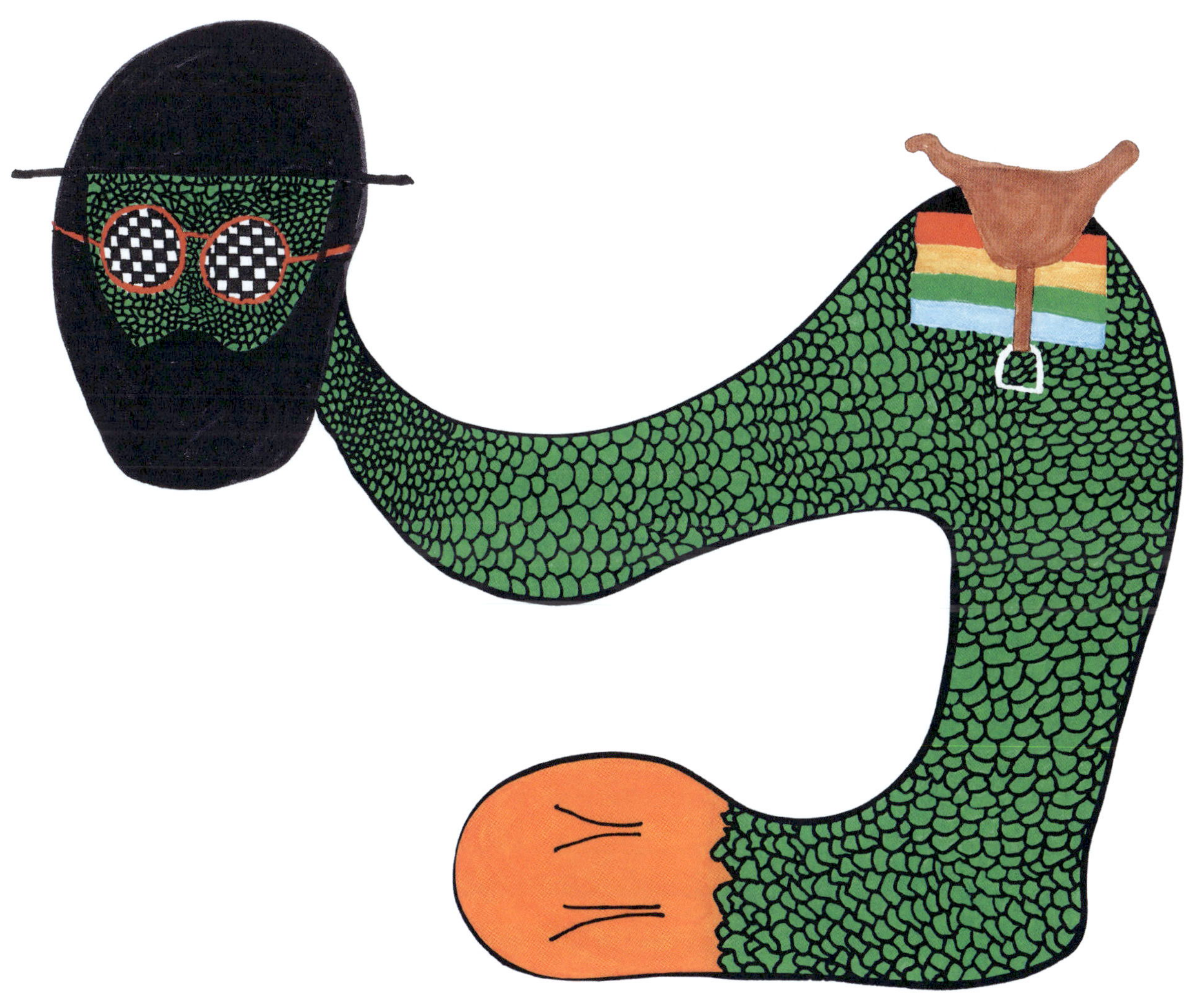

Just Waiting Can Be Nice, 2010

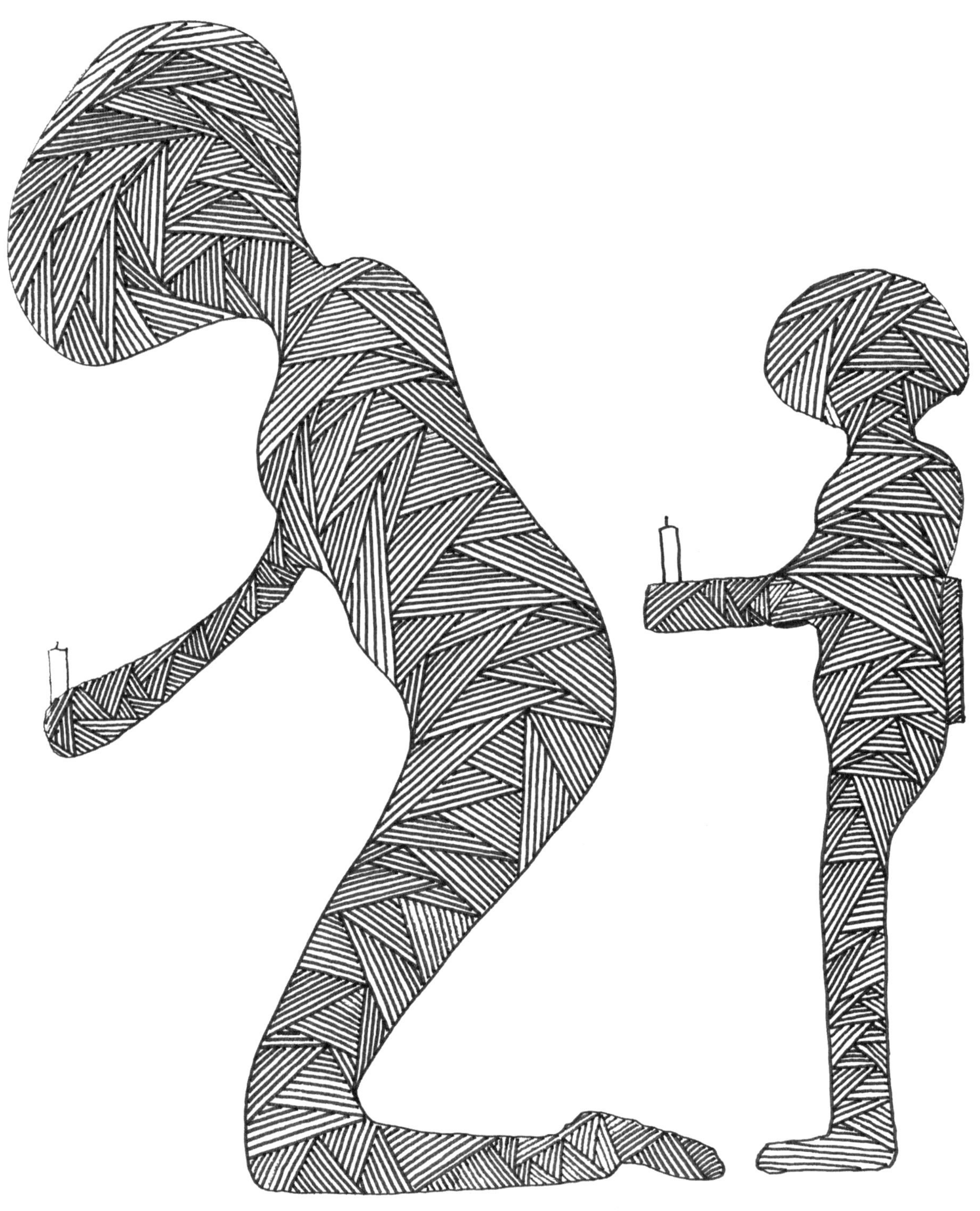

The Candle Lighters, 2012

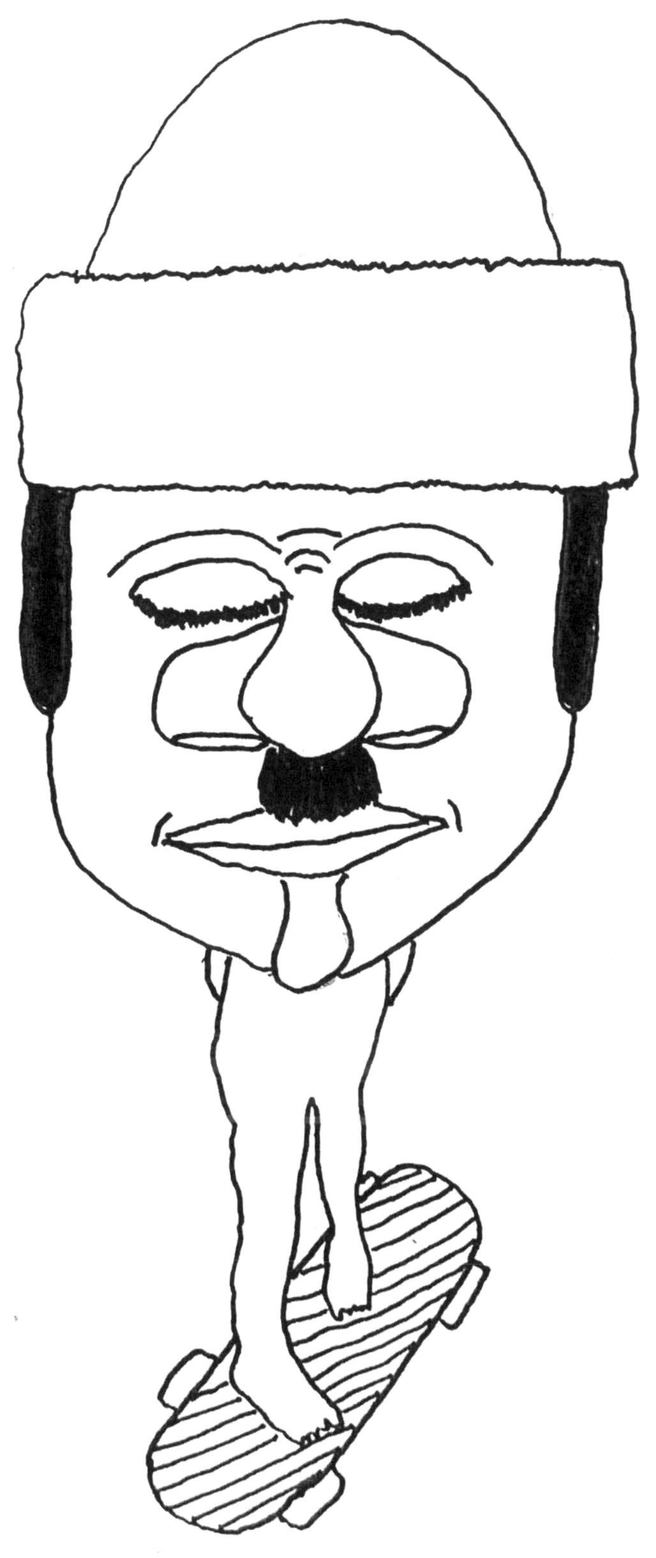

Meditation, 2018

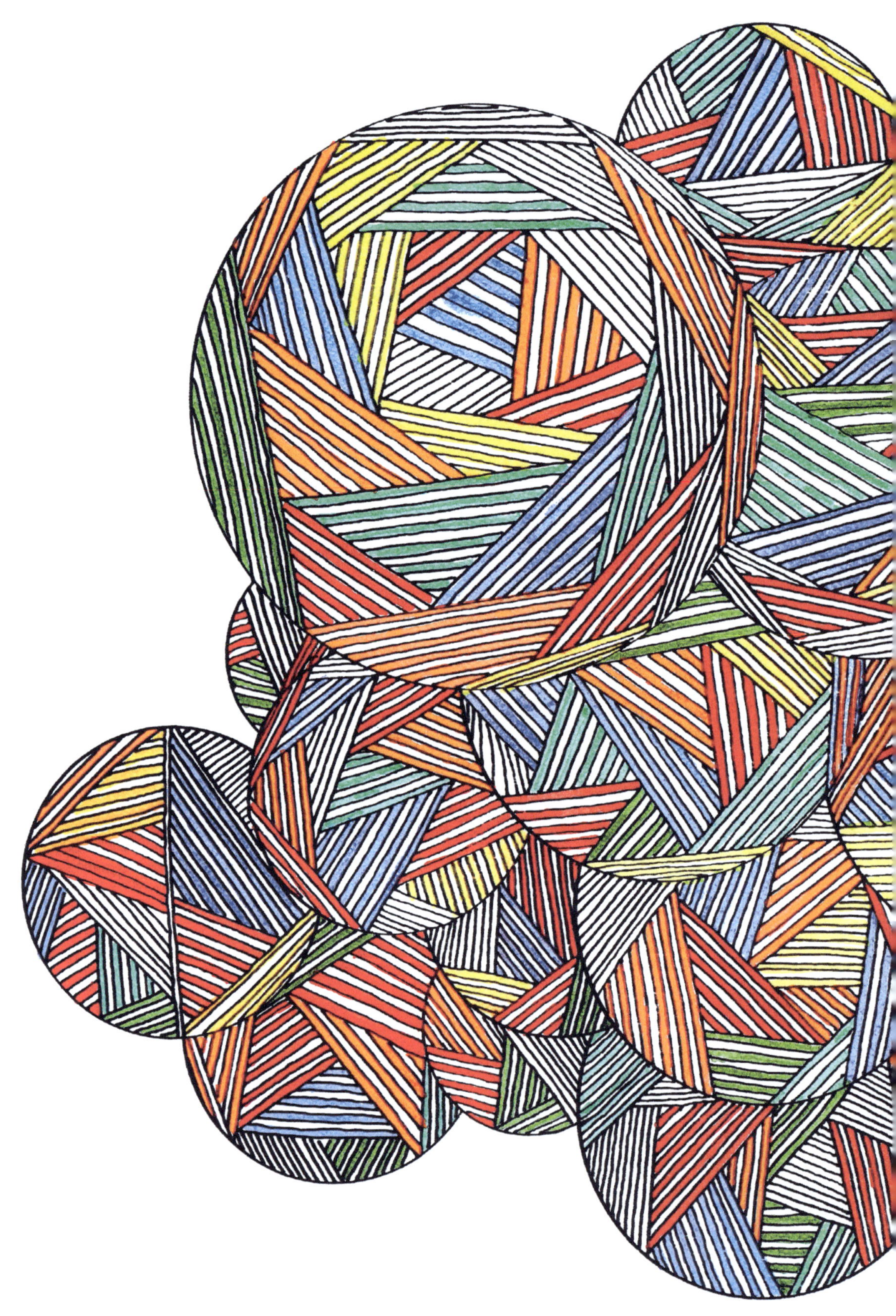

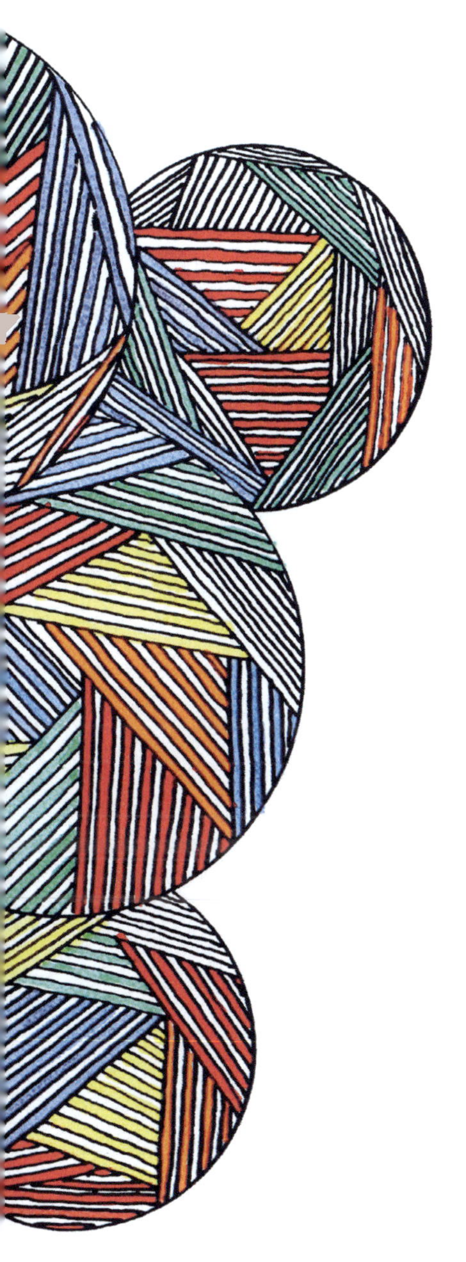

I couldn't think of a name for this piece as I started to draw it, so I thought *A Load Of Old Bollocks* would cover it nicely. It's a lovely statement — a load of old bollocks. You can say it wherever you like, you can say it about Shakespeare — 'what a load of old bollocks!' You can say it about songs, poems — 'a load of old bollocks!' And it just sums things up. It's a nice thing, that basket of balls; it'll never have a use. It's a load of old bollocks! It'll never be welded, it'll never be riveted, it'll never mean anything to anybody. It's a load of old bollocks, and it pleases me greatly.

A Load Of Old Bollocks, 2021

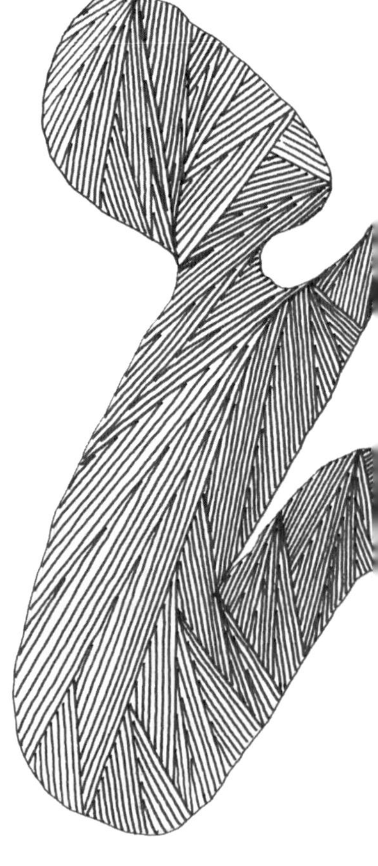

Concentrate, 2012

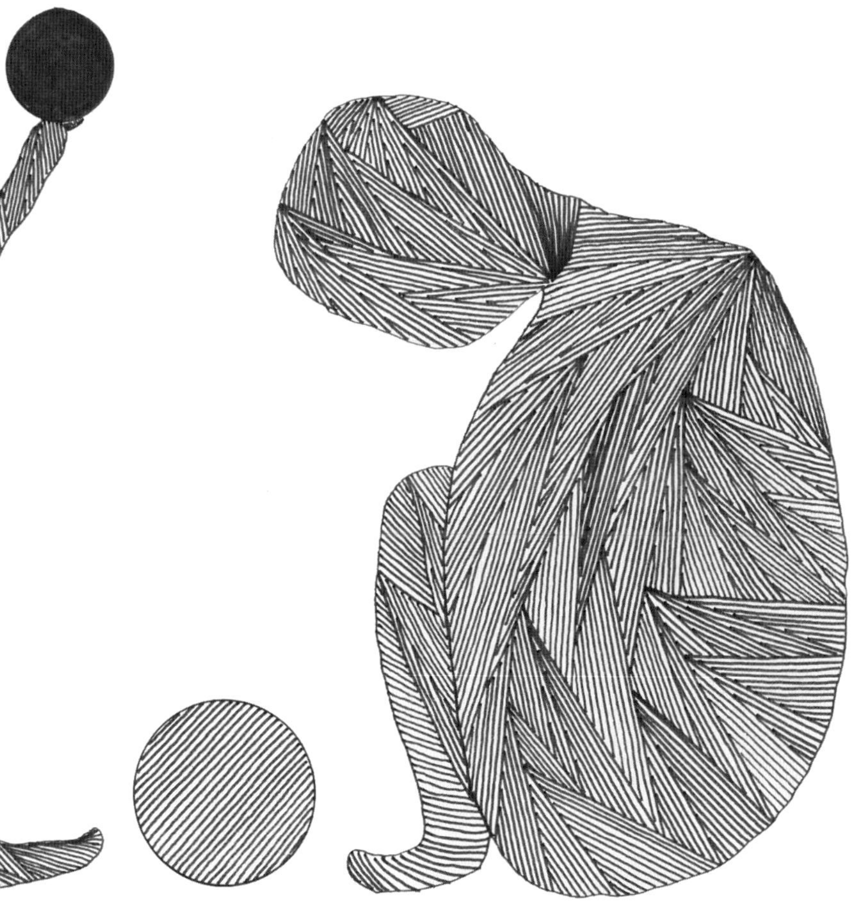

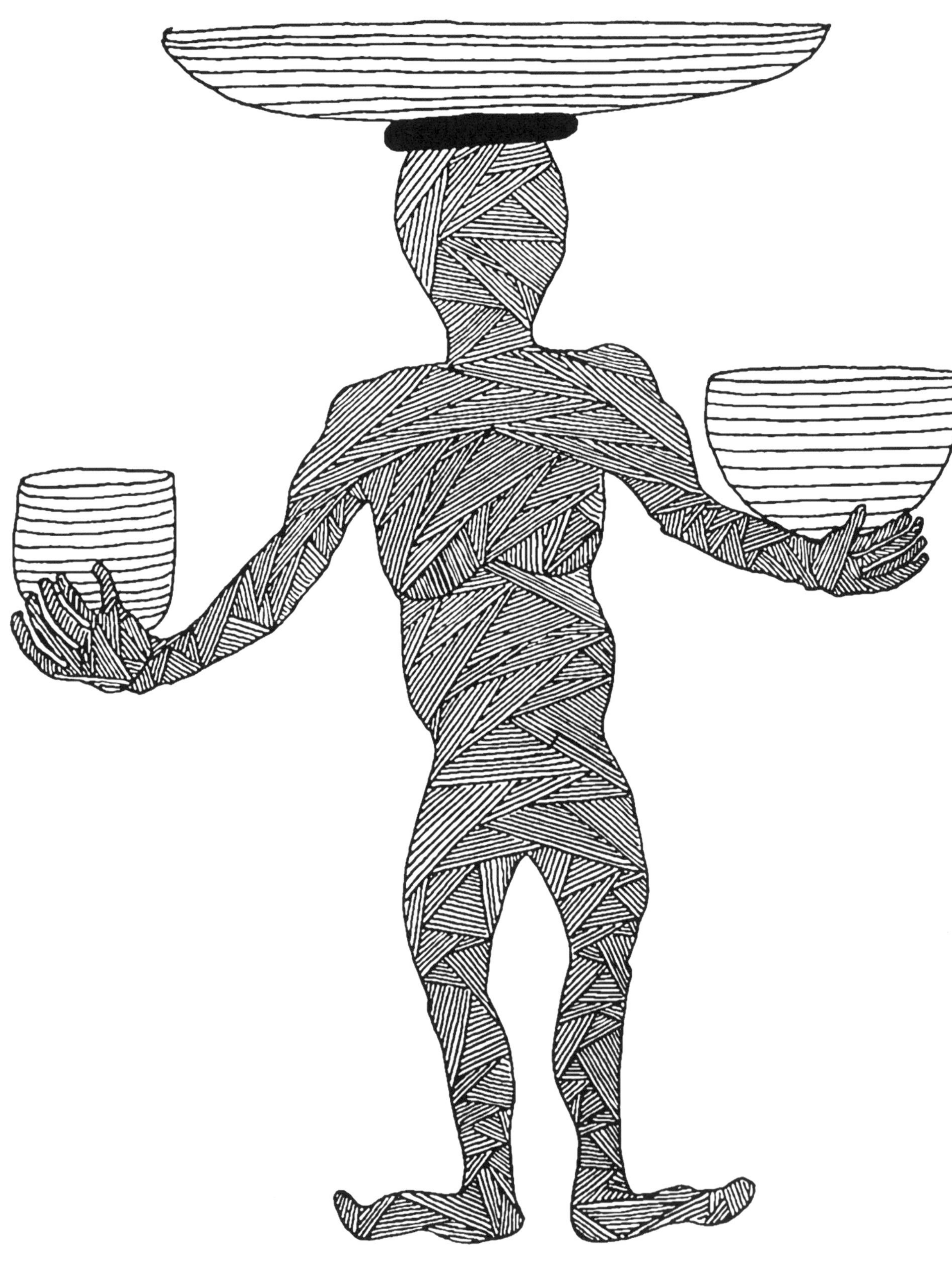

It's Raining On The Moon, 2018

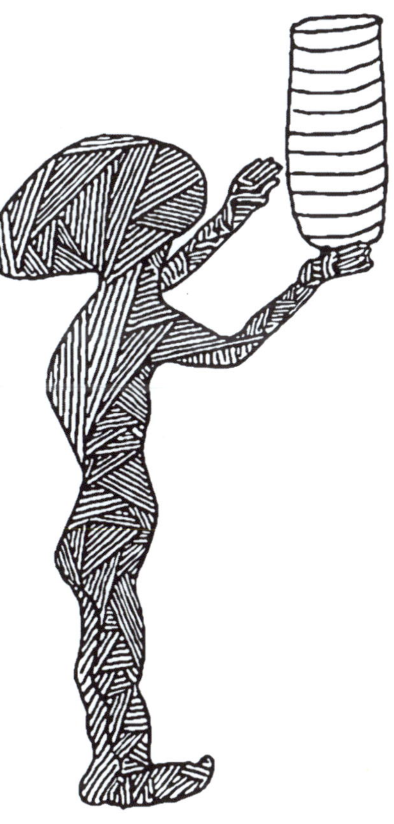

A well-balanced
person has a drink
in each hand.

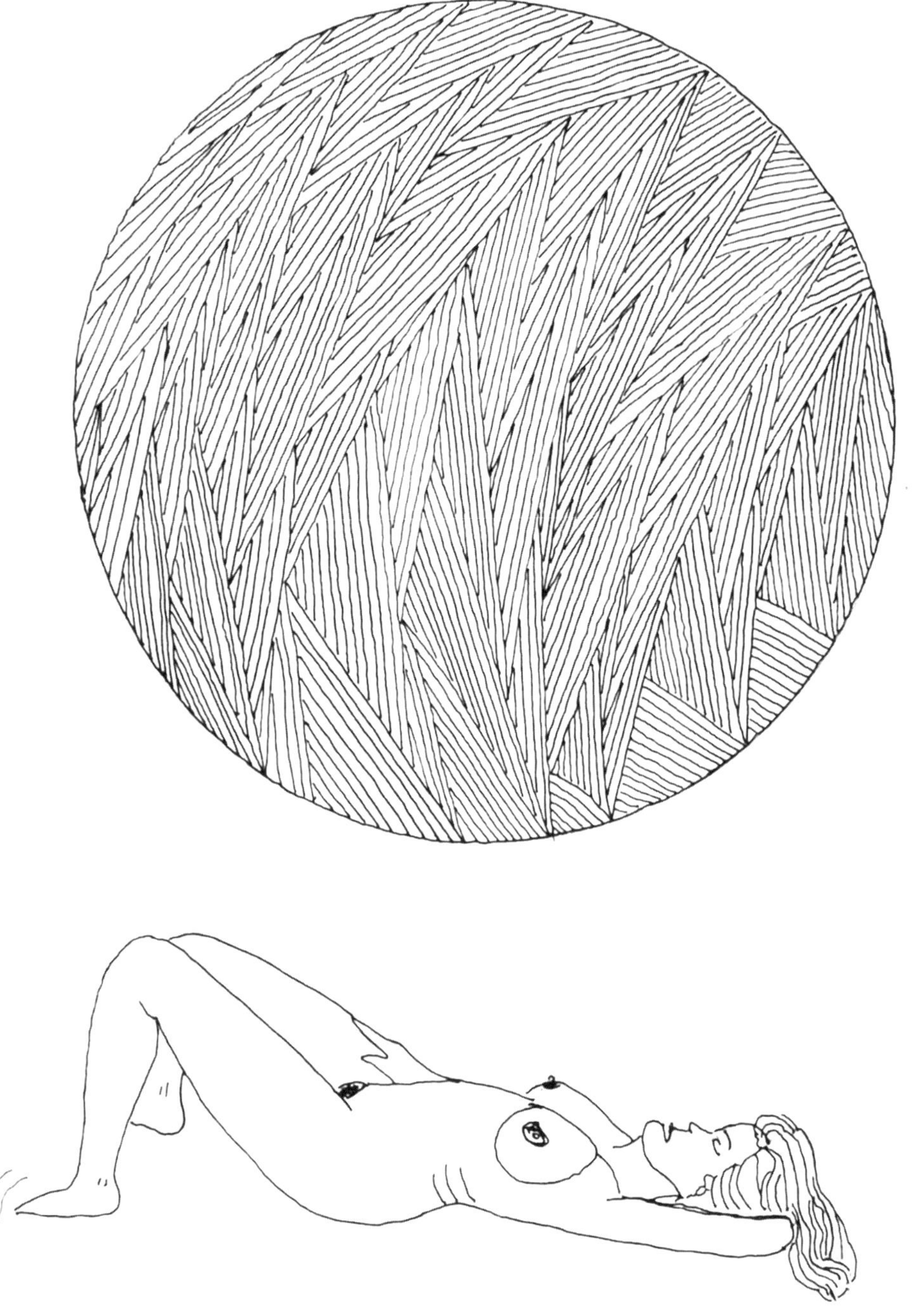

Weight Of The World, 2019

I haven't made up my mind about my burial place, but I'm thinking that instead of a headstone, a table on an island in Loch Lomond for fishermen to picnic on would be nice. During *The Big Send Off* I especially liked visiting the 'green' graveyard, a nine-acre plot of land in Texas, called Eloise Woods. It was opened by a woman called Ellen Macdonald, who was a neuroscientist. It was a very simple concept — you could be buried in a very organic way. Someone would dig a hole, drop you in it, and invite your friends to say 'Cheerio'. If you want, you can get buried with your pet ... although he might not like it if he's not dead. It's charming. Clean. Good. Everything about it is good. One guy was buried in his chair. They just sat him in his chair and covered him with earth. Five million gallons of embalming fluid are poured into the ground every year, which isn't doing the planet any good, so this is the answer — a green burial ground. Families can dig the grave themselves and can mark the grave with something simple like a flat stone. It seemed a refreshing change from the denial of death in our culture where you put make-up on people to look like they are alive and simply sleeping.

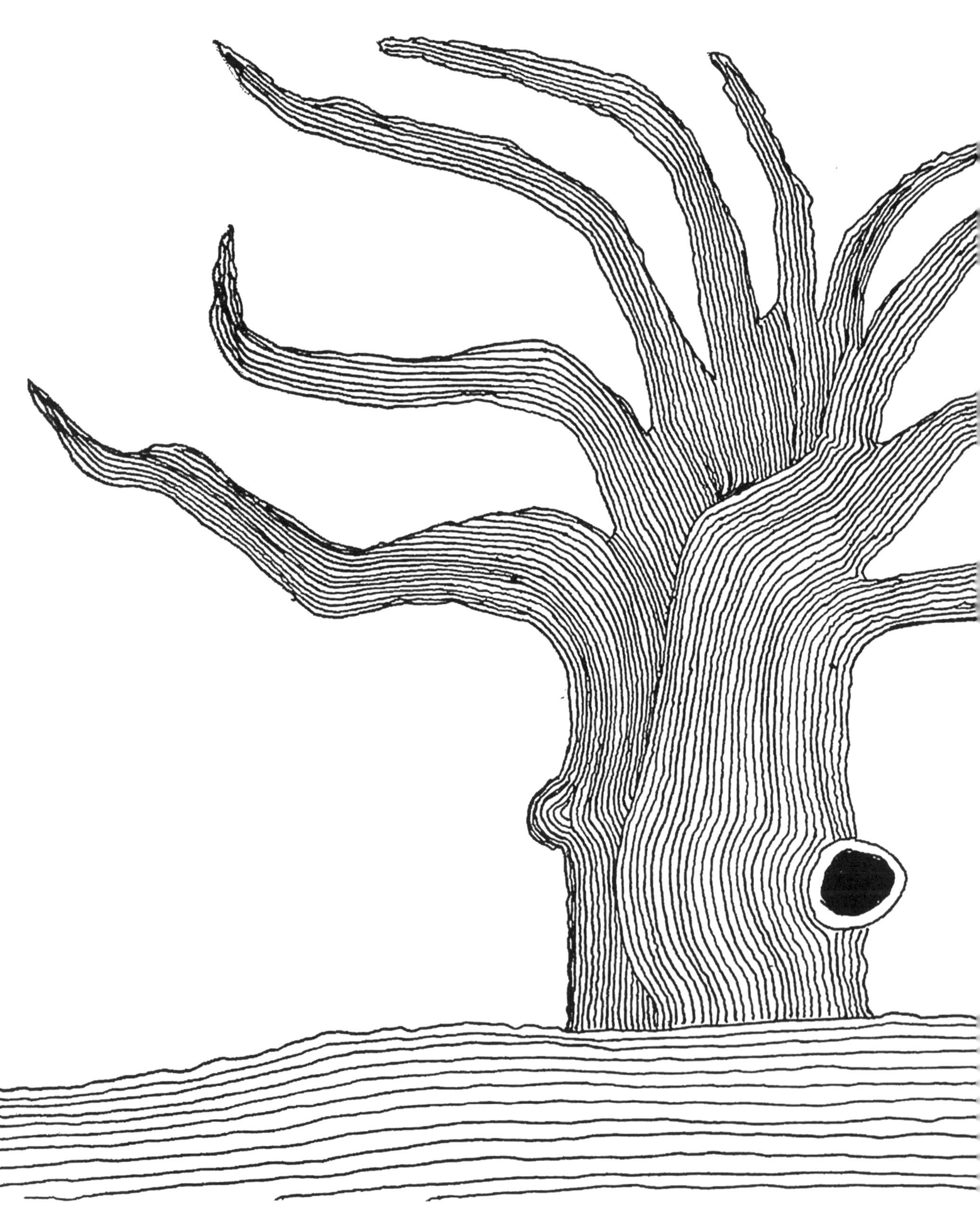

Lifeless, 2016

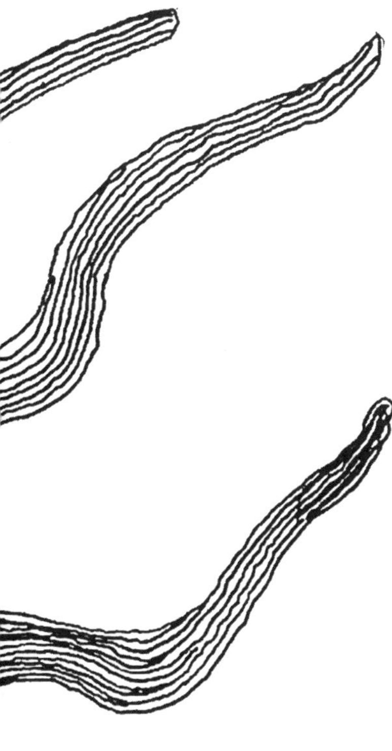

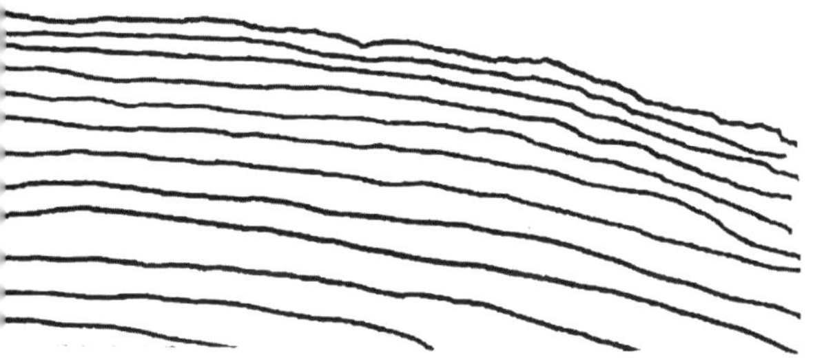

I also liked the Columbarium I saw in San Francisco, a huge structure that is a repository for human ashes. There are walls of remembrances where people can leave things the deceased person liked, displayed as dioramas – little plastic soldiers, flowers – things that meant something to both of them – on a little shelf. There were lots of snow globes – from Hawaii, for example, to remember a great holiday. And pictures of Scottish guys in kilts who'd died a long way from home. People do lovely things when they're left to their own devices. Some people are so imaginative and playful – even when it comes to their own death. The best headstone I ever saw was a hat and beer-keg. This man had his own coffin made while he was alive – out of corrugated iron. He used it as a wine-rack in his living room while he was alive, and then he was buried in it.

Making that documentary changed me. I used to think about death, and about the life I led, and would ask myself, 'How will I be held responsible for it when I come to judgment before God?' I don't believe that any more, although the whole thing is still a mystery to me. It was very comforting meeting those people I spoke to during the series. They were all lovely; there wasn't a single nasty person I encountered. The drive-through funeral parlour in Compton, Los Angeles, was a gas. Mourners could sign the visitors' book outside, then drive through to pay their respects. There was a dead woman in a coffin in the window. They sat the coffin up a bit so you could see her better. Peggy Scott Adams was the proprietor of the parlour. She said: 'Death is a part of life'. I like that.

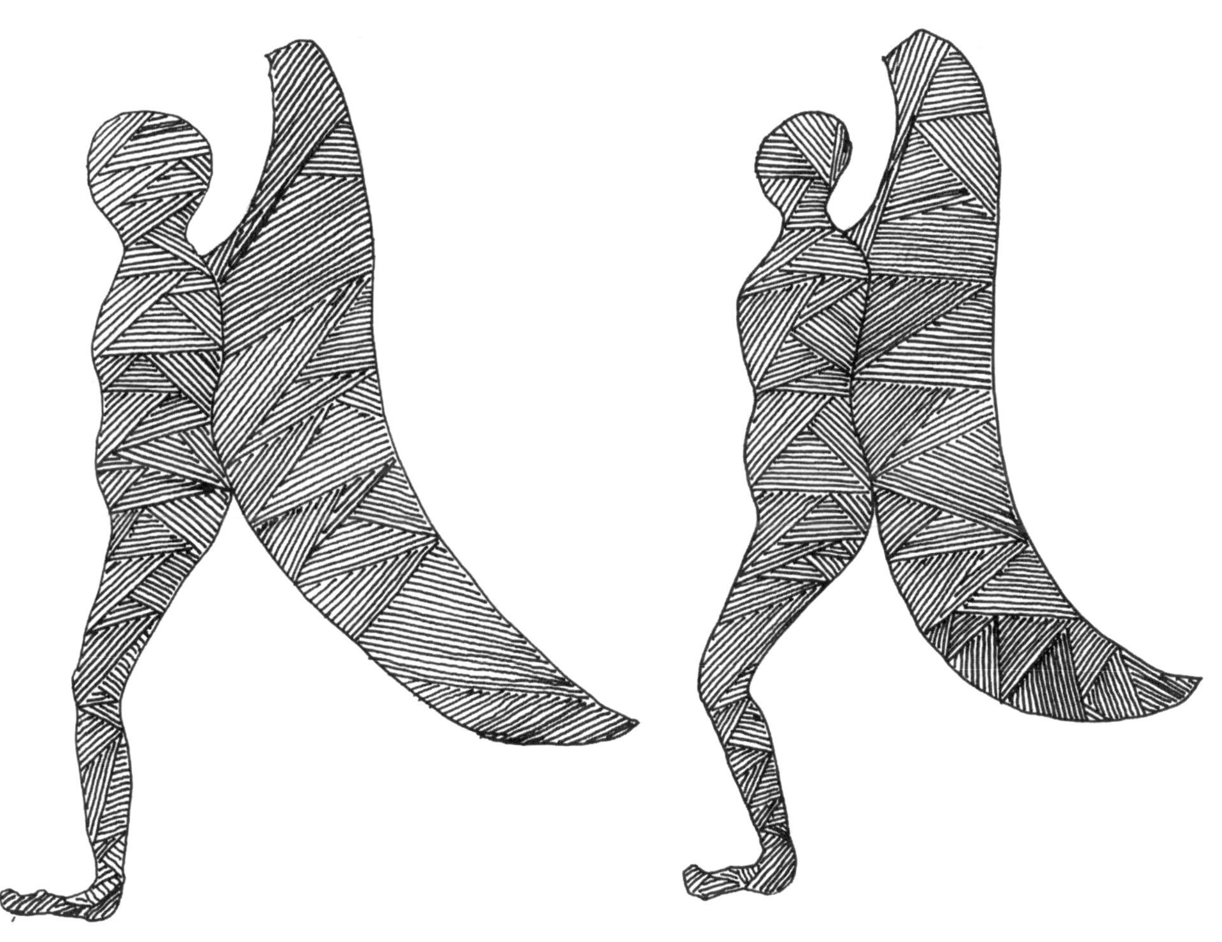

Meek & Mild, 2013

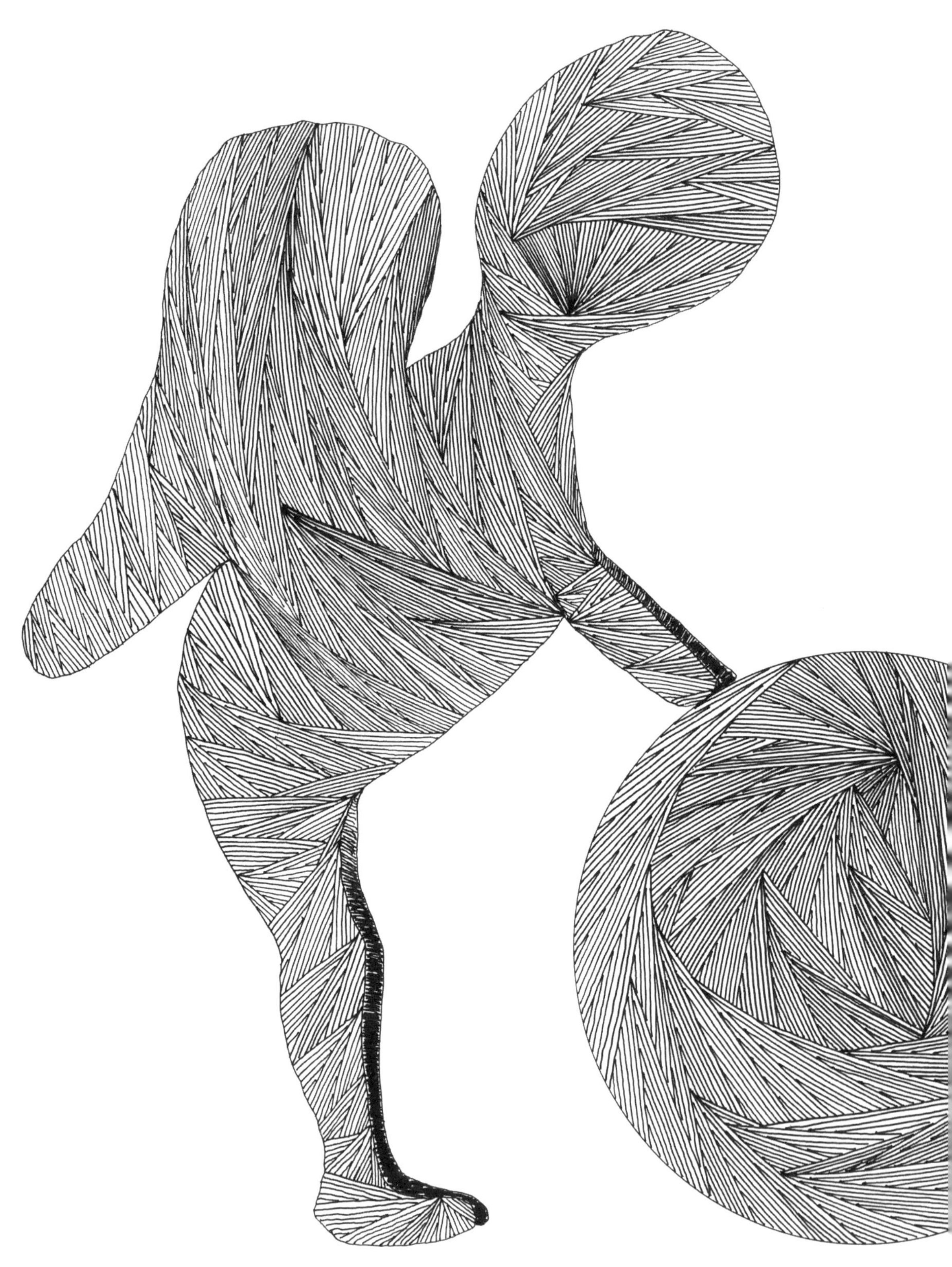

Stone Floaters, 2012

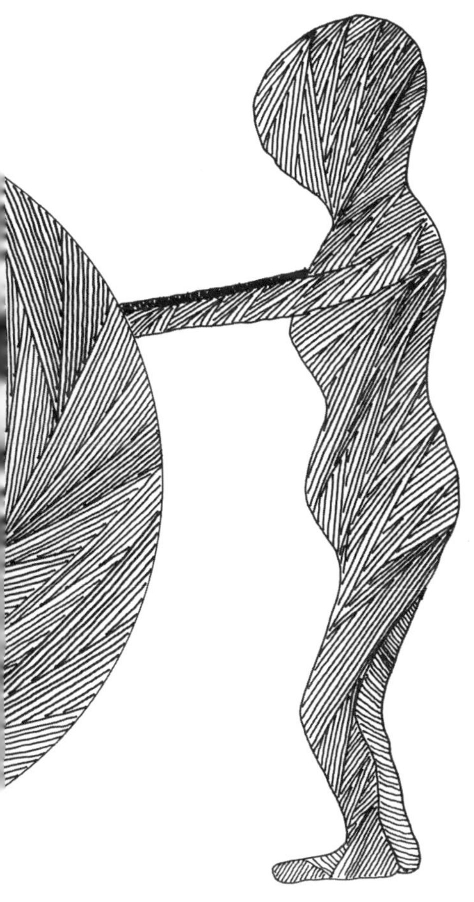

I'm a lucky bugger. I survived a lot of shit — much of it brought on by myself. I probably shouldn't have escaped … but I did. Maybe what doesn't kill you fucks you up for life — but at least I'm still here. I'm fishing happily in Florida, and I'm not yet dead or broken. I once ran into the Geordie writer Ian La Frenais in Tramp nightclub in London. I was wearing my leather jodhpurs and a leather jacket. Pink socks and mules. I was sashaying towards him, and he said, 'You know what you look like?' I said, 'What?' He said, 'A welder who got away with it.'

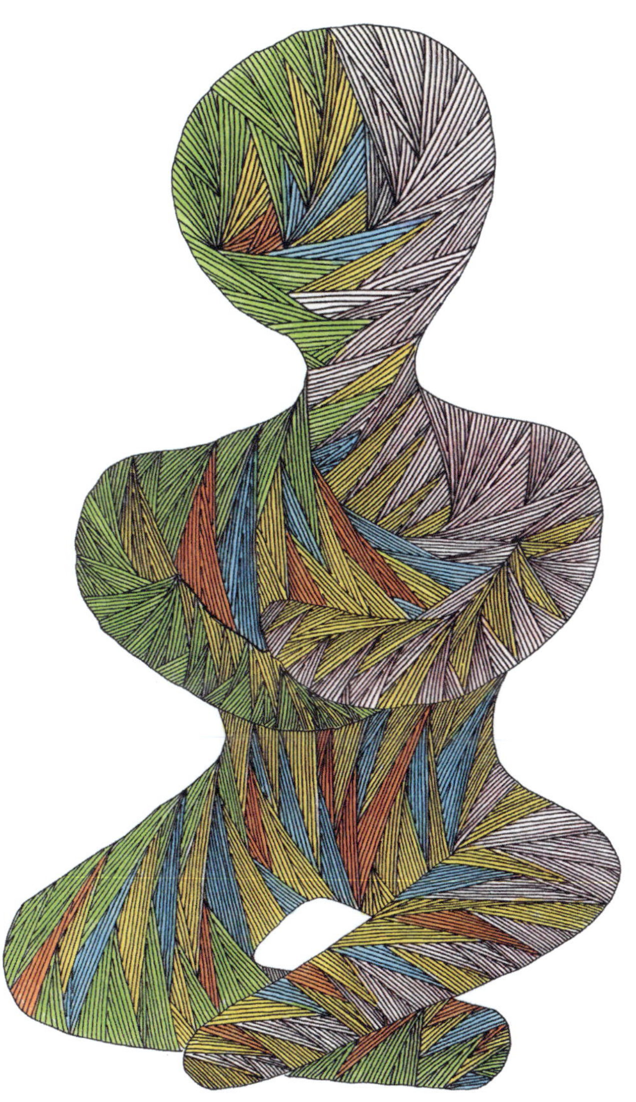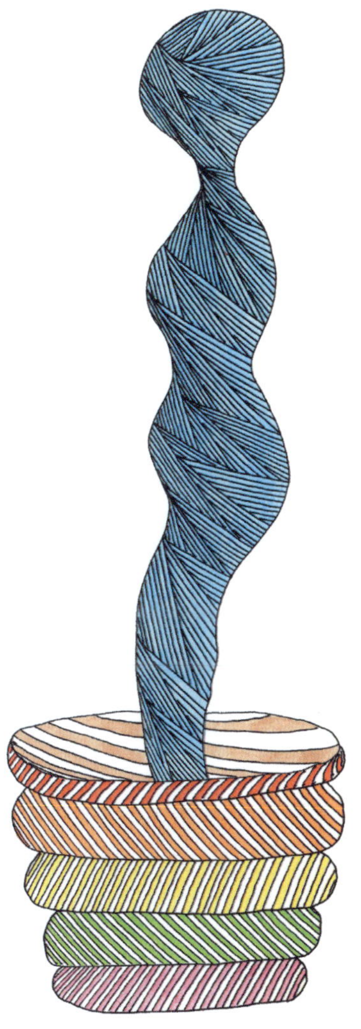

The Charmer, 2023

PICTURE INDEX

CREDITS

Pictures

Courtesy of Castle Fine Art: Page v; © James McCauley: Page 15. Mirrorpix: Page 16. Author's own: Page 56. ITV/ Shutterstock: Page 116 and page 182. Nobby Clark/ Popperfoto via Getty Images: Page 232.

Text

Pages 3–7, 39: Extracts from *Born on a Rainy Day* by Billy Connolly, 2023, courtesy of Castle Fine Art. Pages 11–14, 22–23, 26, 28 (top paragraph), 40, 45 (bottom paragraph), 51, 94, 96, 102–103, 167, 170, 209, 242, 248, 253, 286. Adapted extracts from *Windswept & Interesting* by Billy Connolly, 2021. Reprinted by permission of John Murray Press. Pages 28 (bottom paragraph), 45 (top paragraph), 61, 64, 68, 83–84, 87, 124–126, 133–134, 159, 162, 170, 172, 179, 239, 262–263, 279, 282. Adapted extracts from *Rambling Man* by Billy Connolly, 2023. Reprinted by permission of John Murray Press. Page 87: Extract from 'Waiting for a Train' by Jimmie Rodgers, 1929. Pages 75–76, 149–151, 186, 188, 195, 198–199, 214, 216, 223, 225–226: Adapted extracts from *Tall Tales and Wee Stories* by Billy Connolly, 2020. Reprinted by permission of John Murray Press.